Software Engineering: An Information Technology Approach

Software Engineering: An Information Technology Approach

Edited by Cheryl Jollymore

CLANRYE
INTERNATIONAL
www.clanryeinternational.com

Clanrye International,
750 Third Avenue, 9th Floor,
New York, NY 10017, USA

ISBN: 978-1-63240-803-7

Cataloging-in-Publication Data

Software engineering : an information technology approach / edited by Cheryl Jollymore.
     p. cm.
Includes bibliographical references and index.
ISBN 978-1-63240-803-7
1. Software engineering. 2. Information technology. I. Jollymore, Cheryl.
QA76.758 .S64 2019
005.1--dc23

For information on all Clanrye International publications
visit our website at www.clanryeinternational.com

Contents

Preface...IX

Chapter 1   **Enhancing the Text Production and Assisting Disable users in Developing Word Prediction and Completion in Afan Oromo** 1
Workineh Tesema and Duresa Tamirat

Chapter 2   **Towards Ontology-based SQA Recommender for Agile Software Development**................................. 5
Nada O Bajnaid, Rachid Benlamri, Algirdas Pakstas and Shahram Salekzamankhani

Chapter 3   **Distributed Deadlock Detection Technique with the Finite Automata**....................................... 19
Shivendra Kumar P, Hari Krishna T and R. K. Kapoor

Chapter 4   **An Approach towards Efficient Ranked Search over Encrypted Cloud** 23
Rajpreet Kaur and Manish Mahajan

Chapter 5   **An Architectural Approach for the Dynamic Adaptation of Services-based Software**... 28
Baroudi Mohammed Yassine, Benammar Abdelkrim and Bendimerad Fethi Tarik

Chapter 6   **Designing a Bio-Capsule Secure Authentication System** 32
Logeshwari R, Karthikayani K, Sindhuja A and Ashok D

Chapter 7   **Design and Analysis of a Two Stage Traffic Light System using Fuzzy Logic**....................................... 36
Javed Alam and Pandey MK

Chapter 8   **Load Balancing Approach in Cloud Computing**... 45
Majid Mehmood, Kinza Sattar, Asif Hussain Khan and Mujahid Afzal

Chapter 9   **Multiple Solutions for Elliptic Problem with Singular Cylindrical Potential and Critical Exponent** 50
Mohammed El Mokhtar Ould El Mokhtar

Chapter 10   **A Dynamic Service Composition on Social Networks**... 56
Pravin BR and Geetha

Chapter 11   **Evaluation Report on e- Government Programme Focusing on Infrastructure/ Internet Gateway and Messaging System**... 60
Odewale OA

Chapter 12   **Achieving Memory-saving Network Update**... 69
Jiyang Liu, Liang Zhu, Weiqiang Sun and Weisheng Hu

Chapter 13   **An Efficient Task Scheduling of Multiprocessor using Genetic Algorithm Based on Task Height**... 76
Ashish Sharma and Mandeep Kaur

Chapter 14   **NAND Flash Memory Organization and Operations**..81
Novotný R, Kadlec J and Kuchta R

Chapter 15   **A Comparative Analysis of Social Networking Analysis Tools**..............................89
Hemant Agrawal, Ajay Thakur, Rajan Slathia and Sumangali K

Chapter 16   **A New Approach to Enhance Avalanche Effect in Aes to Improve Computer Security**..98
Ajeet Singh

Chapter 17   **Design and Implementation of an Android Game: Duelling Phone**....................103
Alaa Hassan

Chapter 18   **Provenance Detection of Online News Article**..111
Ruba Ali Alsuhaymi

Chapter 19   **Thermodynamic and Quantum Mechanical Limitations of Electronic Computation**..117
Fayez Fok Al Adeh

Chapter 20   **Design and Simulation of a Linear Prolate Filter for a Baseband Receiver**...........122
Sagar Soman and Michael Cada

Chapter 21   **Root Causes for the Failure of Communication in GSD**....................................127
Hassan Khalid, Farhat-ul-ain and Kokab Khushboo

Chapter 22   **A Critique of Museum's Web Presence in the Kingdom of Saudi Arabia: A Study of Selected Museums**...135
Hamed M and Higgett N

Chapter 23   **Investigating and Criticizing Software Engineering Practices in Palestine**............140
Mohamed D Almadhoun

Chapter 24   **Toward Securing Cyber-Physical Systems using Exact Cover Set**........................144
Sameer Kumar Bisoyi and Hassan Reza

Chapter 25   **Assessing and Ranking the Corporate Social Responsibility Behavior of Five Star Hotels in Tehran using the AHP and FTOPSIS Methods**............................153
Jamal Kheiri

Chapter 26   **GSM Based E-Notice Board: With Software Interfacing using ASM Tools**.............161
Sachin M Dandage

Chapter 27   **An Automated Approach for Web Services Architectural Style Selection**...............166
Mohsin A, Fatima S, Khan AU and Nawaz F

Chapter 28   **Job Scheduling based on Harmonization between the Requested and Available Processing Power in the Cloud Computing Environment**........................174
Elhossiny Ibrahim, Nirmeen A El-Bahnasawy and Fatma A Omara

Chapter 29   **Software Architecture Methodology in Agile Environments**...............................178
Mehdi Mekni, Mounika G, Sandeep C and Gayathri B

Chapter 30   **Server Side Protection against Cross Site Request Forgery using CSRF Gateway**.................................186
Jaya Gupta and Suneeta Gola

Chapter 31   **Sw Quality Process Models: An Appraisal**..194
Tanzila Kehkashan, Shahid Yaqub Tabassam and Nayyar Manzoor

Chapter 32   **Feature-Based Three-Dimensional Registration for Repetitive Geometry in Machine Vision**..200
Yuanzheng Gong and Eric J Seibel

Chapter 33   **Evaluation of Penetration of Electronic Tools for Pedagogical Purposes in Nigerian Universities Compared to British Universities**...205
Folayan GB and Folayan KT

Permissions

List of Contributors

Index

Preface

In my initial years as a student, I used to run to the library at every possible instance to grab a book and learn something new. Books were my primary source of knowledge and I would not have come such a long way without all that I learnt from them. Thus, when I was approached to edit this book; I became understandably nostalgic. It was an absolute honor to be considered worthy of guiding the current generation as well as those to come. I put all my knowledge and hard work into making this book most beneficial for its readers.

Software engineering is a branch of engineering that is concerned with the application of technical knowledge to the design, implementation and testing of software for various functions. The field of software engineering branches out into several sub-domains such as software design, testing, maintenance, configuration management, quality, etc. This book includes some of the vital pieces of work being conducted across the world, on various topics related to software engineering. Chapters herein are compiled to provide detailed information about the advanced theories related to this field. This book, with its detailed analyses and data, will prove immensely beneficial to professionals and students involved in this area at various levels.

I wish to thank my publisher for supporting me at every step. I would also like to thank all the authors who have contributed their researches in this book. I hope this book will be a valuable contribution to the progress of the field.

Editor

Enhancing the Text Production and Assisting Disable Users in Developing Word Prediction and Completion in Afan Oromo

Workineh Tesema[1]* and Duresa Tamirat[2]

[1]*Department of Information Science, Jimma University, Jimma, Ethiopia*
[2]*Department of Information Science, Medawolabu University, Robe, Ethiopia*

Abstract

This work presents a word prediction and completion for disable users. The idea behind this work is to open a chance to interact with computer software and file editing for disable users in their mother tongue languages. Like normal persons, disable users are also needs to access technology in their life. In order to develop the model we have used unsupervised machine learning. The algorithm that used in this work was N-grams algorithms (Unigram, Bigram and Trigram) for auto completing a word by predicting a correct word in a sentence which saves time, reduces misspelling, keystrokes of typing and assisting disables. This work describes how we improve word entry information, through word prediction, as an assistive technology for people with motion impairment using the regular keyboard, to eliminate the overhead needed for the learning process. We also present evaluation metrics to compare different models being used in our work. The result argued that prediction yields an accuracy of 90% in unsupervised machine learning approach. This work particularly helps disable users who have poor spelling knowledge or printing press, institutions or government organizations, repetitive stress injuries to their (wrist, hand and arm) but it needs more further investigation for users who have visual problems.

Keywords: Afan oromo; Word prediction; Word completion; Text production; Disable users

Introduction

As a technology growing fast, Natural Language Processing (NLP) plays a great role in our day to day activity especially in relation to word prediction and auto completion. In Ethiopia, there are more than 80 languages are used as regional and few of it as federal communication. Many people's are using their handheld devices or computers to create different files by their own mother tongue. While writing the files, especially using local languages, it takes time and resource, hence most of file editors are using the English and other language. For example, Afan Oromo which has more than half of the population of a country used as their mother tongue and where there is long vowels and short vowels, needs assisting technology to edit files. In case of long vowels which is vowel repetition, it needs to prediction and completion to save time and resources of users, particularly for disables, poor knowledge of spelling [1].

The absences of these applications in the local languages bring a challenging problem in the society. In rural and urban areas where Hotels, Private Companies and Governmental Organizations are facing a problem while making their identity name, trademark or advertising their product. For example, instead of saying *Daabboo* [Bread], they are saying *Daboo* [Cooperation] with the absence of the letter 'b' which makes completely different spelling, sense, speech and form of the language. In word prediction text entry on mobile phone which is limited to only hand devices [2]. His work presents a word prediction approach based on context features and machine learning. As the result, it shows that the accuracy performance of his system 56.8%. However, in our case we have used different techniques of the n-gram (unigram, bigram, trigram) when there is lack trained data like Afan Oromo.

Additionally, the speed of typing of many secretaries (disable users in this case) when they write Afan Oromo texts is very low and misspelled word that create miscommunication between authors and readers. Hence, the single letter may changes the meaning of the word if misspelled. Furthermore lack of Afan Oromo word auto completion impacts non-native speakers from learning Afan Oromo language. Due to misspelling and low speed of typing, the new Afan Oromo speakers are ashamed from practicing the language. Therefore this study is undertaken to solve the disables problems by providing Afan Oromo word prediction and auto completion.

The developed system was only useful for disable peoples who have lack of fingers to typing and other problems at their hands. And also it can support normal users who want to type their files and want to save their time. As this work describes that targets people with physical disabilities and motion impairments like cerebral palsy, muscular dystrophy, spinal injuries, and other muscular deficiencies. One of the main difficulties faced by such people in interacting with computers is that their word entry is very slow, and the typing process can be tiring. Based on this, our system was cannot be helpful for other patients. And also this system was developed for computer users. However, it cannot be support android, IOS and other environments.

This study was conceptually developed prototype for Afan Oromo words that predict and auto complete words. To develop Afan Oromo word prediction for disabled users and others, we have used java software environment. The researcher used Java program as tool in order to build user interface and it is a platform independent language. As it shown in the result and discussion section, the GUI of this system was developed as it was very easy to use. Hence, the users are may be disabled the researcher consider the issues and make user friendly.

Consequently, the main objective of this work was to develop word prediction prototype for Afan Oromo specifically at word level. Afan Oromo uses Latin based script called Qubee and it has 26 basic characters. The method that used in this work was unsupervised machine learning; hence there is no standardized annotated corpus for training the machines. Generally, guessing the next character or

*Corresponding author: Workineh Tesema, Department of Information Science, Jimma University, Jimma, 378, Ethiopia, E-mail: workineh.tesema@ju.edu.et

word (or word prediction) is an essential subtask of NLP application, handwriting recognition, augmentative communication for the disabled, and spelling error detection. The motivation behind this work was to bring technology to disable peoples and allow the users to use word prediction present in their language.

Materials and Methods

This section presents the proposed method employed in this work. In order to develop word prediction model for Afan Oromo we followed various step process which involve: (a) text preprocessing which take input and corpus, tokenize to remove stop words and perform normalization. The other one is to (b) extract words to providing the clue about the predicted term using two techniques (Frequency and Recency). Based on the frequency of co-occurrences of the words most frequencies will be listed, to select the candidate won. On the other hand, the word was listed which are recently accessed, then select if it is the candidate words and correct to make complete the misspelled words. In order to guess the next word or term the users should press one or more the starting letter of the term. Hence we have used the most frequently occurring words in the corpus to predict.

This approach was statistically driven, as have been virtually all of the predictive models developed since then. Statistical methods generally suggest words based on:

1. Frequency, either in the relevant corpora or what the user has typed in the past; or

2. Recency, where suggested words are those the user has most recently typed. Such approaches reduce keystrokes and increase efficiency. Even with the best possible language models, these methods are limited by their ability to represent language statistically. In contrast, by using common sense knowledge to generate words that are semantically related to what is being typed, text can be accurately predicted where statistical methods fail.

Training data

To this end, the machine which is an unsupervised approach was trained on the free text corpus. As discussed on the above sections, after the machine trained on the corpus, the system preprocessed the corpus as it discussed. Then, simply the users can press the first letter or letters of his candidate word. According to the nature the algorithm, it will apply and show the words start with the entered letters. Assume that the user enter the first letter of a word, then the system was counted the frequent occurrence of words started with entered letter and make a rank at first. On the other hand, the system can show the recently predicted words as first predicted word. Finally, the system shows the list of predicted words according to their frequency and recency. Then the user can select the words, to make auto-complete and meaningful terms to edit the file.

Implementation tools

As it discussed on the above sections, to develop this system the algorithms were implemented in Java Net Beans IDE 8.02 version software which was open and run on the prepared corpus. The reason why the researcher used this tool is hence Java is free and help us to develop user interface. And also, Java is a general purpose and open source programming language. Moreover, it is optimized for software quality, developer productivity, program portability, and component integration. Lastly, the reason why java selected for this work was it is platform independent language which is after application developed we can run on different operating system of the users.

Results and Discussion

This section describes the result and discussion of the work. A prediction and auto-completion were systems which assist disabled users who have poor knowledge of spelling and physically injured in Afan Oromo. Consequently, an unsupervised machine learning method and N-gram algorithm were used in this work. The given corpus is a sequence of sentences, tries to predict the succeeding word. In the current context, no grammar model or parse trees are used in order to gauge the morphology of the words to be predicted. For every word to be predicted, the algorithm needs to scan through the entire training corpus (Figure 1).

This experiment describes that people with physical disabilities and motion impairments like wrist, hand, arm, fingers, cripple and other muscular deficiencies faced challenging problems. One of the main difficulties faced by such people in interacting with computers is that their word entry is very slow, and the typing process can be tiring [3].

Based on the experimental result, auto complete is a word completion task, so that the user types the first letter or letters of a word and the program provides one or more higher probable words. If the user intended to type is included in the list, the user can select it for example by using the keys (complete button (F7) in our case). If the word that the user want is not predicted, the user must type the next letter of the predicting word. At this time, the word choice(s) is altered so that the words provided begin with the same letters as those that have been selected or the word that the user wants appears it is completed. Word prediction technique predicts word by analyzing the previous word flow for auto completing a word with more accuracy by saving maximum keystroke of any users and reduces misspelling. N-gram language model is an important technique for predicting correct word to complete Afan Oromo word with more accuracy [4].

Many researchers have also tried to incorporate linguistic knowledge by employing other grammatical information like the parts-of-speech tags, parsing trees, root and stem of the words of the English language [5] in order to boost performance of the N-gram prediction. However, in this work, such higher level linguistic information which requires annotated data is not used. The only input and features are the sequence of words from the given corpus. As the experiment shows that in most cases, the N-gram model, with N equal to 1 or 2, seem to work the best word prediction for Afan Oromo.

Since the finding of this work, if the users enter three more letters the accuracy of prediction system is fewer lists of words; hence at Afan Oromo three or more extra letters can make one word. Now if any of these three or four words are not in the training corpus, then the frequency of the word will be zero that means that the word does not exist in our corpus. So in this statistical method if we want to consider these words, then we need a huge data corpus that must contain all the words of the language [3]. So there may arise the problems like many entries in the corpus are with zero frequency and the frequency of a word sequence will be very low [4].

As the experiment shows that a typical interface to a word prediction would be a list holding a number of relevant words picked out by the prediction. The list is then modified and pruned from incorrect alternatives as the user types more letters of the word. If the word prediction list contains the correct word the user can select it and go on to type the next word. For example, a user may have typed the word that has started by "a" and a word prediction presents the possible list shown in Figure 2.

As the experiment shows that, the average accuracy of test terms was 56.2% for the machine learning approach. From the Figure 2 above shows the predicted word displayed in the provided graphical user interface. If the listed words, does not listed in the predicted list by the user must know as the word is not present in the prepared corpus, the user can still write the next character to the next word. Sometimes, hence the dataset collected from multi resources, there are spelling errors. Unfortunately, our system cannot recognize the problem of misspelling due it needs Afan Oromo spelling checker system. However, if the word is spelled correctly and available in the corpus the performance is very good.

Additionally, our work gives other alternatives for users; hence they are physically limited to writing. This makes our work an easy and user friendly, hence by only one button pressing, users can text product as his/her interest. For instance, to Move Up (F5), to Move Down (F6), to Complete alternative (F7) the work was helpful.

Based on Figure 2, the result shows that the predicted words are predicted based on their frequency occurrences which are ranked according to frequency in the corpus as it shown in the Table 1.

Assume that the user wanted to type the word "*karaa*". Simply the user can press the first spelling of the word on providing interface of the users. After that the system will list all the words started by "*k*". The system inside will count the words started by this spelling and rank it at first if it has a high frequency of occurrence in the corpus. The user can choose the word directly from the list, for example, with the mouse or by pressing the correct spelling. If the word is not in the suggestion list the user can type the next letter of the word, in the case "*k*" and then get a new list with suggestions. Often a space is inserted after the suggested word, which allows the user to continue typing immediately after the prediction. A possible and often used, the choice when implementing a word prediction could be to make the insertion of an alternative automatic when there is enough information to make the decision (Figure 3).

As the experiment shows that, the result apart from being for people with physical disabilities word prediction can also assist individuals with poor spelling to use a greater variety of words [6]. However, although

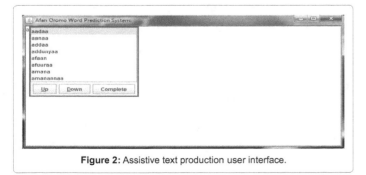

Figure 1: Text editor user interface for afan oromo.

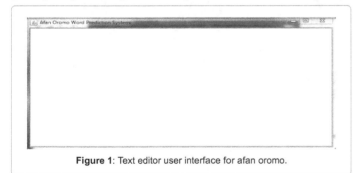

Figure 2: Assistive text production user interface.

Rank	Words
1	Aadaa
2	Afaan
3	Addaa
4	Addunyaa
5	Afuura
6	Ammana
7	Amanannaa

Table 1: Example of word prediction suggestion list.

Figure 3: Sample example after three spelling pressed.

this word prediction can develop writing skills regarding aspects such as word fluency, a variety of words and motivation of writing, the tests completed so far have been inadequate in scope and design [7].

Based on the above experiment, the system shows that in Afan Oromo correctly predicted after the users enter two letters [8,9]. To be honest our system can work at one, two, three or four letters, even it was work at sequence of words to make a sentence, but the accurate performance of the system was not much surprising as the experiment argued, that is 83.84%, 61.4%, 54.8% of unigram, bigram and trigram respectively.

Evaluation methods

As a result revealed that word prediction can be a sequential process over time with an input stream of characters. The task is to predict the next character given a string representing the input history. In this work the first character of a string represents oldest input and the last character represents the newest input [10,11]. For example, given the string "*abaaboo*" a good guess for the next character would be 'b' since 'b' follows 'a' which is a prefix of 'b' in the input history. It is well established that there is a close relationship between the tasks of prediction and auto-completion [12].

$$\text{Accuracy} = \frac{\text{Total number of words predicted correctly}}{\text{Total number of words}} \times 100$$

It is not only important to predict the succeeding word theoretically, but sometimes it is possible to calculate the accuracy of the system which is the probability of several possible words is also important. In our case, the frequency of the words helps us to compute the possible probability of the words. The probability of the succeeding word is used in different applications [13]. This measure gives an indication about what is the probability assigned to the correct word as compared to what is the most likely word according to the algorithm (Table 2).

We have used the two metrics of the evaluation method which are precision and recall metrics. The evaluation component exists on its own in order to have the possibility to automatically evaluate the system [14]. It allows testing the predictions under different metrics and formally, its interface is similar to that of the GUI component (Table 3).

Accuracy of Algorithms			
Number of Words Predicted	Unigram	Bigram	Trigram
1	83.84%	61.4%	54.8%
2	75.4%	59.77%	40.7%
3	70.1%	54.9%	31.8%
4	67.9%	52.68%	29.53%
5	61.8%	50.6%	26.89%

Table 2: Accuracy of the model.

No	Accuracy Performance	
	Precision	Recall
Number of Correctly predicted	90%	73.34%

Table 3: Evaluation of the model.

Conclusion

The overall focus of this research is to investigate word prediction and auto-complete which addresses the problem of poor spelling and completion. Ideally, this can speed up and ease the user's typing of word production. This work is improving and enhancing textual information entry for disabled users has been investigated, with unsupervised approach and user interface proposed and implemented to facilitate and simplify text input for such people. In this work the unsupervised machine learning achieved an accuracy of 90%, 73.34% of precision and recall respectively.

References

1. Yarowsky D (1995) Unsupervised word sense disambiguation rivaling supervised methods. In Proceedings of the 33rd Annual Meeting of the Association for Computational Linguistics, Cambridge, M.A. pp: 189-196.

2. Gudisa T (2013) Design and implementation of predictive text entry method for Afan Oromo on mobile phone, Addis Ababa, Ethiopia.

3. Cockburn A, Siresena A (2003) evaluating mobile text entry with the fasta keypad, people and computers: British computer society conference on human computer interaction, Bath, England.

4. Masudul H, Tarek H, Mokhlesur R (2015). Automated word prediction in bangla language using stochastic language models, bangla. IJFCST 5: 67-75.

5. Wu D, Sui Z, Zhao J (1999) An information-based method for selecting feature types for word prediction. Proc Eurospeech.

6. Sutherland BM (2004) Predictive text entry in immersive environments. Proceedings of the IEEE Virtual Reality.

7. Even-Zohar Y, Roth D (2003) A classification of approach to word prediction. Proceedings of the 1st North American Chapter.

8. Debela T, Ermias A (2011) Designing a rule based stemmer for afaan oromo text. IJCL.

9. Gudisa T (2013) Design and implementation of predictive text entry method for afan oromo on mobile phone.

10. Muzeyn KB (2012) Development of stemming algorithm for Silt'e language text. Thesis faculty of informatics, Addis Ababa University, Addis Ababa.

11. Nancy I, Veronis J (1998). Word sense disambiguation, the state of the art. Computational Linguistics.

12. Tesema W (2016) Afan Oromo sense clustering in hierarchical and partitional techniques. Journal of Information Technology and Software Engineering.

13. Longkai, Li L, Houfeng W, Sun X (2014) Predicting chinese abbreviations with minimum semantic unit and global constraints. Empirical Methods in Natural Language Processing (EMNLP), pp: 1405-1414.

14. Tesema W (2015) Towards the sense disambiguation of afan oromo words using hybrid approach. Jimma University, Jimma, Ethiopia.

Towards Ontology-based SQA Recommender for Agile Software Development

Nada O Bajnaid[1]*, Rachid Benlamri[2], Algirdas Pakstas[3] and Shahram Salekzamankhani[4]

[1]*King Abdulaziz University, Saudi Arabia*
[2]*Lakehead University, Ontario, Canada*
[3,4]*London Metropolitan University, UK*

Abstract

Agility is heavily dependent on tacit knowledge, skilled and motivated employees, and frequent communications. Although, the Agile Manifesto claims fast and light software development process while maintaining high quality, it is however not very clear how current agile practices and methods attain quality under time pressure and unstable requirements. In this paper, we present an ontological approach for process-driven Quality Assurance support for agile software development. Challenges related to the role of Quality Assurance in agile projects are addressed by developing a process-driven recommender that provides tailored resources to user's queries. The proposed ontological model embeds both conceptual and operational SQA knowledge about software processes and their requirements, including quality attributes, SQA measurements, SQA metrics and related SQA techniques and procedures.

Keywords: Agile software development; Context-awareness; E-learning; Ontology-based reasoning; Software quality assurance

Introduction

Software is a key element in daily human activities. Areas such as communications, transportation, health, finances, and education are highly dependent on software systems that range from simple to highly complex life critical systems. People are increasingly relying on software and demanding higher quality products than ever before. Therefore, producing high quality software based on Software Quality Assurance (SQA) techniques and standards becomes one of the most important objectives of software development and maintenance activities. Furthermore, as the complexity of producing software increases, the need for training highly qualified software engineers became critical. This is mainly due to: (a) the fast changing discipline; (b) inability to deal with large complex problems in a limited educational setup; and (c) the variety of methods, techniques, and technological tools used in this field [1,2]. Moreover, educators in this area have different backgrounds, programming language preferences, and usually use different jargons which lead to a variety of understanding and overlapping of meanings of the same software engineering terms or concepts. This may results in a lack of communication between the same team members and ambiguity in understanding requirements and defining system specifications. Therefore, the need for new support learning tools in the workplace is crucial.

Another challenge for software development is related to current rapid changes in technical and business environments with the need to deliver high quality software quickly which resulted in moving from traditional software development methods to agile development methods [3]. Although, the Agile Manifesto claims fast and light software development process while maintaining high quality, it is however, not very clear how current agile practices and methods attain quality under time pressure and unstable requirements. Developers need to know how to revise or tailor their agile methods in order to attain the required level of quality [4]. Knowledge quickly becomes outdated as a result of the shortened product life spans. In such rapidly changing environments, while companies struggle to keep their staff knowledgeable about the new technologies, training departments have to provide training and learning tools at the workplace that are efficient and adapted to current technological needs [5]. One way of achieving this goal is to embed quality tasks in every action and step of the software development process from requirement definition to post-delivery evolution [6]. In practice, this is a challenging task, due to the fact that developing software within schedule and budget has usually higher priority than achieving quality characteristics. In addition, achieving quality requires combining knowledge of different Software Engineering (SE) sub-disciplines, from software analyst to SQA experts [7].

In this paper an attempt is made to address the above-mentioned problems using an ontological approach in developing a process-driven recommender system that supports practitioners towards developing SQA compliant software. The focus of the paper is on the SQA ontology development that includes both domain (SQA concepts) and operational (SQA Processes) knowledge. Such ontology is used as the backbone to build a context-aware SQA recommender system that suggests useful resources, called in this paper Learning Objects (LOs) that deal with all SQA aspects of learner's current software development process [8]. The proposed process-driven recommender provides, just-in-time, and in a contextualized way, all necessary resources to enable software developers deal with SQA issues immediately after coding so that they can refactor while the code is still fresh in their mind. Such facility is a key requirement to address the role of SQA in agile software development.

The rest of the paper is organized as follows: the proposed SQA ontology model is presented in section 2 and an evaluation of the model is discussed in section 3. Section 4 presents experimental results of the developed system. Related work is given in section 5, and finally, section 6 summarizes the main findings of this study and suggests furthers research work.

Modelling the SQA Domain Knowledge

Standardization plays an important role in software engineering

---

*Corresponding author: Nada O Bajnaid, King Abdulaziz University, Saudi Arabia, E-mail: nbajnaid@kau.edu.sa

by providing organizations with agreed upon and well-organized practices that assists users of software development methods in their work. There has been many progress made by different bodies to develop Software Engineering standards, resulting in the forming of the ISO/IEC Joint Technical Committee 1 (JTC1) workgroup in order to guarantee consistency and coherency among standards. Moreover, the IEEE Computer Society and the ISOJTC1-SC7 agreed to harmonize terminology among their standards. However, despite all these efforts, inconsistencies and terminology conflicts still appear between standards even within the same organization. Besides, there is still no single standard that embraces the whole Software Quality Assurance (SQA) knowledge. This paper presents two main contributions. The first contribution is an SQA ontology model that includes new conceptual knowledge based on the latest quality standards (ISO/IEC 20510 [9] and ISO/IEC 20523 [10]) and operational knowledge about SQA software development with special focus on agility. The second contribution however, is a recommender system that provides contextual SQA knowledge to support the software process being developed.

In this study we have used the ISO, all IEEE standards (ISO 20510, ISO 20523, IEEE 12207, IEEE 610.12, IEEE 00100, PMBOK 2008, CMMI v1.2) and SWEBOK to build a consistent SQA ontology that includes both domain and operational knowledge. Table 1 shows the main SQA-related classes that were extracted from the SWEBOK with their instances. The conceptual structure of the proposed SQA ontology is illustrated in Figure 1. The latter shows the various relationships used to define all SQA concepts, SQA-related software development processes, SQA measurements and SQA metrics. The main class in the domain ontology is SQA Concept class which is used to conceptualize and to represent the knowledge of the SQA domain. The figure also shows the major sub-classes of "SQA Concept". The arrows represent relationships (object properties) between domain classes (head of the arrow) and range classes (tail of the arrow). The "is-a" property linksan SQA concepts to its instances (individuals).

Figure 1 does not show all instances of the SQA measures due to space limitation and readability purpose. Also, applicable SQA sub-characteristics and measures are not limited to the ones listed in the ontology. The ontology is designed so that additional measures can be easily added for particular purposes to allow the ontology to evolve.

In Table 2, we provide details of the various properties used in the SQA ontology. For each property, the table presents its domain, range, inverse property (if any) and cardinality. Quality sub-characteristics and their measures are crucial aspects of the SQA ontology. Measurement (quality sub-characteristics in ISO/IEC 20510) plays an important part in software development as it indicates the quality of the product being developed [11]. For any software quality product, measures associated with its attributes should collectively reflect likely user satisfaction with the use of the product and therefore the product entire quality [12] (Tables 1 and 2) (Figure 1).

According to Pressman's categorization of software metrics, quality metrics measure the extent to which customer requirements are fulfilled and indicate how closely software conforms to explicit (Functional Requirements - FR) and implicit (Non-FR) customer requirements. In this study, software measurements and measures are at the heart of the SQA ontology design. All aspects of SQA measurement and measures, as described in the ISO/IEC 25010 and ISO/IEC 25023 standards, are reflected in the proposed SQA ontology. In practice, these are instantly retrieved at the request of the software developer while engaging in a related software process. To the best of our knowledge, the proposed SQA ontology is the first to cover all SQA measurements and measures of the ISO/IEC quality standard. Due to space limitation, only measurements associated with "Maintainability" and "Reliability" quality attributes are chosen for illustration in Table 3.

SQA conceptualization is supplemented with an additional semantic layer that describes SQA operational knowledge, mainly SQA processes for both standard and agile software development. To support agility which relies on individual's tacit knowledge that is very much based on usual work practices and methods, some agile software development resources [13,14] were used to encode related SQA processes in the ontology as shown in Table 4 and highlighted in boldface font in Figure 1 (Tables 3 and 4).

Evaluating the SQA Ontology

High quality ontology can easily be reused and shared with confidence among applications and domains. Additionally, in case of re-use, the ontology may help to decrease maintenance costs [15]. To assess these two qualities, it is important to conduct an evaluation study that should also include assessing the usefulness of the ontology

SQA Ontology Class	List of Individuals
SQAProcess	Validation, verification, audit, review, inspection, joint review, technical review, management review, testing, quality assurance, SW design quality evaluation.
Quality Characteristic	Functional Suitability, Performance Efficiency, Compatibility, Usability, Reliability, Security, Portability
Sub-characteristic	Functional Completeness, Functional Correctness, Maturity, Capacity, Fault Tolerance, Recoverability, Learnability, Operability, Installability, Interoperability, Appropriateness Recognizability, Time Behavior, Resource Utilization, Accessibility, User Error Protection, Availability, Functional Appropriateness, Adaptability, User Interface aesthetics, Analyzability, Modifiability, Testability, Non-repudiation, Replaceability, Coexistence, Confidentiality, Integrity, Accountability, Authenticity, Modularity, Reusability
Measure	Functional implementation coverage, Correctness, Computational accuracy, Functional appropriateness measure, Response time, Turnaround time, Throughput, CPU utilization, Memory utilization, I/O devices utilization, No. of online requests, No. of simultaneous access, Bandwidth of transmission system, Available coexistence, Connectivity with external system, Data exchangeability, Description completeness, Demonstration capability, Completeness of user documentation, Operational consistency, Message clarity, Customizing possibility, Input validity checking, Avoidance of incorrect operation, Appearance customizability of user interface, Physical accessibility, Fault removal, Test coverage, Mean time between failure MTBF, Service time ratio, Mean down time, Failure avoidance, Redundancy, Mean recovery time, Access controllability, Data encryption, Data corruption prevention, Utilization of digital signature, Access auditability, Authentication methods, Condensability, Execution of reusability, Audit trial capability, Diagnosis function sufficiency, Localization degree of correction impact, Modification complexity, Modification success rate, Functional completeness of embedded test functions, Autonomous testability, Test restartability, Hardware environment adaptability, System software environmental adaptability, Organizational environment adaptability, Installation time efficiency, Ease of Installation, User support function consistency, Functional inclusiveness, Continuous usage of data,
Deliverable	Operation report, problem report, audit strategy, design, fault removal report, requirement specification, QA plan, source code, review report, test cases, test report, test specification, user manual, user monitoring record, validation plan, verification plan.
Resource	Check list, complexity analysis, control flow analysis, meeting, prototyping, simulation, use cases, walk through.

Table 1: List of SQA Ontology Classes and their Instances.

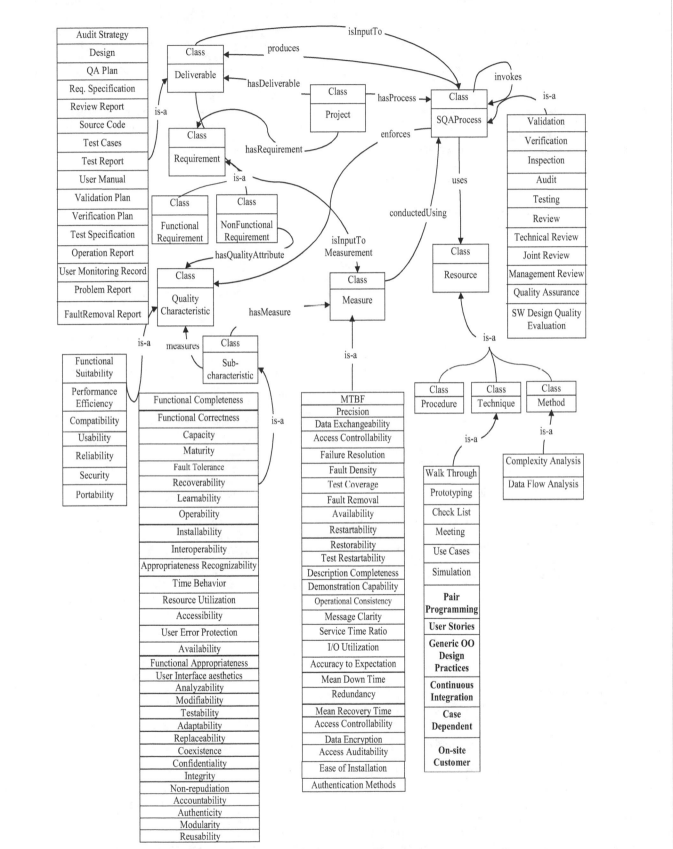

Figure 1: The SQA Conceptual Model.

Name	Domain	Range	Cardinality	Inverse Property
hasProcess	Project	SQAProcess	Multiple: a project may have more than one process	-
Enforces	SQAProcess	Quality Characteristic	Multiple: a process may have more than one attribute	enforced By
uses	SQAProcess	Resource	Multiple: a process may use more than one resource	is Used By
isInputTo	Deliverable	SQAProcess	Multiple: a process may have more than one deliverable as input	has Input
measures	Sub-characteristic	Quality Characteristic	Single: a quality sub-characteristic can be used to measure specific quality characteristic	is Measured By
invokes	SQAProcess	SQAProcess	Multiple: a process might invoke other processes	-
produces	SQAProcess	Deliverable	Multiple: A process might produce one or more products	is Produced By
hasMeasure	Quality Characteristic	Measure	Multiple: a quality sub-characteristic may have one or more measures	is Measurement Metric of
conductedUsing	Measure	SQAProcess	Multiple: a quality measure may be conducted using one or more process(es)	-

Table 2: SQA Ontology Properties.

Quality characteristic	Sub-characteristic	Measure	Input to measure	ISO/IEC 12207 Ref.
Maintainability	Analyzability	Audit trial capability	Problem report Operation report	Testing
		Diagnostic function support	Problem report Operation report	Testing
	Modifiability	Change access rate		
		Modification complexity	Problem report Operation report Maintenance report	Testing
		Localization degree		
	Testability	Test restartability		
Reliability	Maturity	Fault removal	Test report	Testing Validation Quality Assurance
		Mean Time Between Failure	Test report Operation report	Testing
		Test Coverage	Req. specification User manual Test report Operation report	Testing Validation Quality Assurance
	Fault tolerance	Failure avoidance	Test report Operation report	Testing Validation
	Recoverability	Mean recovery time	Test report Operation report	Testing Validation
		Restartability	Test report Operation report	Testing Validation

Table 3: Maintainability and Reliability Knowledge as in ISO/IEC 20510/25023.

Term	Ontology Concept	Related Ontology Concepts
User Stories	Technique	usedBy→ joint review and Verification
Pair Programming	Technique	usedBy→ Quality Assurance
Generic OO Design Practices	Technique	usedBy→ Quality Assurance
Continuous Integration	Technique	usedBy→ Validation and Verification
Case Dependent	Technique	usedBy→ Quality Assurance
On-site Customer	Technique	usedBy→ Joint Review
Iterative Incremental Development (IID)	Technique	usedBy→ Verification, Validation, Qualification Testing, and Joint Review

Table 4: Agile Terminology and SQA Processes.

for the purpose it was built for, and evaluating other attributes such conceptual coverage and clearness. A common approach is to evaluate the ontology according to a set of ontology design principles and criteria, such as those reported [16,17]. For example, it should be possible to extend the ontology to cover new needs and uses. Also, it is important to leave some representational choices (such as concept roles, relations, and constraints) open so that they can be made available at a late stage based on the actual needs of the problem solving or application. However, the most important three assessments according to Corcho [17] that should be conducted to evaluate an ontology are

verification, validation and assessment. Verification refers to building the ontology correctly. In other word, it ensures that the ontology functions correctly in the real world. Validation refers to whether the ontology definitions really model the domain for which the ontology was created for. Ontology validation ensures that the correct ontology was built. The goal is to show that the world model is compliant with the formal model. Finally, assessment focuses on judging the ontology from users' points of view (human judgment).

Many attributes were used to develop the above-mentioned three ontology assessments. The most used attributes are:

- **Completeness**: all knowledge that is expected to be in the ontology is either explicitly stated in it or can be inferred.

- **Consistency**: refers to whether a contradictory knowledge can be inferred from a valid input definition.

- **Conciseness**: ensures that the ontology is free from any unnecessary, useless, or redundant definitions.

- **Expandability**: refers to the ability to add new definitions without altering the already stated semantic.

Many ontology evaluation approaches have been adopted in the literature depending on the purpose of the evaluation and the type of the ontology being evaluated [18]. In survey ontology evaluation approaches are classified as follows [18]:

1. Those based on comparing the ontology to a "golden standard" which might be an ontology itself;

2. Those based on using the ontology in an application and evaluating the results (application-based ontology evaluation);

3. Those involving comparison with a source of data (e.g. a collection of documents) about the domain to be modeled by the ontology; and

4. Those where evaluation is done by humans who try, through a survey for instance, to assess how well the ontology meets a set of predefined user requirements and standards.

The first approach is not applicable in our case due to the lack of a "golden standard" Software Engineering ontology. However, the remaining three evaluation techniques have been used to assess the proposed SQA ontological model. An application-based ontology evaluation was conducted using the developed prototype recommender system as shown in section 4.2. The third approach was adopted during the ontology development stage where the evolving conceptual model (shown in Figure 1) was compared to the sources of knowledge as shown in section 4.1. The fourth approach was also used in this study by developing an ontology assessment questionnaire that was distributed among SE specialists. The results of the survey are presented in section 4.3.

Verifying the developed ontology

During implementation, the developed ontology was verified for consistency using the Protégé consistency checker tool which automatically checks the consistency and conciseness of the developed ontology. Only inconsistent classes will be displayed by the tool. Figure 2 shows the result generated by Protégé and the Racer Pro reasoning for the consistency checking [19] where no inconsistence classes are listed. Syntax checking is performed by Protégé OWL (Web Ontology Language) plug in which generates OWL statements during creation of the ontology using the Graphical User Interface. The plug in ensures that the generated OWL statements adhere to the rules of the OWL language.

In addition, the visualization tab (another Protégé plug in), enables a view of the graph representation of the ontology to ensure the ontology is consistent with the conceptual model (Figure 2).

Validating the ontology using the SQAES web application

Application-based (or task-based) evaluations offer a useful framework for measuring practical aspects of ontology deployment such as the responses provided by the system, the degree of explanation capability offered by the system, and the ease of use of the query component [20]. A proof of concept prototype consisting of an SQA recommender system has been designed and implemented [8]. To develop some scenarios, we have built an upper ontology, mainly for modeling learners' profile and learners' context. The upper ontology consists of three interrelated sub-ontologies, namely Developer (learner) Sub-ontology, Software Development Sub-ontology, and the SQA Domain Sub-ontology. Figure 3 shows the general structure of the upper ontology with the relationships among the sub-ontologies. The Developer Sub-ontology represents the developer's activity profile, which consists of already consumed learning resources. The developer's activity profile and related knowledge are organized into ontology concepts and relationships. This allows adapting and delivering LOs relevant to the software process currently in hand.

The SQA Domain Sub ontology captures general concepts and properties about the SQA knowledge domain. The main class in this ontology is SQA Concept that is used to conceptualize and represent

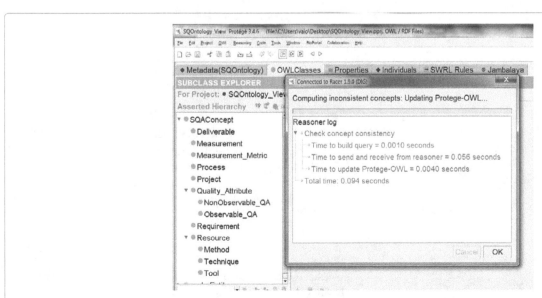

Figure 2: Protégé Consistency Checking Result for SQA Concepts.

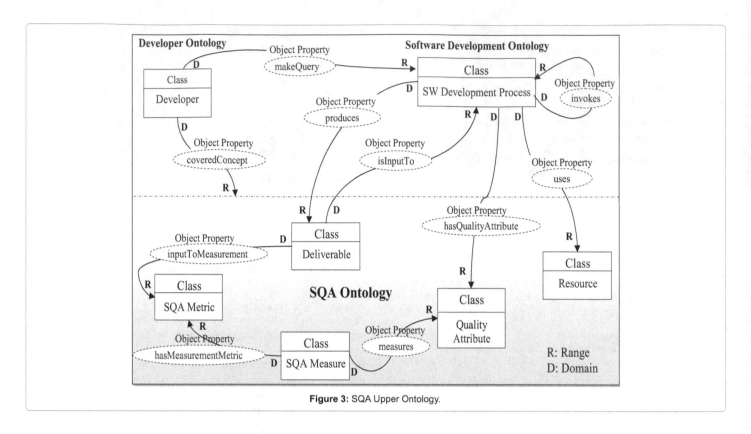

Figure 3: SQA Upper Ontology.

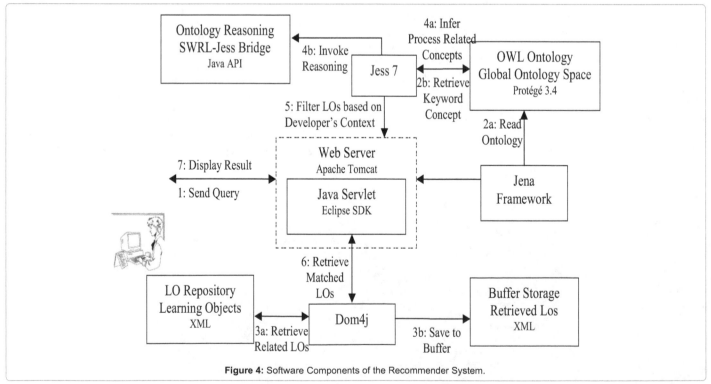

Figure 4: Software Components of the Recommender System.

all concepts of the software quality ontology and related operational knowledge. The property make Query associates process-related keywords entered by the developer to the most relevant concept in the Software Development Process Sub-ontology. The property is Mapped To links the concept class to the learning object class. The property is Mapped To is used to map learning objects' metadata to the SQA

ontology concepts and thus allow sharing of resources. The property Consumed Learning Object tracks LOs previously consumed by a specific learner. The sequence of steps in a typical learning scenario is illustrated in Figure 4 (Figures 3 and 4).

As illustrated in Figure 4, the sequence of steps in a typical learning scenario is given below:

1. The developer navigates (or queries for) an SQA concept.

2. The system retrieves the SQA concept(s) related to the developer's queried one.

3. Then, the system retrieves associated LOs from the LO repository using the term(s) extracted in step 2.

4. The system then infers other SQA related concepts using relationships such as Necessary Requirement, Optional Requirement, Used Resource, ensures QA, Produced Product, and Invoked Process.

5. LOs associated to new terms extracted in step 4 are retrieved from the LO repository.

6. The system will then check for previously covered concepts and LOs, which are then removed from the list of recommendations.

7. The suggested LOs are then provided to the developer for investigation, and then the same cycle can be repeated again.

In the developed prototype recommender system, ontology reasoning is performed to personalize software development services based on the developer's context. The system filters out the available LOs based on the developer's usage profile and guided by related ontology-based reasoning. The output is a set of SQA resources that are directly related to the developer selected query (i.e. SQA process being developed). This developer centric adaptation is enabled by integrating knowledge components from the three sub-ontologies. Ontological rules are applied to dynamically infer metadata that can be used to customize offered LOs.

Besides the OWL ontology reasoning rules (sub Class of, sub Property of, inverse of, etc.) which are necessary to navigate and search for ontology concepts and properties, the SQA knowledge base is extended with a set of user defined rules to allow inferring higher-level conceptual context from relevant low-level ones.

The prototype system aims at guiding software developers through the necessary SQA practices by providing resources that deal with SQA related aspects of the software process in hand and hence improves product quality in an agile software development environment. This is achieved by sensing the developer's current activity and suggesting relevant LOs (e.g. recommendations for good practices, example code, and graphical description of a related methodology/process) that deal with all SQA aspects related to the currently developed software process. The developer centric adaptation achieves its functionality in two steps. First, the reasoning unit of the proposed recommender system infers the core LOs that are directly related to the queried concept through the object property is Mapped To using the Core Learning Object rule illustrated by:

Developer (?D) ^ make Query (?D,?C) ^ is Mapped To (?C,?LO) ^ consumed Learning Object (?D,?LO) → core Learning Object (?C,?LO)

Related LOs are then inferred using different user defined SWRL (Semantic Web Rule Language) rules and depending on user's task. The output is a sequence of LOs that are generated as learning recommendations. Second, recommendations generated from the previous step are then semantically refined and adjusted according to the developer's profile where the system removes LOs that have already been consumed by the developer. The property consumed Learning Object links the learner (Software developer) to the learning objects that have already been consumed by the learner. The ontology model has been validated by developing many user scenarios using the

prototype recommender system. Appendix A shows some of the SWRL rules that have been used to infer learning resources for all possible scenarios.

Ontology conciseness: The prototype recommender system provides the developer with a list of recommended LOs based on the initial query. However, this list may include many LOs that are out of context and therefore, might not be necessary for the user. To ensure conciseness, ontology axioms (i.e. a declaratively and rigorously represented knowledge which has to be accepted without proof) were added to prevent unnecessary knowledge. In ontology representation, axioms can be used to represent the meaning of concepts rigorously, and to answer questions on the capability of the built ontology using the ontology concepts. For example when the user queries the Validation concept, which is a process according to the SQA ontology, the system retrieves the core LOs associated with the Validation concept from the LO repository. Related concepts represent the list of recommended SQA concepts to be provided to the user for further investigation. However, this list may include some irrelevant LOs. In the example of Validation, by firing the Invokes rule, LOs associated with all software processes will be added to the list of recommendations. In theory (i.e. as per IEEE 12207 standard), only those processes that are associated with Review and Audit should have been added to the list and not all those listed in Figure 5.

To prevent such situation, recommendation refining is guaranteed by adding the so called "blocking axioms" to the ontology model. By referring back to our example related to Validation concept and according to ISO/IEC 9126 [21] standard, a Validation process produces Test Report and Validation Plan and requires Requirement Specification, Source Code, Test Report and User Manual as inputs. In addition, Validation has Efficiency and Functionality as quality attributes and uses Use-Cases, Iterative Incremental Development, Prototyping, Testing, Measurement, and Continuous Integration as resources. The above knowledge can be represented with the following axioms added to the Validation concept of the SQA ontology model:

∀ Produces only (Test Report or Validation Plan)

∀ invokes only (Review or Audit)

∀ ensures QA only (Efficiency or Functionality)

∀ uses only (Continuous Integration or Use case or Testing or Iterative Incremental Development or Prototyping or Measurement)

∀ has Input only (Requirement Specification or Source Code or Test Report or User manual)

In Table 5 we show few more axioms added to some of the concepts in the SQA ontology. The complete list of axioms cannot be presented due to space limitation (Figures 5 and 6) (Table 5).

Assessing the quality of the SQA ontology

Ontology assessment was conducted by judging the ontology content from SE specialists' point of view. The ontological conceptual model summarized in Figure 1 with a link to an assessment questionnaire has been sent to domain specialists inviting them to participate in the SQA ontology assessment process in order to verify its SQA domain coverage, structure, clarity, and extendibility. Collecting responses from domain experts was a challenging task due to the limited number of available experts in the SQA domain. It took more than seven months to get 16 responses out of a large number of invitations to participate in the online assessment. Although the sample is small, it is considered fairly acceptable to judge the developed SQA

Concept	Axioms
Efficiency	∀ is Ensured By only (Validation or Verification or SW_Design_Quality_Evaluation) ∀ measured By (Efficiency_Compliance or Resource_Utilization or Time_Behavior)
Failure Avoidance	∀ Conducted Using only (Joint_Review or Qualification_Testing or Validation or Verification) ∀ is Measurement Metric of only (Fault_Tolerance) ∀ has Measurement MetricInput only (Requirement_Specification or Review_Report or Test_Report)
Data Exchangeability	∀ Conducted Using only (Joint_Review or quality_Assurance or Validation) ∀ is Measurement Metric of only (Security) ∀ has Measurement MetricInput only (Requirement_Specification or Review_Report or Test_Report or Design or Operation_Report or Source_Code)
Test Coverage	∀ Conducted Using only (Qualification_Testing or quality_Assurance or Validation) ∀ is Measurement Metric of only (Maturity) ∀ has Measurement MetricInput only (Test_Report or Requirement_Specification or User_Manual)

Table 5: Some SQA Concepts with Related Axioms.

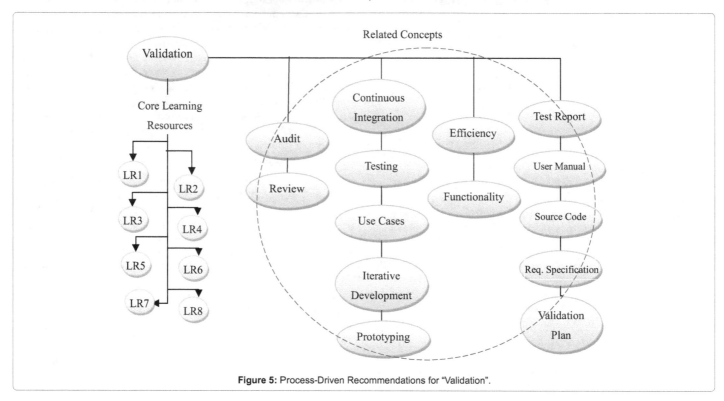

Figure 5: Process-Driven Recommendations for "Validation".

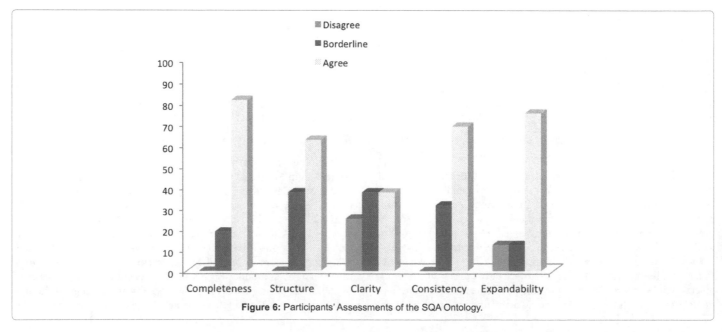

Figure 6: Participants' Assessments of the SQA Ontology.

domain ontology. The results of the survey are summarized in Figure 6 and an analysis is presented below, including experts' suggestions to enhance the SQA ontology.

Completeness: The majority of participants (81.3%) agreed that the ontology developed in this research covers the major concepts of the SQA domain. Few respondents however, think that it is missing "Testing" related concepts (unit testing, black and white box testing, system testing, etc.). Though, the current ontology is not heavily focused on testing techniques, it is worth investigating this aspect in future developments. Another suggestion was made to add concepts such as Software type, Software life cycle model, Architecture, Configuration management. However, we strongly believe that these are not SQA concepts. Nevertheless, these concepts can be added to the ontology if the latter is to be mapped to other SE areas or to an upper-level general purpose SE ontology.

Structure: A reasonable majority of the respondents (62.5%) agreed with the ontology taxonomy as is, while the remaining respondents did not have real disagreements. There were few remarks such as having Design comes after Review Report in the list of instances of the class Deliverable, which we consider semantically insignificant.

Clarity: This criterion obtained a borderline score (50%), just around the mean (3.13). However, we believe that this is a reasonably fair opinion due to the large number of overlapped and redundant SQA terms in available proposals and sources of SQA knowledge. It was noted that most reported disagreements were related to the confusion between Measurements and Metrics. A significant suggestion, which we have taken into consideration and have been incorporated in the ontology design, is to use the terms Quality Characteristic and Sub-characteristic instead of Quality Attribute and Measurements respectively. It was also suggested to replace the term Measurement Metric with the term Measure as per the latest quality standard ISO/IEC 25010. These recommendations were very useful in enhancing the ontology for clarity purpose.

Consistency: A reasonable majority of the responses (68.8) agreed that the developed ontology is consistent. Ontology consistency was verified using the Protégé consistency checker plug in.

Expandability: A good ontology is assumed to cover necessary concepts of the domain and structure them in a way that adding evolving concepts would not affect the existing structure. A satisfactory result was obtained for this criterion as the majority (75%) agreed on the expandability of the developed ontology. Some suggestions to include agile terminology with new quality measurements and metrics (as in ISO/IEC 25010) were taken into consideration and incorporated into the current SQA ontology design.

Experimental Results

In this section, we first present few working scenarios to show the most important features of the system. Then, we focus on another scenario that shows agile-based SQA software support features.

Working scenarios

In the first scenario we show the importance of using axioms in filtering relevant learning resources. The prototype recommender system provides the user with a recommendation list based on the initial query. The recommendations of the LOs suggested by the system include the core LOs of the queried concept and a few related topics based on the inferred SWRL rules. Figure 7 is a screen shot of the system when the user queries about the Validation process without the use of the ontology axioms.

In Figure 7 the system displays all SQA processes as invoked processes by the Validation process. Irrelevant knowledge have been prevented by adding axioms to the SQA ontology model. The results in Figure 8 show the system robustness when using ontology axioms as only contextually relevant resources are filtered. This validates the ontology conciseness and correctness when using ontology axioms (Figures 7 and 8).

In another scenario, the learner wants to know more about the Software Failure Avoidance concept. The screen shots shown in

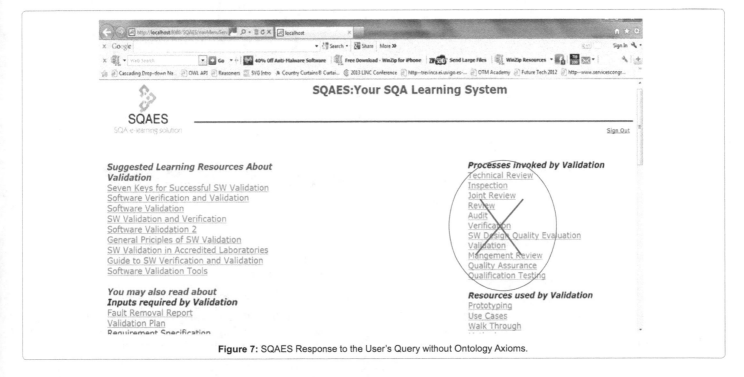

Figure 7: SQAES Response to the User's Query without Ontology Axioms.

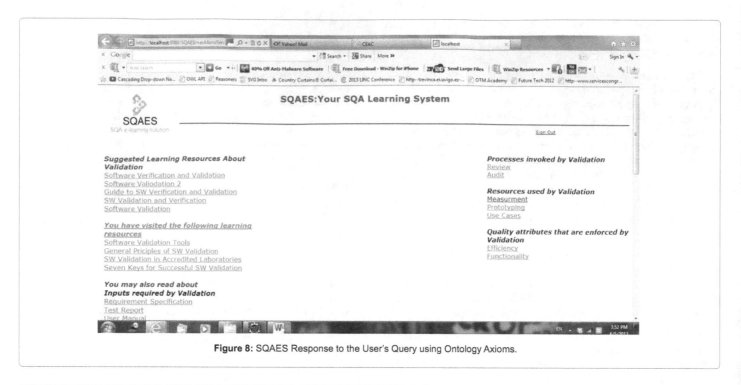

Figure 8: SQAES Response to the User's Query using Ontology Axioms.

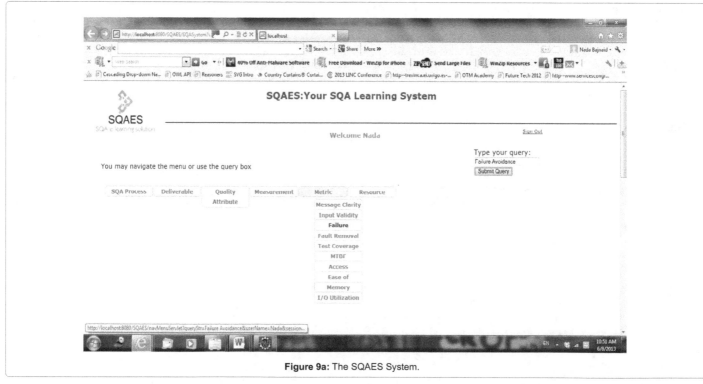

Figure 9a: The SQAES System.

Figures 9a-9d present the results from the system when the user queries "Software Failure Avoidance". The system initially provides all core LOs of the queried concept and a few related LOs generated when the reasoning system infers processes used to conduct the Failure Avoidance concept. These are related to software quality sub-characteristic that uses the Failure Avoidance measure and inputs to the Failure Avoidance measure. In this learning scenario (Figures 9a-9d), we show the system recommendations when the user viewed

a LO related to the core knowledge of Failure Avoidance, and then, the learner further investigation about the SQA concept "Validation" where already consumed LOs are shown (Figures 9a-9d).

Agile software development scenario

Although agile methods produce software faster, they need to attain quality products. While quality software is the output of quality process, it is not clear how current agile practices and methods attain

15

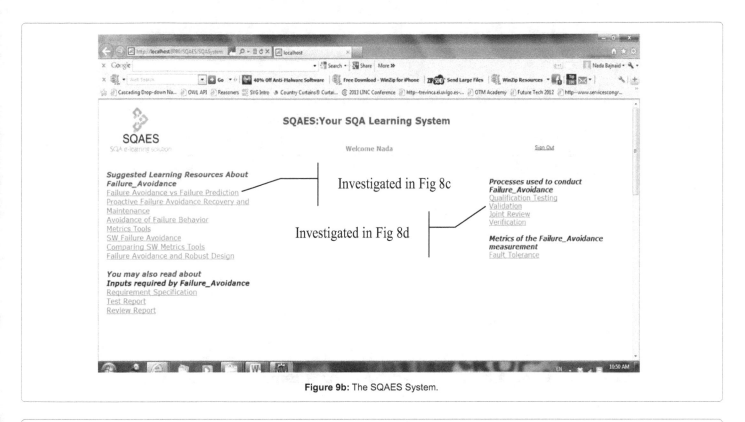

Figure 9b: The SQAES System.

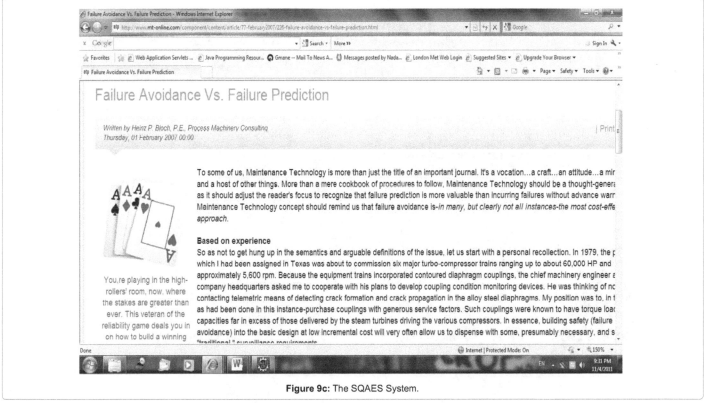

Figure 9c: The SQAES System.

quality under time pressure and in an unpredictable requirements environment. As an extension of the use of the prototype recommender system, the latter can be used to provide agile developers with, just-in-time and in a contextualized way, all necessary resources that deal with SQA related aspects of the software process at hand and hence improve quality in an agile software development environment. To support agility, which relies on individual's tacit knowledge that is very much based on usual work practices and methods, some agile software development resources [12,13] were used to encode related SQA concepts in the developed ontology. It should be noted that the

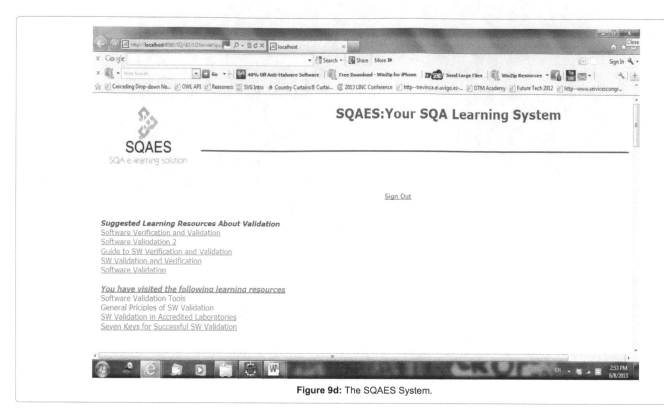

Figure 9d: The SQAES System.

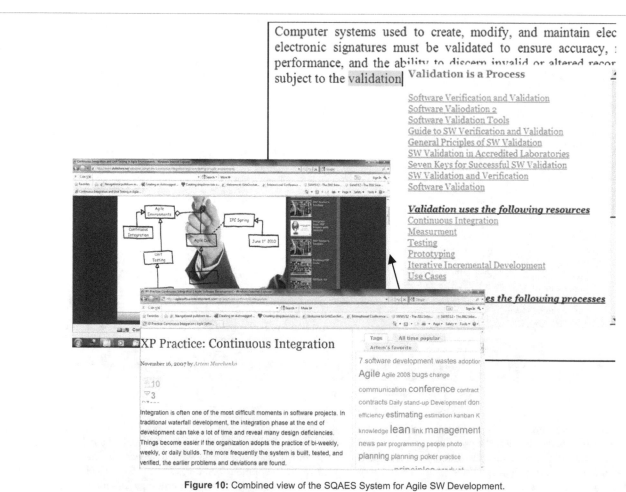

Figure 10: Combined view of the SQAES System for Agile SW Development.

inclusion of the agile terminology into the SQA ontology did not affect the concepts and relationships of the original ontology and thus confirms the expandability of the ontology.

To use the system in an agile development environment, the ontology is first used to annotate software development related keywords. Once a keyword is annotated, the system triggers a drop-down menu with all possible queries that can be generated from the ontology concept that is related to that keyword as shown in Figure 10. The example in Figure 10 shows a combined view with the drop-down menu displaying learning resources related to Validation and its SQA related concepts (invoked processes, produced deliverables, required inputs and used resources). In this case, the user would like to know more about Continuous Integration techniques that are used by the Validation process (Figure 10).

Related Work

In this section we survey recent work in the area of developing ontologies for SE knowledge representation with special focus on those developed for the SQA domain. Software Engineering Body Of Knowledge - SWEBOK-guide provides an international recognized consensus in software engineering terminology. SWEBOK has been used by many researchers to develop partial or sub-domain ontologies tailored to different purposes. However, comprehensive domain ontology in SE does not yet exist. Wille et al. [22] were the first to present a formal approach for designing ontology for SWEBOK. Their work was limited to modeling the taxonomy of software engineering as defined by SWEBOK knowledge areas. Also, their ontology is tightly designed to the SWEBOK naming space, which makes it difficult for mapping with externally defined concepts. Calero et al. [23] have developed a Software Measurement Ontology (SMO) to provide a coherent terminology among different software measurement proposals and standards. Unlike the ontology developed by Wille [22], the SMO ontology includes detailed knowledge about the measurement process, their attributes and results, while it does not link them to their SQA metrics and standards.

In the area of software testing, Barbosa et al. [24] have used the ISO/IEC 12207 [25] standard to develop Onto Test, an ontology based on a common well-defined vocabulary for software testing that can be useful to develop supporting tools and to increase interoperability among software testing tools. In our paper, we have borrowed few aspects of the Onto Test ontology, especially those related to testing processes, resources, and procedures [24]. In another related area, Kassab [26] proposed an ontological representation of the software Non-Functional Requirements (NFRs), their refinements, and their interdependencies. The ontology focuses mainly on the SQA measurement process, highlighting the mechanisms for measurable NFRs. For a complete classification of developed ontologies for software engineering [27].

Conclusion

In this paper we presented an ontological approach for developing a process-driven context-aware recommender to support agile software development. The SQA ontology developed in this study embeds both domain and operation knowledge about SQA processes and their requirements, including SQA quality attributes, metrics and SQA measurements based on the ISO/IEC 25010 and ISO/IEC 25023 standards. The system provides users with tailored SQA resources to support them developing the software process in hand in a timely manner. Context-awareness is achieved through a set of reasoning tools that take into account user's profile and learning history to recommend SQA resources needed for the task in hand. Also, reasoning axioms are

dynamically added to the ontology for refining the list of recommended LOs. An evaluation study was performed to check the developed SQA ontology in terms of consistency, clarity, and completeness and the results were very promising. Future research is directed towards developing an excessive ontology assessment from experts' point of view. An ontology evaluation questionnaire has been developed and the ontology is currently being extended based on suggestions provided by SQA specialists.

Acknowledgment

The authors would like to thanks reviewers for their assessments, comments, and suggestions that helped improve the current work.

References

1. Boehm B, Chulani S, Verner J, Wong B (2009) Seventh workshop on Software Quality. International Conference on Software Engineering, ICSE-Companion, Vancouver, Canada 449-450.

2. Saiedian H, Weide B (2005) The New Context for Software Engineering Education and Training. The Journal of Systems and Software 74: 109-111.

3. Kalermo J, Rissanen J (2002) Agile Software Development in Theory and Practice. Software Business program, Masters Thesis.

4. Huo M, Verner J, Babar AM, Zhu L (2004) How Does Agility Ensure Quality? Proc. 2nd Workshop on Software Quality, Scotland.

5. Wang M, Jia H, Sugumaran V, Ran W, Liao J (2011) A Web-based Learning System for Software Test Professionals. IEEE Transactions on Education 54: 263-272.

6. Bourque P, Dupuis R (2004) Guide to the Software Engineering Body of Knowledge. SWEBOK, Computer Society Press.

7. Kusters RJ, Van Solingen R, Trienekens JJM (1999) Strategies for the Identification and Specification of Embedded Software Quality. Proc. STEP'99: Software Technology and Engineering Practice 33-39.

8. Bajnaid N, Benlamri R, Cogan B (2011) Context-Aware SQA E-learning System. Proc. of the Sixth International Conference on Digital Information Management ICDIM 2011, Melbourne, Australia.

9. (2011) Systems and Software Engineering-Systems and software Quality Requirements and Evaluation (SQuaRE)-System and software quality models ISO/IEC 25010.

10. (2011) Systems and Software Engineering-Systems and software Quality Requirements and Evaluation (SQuaRE) – Measurement of system and software product quality ISO/IEC 25023.

11. Pressman RS (2005) Software Engineering: a Practitioner's Approach, (6thedn). McGraw-Hill Inc.

12. Bishop R, Lehman MM (1991) A View of Software Quality. IEEE Col. on Designing Quality into Software Based Systems. London.

13. Mnkandla E, Dwolatzky B (2006) Defining Agile Quality Assurance. Proc. ICSEA-International Conference on Software Engineering Advances, Tahiti.

14. Abrahamsson P, Salo O, Ronkainen J, Warsta J (2002) Agile Software Development Methods: Review and Analysis. (VTT Publication 478). Technical Research Centre of Finland, Espoo, Finland.

15. Vrandečić D (2009) Ontology Evaluation. Handbook on Ontologies. International Handbooks in Information Systems, (2ndedn), Springer, Heidelberg 293-313.

16. Gruber T (1995) Towards principles for the design of ontologies used for knowledge sharing. Int. Journal of Human-Computer Studies 43: 907-928.

17. Pérez G, Lopez F, Corcho O (2004) Ontological engineering: with examples from the areas of knowledge management, e-commerce and the semantic Web. Springer-Verlag, New York, London.

18. Brank J, Grobelnik M, Mladenic D (2005) A survey of ontology evaluation techniques. Proc. of 8th Int. multi-conf. Information Society, Ljubljana, Slovenia.

19. Haarslev V, Hidde K, Möller R, Wessel M (2011) The RacerPro Knowledge Representation and Reasoning System. Semantic Web 1: 1-5.

20. Obrst L, Ceusters W, Mani I, Ray S, Smith B (2007) The Evaluation of Ontologies: Toward Improved Semantic Interoperability. Chapter in: Semantic

Web 139-158.

21. (2003) Software Engineering – Product Quality, Part1: Internal Metrics ISO/IEC 9126-9133.

22. Wille C, Dumke RR, Abran A, Desharnais E (2004) E-Learning Infrastructure for Software Engineering Education: Steps on Ontology Modeling for SWEBOK. Proceedings of the IASTED International Conference on Software Engineering 520-525.

23. Calero C, Ruiz F, Piattini M (2006) Ontolgies in Software Engineering and Software Technology. Springer.

24. Barbosa EF, Nakagawa EY, Maldonado JC (2006) Towards the establishment of an ontology of software testing. 18th Int. Conf. on Soft. Engineering and Knowledge Engineering (SEKE'06) , San Francisco.

25. (2008) System and Software Engineering – Software Life Cycle Processes. JTC 1 Information technology ISO/IEC 12207.

26. Kassab M (2009) Formal and quantitative approach to non-functional requirements modeling and assessment in software engineering. PhD thesis, Concordia University, Canadas.

27. Zhao Y, Dong J, Peng T (2009) Ontology Classification for Semantic-Web-Based Software Engineering. IEEE Transactions on Services Computing 2: 303-317.

3

Distributed Deadlock Detection Technique with the Finite Automata

Shivendra Kumar P*, Hari Krishna T and R. K. Kapoor

Department of Computer Application and Research, National Institute of Technical Teachers Training and Research, Bhopal, India.

Abstract

In the distributed, system deadlocks is a fundamental problem. A process may request resources in any order, which may not be known in advance and a process can request resource while holding others. Deadlocks can occur if the sequence of the allocations of resources to the processes is not controlled. Fast and efficient deadlock detection is very challenging and difficult task in distributed systems. In this paper distributed deadlock is detected by the distributed control manager. We proposed a distributed deadlock detection algorithm based on the finite automata to detect deadlock in a distributed environment. In this proposed solution we draw the wait for graph for the distributed transaction with the help of finite automata. Our proposed algorithm avoids the transmitting massage to other nodes; it is based on the expansion of an unvisited node in the wait for graph with the help of finite automata. This finite automaton based deadlock detection technique works fast and takes less number of comparisons to detect the deadlock in the wait for graph.

Keywords: Distributed systems; Deadlock detection algorithm; Wait for graph; Finite automata.

Introduction

In a distributed system, deadlock is a situation which occurs when a process enters a waiting state because a resource requested is being held by another waiting process, which in turn is waiting for another resource [1]. If the process is unable to get full filled their request forever because the resource is requested by it is being held by another process, then the system is said to be in a deadlock [2]. Two common places where deadlocks may occur are with processes in an operating system (distributed or centralized) and with transactions in a database [3]. Deadlock is a common problem multiprocessing systems, parallel computing and distributed systems, where software resources and hardware resources are used to perform the task [4]. There are two major types of model available for the deadlock that is the AND model (also called the multiple-resource model), a process is allowed to make several resource requests, and it is blocked until all of the requests are granted. Processes in this model can be involved in several deadlock cycles at once [5,6]. In the OR model (also called the communication model), a process makes several requests and is blocked until any one of them is granted [6]. The AND-OR model allows a combination of request types, such as a request for resource X and either Y or Z [5]. Our proposed model is based totally on the AND model.

Necessary Conditions for Deadlock

Mutual exclusion

There must be some non-sharable resource. That only one process can access at a time [7].

Hold and wait

A process is holding a resource and requesting an additional resource which already held by other processes [5].

Ti-h (RI and Ti-w Rj) Where

Ti: Transaction i

Ri, Rj: Resources respectively i^{th} and j^{th}

h: resource in hold.

w: resource in wait.

No preemption

A resource can be only when the process has completed (voluntarily) its task.

Circular wait

A process must be waiting for a resource which is being held by another process, which in turn is waiting for the first process to release the resource [8].

Ti→Tj→Tk→Ti

Under deadlock detection technique, the manager allows for the system to occur deadlock. Then apply the detection algorithm to detect that a deadlock has occurred or not, occurred and subsequently it is recovered if there is a deadlock in the system [8].

Detecting a deadlock that has already occurred is easily possible since the resources that each process has locked and/or currently requested are known to the resource scheduler of the operating system. After a deadlock is detected, it can be recovered by using any of the two methods:

Process termination

When one or more processes involved in the deadlock maybe aborted or process has been killed. We can choose to abort all processes involved in the deadlock on the basis of utilization of CPU, resources held by the process and etc.

Resource preemption

This is the way to remove the deadlock from the system. So in this way Resources allocated to different processes is preempted and allocated to other processes until the deadlock is broken [5]. There are several variations to these algorithms that seek to optimize different parameters like, number of messages, length of messages, and frequency of detection.

In the proposed algorithm we have taken a number of probe

---

*Corresponding author: Shivendra Kumar P, Department of Computer Application and Research, National Institute of Technical Teachers Training and Research, Bhopal, India, Email: shivendrapandey786@gmail.com

massage comparisons and size of the message as a parameter to optimize the deadlock detection technique. In the paper, we have used the state transitions to find out the deadlock in the distributed system. We also have avoided sending a triple probe massage [4]. The number of massage comparisons with probe message is more and it is difficult to manage the probe massage [6]. In this paper we have shown that with the use of finite automata concept we need not to send the probe message in the outgoing link. In the Chandy Misra Haas model the concept of sending the number of probe massage has been used to find out deadlock and so the number of probe massage and their comparison is high in the AND model. In our proposed algorithm, there is no overhead for sending and waiting for the probe massage for the initiator and there is a very less number of transition it takes to detect the deadlock in the system because with the use of finite automata in the proposed algorithm, this decrease not only the comparisons of massages but also remove the concept of probe massage overhead.

Literature Survey

In the distributed deadlock detection techniques, there are many algorithms in practice. Some widely used algorithms are Obermarck's Path Pushing Algorithm, Chandy-Misra-Haas Edge-Chasing Algorithm

Obermarck's Path-Pushing Algorithm

In the Path Pushing algorithm the information about the global wait for graph is distributed in the form of paths from one site to another site [9]. In this algorithm, there is number of Processes (T1, T2, T3...... TN) and There is a special virtual node Ex. The transaction is totally ordered. The following steps show the process of Obermarck's path-pushing algorithm:

For each site S,

- Construct a wait-for-graph using the transaction-to-transaction wait-for relationships.

- Receive any strings of nodes transmitted from other sites and add them into the wait-for-graph.

a. For each transaction identified in the string, create a node of the TWFG if none exists at this site.

b. For each transaction identified in the string, starting with the first, create an edge to the node representing the next transaction in the string.

- Create wait-for edges from EXTERNAL to each node representing a transaction's agent that is expected to receive on a communication link.

- Create wait-for edges to EXTERNAL from each node representing a transaction's agent that is expected to send on a communication link.

- Analyze the resulting graph, listing all elementary cycles.

- Select a victim to break each cycle that does not contain the node external. As each victim is chosen for a given cycle, remove all cycles that include the victim.

a. Site must remember the transaction identifier of the victim such that it can discard strings received involves the victim.

b. If the victim transaction has an agent at this site, then the fact that the transaction was chosen as a victim must be transmitted to each site known to contain an agent of the victim transaction. Otherwise, the site has to transmit the fact to each site that

sends a string containing the victim's identifier to S.

- Examine each remaining cycle that contains the node External. If the transaction identifier of the node External is waiting for is greater than the node that waits for external, then

a. Transform the cycle into a string, which starts with "EX" and terminates with a node identifier that identify the node waiting for External on the site.

b. Send the string to each site which the terminating node in the string is waiting for.

- O (n (n-1)/2) messages

- O (n) message size

- O (n) detect deadlock

Chandy-Misra-Haas Edge-Chasing Algorithm

The scheme proposed by Chandy, Misra and Haas uses local WFGs to detect local deadlocks and probes to determine the existence of global deadlocks [4]. Chandy-Misra-Haas edge-chasing algorithm uses a probe message (i,j,k) deadlock detection initiated for process 'Pi' and send to and is sent by the site of 'Pj' to the site of Pk [4].

Deadlock initiated at pi: If

Pi is locally dependent on itself, then declares a deadlock else

send probe (i, j, k) to home site of Pk for each j, k such that all of the following hold

Pi is locally dependent on PjPj is waiting on Pk

Pj and Pk are on different sites

Receipt of probe (I, j, k) by node of Pk: check the following conditions:

Pk is blocked dependentk(i)=false

(Pk does not yet know that Pi is dependent on Pk)\Pk has not replied to all requests of Pj

if these are all true, do the following

setdependentk(i)=true(Pk now knows that Pi is dependent on Pk) if k=i declare that Pi is deadlocked

else

send probe (i,m,n) to the home site of Pn for every m and n such that the following all hold

Pk is locally dependent on Pm

Pm is waiting on Pn

Pm and Pn are on different sites

Performance of Chandy-Misra-Haas edge-chasing algorithm

- m(n-1)/2 messages for m processes at n sites

- 3-word message length

- O(n) delay to detect

The Proposed Algorithm

In our proposed algorithm, we have devised an approach to detect the deadlock with the help of finite automata. In this approach the process id is taken as an input (sigma) and the process is as a state. With the help of transition function, we draw the transition table; this helps us to detect the deadlock in the distributed system [10-13]. In the process of transition the unvisited or unexpended vertex/transition is selected to visit and we fully expand (visits its neighbors through directededge) the selected node/transition. And again one of the unvisited nodes from thetransition table is selected. If any node/transition has been visited once, we need not to explore it further. The process of expansions of vertices/transition is repeated until either we get the deadlock in the transition table or all the nodes have been expanded. A flag value has been given to the starting node of the transition so whenever we have fully expanded a node (visited all its neighbours through direct edge), we check the flag value to decide whether there is a deadlock in the system or not. If we do not get the deadlock for the first time, then we take the second node and repeat whole process for this node also. Continue the same process for all available nodes in the distributed system.

This is illustrated with the help of following example: Suppose we have 10 resources (A,B,C,D,E,F,G,H,I,J) and

4 Processes (P0, P1, P2, P3)

Here h denotes resource in hold and w denote wait for the resource. With reference to figure 1 below:

P0—h→A, P0—w→C;

P1—w→A, P1—h→B, P1—w→D;

P2—h→C, P2—w→H, P2—h→J;

P3—w→B, P3—w→F, P3—h→H, P3-h→G;

P4—w→E, P4—f→F;

P5—h→D, P5—h→E, P5—w→I;

P6—h→I, P6—w→G, P6—w→J;

In this proposed algorithm the wait for graph is based on transition input and current state.

Here we have taken the transition input from the resource allocated process, for which the current process is in waiting state (Figure1).

Distributed Deadlock Detection

In this proposed algorithm we have used distributed control system to detect the deadlock where the wait for graph (WFG) is spread over different sites. Any site can initiate the deadlock detection process by constructing a global wait-for graph from local wait-for graphs at a deadlock detector or by a distributed algorithm like edge chasing [14,15]. The control manager will decide when to take the decision to go for detecting the deadlock. It might be based on some threshold value for the CPU utilization, throughput, and/or some other parameter, or when the system is irresponsive. A distributed system is an environment where a number of heterogeneous machines are running parallel and performing the task, so when request are made in the distributed environment, these machines uses mutually exclusive resource so sometimes for a resource it is possible that one process using it and another process for the same resource. So in the distributed system, it is very difficult for the distributed system manager to manage the resource. So while keeping one resource and waiting for the other resource will lead to the wastage of resource and processor utilization too. Some it is also possible where there are more than one process holding a resource and waiting for another which is held by another process and the other process is also waiting for the resource that is held by the first process; under such situation deadlock situation occurs.

This type of situation is very common in the distributed environment. We have taken an example of distributed systems; in the example there are four machines that are running in the distributed environment, fashion and processes are requesting the resources from the distributed manager and distributed manager grant them the required resources (Figure 2). In our algorithm we have setup a flag value with the initiator of the transition table. So every time when we fully expand (visit all the outgoing edges) the process we check the flag value .And according to the flag value we decide the deadlock. If there is change in the flag value then it indicate the deadlock and if there is no change in the flag value then check with the others.

Distributed deadlock detection algorithm:

M (Q, δ, Σ)

Q=Set Of Processes;

Q=P1, P2.............Pn;

Σ=Set Of Input Symbol;

Σ=1, 2,...n;

δ=Transition Function

δ: Q × Σ→Q

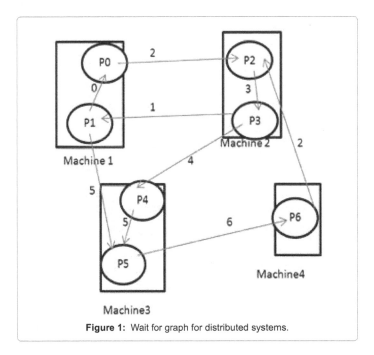

Figure 1: Wait for graph for distributed systems.

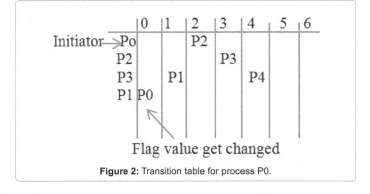

Flag value get changed

Figure 2: Transition table for process P0.

Step1: Select a process (Qi);

Step2: Initially create a matrix of size $1 \times \Sigma$;

$Qi \times \Sigma$;

Where: Qi is the selected state for deadlock detection;

Initialize: Flag=0: for process Qi;

Step3: Make transitions for Qi,

We have transition function

$\delta: Q \times \Sigma \rightarrow Q$

$\delta: Qi \times \Sigma \rightarrow Q$

Repeat step 3 for All Σ for state Qi;

Step 4: Select one of the unvisited process Qk to visit, from the Qi;

Select a state from

$\delta: Qi \times \Sigma \rightarrow Qk$;

We have transition function:-

$\delta: Q \times \Sigma \rightarrow Q$

$\delta: Qk \times \Sigma \rightarrow Q$

For all Σ state Qk;

If ($Qk \times \Sigma \rightarrow Qi$)

{Set flag=1; Go to step 6;}

Else if (there is a unvisited process) Go to step 4;

Else go to step 7;

Step 6: report there is deadlock,

Go to step 8;

Step 7: report there is no deadlock,

Go to step 8;

Step 8: exit;

Performance of Proposed Algorithm

The time complexity of our proposed algorithm is based on number of process 'n' in the distributed system. Our proposed algorithm takes less number of comparisons in average case and in best case it takes very less comparisons [13-16].

Analysis of Comparisons to Find Out the Deadlock in the System

For the initiator's transmission there is zero comparison. Otherwise when we select one of the processes to visit and after transmitting all the transitions, we check two things,

1. Is there is change in flag value; if yes then report deadlock

2. Else (go for another comparison) If the flag value is not changed but there is some process to visit then go and select another process and visit it. Else report deadlock

Here for the 1st process no comparison is made and for remaining (n-1) processes it will take 2 comparisons each time,

Thus total number of comparisons is, 0+2(n-1) i.e. 2(n-1)

Analysis of Number of Transmissions to Find Out the Deadlock in the System

First process can take transmission up to (n-1) nodes, and second can take all the transmission (n-2) and third can take all the transmission (n-3) and the n-1st node will take 1 transmission so it will take [13].

(n-1)+ (n-2) + (n-3) +..........................+ 1=n(n-1)/2 Therefore, total number of transmission are n(n-1)/2

For summary of performance of proposed algorithm, refer table at appendix 1. Since we have not used any message thus message size is zero.

Conclusion

In this paper we have investigated Obermarck's path pushing algorithm, Chandy-Misra-Haas edge-chasing algorithm for distributed deadlock detection techniques [15-16]. We have proposed a deadlock detection algorithm in distributed environment. Our deadlock detection algorithm is totally based on finite automata concept so execution of algorithm is based on the transition function of detection algorithm. By this algorithm, we have avoided the phantom deadlock problem in the distributed environment and so our deadlock detection approach detects only the real deadlocks and reports this. This proposed algorithm is more efficient due to reduced overheads.

References

1. Farajzadeha N, Hashemzadeha M, Mousakhania M, Haghighata AT (2005) An Efficient Generalized Deadlock Detection and Resolution Algorithm in Distributed Systems. The Fifth International Conference on Computer and Information Technology. Shanghai.

2. Yeung CF, Hung SH , Lam KY, Law CK (1994) A New Distributed Deadlock Detection Algorithm ForDistributed Database Systems. Browse Conference Publications 1: 506-510.

3. Brzezirislti J, Helary JM, Raynal M (1995) Deadlocks in Distributed Systems: Request Models andDefinitions. IEEE 186-193 Cheju Island.

4. Chendy M, Misra J, Haas LM (1983) Distributed Deadlock Detection. ACMTmns. Comput Syst 1: 143-156

5. Holliday JL, Abbadi EA (2000) Distributed Deadlock Detection. University of California at Santa Barbara.

6. Lee S, Lee Y A (1999) Distributed Algorithm for Deadlock Detection under OR-request Model. Conference: Reliable Distributed Systems, IEEE.

7. Obermarck, R (1982) Distributed Deadlock Detection Algorithm ACM Trans.on Database Systems

8. Chen S, Deng Y, Attie P, Sun W (1996) Optimal deadlock detection in distributed systems based on locally constructed wait-for graphs. Proc. Int'l Conf. Distributed Computing Systems. IEEE, pp. 613-619.

9. Knapp E (1987) Deadlock Detestion in Distributed Database. ACM Comp.Sur 19: 302- 328

10. Ajay DK, Singhal M (1997) Distributed Detection of Generalized Deadlocks. IEEE 553-560 Baltimore.

11. Kawazu S, Minami S, Itoh K, Teranaka K (1979) Two-Phase Deadlock Detection Algorithm in Distributed Databases. IEEE 5: 360-367.

12. Kshemkalyani A, Singhal M (1989) Deadlock detection in distributed systems. IEEE Computer 22: 37-48.

13. Lee S (2002) Fast Detection and Resolution of Generalized Distributed Deadlocks. IEEE, pp. 429-436.

14. Lee S (2004) Fast, Centralized Detection and Resolution of Distributed Deadlocks in the Generalized Model IEEE Trans. On Software Engineering 30: 561-573.

15. Shyam B, Dhamdhere DM (1990) A New PriorityBased Probe Algorithm for Distributed DeadlockDetection," Indian Inst. of Technology, Bombay, Technical Report.

16. Roesler M, Burkhard WA (1989) Resolution of Deadlocks in Object-Oriented Distributed Systems. IEEE Trans. Computers 38: 1212-1224.

4

An Approach towards Efficient Ranked Search over Encrypted Cloud

Rajpreet Kaur[1]*and Manish Mahajan[2]

[1]CGC, Landran Mohali, Punjab, India
[2]Computer Science and Engineering, CGC, Landran Mohali, Punjab, India

Abstract

In present, Cloud computing is a dominant field in information technology. With the increased rate of data outsourcing over cloud data privacy of sensitive data becomes a big issue. For the security purpose data is encrypted before outsourcing. But encrypted data is very difficult to be retrieved efficiently. Although some traditional search schemes are available for searching encrypted data, but these techniques are merely base on Boolean search and not deals with the relevance of files. These approaches suffer from two main shortcomings. Firstly, if one user has no pre-knowledge of encrypted data, has to process every retrieved file to find results of his use. Secondly, every time retrieving all the files containing query keyword increases network traffic. This work is dedicated to develop an approach for secure and effective retrieval of cloud data. Ranked search greatly improves the performance by returning the files in ranked order based on some similarity relevance criteria. To achieve more practical performance, system demonstrates an approach for symmetric searchable encryption (SSE) which utilizes information retrieval and cryptography primitives. Hence the implementation is based on order-preserving symmetric encryption (OPSE).

Keywords: Cloud; Data privacy; Similarity relevance; Ranking; SSE

Introduction

Cloud computing can be assumed as a model for delivering information technology services (like storage space, networking, applications etc) in which resources are retrieved from internet using web based tools, rather than a direct connection to server. Cloud computing provides hardware and software resources from a shared pool of resources on rent according to user's demand. So this technology releases user from burdens of management efforts and also from headaches of installation and maintenance.

Service model

Cloud software as a service (SaaS): In this software is made available to the user as service. Cloud applications are generally accessible from various devices like mobile, tablet, laptop, PC, workstations, servers etc. The user has no control over the underlying platform and infrastructure. Examples are Dropbox, Gmail, Gtalk etc.

Cloud platform as a service (PaaS): In this software is made available to the user as service. Programming languages and tools are provided by service provider to develop and deployment services. A user has no control over underlying infrastructure but has control over the deployed applications. Examples are Windows Azure, Google App Engine.

Cloud infrastructure as a service (IaaS): In this Software is made available to the user as a service. A user can demand computing infrastructure, storage infrastructure and network infrastructure etc from service provider. User is not the actual owner of the infrastructure but has control over operating systems, storage, deployed applications etc. For example Amazon, Rack space cloud.

Searching Cloud Data

As cloud computing has become a prevalent platform in information technology, the amount of sensitive information centralized over cloud is also increasing. These information files contain confidential data like personal medical records, government documents, private photos etc. To protect privacy of data and to prevent unauthorized access, it becomes very necessary to encrypt data before outsourcing to ensure data integrity and confidentiality. Along with this, data owner may share their outsourced data with a number of users. But, each user desires to retrieve files of his own interest during a given time period,

which makes data utilization very challenging. From the existing approaches, most common is using keyword based search technique. These techniques are commonly applied for plaintext search scenarios where user can retrieve the files of interest by giving keyword in query. Unluckily, data encryption for securing outsourced data makes these traditional methods to become fail for searching cloud data. Although, some traditional encryption techniques facilitate user to search over encrypted data without first decrypting it. But these techniques only support Boolean search, where files are retrieved according to presence or absence of keyword in file and don't consider relevance of files (Figure 1).

Many existing approaches for ranked order search and relevance score of files are being used by Information retrieval (IR) community for searching cloud data. Although the importance of ranked search is

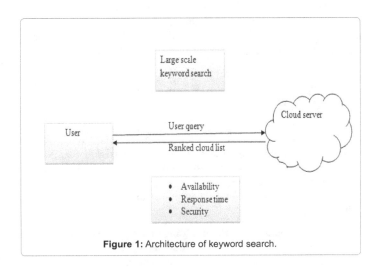

Figure 1: Architecture of keyword search.

*Corresponding author: Rajpreet Kaur, Research Scholar, CGC, Landran Mohali, Punjab, India, Email: Preet.billing00@gmail.com

receiving attention from a long time, yet the topic of encrypted search is not addressed much. Therefore enabling a mechanism for secure symmetric encryption and ranked search is a problem tackled in this work.

Related Work

Early searchable encryption techniques were only base on exact keyword search [1-6]. Song et al. gave an SE scheme for symmetric keyword search. In which each file in the file is encrypted using two-layered encryption method [1]. Index creation is used by some researchers for efficiency improvement. In index based techniques secure index is constructed for every unique word in a file [2,6]. In the work proposed by Curtmola et al., for each keyword index construction, entries are done to hash table. Each entry contains index for unique word and their trapdoor file identifier [5].

Further, some researchers stepped towards ranked search to improve usability. Wang et al. [7,8] proposed ranked search mechanism based on certain relevance scores to identify similarity of files with queried keyword. This approach was single-keyword based. Moving a step ahead, multi-keyword search is elaborated by Yang et al. and Cao et al. [9,10]. They used "similarity based inner product for result ranking.

However, all above schemes are exact keyword search based. For enhancing search flexibility, fuzzy- keyword based search is introduced by some authors [11-13]. Edit distance concept is used for calculating similarity of keywords with each other for generating fuzzy keyword sets for indexes. Li et al. and Wang et al. [11,14] presented this edit distance procedure. In this paper an implementation is given for secure symmetric search encryption and ranking of results in a particular order according to some relevance criteria.

Searchable Symmetric Encryption

System Model- Basic model involves three types of entities which are represented in the Fig. These entities are named as Data owner (O), cloud server (CS) and user (U). A collection of n data files $C=(F_1, F_2, \ldots , F_n)$ is outsourced by data owner onto the cloud into encrypted format. However for effective utilization of encrypted files data owner creates secure index I using a set m of different keywords given by $W=(w_1, w_2, ..., w_m)$, which are extracted from file collection C. After this both encrypted data and indexes are outsourced onto the cloud server.

When an authorized user wants to retrieve some data file which contains some keyword w, a secret search trapdoor is created by user to the cloud server.

When server receives the search request T_w, all the computation is done by server. After checking the index I, server returns the matching files to user. Project considers the secure ranked keyword search problem as follows: the search result should be returned according to certain ranked relevance criteria (e.g., keyword frequency), to improve file retrieval accuracy for users without prior knowledge on the file collection C. w (Figure 2).

All the computation work for finding search results and generating relevance score of files is done at cloud server. Hence the server has the access to all the files which are stored. For security purpose server should act in an "honest" manner and strictly follows the assigned protocols.

It considers an "honest-but-curious" server in our model. In other words, the cloud server has no intention to actively modify the message flow or disrupt any other kind of services.

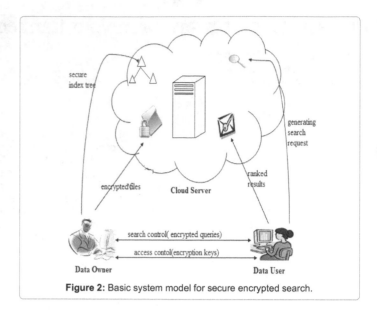

Figure 2: Basic system model for secure encrypted search.

Index and semantic relationship library (SRL) for various unique words is constructed using metadata created. When user gives some query keyword, server expands it on the basis of SRL. After searching index, it returns the relevant files to user.

Design goals

To enable ranked searchable symmetric encryption for effective utilization of outsourced cloud data under the aforementioned model, project design should achieve the following security and performance guarantee. Specifically, it has the following goals:

- Ranked keyword search: To explore various existing mechanisms for secure searchable encryption and to build a framework for effective ranked search.

- Security guarantee: To making the outsourced data secure by preventing cloud server from learning plaintext of files.

- Achieving Efficiency: Above goals should be achieved with minimum communication and computation overhead.

Notation and preliminaries

- C – the file collection to be outsourced, denoted as a set of n data files $C=(F_1, F_2, \ldots , F_n)$.

- W – the distinct keywords extracted from file collection C, denoted as a set of m words $W=(w_1, w_2, ..., w_m)$.

- $\text{id}(F_j)$ – the identifier of file F_j that can help uniquely locate the actual file.

- I – the index built from the file collection, including a set of posting lists $\{I(w_i)\}$, as introduced below.

- T_{wi} – the trapdoor generated by a user as a search request of keyword w_i.

- $F(w_i)$ – the set of identifiers of files in C that contain keyword w_i.

- N_i – the number of files containing the keyword w_i and

- $N_i=|F(w_i)|$.

Further project introduces some necessary information retrieval background for our proposed system:

Inverted index

Inverted index (also referred as posting files) is widely used indexing scheme in information retrieval. In inverted index structure a unique index value is given to every keyword and list of mappings is generated from keywords to the files in which word is present. For enabling ranked search, a relevance score for files is calculated using some mathematical assumptions.

Ranking function

A ranking function is used to compute similarity of terms by calculating relevance score. For a given search request, score is generated for matching files which are relevant to queried keyword. The most widely used statistical measurement for evaluating relevance score in the information retrieval community uses the TF × IDF rule, where TF (term frequency) is simply the number of times a given term or keyword appears within a file (to measure the importance of the term within the particular file), and IDF (inverse document frequency) is obtained by dividing the number of files in the whole collection by the number of files containing the term (to measure the overall importance of the term within the whole collection).

Order preserving symmetric encryption

The OPSE is a deterministic encryption scheme where the numerical ordering of the plaintexts gets preserved by the encryption function. Boldyreva et al. [15] gives the first cryptographic study of OPSE primitive and implements a secure search framework using pseudorandom function and permutation. This work considers an order-preserving function $g(\cdot)$ from domain $D=\{1, \ldots, M \}$ to range $R=\{1, \ldots, N \}$, which can be uniquely defined by a combination of M out of N ordered items. An OPSE can be said secure only if an attacker has to perform a brute force search over all the possible combinations of M out of N to break the encryption scheme. If the security level chosen is of 64 bits, then it is good to choose $M=N/2 > 64$, in order to create number of combinations so that the total number of combinations will be greater than 264. This construction is based on relationship between order preserving function and hyper geometric probability distribution (HGD). Their construction is based on an uncovered relationship between a random order-preserving function (which meets the above security notion) and the hyper geometric probability distribution, which will later be denoted as HGD. Readers can refer [15] for more details of OPSE. As first look, It seems changing relevance based encryption from earlier search schemes to OPSE is very efficient. But OPSE is deterministic encryption scheme, in which if data is not handled appropriately, then a little mistake can leaks lots of information.

Problem Statement

Problem formulation

In the early techniques for symmetric search like fuzzy keyword search etc, were mainly used for searching. However, these techniques enhance search flexibility and usability. They consider structure of terms and edit distance between terms to calculate similarity [16]. But don't consider the terms semantically related to search keyword. The results were only based on presence or absence of keyword. For example these schemes only consider certain misspelling or inconsistencies like "Written" or "written" are considered to be similar. The most important thing which was Result-ranking was still out of ordering.

Implementation of system

Semantic expansion based similar search enhances usability by returning exactly matching files and also returns the files which are relevant to given query keyword. From the metadata set cloud server generates the inverted index and constructs the semantic relationship library (SRL) for keywords set. Cloud server automatically finds all relevance files using SRL, when user makes a search request.

In the implemented system, to ensure security and final result ranking, order-preserving encryption is used to preserve numerical ordering for protecting relevance score.

The above straightforward approach demonstrates the core problem that causes the inefficiency of ranked searchable encryption. Server should perform searching and ranking quickly by not knowing relevance score and other information of files.

The main objectives of the given scheme are discussed below:

- To design a search scheme for encrypted cloud data that gives relevance score to files with query keyword and returns the retrieved files in order.

- To enable efficient utilization of data files using ranked searchable encryption scheme.

- To enable security by preventing cloud server from learning plaintext of data files.

Methodology

Implementation of discussed work is shown by the flowchart in the figure given below (Figures 3 and 4).

Steps of implementation

1. In first step, encryption of data is done using AES (Asymmetric encryption standard) algorithm. The implementation is done by generating local environment in MATLAB. Different GUI (Graphical user interface) are created for user interaction. This algorithm encrypts the data file and also creates index value for every unique keyword [17] (Figure 5).

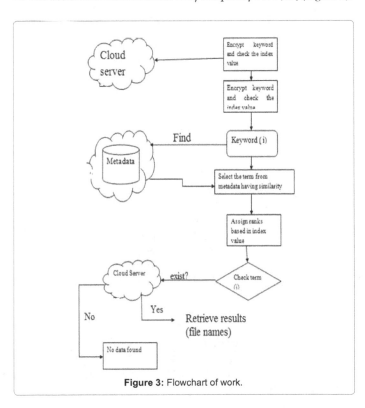

Figure 3: Flowchart of work.

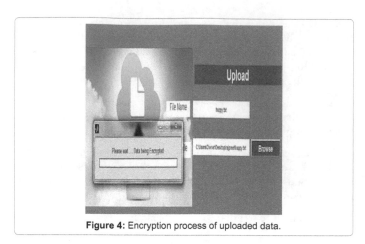

Figure 4: Encryption process of uploaded data.

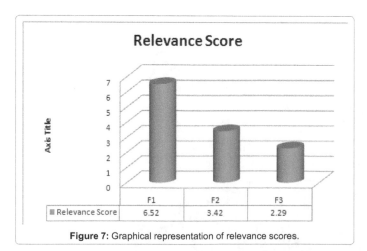

Figure 5: Encrypted file.

File ID	Relevance Score
F1	6.52
F2	3.42
F3	2.29

Figure 6: Table for relevance score.

Relevance Score

	F1	F2	F3
▪ Relevance Score	6.52	3.42	2.29

Figure 7: Graphical representation of relevance scores.

2. After encryption and indexing Metadata is created for keywords. In metadata relative terms are represented.

3. Now if a user searches a term by giving query keyword, then SSE (Secure symmetric encryption) and OPSE are used for giving results in ranked order.

Result Analysis

The experimental results can be explained with the set of some snapshots.

1. First of all a data owner uploads some data file, which is encrypted using AES algorithm.

2. The uploaded on cloud server can be searched in a secure way using SSE (secure symmetric encryption) algorithm. The search results are displayed in ranked form using OPSE (order preserving symmetric encryption

3. Algorithm generate the relevance score of files based on term frequency (TF) and inverse domain frequency (IDF), using the equation TF×IDF. Where TF can be defined as the number of times given keyword or term exists in a given file. IDF can be calculated by dividing the number of files in whole collection by number of files containing that keyword (Figures 6 and 7).

4. Hence based on relevance score files can be ranked for more symmetry.

References

1. Song DX, Wagner D, Perrig A (2000) Practical techniques for searches on encrypted data. Proceedings of IEEE Symposium on Security and Privacy, IEEE, Berkeley, California.

2. Goh EJ (2003) Secure indexes. Cryptology ePrint Archive, Report 2003/216

3. Boneh D, Cresecenzo G, Ostrovsky R, Persiano G (2004) Public key encryption with keyword search. Advances in Cryptology- Eurocrypt 3027: 506-522.

4. Chang YC, Mitzenmacher M (2005) Privacy preserving keyword searches on remote encrypted data. Applied Cryptography and Network Security 3531: 442-455.

5. Curtmola R, Garay J, Kamara S, Ostrovsky R (2006) Searchable symmetric encryption: improved definitions and efficient constructions. Proceedings of the 13th ACM conference on Computer and communications security, ACM, Alexandria, VA, USA.

6. Bellare M, Boldyreva A, O'Neill A (2007) Deterministic and efficiently searchable encryption. In Advances in Cryptology-CRYPTO 4622: 535-552.

7. Wang C, Cao N, Li J, Ren K, Lou W (2010) Secure ranked keyword search over encrypted cloud data. 30th IEEE International Conference on Distributed Computing Systems (ICDCS), IEEE Comp Society Washington, DC, USA.

8. Wang C, Cao N, Ren K, Lou W (2012) Enabling secure and efficient ranked keyword search over outsourced cloud data. IEEE Trans Parallel Distrib Syst 23:1467-1479.

9. Cao N, Wang C, Li M, Ren K, Lou W (2011) Privacy-preserving multi-keyword ranked search over encrypted cloud data. Proceedings of IEEE INFOCOM. IEEE, Shanghai.

10. Yang C, Zhang W, Xu J, Xu J, Yu N (2012) A Fast Privacy-Preserving Multi-keyword Search Scheme on Cloud Data. International Conference on Cloud and Service Computing (CSC). IEEE, Shanghai, China.

11. Wang C, Ren K, Yu S, Urs, KMR (2012) Achieving Usable And Privacy-assured similarity search over outsourced cloud data. Proceeding of IEEE INFOCOM, Orlando, Florida, USA.

12. Li J, Wang Q, Wang C, Cao N, Ren K, et al. (2010) Fuzzy keyword search over encrypted data in cloud computing. Proceedings of IEEE INFOCOM. IEEE, San Diego, CA, USA.

13. Xia Z, Zhu Y, Sun X, Chen L (2014) Secure semantic expansion based search over encrypted cloud data supporting similarity ranking. Journal of Cloud Computing 3.

14. Stefanov E, Papamanthou C, Shi E (2014) Practical Dynamic Searchable Encryption with Small Leakage. NDSS '14, San Diego, CA, USA, pp. 23-26.

15. Boldreva A, Chenette N, Lee Y, O'neill A (2009) Order-preserving Symmetric encryption. Advances in Cryptology EUROCRYPT 2009 Springer, Berlin, Heidelberg 5479: 224-241.

16. Bellare M, Boldyreva A, O'Neill A (2007) Deterministic and efficiently searchable encryption. Advances in Cryptology CRYPTO, Springer, Berlin,Heidelberg 4622: 535- 552.

17. Chuah M, Hu W (2011) Privacy-aware bed tree based solution for fuzzy multi-keyword search over encrypted data. 31st International Conference on Distributed Computing Systems Workshops (ICDCSW). IEEE, Minneapolis, Minnesota, USA.

5

An Architectural Approach for the Dynamic Adaptation of Services-based Software

Baroudi Mohammed Yassine*, Benammar Abdelkrim and Bendimerad Fethi Tarik

Department of Electrical Engineering and Electronics, University Aboubakr BELKAID Tlemcen, Algeria

Abstract

Services are very important component of software which will be essential part for future internet applications. Development of several applications considering the need of open environment and large scale usage is the need of the hours. Alternative intelligent presence and absence of services along with maintaining the quality is important. Dynamic adaptations and their optimum efficiency are mandatory to have a better application and solution. Moreover, novel application development requires other factors to be considered, such as, cost effectiveness and reusability of the existing components in a better and effective manner. This article proposes specific software architecture for dynamical service adaptation. The services are constituted by reusable software components. The adaptation's goal is to optimize the service function of their execution context. For a first step, the context will take into account just the user needs but other elements will be added. A particular feature in our proposition is the profiles that are used not only to describe the context's elements but also the components itself. An Adapter analyzes the compatibility between all these profiles and detects the points where the profiles are not compatibles. The same Adapter search and apply the possible adaptation solutions: component customization, insertion, extraction or replacement.

Keywords: Adaptive service; Software component; Service; Dynamic adaptation

Introduction

The operation of a service application must consider different elements that interact with its operation which are provided as following:

A service application is generally constructed by assembling a variety of software components. These pre-existing software components are being reused to build the application. Productions are continued by different manufacturers. Such components are adapted depending on the specific context of their use. In the present days, the Internet has become a free and dynamic market of reusable components.

During the daily usage of these applications, they use different types of terminals. They appear continuously in the market and it is impossible to predict at prior all target platforms, especially, in the field of mobile terminals. We assume that, all such systems have a computing capacity and sufficient RAM, and various means of connection (GSM, GPRS, LAN or Bluetooth).

User needs are diverse and evolving continuously. Some of these depend on the physical context, i.e., location, external noise etc. or the social context, such as, human issues. For example, it may be necessary to complete a service to suit the specific requirements of the user. A visually impaired person in need of a suitable IHM child requires simple vocabulary French speakers quite literate than French.

We grouped all of these items listed in the notion of context of the service. This context is variable and constantly influences the services from different point of views. The context adaptation service is an important problem whose expected solution is variable with time. Considering a service application is built by assembling components, we believe that the adaptation of the latter should be carried out at its architecture level either by adding, removing, or replacement of its components.

Relevant Literature Evidences

It has been observed that several researches have been carried out dealing with dynamic adaptation problems in the past, hence, allowed the emergence of several approaches. In the model driven approach, the dynamic adaptation is based on a component model that is designed to support this kind of adaptation.

Dynamic Component Updating (DCUP) [1] is an example of such approach. In DCUP, the component is divided into two parts: permanent part and replaceable part. Adapting a component refers to the alteration of its replaceable part by a new version at run-time.

In the reflexive approach, an application contains an abstract level (meta-level) that reify the real system. Under such circumstances, the adaptation is made first on the meta-level, after that, the changes are reflected on the executed applications. Thanks to the causal connection between the meta-level and the real system. An example of this system is DYVA [2]: a reflexive framework for dynamic reconfiguration of components-based applications. The framework is decomposed in two main parts: The base-level represents the concrete application that provides the expected functionalities and its execution environment and the reconfiguration of the machine that contains two major characteristics. The different operational modules responsible for achieving the reconfiguration in a major characteristic and the other issue is the meta-level which represents the reification of the concrete application.

Architectures for Adaptation Services

Many systems that support services associated with dynamic adaptation usually consist of three parts:

1.   The formed part of the service that can be adapted dynamically according to wide variety of techniques [3].

*Corresponding author: Baroudi Mohammed Yassine, Department of Electrical Engineering and Electronics, University Aboubakr BELKAID Tlemcen, Algeria
E-mail: yassinebaroudi@hotmail.com

2.   The party responsible for evaluating continuously the group consisting of the service and its context and performs a monitoring task.

3.   The control part generating a logic that is specific to the user's/developer's reconfiguration commands.

These three parts are physically distinct. In some proposals, all the three parts are present in each component. For example, the model proposed by Segara and André [4] allows each component to be adapted, to possess a part related to the observation and possibly generate reconfiguration commands.

Aksit and Choukair [5] proposed an overview of the dynamic reconfiguration and adaptation techniques. Some techniques for dynamic adaptation are as follows: insertable components, alternative algorithms, oriented programming aspects-AOP, composition filters, connectors changeable, interaction patterns as described by Blay-Fornarino et al. [6], reflexive middleware [7], behavior injectors, and adaptive interface.

Objective

In this article, our goal is to propose a software architecture that enables the dynamic adaptation of services built by assembling components depending on a variety of usage contexts. As part of this first experiment, the context relates to the user's needs.

The main feature of our proposal is the behavior of each service in relation to its context of use which is evaluated by the analysis of the behavior of each component constituting the service.

For this, we used profiles that describe not only the elements of context but also each component constituting the service. An adapter analyzes the consistency of different profiles for each component and the contextual elements of the profiles.

The adapter detects the mismatch points through seeking and applying various components of the service changes which are required to restore. Based on such compatibility issues and by changing configuration settings through adding, removing, or replacing components, adapters aid in restoring the service.

Architecture for Dynamic Adaptation of Service

The proposed architecture is consists of three parts which are described in the following section:

•   Modifiable part: This part consists of the service containing an assembly of components. The modifiable elements are the components, and the various interconnections between these components.

•   Monitoring part: This part is represented by monitors who observe the resources and user profiles. These elements provide the necessary data for a complete description of the service called meta-description of all petrol contexts.

•   Control part: This part is represented by the Adapter which from the description of all petrol contexts decides the necessary modification to accommodate the service. In this context, an assembler dictates adapter. The adapter uses existing components found within the basic components, such as, adaptation options (Figure 1).

Illustrative example

A bulletin board service allows a community of students to exchange information on scientific and cultural activities within the university. For customary reasons, the language focus is French. Student members

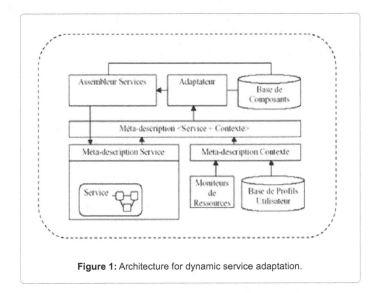

Figure 1: Architecture for dynamic service adaptation.

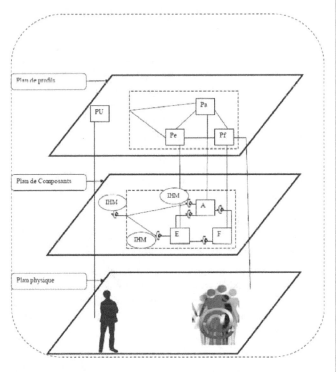

Figure 2: The meta-description of all Service-context "different planes of view.

have the opportunity to write and read on the forum.

Meta-description of all service-context

Figure 2 shows a perspective on the meta-description of all corresponding context-service scenario presented in the illustrative example.

We find three different levels in this:

•   The user plane containing the physical elements of context.

•   The plan components containing the architecture description language (ADL) service and

- Interface definition language (IDL) components.

- The ADLs describe software architectures. Rewriting the rules capture and consolidate adaptations as sets of rules (patterns) and facilitate their selection.

- The profile plan that meets the service profile and the context profile indicates how the service is.

User plane – physical elements of the context: Physical layer contains the physical elements of the context. In this case, they are the users of the forum service. The items found in this plan have projections in the profile plan. These projections form the meta-description of the context.

The plan components – service components assembly: The plan contains component's "S" service as assembly of software components that are the basis of bundles of OSGI platform. For our example it consists of:

- Component A: Display messages posted on the forum,

- Component E: Writing new message

- Component F: Forum contains all the messages posted on the forum.

The IHM service "S" is constructed from a composition IHM components E and A. This plan components represent the syntactic part of the meta-description of the service. To describe the service in this plan we use ADL type of language that describes the internal architecture of the service, IDL descriptors and interconnections that are MANIFEST. MF files for the components. We have also included the IHM interconnections (or connectors).

The profiles plan – user profile, profile components, composition profiles: The profiles of the plan are essential for adaptation because it represents the semantics of the meta-description of the set service-context. For the example chosen it contains:

The profile of the PS service, the user profile Pu. PS is the result of the composition profiles of the components that make up the service "S"Pe, Pa, Pf. This plan contains the semantics of all service context.

The user profile contains, in our example, a single parameter: language = 'Ar', indicating a user writing in English. The profile of a component indicates how the component works with respect to the parameters of context. The profile of a component translation for Arabic to French:

```
<profile>
<component>Translation AR_FR</component><point>
<interface>Translation</interface>
<method>translate</method>
<argument>text</argument>
<argtype>String</argtype><precondition>langue = 'AR' </precondition>
</point>
<point>
<interface>Translation</interface>
<method>translate</method>
<returntype>String</returntype>
```

```
<function>=</function><postcondition>langue = 'FR' </postcondition>
</point>
</profile>
```

This profile shows the behavior of the component with respect to the language, the interface to the "Translation" component "TranslationAR_FR" remains as a precondition to the parameter "language" which calls for the "AR" value.

The return value will be "FR" value. This component, therefore, modifies the language and thanks to the profile Adapter which can discover this fact.

The profile of the service which is a composite component resulting from the composition profiles of components I, Q, F: F requires language = 'FR' by convention."F" is connected with "E", but "E" expresses language neutral point of view via the assigned condition extended to "E". The IHM "E" is connected to the IHM "S" and the condition extended to the IHM "S" (Figure 2).

Adaptation of axioms all service-context: For the semantic part of the set service-context, one that corresponds to the profile level, we need to define the axioms (conditions) which are checked if a service is appropriate for its context. As an example, one axiom we need to have to represent the adaptation of all petrol context if the profiles parameter values are contradictory. In our example, if the user writes in Arabic, there is a contradiction for the parameter "language" (Ar<>Fr) at the IHM Service "S". In this case, the adaptation axiom is not verified.

The adapter-algorithm

The adapter must be able to adapt the service to the condition provided, it must perform the following:

- Verification: For each parameter profile adaptation axioms should get satisfied, especially, when we all followed a suitable service.

- Search an adaptation solution: If at least one parameter is in use, an axiom does not provide proper output, thus it must be adapted to search.

- For each parameter that does not satisfy the axioms, the adapter builds a graph that has nodes of the component interfaces which have a relationship with this parameter and referring the arcs as the interconnections.

- In this graph the adapter associated branches (sequence of nodes) which are of unequal value are represented for each branch adapter looking components, inserting these into the branch, restores equal values.

- Application of the solution: If the adapter able to find the solution, it can apply the solution found.

Prototype

We propose in the prototype (Figure 3), the service consists of the components which contain the following.

A- View forum

E - Write a message

Proxy F - a local connection to the remote component

F - Forum.

T component - Translation is dynamically added to the request of

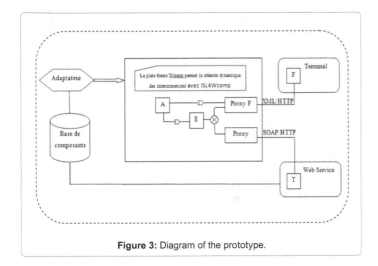

Figure 3: Diagram of the prototype.

the adapter which uses the following:

• The platform Wcomp [8]: This platform provides a development environment based on software components, it allows the dynamic creation of interconnections with ISL4Wcomp. The dynamic adaptation of Wcomp is done by adding, removing, the connection and disconnection of software components during the execution of the application.

• The language of ISL4Wcomp (Interaction Specification Language for Wcomp) interactions [9]: It is based on the interaction specification language called ISL (Interaction Specification Language), which we used to describe patterns of interactions objects [10]. ISL4Wcomp meanwhile fits these specifications for the consideration of interactions based on messages or events in the components in the assembly.

The adapter is the component in the components directory that is searched from the profile of the component by typing connections.

Conclusion

In this paper we presented an architecture that allows dynamic service adaptation. Our proposal is based on a meta-description of the overall context where in the service we have a limited set of axioms adaptation based on the semantics of the service. As it is not mandatory to describe the different rules of evolution which will be discovered by analyzing case of inadequacy subject only considering each component described with its profile.

To demonstrate the architecture, we implemented a prototype board service. This service is initially created for French-speaking users, but the proposed architecture can adapt other service by adding a dynamic translation component if the user language is not French. The main disadvantage of this architecture is its complexity. Generalization and further simplification of the model is required so that different profile settings could be assessed for the expression of adaptation axioms.

Despite these limitations and difficulties, we believe that the future belongs to adapting semantic service composition. To achieve this, the functioning of the whole context Service must be understandable for the machine, not just the human being who is building the services.

References

1. Plasil F, Balek D, Janecek R (1997) DCUP: Dynamic Component Updating in Java/CORBA Environment.

2. Ketfi A (2004) UneApprocheGénérique Pour La Reconfiguration Dynamique Des Applications A Base De ComposantsLogiciels. Thèse de doctorat de l'Université. Joseph Fourier de Grenoble.

3. Ledoux T (2001) Projet RNTL ARCAD D.1.1 Etat de l'artsurl'adaptabilité. Ecole de Mines de Nantes, 4, rue Alfred Kastler, 44307 Nantes Cedex.

4. Segara MT, André F (2000) A Framework for Dynamic Adaptation in Wireless Environments. IRISA Research Insitute, Technology of Object Oriented Languages and systems (TOOLS 33), St. Malo, France.

5. Aksit M, Choukair Z (2003) Dynamic, Adaptive and Reconfigurable Systems Overview and Prospective Vision. ICDCSW'03, Providence, Rhode Island, USA.

6. Blay-Fornarino M, Ensellem D, Occello A, Pinna-Dery A-M, Riveill M, et al. (2002) Un service d'interactions : principes et implémentation . Journées composants 1: 16.

7. Kon F, Costa F, Blair GS, Campbell R (2002) The Case for Reflective Middleware: Building middleware that is flexible, reconfigurable, and yet simple to use. ACM Comminications 45.

8. Cheung-Foo-Wo D, Blay-Fornarino M, Tigli J-Y, Lavirotte S, Riveill M (2006) Adaptation dynamiqued'assemblage de dispositifs par des modèles. 2ème journéesurl'ingénieriedirigée par les modèles (IDM).

9. Blay-Fornarino M, Charfi A, Emsellem D, Pinna-Dery A-M, Riveill M (2004) Software interactions. Journal of Object Technology 3 : 161-180.

10. Berger L (2001) Mise en Oeuvre des Interactions en EnvironnementsDistribués, Compilés et FortementTypés: le Modèle MICADO. Thèse de doctorat, Université de Nice-SophiaAntipolis - Faculté des sciences et techniques, Ecoledoctorale.

6

Designing a Bio-Capsule Secure Authentication System

Logeshwari R[1]*, Karthikayani K[1], Sindhuja A[2] and Ashok D[1]

[1]Assistant Professor, Department of Computer Science, SRM University, Chennai, India
[2]Assistant Professor, Department of Information Technology, Prathyusha Institute of Technology and Management, Thiruvallur, India

Abstract

In this modern world, especially on the Internet, user might have more and more usernames or IDs and passwords, which contains his/her private information. There are too many for user to remember and it is unsafe to write them down on you notebook. To solve this problem, this paper made a designed a User data Management System (UMS), by which user can manage his/her private information's efficiently. With the fast evolution in sensor technology biometric authentication system becomes more popular in daily lives. The biometrics is improving the capability to recognize the persons. The construction of Bio-Capsule from biometrics is used generally to secure the system. The biometrics used in this paper is fingerprint and iris. These two features are combined with the help of fusion algorithm. From the combined features, Bio-Capsule is generated which used for authenticating User data Management Systems.

Keywords: Biometrics; Bio-capsule generation; Minutiae points; Morphological operation; Histogram Equalization; Weiner filtering; Fusion algorithm

Introduction

Information security and privacy has become an important factor in the present world. As an individual, everyone has the security problem on their private information"s, which is accompanied by password protection. With the services on the internet increased, user may become a member of different websites, and also use many other network services and online transactions, thus the password setting problem occurs. For the convenience, some users may assign same passwords for all the internet services, resulting in onelost- all-lost security risk. Also some users may have high awareness of security, so they passwords for each service. But he/she may likely forget some of them when they have not been used for long time. To effectively alleviate the contradiction between password security and memory defects of human beings, a design of User Data Management System (UMS) is needed to manage user"s data. A biometric system is a standard method for identification and verification of a human being based on the personal or physical identification of characteristics. Biometric cryptosystems is a new technique which combines biometrics and cryptography, and is popularly known as crypto-biometric systems. The integration of biometrics and cryptography is broadly carried now-a-days. In biometrics bio-capsule resetting is very much complicated. This paper uses two biometrics features to generate the bio-capsule. The biometrics used in this paper is fingerprint and iris. These two biometrics features are combined using a technique called fusion. From these combined features, bio-capsule is generated which is used for authenticating UMS.

Related works

Biometrics is a powerful tool for human verification and authentication. It is done with the help of human biometric templates namely Finger-Knuckle- Print, Finger Print, Iris, Palm Print etc. Recently more research going on hand based samples, because it is highly sensitive and distinct. Cryptography needs for reliable communication (Figure 1), but cryptography alone is not enough to achieve it. In such a way, cryptography deals with security levels and biometric handles identity of human. Biometric key generation is mainly used for user identification. The generated key is totally differs from biometric features. So the key is never ever overridden with cryptographic systems. Each biometric feature has its own strengths and weaknesses and the choice typically depends on the application. The better biometric characteristic has five qualities: robustness,

distinctiveness, availability, accessibility and acceptability. Fingerprints are unique and it is most widely used to identify the person. Its matching accuracy was very high [1]. Iris is the ideal part of the eye in human body. It contains many distinctive features such as furrows, ridges and rings etc. [2]. Iris technology provides greater unique identification. According to the above features

Fingerprint and iris are taken to develop the proposed system. A Multi biometric system combines characteristics from different biometric traits [3] uses approach to making a feature vector compact and efficient by using Haar wavelet transform, and two straightforward but efficient mechanisms for a competitive learning method such as a weight vector initialization and the winner selection. The system proposed by Tisse [4]. Uses gradient decomposed Hough transform integro-differential operators combination for iris localization and the "analytic image" concept (2D Hilbert transform) to extract pertinent information from iris texture. The concept of multimodal biometric system has been proposed by Ross and Jain [5] where apart from fusion strategies various levels of integration are also presented. In [6] fusion of iris and face biometrics has been proposed. The score level fusion in multimodal biometrics system is proposed in [7]. A novel fusion at feature level for face and palm-print has been presented in [8].

A proposed bio-capsule generation: Biometric cryptosystems combines cryptography and biometrics to afford the advantages of both for security [9]. This technique will provide the advantages like better and modifiable security levels which are the advantages of cryptography and advantages like eliminating the must to memorize passwords or to carry tokens etc. which are the advantages of using biometrics. This paper combines the features of fingerprint and iris and with that combined feature; Bio-capsule generated which provides secure authentication to UMS as shown in (Figure 1).

Over view of fingerprint: A fingerprint is made of a number of

---
*Corresponding author: Logeshwari R, Assistant Professor, Department of Computer Science, SRM University, Chennai, India, E-mail: Loge.shwari54@gmail.com

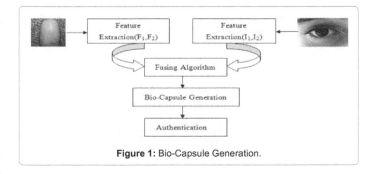

Figure 1: Bio-Capsule Generation.

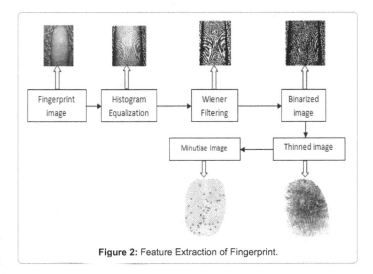

Figure 2: Feature Extraction of Fingerprint.

ridges and valleys on the surface of the finger. Ridges are the upper skin layer segments of the finger and valleys are the lower segments. The ridges form so-called minutia points: ridge endings (where a ridge end) and ridge bifurcations (where a ridge splits in two). Many types of minutiae exist,

- Dots-Very small ridges
- Islands-Ridges slightly longer than dots, occupying a middle space between two temporarily divergent ridges
- Ponds or lakes-Empty spaces between two temporarily divergent ridges
- Spurs-A notch protruding from a ridge
- Bridges-Small ridges joining two longer adjacent ridges
- Crossovers-Two ridges which cross each other.

Feature extraction from fingerprint: We have selected fingerprint as the biometrics feature for generating Bio-Capsule. We have extracted minutiae points from the fingerprint and used that point set for generating capsule [10].

Fingerprint image preprocessing: For image preprocessing Histogram Equalization and Filters are used to enhance the image. Binarization is applied on fingerprint image. Then Morphological operation is used to extract Region of Interest (Figure 2).

Histogram equalization

Histogram equalization defines a mapping of gray level p into gray level q such that the distribution of gray level q is uniform. This mapping stretches contrast (expands the range of gray levels) for gray

level near the histogram maxima. Since contrast is expanded for most of the image pixels. The transformation improves the delectability of many image features. The probability density functions of pixel intensity level rkis given by:

$Pr(rk)=nk/n$ (1) Where $0 \le rk \le 1$ where k=0,1,2…255 nk is the number of pixels at the intensity level rk and n is the total number of pixels.

Wiener filtering noise reduction

We proposed to use a pixel-wise adaptive Wiener method for noise reduction. T the filter is based on local statistics estimated from a local neighborhood of size 3×3 of each pixel, $W(n1,n2)=\mu+ (\sigma2 – v2)/\sigma2(I(n1,n2)-\mu)$ (3) When v2 is noise variance and σ2 are local mean and variance, I represent the gray level intensity in n1, n2∈ ∩.

Binarization: The operation that converts a grayscale image into a binary image is known as binarization by computing the mean value of each 32-by-32 input block matrix and transferring the pixel value to 1 if larger than the mean or to 0 if smaller [11].

Thinning: The final image improvement pace normally performed before minutiae extraction is thinning. Thinning is a morphological process that consecutively takes away the foreground pixels till they are one pixel apart. By applying the thinning technique to a fingerprint image maintains the connectivity of the ridge structures during the formation of a skeleton stage of the binary image. This skeleton image is subsequently utilized in the following extraction of minutiae. Inew(n1 , n2,)={1 if I old(n1,n2)≥ local mean (4) Thinned (one pixel 1 thickness) ridgelines are obtained using morphological thinning operations.

Minutiae feature extraction

The next step is to obtain the minutiae from the thinned image. The most commonly used technique of minutiae extraction is the Crossing Number (CN) model. This process involves the utilization of the skeleton image in which the ridge flow pattern is eight-connected [12]. The minutiae are obtained by examining the local neighborhood of every ridge pixel in the image by means of a 3×3 window. The CN value is then calculated which is defined as partially the addition of the differences among the pairs of neighboring pixels in the eight-neighborhood indicates the list of minutiae in a fingerprint image.

Mapping function

The coordinate system utilized for the purpose articulating the minutiae point locations of a fingerprint is a Cartesian coordinate system. The X and Y coordinate of the minutiae points are in pixel units. Angles are represented in regular mathematical format, with zero degrees to the right and angles rising in the counter-clockwise direction [13]. The obtained minutiae points are stored as below F1 = [x1,x2,x3,……xn] F2 = [y1,y2,y3,…..yn]

Overview of iris: The iris is a thin circular diaphragm, which lies between the cornea and the lens of the human eye. The average diameter of the iris is 12 mm, and the pupil size can vary from 10% to 80% of the iris diameter. Due to epigenetic nature of iris patterns, the two eyes of an individual contain completely independent IRIS patterns and identical twins possess uncorrelated iris patterns.

IRIS image processing

Iris localization: The acquired iris image has to be preprocessed to detect the iris, which is an annular portion between the pupil (inner boundary) and the sclera (outer boundary). The first step in iris localization is to detect pupil which is the black circular part surrounded by iris tissues [14]. The center of pupil can be used to detect the outer radius of iris patterns. The important steps involved are:

1. Pupil detection

2. Outer iris localization

Pupil detection: The iris image is converted into grayscale to remove the effect of illumination. As pupil is the largest black area in the intensity image, its edges can be detected easily from the binarized image by using suitable threshold on the intensity image. But the problem of binarization arises in case of persons having dark iris. Thus the localization of pupil fails in such cases. In order to overcome these problems Circular Hough Transformation for pupil detection can be used. The basic idea of this technique is to find curves that can be parameterized like straight lines, polynomials, circles, etc., in a suitable parameter space. The transformation is able to overcome artifacts such as shadows and noise as shown in (Figure 3).

Outer Iris localization: External noise is removed by blurring the intensity image. But too much blurring may dilate the boundaries of the edge or may make it difficult to detect the outer iris boundary, separating the eyeball and sclera. Thus a special smoothing filter such as the median filter is used on the original intensity image. After filtering, the contrast of image is enhanced to have sharp variation at image boundaries using histogram equalization as shown in (Figure 4) shows an example of localized iris image.

Iris normalization: When the iris image is proficiently localized, then the subsequent step is to transform it into the rectangular sized fixed image.

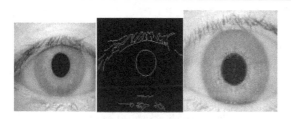

Figure 3: Steps involved in detection of inner pupil boundary.

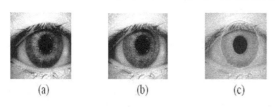

(a)   (b)   (c)

Figure 4: (a) Contrast enhanced image (b) Concentric circles of different radii (c) Localized Iris image.

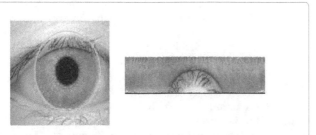

Figure 5: Daugman"s Rubber Sheet Model–Normalisation.

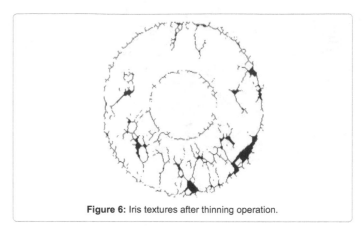

Figure 6: Iris textures after thinning operation.

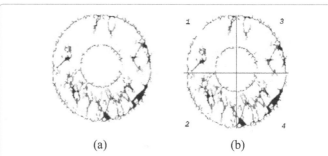

(a)   (b)

Figure 7: Minutiae representation (a) Nodes are shown in pink dots and end points are shown in blue dots (b) Iris rim divided into 4 quadrants.

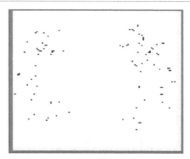

Figure 8: Minutiae representation of Nodes and endpoints are shown in circles.

Daugman's rubber sheet model: Normalization process includes unwrapping the iris and transforming it into its polar equivalent. It is performed utilizing Daugman"s Rubber sheet model and is depicted in the following (Figure 5).

Extraction of Iris texture

For appropriate representation of structures, thinning is used so that every structure presents itself as an agglomerate of pixels as shown in (Figure 6).

From the above iris rim containing iris pseudo textures, the polar coordinates of minutiae (nodes and end points of iris textures)are extracted by resizing the image into a standard format of 256×256 as shown in (Figure 7).

From the above iris rim containing iris pseudo textures, the polar coordinates of minutiae (nodes and end points of iris textures) are obtained by resizing the image into a standard format as represented in (Figure 8).

These obtained Minutiae points are kept as I1 = [x1,x2,x3,......xn] I2 = [y1,y2,y3,.....yn]

Algorithm for feature fusion: This phase will perform the fusion process for the gathered fingerprint and iris features. The input to the fusion process will be four vectors F1, F2, I1 and I2 which are obtained from fingerprint and iris.

The steps involved in fusion of biometric feature vectors are as follows.

Shuffling of individual vectors: 1. Initialize a Random vector RVi (Size of F1)

2. J=RVi×Large Integer Value

3. Interchange ithand jthIndex Values

Above steps are repeated for all the components of F1 which given as S1. This procedure is repeated for all vectors F2, I1 and I2 to produce S2, S3 and S4.

Concatenation of shuffled vectors: In this process the shuffled Fingerprint vectors S1 and S2 is concatenated with Iris vectors S3 and S4.

1. Initialize a vector M1 (size of |S1| + |S3|) and Initial values of |S3| is filled with S3 for S1

2. Select „t‟ (size of M1)

3. Do logical right shift operation in M1 from index t

4. The components of S1 are inserted into emptied th index of M1. The above mentioned procedure is performed among shuffled vectors S2 and S4 to obtain a vector M2. In this manner, the concatenation process yields two vector M1 and M2.

Merging of concatenated vectors: The final process in creating the biometric template BT is the merging of two vectors M1 and M2

1. The component M1 and M2 are converted to binary form M11 and M21.

2. Do Binary NOR operation on M11and M21.

3. Convert the binary value into decimal form.

4. Store these decimal values in vector BT.

Generation of Bio-capsule–UMS authentication: The final process of the proposed technique is the creation of Bio-Capsule from the biometric template BT.

BT=[bT1, bT2, bT3 ...bTh] The set of different components in the template vector BT are recognized and are stored in another vector UBT. UBT=[u1, u2, u3, ...ud] |UBT| ≤ |BT| The vector UBT is then resized to k components appropriate for creating the k-bit Bio-Capsule.

u1, u2, … . uk, if $UBT > k$

u1 u2 … ud $\ll ui$; $d + 1 \geq i \geq k$

if $|UBT| < k$

Where,

Ui=1 $duj\ dj$=1

Finally, the key K

B

is created from the vector BT.

KB<<Bi mod 2, i = 1,2,3…k

This finally obtained key serves as an authentication Bio-capsule for the individual in the system. This key is definitely very difficult for the theft to generate. Therefore, a better secure system is created using the proposed technique.

Conclusion

In this paper, we propose a novel Bio-Capsule authentication to provide security to his/her private information's. To effectively alleviate the contradiction between password security and memory defects of human beings, a design of User data Management System (UMS) is needed to manage user's data. Securing the information system becomes most challenging task because of the increased number of theft. To overcome these issues, biometrics of a person is used to secure the system. This paper used fingerprint and iris biometrics to secure the system. The features obtained from these two biometrics are combined using fusion technique. From these fused features, bio capsule is generated which is more secure than other techniques. In future it will be extended with other biometric samples like finger knuckle print, retina, palm-print etc.

References

1. Chih L, Sheng W (1999) WFingerprint feature extraction usinggabor filters. Electron. Lett volume 35: 288-290.

2. Xiang C, Fan XA, Lee TH (2006) Face recognition using Recursive Fisher of Linear Discriminant. IEEE Trans. ImageProcess 15: 2097-2105.

3. Lee BK, Byeon O, Lim S, Lee K, Kim T (2001) "EfficientIris Recognition through Improvement of Feature Vector and Classifier". ETRI Journal 23: 61-70.

4. LocTisse C, Martin L, Torres L, Robert M (2002) Person Identification Technique using Human Iris Recognition. International Conference on Vision Interface, Canada.

5. Arun R, Sarat D, Anil J (2005) "A deformable model for fingerprint matching." Pattern Recognition. 38:95-103.

6. Chen X, Tian J, Yang X, Zhang Y (2006) "An algorithm fordistorted the fingerprint matching based on local triangle feature set." IEEE Trans. Inf. Forensics Security 1: 169–177.

7. Vajna ZMK (2000) "A fingerprint verification system based ontriangular matching and dynamic time Warping." IEEE Trans.Pattern Anal. Mach. Intell 22: 1266-1276.

8. Hong L, Yifei W, Anil J (1998) "Fingerprint image enhancement: Algorithm and performance evaluation." IEEE Trans. Pattern Anal. Mach. Intell 20: 777–789.

9. Schreiner K (1997) Biometrics Prospects for going the distance. IEEE Intelligent Systems, Nov./Dec.1999.

10. Wildes RP, Corp S (1997) Iris Recognition: An Emerging Biometric Technology. IEEE 85: 1348-1363.

11. Arul P, Shanmugam A (2009) Generate a Key For AES Using Biometric For VOIP Network Security. Journal of Theoretical and Applied Information Technology

12. Dodis Y, Ostrovsky R, Reyzin L, Smith A (2004) Fuzzy Extractors: How to generate Strong Keys from Biometrics and other Noisy Data. Proceedings of International Conference on Theory and Applications of Cryptographic Techniques.

13. Chang YJ, Zhang W, Chen T (2004) Biometrics based cryptographic key generation. IEEE International Conference on Multimedia and Expo.

14. Chen B, Chandran V (2007) "Biometric Based Cryptographic Key Generation from Faces," Proceedings of the 9th Biennial Conference of the Australian Pattern Recognition Society on Digital Image Computing Techniques and Applications, Usa.

7

Design and Analysis of a Two Stage Traffic Light System Using Fuzzy Logic

Javed Alam[1]* and Pandey MK[2]

[1]Research Scholar, Dept. of CS,Mewar University, Gangrar, Chittorgarh, Rajasthan, India
[2]Director, Computer Science and Applications, AIMCA, Haldwani, Uttrakhand, India

Abstract

Traffic congestion is a growing problem in many countries especially in large urban areas. The reason behind this is the increase in number of vehicles all over the world. Due to this vehicles do not run efficiently which increasestravel time, noise pollution, carbon dioxide emissions and fuel usages.In large urban cities, traffic signal controller plays an important role to improve the efficiency of vehicles, traffic congestion and hence reduces travel time, noise pollution, carbon dioxide emission and fuel used. In this paper, a two stage traffic light system for real-time traffic monitoring has been proposed to dynamically manage both the phase and green time of traffic lights for an isolated signalized intersection with the objective of minimizing the average vehicle delay in different traffic flow rate. There are two different modules namely traffic urgency decision module (TUDM) and extension time decision module (ETDM). In the first stage TUDM, calculates urgency for all red phases. On the bases of urgency degree, proposed system selects the red light phase with large traffic urgency as the next phase to switch. In second stage ETDM, calculatesgreen light time i.e., extension time of the phase which has higher urgencyaccording to the number of vehicles. Software has been developed in MATLAB to simulate the situation of an isolated signalized intersection based on fuzzy logic. Simulation results verify the performance of our proposed two stage traffic light system using fuzzy logic.

Keywords: Traffic congestion; Traffic urgency; TSTLS; TUDM; DTDM

Introduction

Traffic congestion of streets and roads constitutes a critical problem which is aggravated by the rise in the number of vehicles and by greater urbanization. The slow pace in the development of new highways and roads and public opposition to the widening of existing streets in some locations has forced the city managers to optimally use the existing infrastructures in order to effectively manage the flow of traffic. Moreover the loss of valuable time during traffic congestion can directly affect the production, productivity, performance and the utilization of fuel. The control of traffic light signal is one of the subjects of intelligent or advance systems being investigated by researchers because this kind of control has a direct impact on the effectiveness of urban transportation systems [1].

Traffic signals operate in pre-timed, actuated or adaptive mode. Pre-timed control consists of a series of intervals that are fixed in duration. They repeat a preset constant cycle. In contrast to pre-timed signals actuated signals have the capability to respond to the presence of vehicles or pedestrians at the intersection. Vehicle actuated signals require actuation by a vehicle on one or more approaches in order for certain phases or traffic movements to be serviced. They are equipped with detectors and the necessary control logic to respond to the demands placed on them. Vehicle-actuated control uses information on current demands and operations obtained from detectors within the intersection to alter one or more aspects of the signal timing on a cycle-by-cycle basis. Timing of the signals is controlled by traffic demand.

Adaptive or area traffic control system sometime called as ATCS. It is the latest generation of traffic control system. ATCS continuously compute optimal signal timings based on this detected volume and simultaneously implement them. ATC system to effectively respond to the rapid changes in dynamic traffic conditions which are designed to have intelligent real-time dynamic traffic control systems. These systems use data from vehicle detectors and optimize traffic signal time in real time that's why ATCS called as adaptive traffic signal. The timing plan of ATCS controller changes automatically for these purpose digital computers are used.

Over the course of performing a literature review, adaptive traffic signal systems have been operating successfully in many countries since the early 1970. Adaptive traffic signal control systems are normally complicated and include prediction and estimation modules. More than twenty Adaptive traffic signal controls are available on the market. They are significant due to their relative acceptance in the field as well as the relative extent of their real world implementation. The most widely deployed control systems are discussed here.In the early 1980, Nathan Gartner at the University of Massachusetts at Lowell proposed a traffic control system called asOptimized Policies for Adaptive Control for the Federal Highway Administration. Optimized Policies for Adaptive Control sometime called as OPAC. The Split Cycle Offset Optimization Technique (SCOOT) was also developed in the early 1980 by the Transport Research Laboratory in the United Kingdom. The Sydney Coordinated Adaptive Traffic System (SCATS) is slightly newer, having been created in the early 1990 by the Roads and Traffic Authority of New South Wales, Australia. A major difference between SCATS and SCOOT is that SCATS does not have a traffic model or a traffic signal control plan optimizer. Timing of signals is controlled by digital computer based control logic. It has ability to modify signal timings on a cycle-by-cycle basis using traffic flow information collected at the intersection. It is not model based but has a library of plans that it selects from and therefore banks extensively on available traffic data. The Real-time Hierarchical Optimized Distributed Effective System (RHODES) is the newest of these four systems, having been produced in the mid-1990 at the University of Arizona at Tucson.

A decentralized adaptive traffic signal control method known as ALLONS-D (Adaptive Limited Look-ahead Optimization of Network Signals – Decentralized) presented by Porche [2] in his dissertation

---

*Corresponding author: Javed Alam, Research Scholar, Dept of CS, Mewar University, Gangrar, Chittorgarh, Rajasthan, India, E-mail: javedalam4u@gmail.com

based on a depth-first branch and bound algorithm.More recently, Yu and Recker [3] developed a stochastic adaptive traffic signal control model. The authors formulated traffic signal control as a Markov Decision Process (MDP) and solved it by dynamic programming. Although dynamic programming algorithm can be used to solve this MDP problem and is guaranteed to find the optimal policy [4], it needs a well-defined state-transition probability function. In practice this state transition probability function is difficultto define. In the case of intersection traffic control state transition probability function are affected by the arrival of actual traffic and often time is different. Thus it is even more difficult to give a precise estimate. An intersection traffic signal control application in addition to the number of states is usually very large. The dynamic programming algorithm to calculate the time could make a serious problem.

However this type of methods still has the problems that under certain circumstances, the excessive computation requirement makes some systems based on dynamic programming and Markov decision process require accurate traffic arrival information for the next one or two minutes to determine the best control plans. This information is very difficult to obtain. These systems take ordinary variable in computation. Therefore it is necessary to improve the traffic controller for effective traffic management and better traffic flow, we use linguistic variable in place of ordinary variable.

Fuzzy logic enables the implementation of rules very similarly to what goes on in the human thinking process. In other words, fuzzy controllers have the ability to take decision even with incomplete information. More and more sophisticated controllers are being developed for traffic control. These algorithms are continually improving the safety and efficiency by reducing the waiting delay of vehicles on signals. This increases the tempo of travel and thus makes signals more effective and traffic flow smooth. The key motivation towards fuzzy logic in traffic signal control is the existence of uncertainties in signal control. Decisions are taken based on imprecise information and the effect of evaluation is not well known.

In this paper we discuss the design and analysis of atwo stage traffic lightsystem for isolated intersectionusing fuzzy logic basedtechnology which has the capability of mimicking human intelligence for controlling traffic light. We used fuzzy logic tools available with MATLAB and developed software to simulate the situation of traffic at an isolated junction. The simulated model used for the analysis of efficiency of traffic light controller. The average vehicle delays will be used to evaluate the performance of a two stage traffic light system using fuzzy logic. The software can also be used as an exercise for undergraduate and graduate students to understand the concept of fuzzy logic and its application to a real life environment. The rules and membership functions of the fuzzy logic controller can be selected and changed their outputs can be compared in terms of several different representations.

Related Work

In this section, we discuss different research work in the field of traffic light system using fuzzy logic. The first attempt made to design fuzzy traffic controller was in 70s by Pappis and Mamdani[5]. Kelsey and Bisset also designed a simulator for signal controlling of an isolated intersection with one lane. Same work was also done by Niittymaki and Pursula [6]. They observed that Fuzzy Controller reduces the vehicle delay when traffic volume was heavy. Niittymaki and Kikuchi developed Fuzzy based algorithm for pedestrians, crossing the road.

Initially fuzzy logic was used to control traffic in multiple

intersections by Chui [7]. In this research only two way streets are evaluated without considering any left or right turn. A two stage traffic light controller proposed by Trabia, et al. [8]. In the first stage, observed approach traffic flows are used to estimate relative traffic intensities. These traffic intensities are then used in the second stage to decide current green signal should be extended or terminated for through movements without considering any left or right turn. The isolatedintersection model proposed by Soh AC, et al. [9], used consists of two lanes in eachphase. There are two inputs i.e., vehicles queue lengthand waiting times for each phase. The maximum values of these inputs are selected for controllerto optimized control of traffic flows. A fuzzy logic traffic system proposed by Zaied ANH, et al. [10], that considers the two two-way intersections and is able to adjust changes in time intervals of a traffic signal based on traffic situation level.

Indrabayul, et al. [11], proposed an adaptive timely traffic light is as solution for congestion in typical area in Indonesia. Makassar City, particularly in the most complex junction is observed for months using static cameras. The condition is mapped into fuzzy logic to have a better time transition of traffic light as opposed to the current conventional traffic light system. Fuzzy logic based traffic light shows significant number of potential reduced in congestion.

Shahraki, et al. [1] a new fuzzy logic based algorithm is proposed in this research not only can reduce the waiting time and the number of vehicles behind a traffic light at an intersection but also can consider the traffic situations at adjacent intersections as well. The fuzzy control system comprises three stages. These three stages include the next green phase, green phase extender, and the decision stage. The inputs are applied through the green phase selector. The next green phase stage selects the most urgent phase from the phases waiting to become green. If necessary, the green phase extender increases the duration of the green light. In the decision making stage, by deciding either to increase the green light duration or to change to another phase, the most urgent stage is selected from the two stages of next green phase and green phase extender.

Collotta, et al. [12], a novel approach to dynamically manage the traffic lights cycles and phases in an isolated intersection. The proposed solution is a traffic lights dynamic control system that combines Wireless Sensor Network for real time traffic monitoring with multiple fuzzy logic controllers, one for each phase that work in parallel. Each fuzzy controller addresses vehicles turning movements and dynamically manages both the phase and the green time of traffic lights.

Wu, et al. [13], a dynamic control technique for traffic lights is presented, which is based on the queue detection in the left and straight lanes assuming that the vehicles in the right lane are not in conflict with the others. For queue detection purposes, two induction coils are used, the first one to detect oncoming vehicles, the second to measure the vehicles that leave the intersection. The work considers 12 phases, scheduled according to the priority of each phase that depends on the queue lengths of the specific phase lanes. The additional green time is then calculated using a fuzzy logic controller that processes two parameters, i.e., the queue length of the lane with the green light and that of the lanes with the red light. The phase duration depends on the traffic flow that the phase should serve and in this respect the main limitation of the works presented by Shahraki, et al. [1] and Wu, et al. [13] is that the green time extension is calculated by a single fuzzy controller for all the phases whereas for better performance, fault-tolerance and flexibility, as explained before a controller for each phase would be needed to determine the green time duration of the specific phase. The same problems in Shahraki, et al. [1] and Wu, et al. [13] also characterize the approach presented in Zaied and Othman [10] whose aim is to dynamically regulate through a fuzzy controller, the green time duration of an 8-phase traffic lights in an isolated intersection. In this case, 8 inputs (i.e., the queues) and 16 outputs (i.e.,, the calculated green time for each allowed direction) have to be handled. This means that the fuzzy controller is characterized by multiple input variables.

Traffic Engineering and Traffic Congestion Estimation

Traffic signals are designed to ensure safe and orderly flow of traffic protect pedestrians and vehicles at busy intersections and reduce the severity and frequency of accidents between vehicles entering intersections. In other words traffic signals are one of the most effective and flexible active control of traffic and is widely used in several cities worldwide. The conflicts arising from movements of traffic in different directions are addressed by time sharing principle. The advantages of traffic signal include an orderly movement of traffic an increased capacity of the intersection and require only simple geometric design. However the disadvantages of the signalized intersection are large stopped delays and complexity in the design and implementation. Although the overall delay may be lesser than a rotary for a high volume a user may experience relatively high stopped delay [14].

Cycle length

According to Mathew [14], a signal cycle is one complete rotation through all of the indications or phases that are provided. Cycle length is the time that it takes a signal to complete one full cycle of indications or phases.

Interval

It indicates the change from one stage to another stage. Intervalis oftwo types i.e., change interval and clearance interval

Change interval: The change interval some time called as yellow time. It is provided after green time for movement. The purpose is to inform a driver approaching the intersection during the end of a green time about the coming of a red signal. They normally have a value of 3 to 6 seconds. Institute of transportation engineers (ITE) has recommended following methodology for computing the appropriate length of change interval

$$Y = t + \frac{v}{2(g_n + a)}$$

Where t is the reaction time (about 1.0 sec), v is the velocity of the approaching vehicles, g is the acceleration due to gravity (9.8 m/sec^2), n is the grade of the approach in decimals and a is the deceleration of Change interval. It can also be approximately computed as $y = SSD/v$, where **SSD** is the stopping sight distance and v is the speed of the vehicle.

Clearance interval: The clearance interval some time called as all-red time. It will facilitate a vehicle just crossed the stop line at the turn of red to clear the intersection without being collided by a vehicle from the next phase. Institute of transportation engineers (ITE) recommends the following policy for the design of all read time, given as

$$R_{AR} = \begin{cases} \dfrac{w+L}{v} & \text{If no pedestrians} \\[2mm] \max\left(\dfrac{w+L}{v}, \dfrac{P}{v}\right) & \text{If pedestrians crossing} \\[2mm] \dfrac{P+L}{v} & \text{If protected} \end{cases}$$

Where **w** is the width of the intersection from stop line to the farthest conflicting traffic, **L** is the length of the vehicle, **v** is the speed of the vehicle, and **P** is the width of the intersection from STOP line to the farthest conflicting pedestrian cross-walk.

Phase

A phase follows the time of green interval plus the change and clearance intervals. Therefore during green interval, non-conflicting movements are assigned into each phase. The objective of phase design is to separate the conflicting movements in an intersection into various phases so that movements in a phase should have no conflicts. If all the movements are to be separated with no conflicts then a large number of phases are required. In such a situation the objective is to design phases with minimum conflicts or with less severe conflicts as discuss by Mathew [14].

Lost time

Lost time is the interval in which there is no effectivemovement at the intersection.

Delay

There are a number of measures used for capacity analysis and simulations for signalized intersection. The most common measures the average delays per vehicle, average queue length and number of stops. The delay is a measure that is most directly related to the experience of the driver. It is the measure of extra time consumption through the intersection. Any time is a useful measure of the queue length and the intersection of an adjacent upstream intersection will begin to hinder the discharge is important in determining. The number of stops made in particular in the air quality model, is an important input parameter. It is directly perceived by the driver. Apart from these three, the effects of delay signalized intersections are the most frequently used measures. Due to the delay estimation is complicated by the arrival of vehicles at random, over saturated flow conditions, lost time due to stopping of vehicles etc. although delay can be quantified in several different ways. Thus, as the most frequently used forms of delay are following-

- Stopped time delay
- Approach delay
- Travel time delay
- Time-in-queue delay
- Control delay

Traffic congestion

Traffic congestion means there are more people trying to use a given transportation facility during a specific period of time than the facility can handle with what are considered to be acceptable levels of delay or inconvenience. Delays at particular locations in a transportation network are certainly provoking to those using the system but these delays are part of a much larger picture of how a transportation system allows people and goods to move around a metropolitan area [15]. Congestion management are designed to improve the operating efficiency of the existing transportation system by increasing the use of alternative transportation modesaltering trip patterns through the application of measures and improving traffic flow through measures such as route guidance systems, traffic signal improvements and incident management.

In TSTLS, four-phase signal are designed as shown in Figure 1. In a cycle, each approach goes through two time intervals, green interval and red interval. The green interval has three timing parameters namely lost time T_{LOST}, minimum time T_{MIN}, and maximum time T_{MAX}.

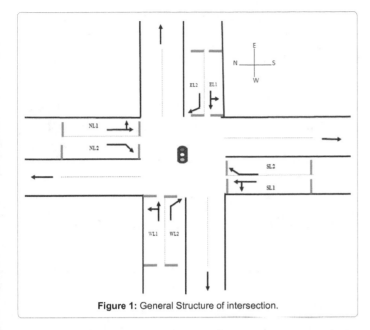

Figure 1: General Structure of intersection.

Lost time T_{LOST} represents the green time not utilized by the vehicles waiting in queue. It consists of startup lost time at the beginning of a green phase and clearance lost time at the end of the phase [16]. In Our proposedTSTLS, we assume that the entire lost time per phase occurs only at the beginning of the green phase. When a phase is initiated minimum green time to be provide and it represented by Minimum time T_{MIN}. This ensures that the green signal stays long enough for safe passage of a single vehicle to clear the intersection. The maximum green time that can be provided to any phase and represented by Maximum time T_{MAX}. In fixed-cycle traffic light system each cycle can be approximated to a periodic task with period T characterized by a fixed green time T_g, yellow time T_y and red time T_r described as

$$T = T_g + T_y + T_r$$

Whenever, a phase has the least Urgency than all other phases in a cycle. This phase can be skip. Therefore green time not provided to this phase because traffic system is based on urgency. If this phase will be skip into this cycle and next one or more consecutive cycle then congestion may occur. In our proposed system this type of congestion can be estimated and hence minimum green time T_{MIN} will be provided to this phase in each cycle.

Description of the Proposed Two Stagetraffic Lightsystem (TSTLS)

Investigation on the driving behaviors indicates that it is dangerous to change dynamic phase compositionbecause this may disturb the drivers' mental status and may get nervous. In our proposed two stage traffic light system using fuzzy logic model it is assumed that phase composition is predetermined and the phase sequence as well as signal timing are changeable.

From the review of literature related with traffic light system it has reported that fuzzy logic controllers perform better than pre-timed, actuated and adaptive controllers. However the phase changes in sequential order without considering the urgency of the red phases. In this paper, a two stage traffic light system using fuzzy logic will not only decide whether to extend or terminate a current green phase but also decide which red phase will be set as green phase then determine the extension time of green phase. Therefore in this traffic light system

the phase sequence is uncertain.The average vehicle delays will be used to evaluate the performance of the two stage traffic light system using fuzzy logic [17].

The general structure of an isolatedintersection is illustrated as in Figure 1. Each lane equipped with two electromagnetic. The first sensor is located behind each traffic light and second sensor is located behind the first sensor at distance S. The first sensor counts the number of cars passing the traffic light and the second sensor counts the number of cars coming to the intersection. The number of cars waiting at the traffic light is determined by the difference of the reading between the two sensors. Each traffic light in front of it is a proximity sensor and can only sense the presence of a car waiting at the junction, which is contrary to the traditional control systems.

The isolated intersection considered as in Figure 1 is characterized by four phases as in Figure 2 with eight lanes. Each phase has two lanes. As we discuss earlier the objective of phase design is to separate the conflicting movements in an intersection into various phases so that movements in a phase should have no conflicts. For example, when Phase 1 is enabled, only the cars of Lane EL1 of the Road directionE and Lane WL1 of the Road direction W can go straight or turn left, while all the other lanes will have the red light to stop [18]. Table 1 summarizes the notation adopted in two stage traffic light system.As shown in Figure 1 the length of each phase is obtained as the maximum of the queue lengths intended as the number of vehicles during the green/red light in their respective lanes as shown

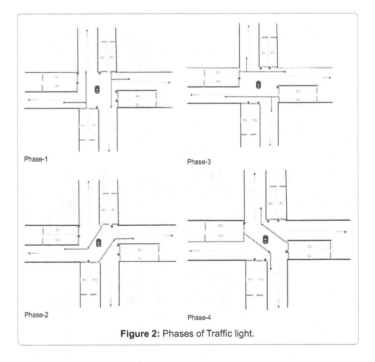

Figure 2: Phases of Traffic light.

Symbol	Lane	Movement Allowed
EL 1	East Lane- 1	Straight and left
EL 2	East Lane- 2	Right
WL 1	West Lane- 1	Straight and left
WL 2	West Lane- 2	Right
NL 1	North Lane- 1	Straight and left
NL 2	North Lane- 2	Right
SL 1	South Lane- 1	Straight and left
SL 2	South Lane- 2	Right

Table 1: Notation.

Phase1 = maximum (WL1, EL1)

Phase2 = maximum (WL2, EL2)

Phase3 = maximum (NL1, SL1)

Phase4 = maximum (NL2, SL2)

Vehicle arrival distribution

There are four phases or approaches in this isolated intersection model with twelve total movements and a server traffic light. Each phase consists of three movements which are through movement, right and left turn movements. This model is based on an M/M/1 queuing theory using three basic concepts of queuing theory i.e., customer, queue, and server. The first and the second M in M/M/1 stand for memory less distribution of inter-arrival times and service times respectively. The "1" indicates that the isolated intersection has single server, which means one traffic signal, to service single signal phase at one time [19].

In this model First-In-First-Out (FIFO) principle is applied to the vehicles queue. The vehicles are known as customers while services time is the time for the vehicles to depart and to cross the intersection. Traffic at the intersection arrival and service time are independent random variables with Poisson distribution. Therefore, the arrival of vehicles at the intersection with arrival rate λ and the average of the inter-arrival times between vehicles are $1/\lambda$. The arrival of the vehicles in a Poisson process and the time period in order to reach the number of vehicles is as follows Poisson distribution.

$$P(x) = \frac{(\lambda t)^x . e^{-\lambda t}}{x!} \qquad x = 0, 1, 2, 3, \ldots\ldots$$

Where P(x) is the probability of vehicles x during counting interval t and λ is the average arrival rate per unit time, t is the duration of each counting interval. The vehicle arrival rate is 0~1 per second.

Put n= λt, where n is the average number of vehicles during counting interval. The equation can be written as follows

$$P(x) = \frac{n^x . e^{-n}}{x!}$$

Computation of the average vehicle delay (AVD)

In this research paper the average delay of vehicles is the performance evaluation for traffic signal control of intersection. If the value of average vehicle delay is small then the traffic signal control effect is better. The amount of queuing vehicles in red light phase at time t i.e.,(t) can be calculated using the following ways-

$$Q_r(t) = \sum_{i=1}^{k} \left(Q_{gi} + \sum_{t_1=1}^{t} q_{it_1} \right)$$

where i is one of the red light phase branches, Q_{gi} is the amount of queuing vehicles in the red light phase branch i when the current green signal ends, t_1 is the time interval during the red light, qi_{t_1} is the amount of arriving vehicles in the red light phase branch i during time interval t_1 k is the number of red phase branch. In our proposed system $k = 6$. The total vehicle delay in red light phase i.e., D_r can be calculated as-

$$D_r = \sum_{t=1}^{t_r} \left[\sum_{i=1}^{k} \left(Q_{gi} + \sum_{t_1=1}^{t} q_{it_1} \right) \right]$$

Where t_r is the red light time of red light phase.

The amount of queuing vehicles at time t seconds during green light i.e.,$Q_g(t)$ can be calculated as follows:

$$Q_g(t) = \sum_{i=1}^{k} z_i \left(Q_t + \sum_{t_1=1}^{t} q_{t_1} - S_f.t \right)$$

Where Q_{ri} is the amount of arriving vehicles in the green light phase branch i during last red light phase, k is the vehicles flow in green light phase, S_f is saturation flow, q_{it_1} is the amount of arriving vehicles in the green light phase branch i during time t_1. In our research paper there are four phases in an intersection. The value z_i can show whether there are queuing vehicles or not in current green light phase branch i. If $Q_t + \sum_{t_1=1}^{t} q_{t_1} - S_f.t > 0$, then $z_i = 1$, otherwise, $z_i = 0$. The total vehicle delay of green light phase i.e.,, D_g can be calculated as follows:

$$D_g = \sum_{t=1}^{t_g} \left[\sum_{i=1}^{k} z_i \left(Q_t + \sum_{t_1=1}^{t} q_{t_1} - q_s.t \right) \right]$$

Where t_E is the green light time i.e., extension time provided by extension time decision module during green light phase. The total vehicle delay in the x cycle i.e.,D_x can be calculated as follows:

$$D_x = D_r + D_g$$

The average vehicle delay (AVD) can be calculated as follows:

$$AVD = \frac{\sum_{x \in cycle} D_x}{A_r}$$

Where A_r is the total amount of arriving vehicles from all directions in an intersection during all cycles.

Traffic urgency decision module

Traffic urgency decision module (TUDM) calculates urgency for all red phases as shown in Figure 3. On the bases of urgency degree, proposed system selects the next red light phase to switch. There are two input variables namely *Queue*, *Time$_r$* and one output variable namely *Urgency*. The input variable *Queue* count the number of vehicles of current red light phase and variable *Time$_r$* count the duration of red light since the last end of the green light. The output variable *Urgency* is traffic urgency of red light phases. Therefore for instance in the case of Phase 1, TUDM will determine the urgency (U1) by processing the queue length and duration of red light since the last end of the green light of phase 1. Similarly, for phase 2, TUDM will determine the urgency (U2) by processing the queue length and duration of red light since the last end of the green light of phase 2 and so on.

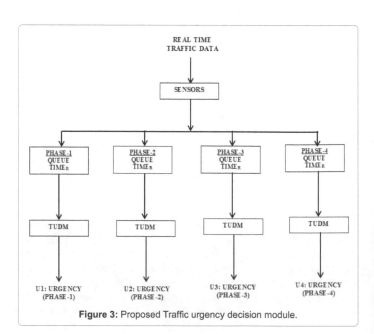

Figure 3: Proposed Traffic urgency decision module.

Extension time decision module

Extension time decision module (ETDM),calculate green light time i.e., extension time of the phase which has higher urgency can be calculated according to the number of vehicles as shown in Figure 4. There are two input variables namely *Queue-Lane-1, Queue-Lane-2* and one output variable *Extension-Time*. The input variable *Queue-Lane-1*count the number of vehicles of lane 1 and input variable *Queue-Lane-2*count number of vehicles of other side i.e., lane 2 of red light phase which has big traffic urgency. The output variable *Extension-Time* is the extension time of current green light phase. Therefore for instance in the case of Phase 1, ETDM will determine the green light duration i.e., extension time (E1) by processing the queue length of the Lane EL1 of the Road direction E and Lane WL1 of the Road direction W. Similarly, for phase 2, ETDM will determine the extension time (E2) by processing the queue length of the Lane EL2 of the Road direction E and Lane WL2 of the Road direction W and so on.

Fuzzy Parameters and Their Membership Functions Design

For a two stage traffic lightsystem, there are five membership functions such as Zero, Small, Medium, Large and Very-Large for each of the input as well asoutput fuzzy variable of the system. There are two input variables *Queue*and *Time$_r$* and one output variable*Urgency*for traffic urgency decision module as shown in Figure 5-7 respectively. For extension time decision module, we designed two input variables namely *Queue-Lane-1, Queue-Lane-2* and one output variable *Extension-Time* as shown in Figure 8-10 respectively. Each input and output fuzzy variable is design using triangular membership function.

Fuzzy Rules and Defuzzification

The inference mechanism in the fuzzy logic controller resembles that of the human reasoning process. Fuzzy logic technology is associated with artificial intelligence. For example, a traffic policeman managing a junction say, one from the east and one from the north he would use his expert opinion in controlling the traffic more or less in the following way:

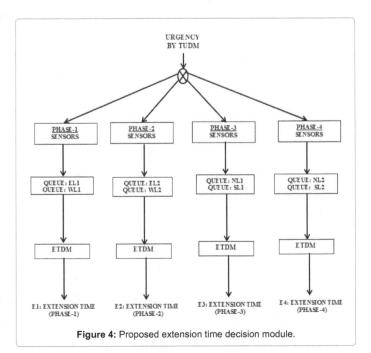

Figure 4: Proposed extension time decision module.

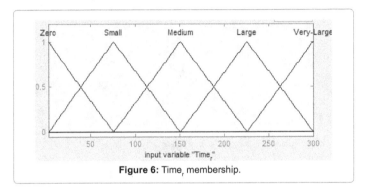

Figure 5: Queue membership.

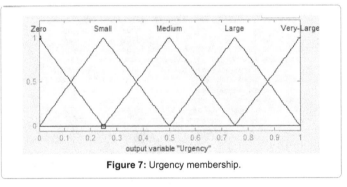

Figure 6: Time$_r$ membership.

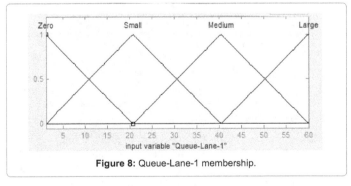

Figure 7: Urgency membership.

Figure 8: Queue-Lane-1 membership.

IF traffic from the east side of the city is VERY-LARGEand traffic from the north sides is SMALLthen allow movement of traffic to the east side LONGER

In two stage traffic light system using fuzzy logic, we develop two different modules namely traffic urgency decision module (TUDM) and extension time decision module (ETDM). In TUDM 25 fuzzy rules have been found and for ETDM 16 rules have been found.The some

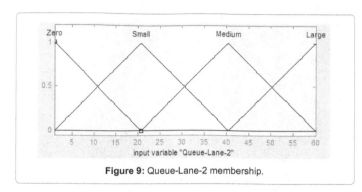

Figure 9: Queue-Lane-2 membership.

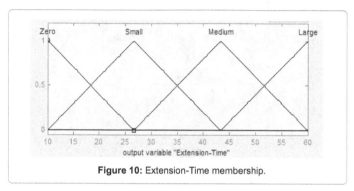

Figure 10: Extension-Time membership.

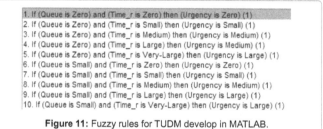

1. If (Queue is Zero) and (Time_r is Zero) then (Urgency is Zero) (1)
2. If (Queue is Zero) and (Time_r is Small) then (Urgency is Small) (1)
3. If (Queue is Zero) and (Time_r is Medium) then (Urgency is Medium) (1)
4. If (Queue is Zero) and (Time_r is Large) then (Urgency is Medium) (1)
5. If (Queue is Zero) and (Time_r is Very-Large) then (Urgency is Large) (1)
6. If (Queue is Small) and (Time_r is Zero) then (Urgency is Zero) (1)
7. If (Queue is Small) and (Time_r is Small) then (Urgency is Small) (1)
8. If (Queue is Small) and (Time_r is Medium) then (Urgency is Medium) (1)
9. If (Queue is Small) and (Time_r is Large) then (Urgency is Large) (1)
10. If (Queue is Small) and (Time_r is Very-Large) then (Urgency is Large) (1)

Figure 11: Fuzzy rules for TUDM develop in MATLAB.

1. If (Queue-Lane-1 is Zero) and (Queue-Lane-2 is Zero) then (Extension-Time is Zero) (1)
2. If (Queue-Lane-1 is Zero) and (Queue-Lane-2 is Small) then (Extension-Time is Small) (1)
3. If (Queue-Lane-1 is Zero) and (Queue-Lane-2 is Medium) then (Extension-Time is Medium) (1)
4. If (Queue-Lane-1 is Zero) and (Queue-Lane-2 is Large) then (Extension-Time is Large) (1)
5. If (Queue-Lane-1 is Small) and (Queue-Lane-2 is Zero) then (Extension-Time is Small) (1)
6. If (Queue-Lane-1 is Small) and (Queue-Lane-2 is Small) then (Extension-Time is Small) (1)
7. If (Queue-Lane-1 is Small) and (Queue-Lane-2 is Medium) then (Extension-Time is Medium) (1)
8. If (Queue-Lane-1 is Small) and (Queue-Lane-2 is Large) then (Extension-Time is Large) (1)
9. If (Queue-Lane-1 is Medium) and (Queue-Lane-2 is Zero) then (Extension-Time is Medium) (1)
10. If (Queue-Lane-1 is Medium) and (Queue-Lane-2 is Small) then (Extension-Time is Medium) (1)

Figure 12: Fuzzy rules for ETDM develop in MATLAB.

fuzzy rules are used for designingTUDM and ETDM shown in the Figure 11 and 12 respectively.

In the fuzzy logic controller once the appropriate rules are fired, the degree of membership of the output fuzzy variable i.e.,, Urgency is determined by encoding the antecedent fuzzy subsets in this case Queue, Time_r and the output fuzzy variable i.e., Extension-time is determined by encoding the antecedent fuzzy subsets, in this case Queue-Lane-1, Queue-Lane-2. In two stage traffic light system using fuzzy logic the max-min implication technique is used. Using this technique the final output membership function for each rule is the fuzzy set assigned to that output by clipping the degree of truth values of the membership functions of the associated antecedents. Once the membership degree of each output fuzzy variable is determined all of the rules that are being fired are then combined and the actual crisp output is obtained through defuzzification. The procedure of converting each aggregated

fuzzy output set into a single crisp value is called defuzzification. In traffic urgency decision module and extension time decision modules we use centroid defuzzification method.

Simulation Result and Discussion

After a two stage traffic light system was carefully designed, we test the system and discuss the impact of the input variables on the output variable.With thehelp ofsimulation we show the effect of the two inputs*Queue, Time_r*and *Queue-Lane-1, Queue-Lane-2*to resulted *Urgency* and*Extension-Time*respectively.

As shown in Figure 13, the Urgency (z-axis) is small when the value of Queue (x-axis) and Time_r (y-axis) have a small value. The urgency grows fastly and gets a maximum value when the queue side is being too many and the time_r density become small. On the other hand, urgency grows fastly and gets a maximum value when the queue side is being small and the time_r density become too large.

As shown in Figure 14 as well as Table 2, the extension time (z-axis)

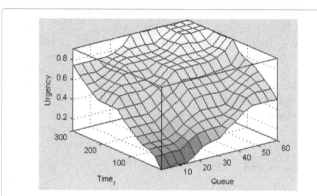

Figure 13: Input variables Queue, Time_r Vs output variable Urgency using centroid defuzzification method.

No of Vehicles (Maximum = 60)		Extension Time (in Seconds)	
Queue Lane-1	Queue Lane- 2	ETDM	Actual Method
3	3	15	10
5	5	18	12
10	10	22	16
15	15	25	21
20	20	26	26
25	25	31	31
30	30	35	36
35	35	38	40
40	40	42	45
10	20	26	26
10	25	31	31
10	30	35	36
10	35	38	40
10	40	42	45
20	10	26	26
25	10	31	31
30	10	35	36
35	10	38	40
40	10	42	45
50	10	46	55
60	10	54	64

Table 2: Comparison of ETDM and Actual method.

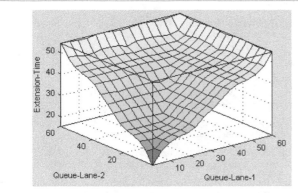

Figure 14: Input variables Queue-Lane-1, Queue-Lane-2 Vs output variable Extension-Time using centroid defuzzification method.

Maximum detectable queue per lane (Vehicles)	60
Maximum Length queue per lane (meters)	160
Maximum Length between parallel stop line (meters)	20
Maximum queue per phase (vehicles)	120
Lost time per phase, T_{LOST} (Seconds)	4
Saturation flow rate (Vehicles/hour/lane)	2400
Maximum allowable green phase, T_{MAX} (Seconds)	60
Maximum allowable green phase, T_{MIN} (Seconds)	8
Low arrival rate (Vehicles/minute)	0-18
Medium arrival rate (Vehicles/minute)	18-36
High arrival rate (Vehicles/minute)	36-60
Fixed yellow time, T_Y (Seconds)	4

Table 3: Simulation parameters for intersection.

is small when the value of queue-lane-1 (x-axis) and queue-lane-2 (y-axis) have a small value. The extension time grow slowly and have a long value when both the queue-lane-1 side and the queue-lane-2 go to medium to large value. If one of the queue-lane sides constant and other side increase then extension time also increase this is equivalent to actual method.

In this research paper, the vehicle arrival rate is Poisson distribution which is divided into three types such as low traffic rate, middle traffic rate and high traffic rate. The ranges of each vehicle rate are as 0~0.3 car per second, 0.3~0.6 car per second and 0.6~ 1 car per second respectively. Table 3 summarizes all the simulation parameters used in TSTLS (Figure 15).

As shown in Table 2 result of extension time decision module and actual method are very close. In maximum situation extension time taken by ETDM is similar to actual method. But ETDM take less time than fixed time controller without making unstable conditions in the traffic flow. Extension time of actual method are found with the help of the following formula-

$$\text{Extension Time} = \frac{\text{Average Distance}}{\text{Average Speed}} = \frac{2.67 \times n + 20}{2.78}$$

Where n is no of vehicles and average distance is 180 meter (160+20) the distance from last vehicle in the queue to cover the intersection and average speed is 10 km/h or 2.78 m/sec (Figure 16 and 17).

The average vehicle delay of pre-timed control system and TSTLS are shown in following tables. The average vehicle delay of low traffic rate, middle traffic rate and high traffic rate is shown in Tables 4, 5 and 6 respectively.

Table 7 shows the improvement percentage of TSTLS with pre-timed control system which is taken with different traffic rate. The average vehicle delay in low traffic rate of TSTLS is reduced by 48.91% compared to pre-timed control system. The average vehicle delay in middle traffic rate of TSTLS is reduced by 58.65% compared to pre-timed control system and the average vehicle delay in high traffic rate of TSTLS is reduced by 39.73% compared to pre-timed control system.

Conclusion and Future Works

The two stage traffic light system using fuzzy logic performed better than the fixed time system or even vehicle actuated system due to its flexibility. The flexibility involves the number of vehicles sensed at the incoming junction and in first stage, determines the maximum urgency

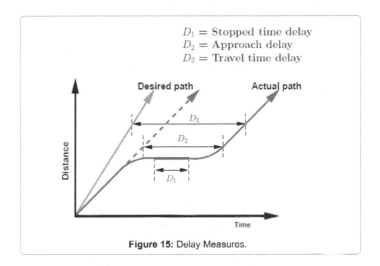

Figure 15: Delay Measures.

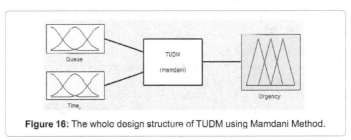

Figure 16: The whole design structure of TUDM using Mamdani Method.

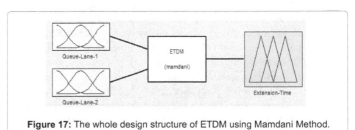

Figure 17: The whole design structure of ETDM using Mamdani Method.

No. of Simulation	Pre-timed control system	Two stage traffic light system (TSTLS)
1	61.98	31.11
2	73.56	39.35
3	69.63	36.69
4	57.33	27.38
5	64.85	32.73
Average	65.47	33.45

Table 4: Average vehicle delay of low arrival rate.

No. of Simulation	Pre-timed control system	Two stage traffic light system (TSTLS)
1	167.56	78.63
2	136.38	59.34
3	156.74	67.21
4	143.23	51.86
5	121.81	42.97
Average	145.14	60.01

Table 5: Average vehicle delay of medium arrival rate.

No. of Simulation	Pre-timed control system	Two stage traffic light system (TSTLS)
1	302.78	186.34
2	290.56	173.67
3	287.45	168.96
4	308.67	189.48
5	293.39	175.18
Average	296.57	178.73

Table 6: Average vehicle delay of high arrival rate.

	Arrival rate		
	Low	Medium	High
Pre-timed control system	65.47	145.14	296.57
TSTLS	33.45	60.01	178.73
Improvement TSTLS vs. Pre-timed Control	48.91%	58.65%	39.73%

Table 7: Improvement TSTLS vs. Pre-timed control system.

degree ofred phases then in second stage, determines the extension time of the green phase. In the fixed time system, being an open loop system phase sequence is not changeable and the green time is not extended whatever the density of carat the junction. In addition to the fuzzy variables as mentioned, the fuzzy system also has an advantage of performing according to linguistics rules in the manner of how a human would use.

It can be observed from the result that a two stage traffic light system (TSTLS) provide better performance in terms of average vehicle delay than pre-timed control system. Therefore TSTLS, improve the efficiency of vehicles, traffic congestion and hence reduce travel time, noise pollution, carbon dioxide emission, fuel used and save the time of human being.

One direction for future research on a proposed two stage traffic light system is that to enhance the system with a neural network which is able to forecast the traffic conditions i.e., to predict the traffic conditions at different times of the day or on different days of the week. This combination would allow the fuzzy control system to make its decision taking into account not only the current traffic situation as detected by the sensor but also the probable short term evolution of the traffic conditions. In this way the choice of the phase would depend on the number of vehicles in the queue while the green time duration of the traffic lights would be determined based on the traffic flow forecast by the neural network.

Moreover,prospect research direction is to provide the system with the ability of detecting emergency situation such as the presence in the queue of ambulance, VIP vehicle and fire trucks etc. through non-expensive sensors and of implementing suitable contingency actions so as to prioritize the phase that hosts those vehicles. A further area of investigation refers to the adoption of low power mechanisms to reduce the sensor node power consumption as shown in Collotta, et al. [20] and hence increase the network lifetime.

References

1. Shahraki AA, Shahraki MN, Mosavi MR (2013) Design and Simulation of a Fuzzy Controller for a Busy Intersection. IEEE: 1-6.

2. Porche IR (1997) Dynamic Traffic Control: Decentralized and Coordinated Methods. Ph.D. Dissertation, Department of Electrical Engineering and Computer Science, The University of Michigan: 930-935.

3. Yu XH, Recker WW (2006) Stochastic Adaptive Control Model for Traffic Signal Systems. Transportation Research Part C 14: 263-282.

4. Gosavi A (2003) Simulation-Based Optimization: Parametric Optimization Techniques and Reinforcement Learning, Springer.

5. Pappis CP, Mamdani EH (1977) A Fuzzy Logic Controller for a Traffic Junction. IEEE Transactions on Systems, Man, and Cybernetics 7: 707-717.

6. Niittymaki J, Pursula M (2000) Signal Control Using Fuzzy Logic. Elsevier fuzzy sets and systems 116: 11-22.

7. Chiu S (1992) Adaptive Traffic Signal Control Using Fuzzy Logic. Proceedings of the IEEE Intelligent Vehicles Symposium: 98-107.

8. Trabia MB, Kaseko MS, Ande M (1999) A two-stage fuzzy logic controller for traffic signals. Elsevier: Transportation Research Part C 7: 353-367.

9. Soh AC, Rhung LG, Sarkan HM (2010) MATLAB Simulation of Fuzzy Traffic Controller for Multilane Isolated Intersection. International Journal on Computer Science and Engineering 2: 924-933.

10. Zaied ANH, Othman WA (2011) Development of a fuzzy logic traffic system for isolated signalized intersections in the State of Kuwait. Elsevier: Expert Systems with Applications 38: 9434- 9441.

11. IndrabayulAreni IS, Makobombang NN, Sidehabi SS (2014) A fuzzy logic approach for timely adaptive traffic light based on traffic load. IEEE: 170-174.

12. Collotta M, Bello LL, Pau G (2015) A novel approach for dynamic traffic lights management based on Wireless Sensor Networks and multiple fuzzy logic controllers. Elsevier: Expert Systems with Applications, pp.5403- 5415, March 2015.

13. Wu L, Zhang X, Shi Z (2010) An intelligent fuzzy control for crossroads traffic light, 2nd WRI global congress-GCIS 3: 28-32.

14. Mathew T V (2014) Design Principles of Traffic Signal.

15. Zhang W, YUE WL (2001) Alternative solutions for urban traffic congestion, Proceedings of the Eastern Asia Society for Transportation Studies 3: 327-342.

16. Barto AG, Mahadevan S (2003) Recent Advances in Hierarchical Reinforcement Learning. Kluwer Academic Publishers 13: 343-379.

17. Wei H, Yong W, Xuanqin W, Yan W (2001) A cooperative fuzzy control method for traffic Lights. IEEE Intelligent Transportation Systems Conference Proceedings-Oakland (CA), USA: 185-188.

18. Nakatsuyama M, Nagahashi H, Nishizuka N (1984) Fuzzy Logic Phase Controller for Traffic Junctions in the One-Way Arterial Road. in Proc. of 9th IFAC-World Congress, Budapest, Hungary: 2865-2870.

19. Niittymaki J, Nevala R, Turunen E (2003) Fuzzy Traffic Signal Control and a New Inference Method Maximal Fuzzy Similarity. Researchgate: 716-728.

20. Collotta M, Pau G, Salerno V, Scata G (2011) A fuzzy based algorithm tomanage power consumption in industrial wireless sensor networks. Industrial informatics 9th IEEE international conference, India: 151-156.

8

Load Balancing Approach in Cloud Computing

Majid Mehmood[1], Kinza Sattar[2], Asif Hussain Khan[3] and Mujahid Afzal[3]

[1]*Department of Information Technology, University of Lahore, Gujrat, Pakistan*
[2]*Department of Computer Science, COMSATS, Abbottabad, Pakistan*
[3]*Department of Information Technology, University of Lahore, Gujrat, Pakistan*

Abstract

Cloud computing is a utility to deliver services and resources to the users through high speed internet. It has a number of types and hybrid cloud is one of them. Delivering services in a hybrid cloud is an uphill task. One of the challenges associated with this paradigm is the even distribution among the resources of a hybrid cloud, often refereed as load balancing. Through load balancing resource utilization and job response time can be improved. This will lead to better performance results. Energy consumption and carbon emission can also be reduced if the load is evenly distributed. Hence, in this paper we have conducted a survey of the load balancing algorithms in order to compare the pros and cons of the most widely used load balancing algorithms.

Keywords: Cloud; Cloud computing; Load balancing

Introduction

Cloud computing

Cloud computing is a utility to deliver services and resources to the users through high speed internet [1]. It has gained immense popularity in recent years. These cloud computing services can be used at individual or corporate level [2,3]. Cloud computing can be summarized as a model that gives access to a pool of recourses with minimal management effort [4].

Types of clouds

Clouds can be classified as private, public and hybrid [6,7,8] on the basis of their architecture. It provides three types of services 1. Infrastructure as a Service (IAAS), that provides the infrastructure a user demands like routers. 2. Software as a Service (SAAS), delivers software services like Google Apps. 3. Platform as a Service, PAAS, as the name suggests provides platforms for program development for example Google's App Engine [5].

Private cloud: A cloud used only within an enterprise is referred as a private cloud [6]. It can also be addressed as internal cloud [8]. They are managed by the organization itself.

Public cloud: A cloud that is made available to the users around the globe through an Internet access is called a public cloud [6]. Organizations providing such cloud services include Google Docs [9], Microsoft's Windows Azure Platform [10], Amazon's Elastic Compute Cloud and Simple Storage Services [11], IBM's Smart Business Services [12].

Hybrid cloud: A union of private and public clouds forms another type of cloud referred as hybrid cloud. As one part of it is private, it is considered to be more secure but designing a hybrid cloud is a challenging job because of the complexities involved in the design phase [8]. The major issues linked with them are that of interoperability and standardization [13]. They are costly as compared to the aforementioned types but it has their best features combined [14].

Benefits of hybrid clouds

Hybrid cloud model provides a seamless integration of public and private infrastructure which allows the use of public resources when local resources run out. The term normally used to refer to this state is called "cloud bursting". An elastic environment is created this way. Some benefits of hybrid clouds are listed as follows [15,16].

Optimal resource utilization: One strategy for handling peak load is to extend the infrastructure that could handle the load when it crosses the average load. The peak load is almost ten times the average load. That's why this strategy would be costly. In hybrid cloud environment, the public cloud is used at the time of peak loads. That saves from unnecessary investment on infrastructure expansion.

Risk transfer: It also reduces the risk of downtime. If some problem occurs in the private cloud the load is transferred to the public infrastructure. This way, hybrid clouds help in increasing the uptime.

Availability: Hybrid clouds provide availability without having to provide redundant and geographically distributed infrastructure.

Reduction in hardware cost: With the help hybrid clouds the need to expand the data centers has reduced as the peak load is faced only occasionally, adding infrastructure to cater this requirement would be a waste of money. As mention before, peak load is ten times the average load.

Better QoS: By using proper scheduling techniques, hybrid clouds can help meet the desired deadlines and execution times hence QoS and SLAs can be delivered as promised.

Challenges and issues of hybrid clouds

However, many challenges are also associated with hybrid clouds as elaborated in [15-17]. Some are briefly discussed here:

Interoperability and portability: Vendor lock-ins is always given importance whenever outsourcing is discussed. Interoperability and Portability is an open research problem in hybrid clouds for the researchers. Interoperability defines the way how communication between different clouds would occur. If we take the example of Amazon and Google, the image of Windows used is the same on both, no change is required, this is called interoperability. On the other hand, portability refers to the capability of a cloud, to move data and

---

*Corresponding author: Majid Mehmood, Department of Information Technology, University of Lahore, Gujrat, Pakistan, E-mail: majidmehmood038@gmail.com

application from one cloud to another. This becomes a possibility only if the dependencies are removed.

Cost: In these environments, on one hand, private infrastructure is to be managed, while on the other hand, you are charged on the basis of pay-per-use for using the public resources. This makes predicting the overall cost an uphill task.

Security: For using public cloud resources certain SLAs are settled first and a lot of trust is placed in the public cloud. Additional security measures are to be taken along with the company's firewalls. That is why security is one of the primary concerns in hybrid cloud environment. To ensure secure computation, some security issues are given prime importance. The list includes: Identification and authentication, authorization, and confidentiality etc. [18].

Reliability: As the communication between a private and public cloud occurs through a network connection, the availability of connection is again an issue as connection often breaks. Are these connections secure or not and would the migration of tasks to the public cloud actually help reduce the response time or not, are the questions that need to be addressed. So ensuring reliability is another challenge.

Monitoring: Organizations monitor the cloud services to ensure the performance is not compromised in any situation. In hybrid clouds, along with monitoring the private cloud, public clouds also need to be monitored.

Denial of service: Another challenge that is inspected by the researchers is the denial of service (DoS) in cloud computing environments. As in normal clouds and even in the hybrid environments resources are allocated dynamically, how would these clouds respond to a DoS attack, is a question given a lot of importance in the recent years. In hybrid clouds if resources are not available to the executing tasks, those tasks are forwarded to the public clouds but in this case the strategy discussed won't be a feasible solution. Finding a solution to this problem is a burning challenge for the researchers.

Load balancing: Load balancing is also one of the main challenges faced in hybrid cloud computing, as there is a need for an even and dynamic distribution of load between the nodes in private and public clouds.

In distributed systems load balancing is defined as the process of distributing load among various nodes to improve the overall resource utilization and job response time. While doing so, it is made sure that nodes are not loaded heavily, left idle or assigned tasks lesser then its capacity [19]. It is ensured that all the nodes should be assigned almost the same amount of load [20].

If resources would be utilized optimally, performance of the system will automatically increase. Not only this, the energy consumption and carbon emission will also reduce tremendously. It also reduces the possibility of bottleneck which occurs due to the load imbalance. Furthermore, it facilitates efficient and fair distribution of resources and helps in the greening of these environments [21,22].

Load balancing algorithms are classified into categories for the ease of understanding. That helps in identifying a suitable algorithm in the time of need. A detailed view of classification is presented below [23].

Related Work

With the emergence of hybrid clouds, the idea of balancing the load between the public and private clouds has gained immense popularity. That is why a lot of research in now being conducted to facilitate this concept. Load balancing has always been given prime importance in cloud environment. Lately, researchers have started expanding this idea to the hybrid clouds as well in order to balance load at peak times while meeting the promised QoS and SLAs.

Load balancing strategies for clouds

Load balancing algorithms can be broadly categorized into static and dynamic load balancing algorithms.

Static load balancing algorithms: Gulati et al. [24] claimed that in cloud environment a lot of work is done on load balancing in homogeneous resources. Research on load balancing in heterogeneous environment is given also under spot light. They studied the effect of round robin technique with dynamic approach by varying host bandwidth, cloudlet long length, VM image size and VM bandwidth. Load is optimized by varying these parameters. CloudSim is used for this implementation.

Dynamic load balancing algorithms: A hybrid load balancing policy was presented by Shu-Ching et al. [25]. This policy comprises of two stages 1) Static load balancing stage 2) Dynamic load balancing stage. It selects suitable node set in the static load balancing stage and keeps a balance of tasks and resources in dynamic load balancing stage. When a request arrives a dispatcher sends out an agent that gathers nodes information like remaining CPU capacity and memory. Hence the duty of the dispatcher is not only to monitor and select effective nodes but also to assign tasks to the nodes accordingly. Their results showed that this policy can provide better results in comparison with min-min and minimum completion time (MCT), in terms of overall performance.

Another algorithm for load balancing in cloud environment is ant colony optimization (ACO) [26]. This work basically proposed a modified version of ACO. Ants move in forward and backward directions in order to keep track of overloaded and under loaded nodes. While doing so ants update the pheromone, which keeps the nodes' resource information. The two types of pheromone updates are 1) Foraging pheromone, which is looked up when an under loaded node is encountered in order to look for the path to an over loaded node. 2) Trailing pheromone is used to find path towards an under loaded node when an over loaded node is encountered. In the previous algorithm ants maintained their own result sets and were combined at a later stage but in this version these result sets are continuously updated. This modification helps this algorithm perform better.

Genetic algorithm [27] is also a nature inspired algorithm. It is modified by Pop et al. [28], to make it a reputation guided algorithm. They evaluated their solution by taking load-balancing as a way to calculate the optimization offered to providers and makespan as a performance metric for the user.

Another such algorithm is the bees life algorithm (BLA) [29], which is inspired by bee's food searching and reproduction. This concept is further extended to specifically address the issue of load balancing in [30]. The Honey bee behavior inspired load balancing (HBB-LB) algorithm basically manages the load across different virtual machines for increasing throughput. Tasks are prioritized so that the waiting time is reduced when they are aligned in queues. The honey bee foraging behavior and some of its variants are listed in [31].

Comparison

A comparative study of different load balancing algorithms is presented in [32]. Load balancing is not only required for meeting users' satisfaction but it also helps in proper utilization of the resources available. The metrics that are used for evaluating different load balancing technologies are: throughput, overhead associated, fault tolerance, migration time, response time, resource utilization, scalability, and performance. According to this study, in honeybee foraging algorithm, throughput does not increase with the increase in system size. Biased random sampling and active clustering do not work well as the system diversity increases. OLB + LBMM shows better results than the algorithms listed so far, in terms of efficient resource utilization. The algorithm Join-Idle-Queue can show optimal performance when hosted for web services but there are some scalability and reliability issues that make its use difficult in today's dynamic-content web services. They further added that min-min algorithm can lead to starvation. They concluded that one can pick any algorithm according to ones needs. There is still room for improvement in all of these algorithms to make them work more efficiently in heterogeneous environments while keeping the cost to a minimum. A somewhat similar analysis of load balancing algorithms is presented by Daryapurkar et al. [33] and Rajguru and Apte [34] as well. Different scheduling algorithms for the hybrid clouds compared by Bittencourt et al. [35], highlights that the maxspan of these algorithms widely depend on the bandwidth provided between the private and public clouds. The channels are usually part of the internet backbone and their bandwidth fluctuates immensely. This makes the designing of the communication aware algorithms quite challenging.

Load Balancing Strategies in Hybrid Clouds

Zhang et al. [36] proposed a design for hybrid cloud is. It allows intelligent workload factoring by dividing it into base and trespassing load. When a system goes into a panic mode the excess load is passed on to the trespassing zone. Fast frequent data item detection algorithm is used for this purpose. It makes use of the least connections balancing algorithm and the Round-Robin balancing algorithm as well. Their results show that there is a decrease in annual bills when hybrid clouds are used. Buyya et al. [37] proposed a concept of federated cloud environment, to maintain the promised QoS even when the load shows a sudden variation. It supports dynamic allocation of VMs, Database, Services and Storage. That allows an application to run on clouds from different vendors. In Social Networks like Facebook, load varies significantly from time to time. For such systems this facility can help scale the load dynamically. No cloud infrastructure provider can

have data centers all around the globe. That's why to meet QoS, any cloud application service provider has to make use of multiple cloud providers. For implementation purpose they used Cloud Sim Tool kit. They made a comparison between federated and non federated cloud environments. Their results showed a considerable gain in performance in terms of response time and cost in case of the former. The turnaround time is reduced by 50% and the make span improves by 20%. Although the overall cost increases with the increase in the public cloud utilization but one has to consider that such peak loads are faced occasionally which makes it acceptable.

Task scheduling plays a vital role in solving the optimization problem in hybrid clouds. A graph-based task scheduling algorithm is proposed by Jiang et al. for this purpose [38]. In order to reduce the cost to a minimum value, like other algorithms, it makes use of the public resources along with the private infrastructure. The key stages of this algorithm are 1) Resource discovery and filtering, for the collection of the status information of the resources that are discovered. 2) Resource selection, this algorithm's main focus is on this stage as this is the decision making stage. Resources are picked keeping in view the demand of the tasks to be performed. 3) Task submission, once the resources are selected the tasks are assigned accordingly. A bipartite graph G=(U,V,E) is used to help elaborate this concept, where U is used for private or public Virtual Machines, V is for the tasks, and E denotes the edges in between. Cloud Report and Cloud Sim 3.0 are used for evaluating this algorithm. Their results showed a 30 % decrease in cost as compared to a non hybrid environment. For improving these figures even more, disk storage and network bandwidth need to be considered as well.

Another algorithm, adaptive-scheduling-with-QoS-satisfaction (AsQ) [39], for the hybrid cloud is proposed that basically reduces the response time and helps increase the resource utilization. To fulfill this goal several fast scheduling strategies and run time estimations are used and resources are then allocated accordingly. If resources are used optimally in the private clouds, the need for transferring tasks to the public clouds decreases and deadlines are fulfilled efficiently but if a task is transferred to the public cloud, minimum cost strategy is used so that the cost of using a public cloud can be reduced. The size of the workload is specially considered in this regard. Their results show that As Q performs better compared to the recent algorithms of similar

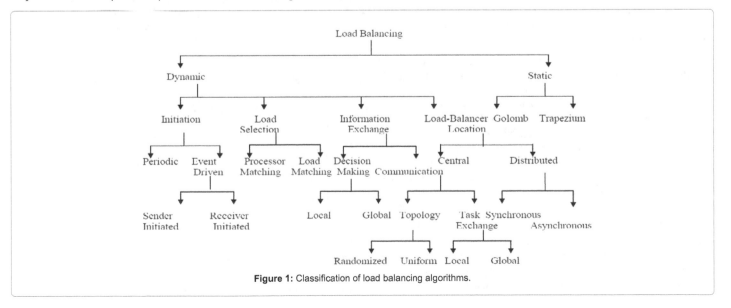

Figure 1: Classification of load balancing algorithms.

Metrics	Honeybee Scheduling	Biased random Sampling	Active Clustering	OLB+ LBMM	Join Idle Queue	Min-Min	Min-Max
Throughput	✗	✗	✗	✗	✗	✓	✓
Overhead	✗	✓	✓	✗	✓	✓	✓
Fault Tolerance	✗	✗	✗	✗	✗	✗	✗
Migration Time	✗	✗	✓	✗	✗	✗	✗
Response Time	✗	✗	✗	✗	✓	✓	✓
Resource Utilization	✓	✓	✓	✓	✗	✓	✓
Scalability	✗	✗	✗	✗	✗	✗	✗
Performance	✗	✓	✗	✓	✓	✓	✓

Figure 2: Comparison of the existing load balancing techniques.

nature in terms of task waiting, execution and finish time. Hence it provides better QoS.

Picking the best resources from the public cloud is a serious concern in hybrid clouds. The Hybrid Cloud Optimized Cost (HCOC) [40], is one such scheduling algorithm. It helps in executing a workflow within the desired execution time. Their results have shown that it reduces the cost while meeting the desired goals. Gives better results in comparison with the other greedy approaches. There is another approach [41], which also deals with directed acyclic graphs (DAG) as in study by Bittencourt and Madeira [40]. It uses integer linear program (ILP) for the workflow scheduling n SaaS/PaaS clouds with two levels of SLA, one with the customer one for the provider. This work can be extended by considering multiple workflows and fault tolerance in view.

Gupta et al. [42], contributed that there are a number of load balancing algorithms that basically help in avoiding situations where a single node is loaded heavily and the rest are either idle or have lesser number of tasks when in reality they can afford to deal with a lot more. But what is overlooked in most of these algorithms is the trust and reliability of the datacenter. A suitable trust model and a load balancing algorithm are proposed. They used VMMs (Virtual Machines Monitors) to generate trust values on the basis of these values nodes are selected and the load is balanced.

A virtual infrastructure management tool is offered by Hoecke et al. [43], that helps to set-up and manage hybrid clouds in an efficient way. This tool automatically balances load between the private and public clouds. It works at the virtual machine level. This tool has two parts 1) a proxy, where different load balancing algorithms are implemented like weighted round robin and forwarding requests to appropriate VMs, and on the other hand a management interface is designed that visualizes the hybrid environment and manages it too for example it can start and stop VMs, can form clusters of VMs, and can also manage the proxy remotely. It can be improved further by using a more efficient algorithm on the proxy for balancing load in a more convenient way.

In workflow applications [44], the cost of execution is kept to a minimum level by allocating the workflow to a private cloud but in case of peak loads, resources from the Public cloud need to be considered as well. As meeting the deadlines is a primary concern in workflow applications. By using cost optimization, this algorithm decides which

resources should be leased from the public cloud for executing the task within the deadline. In this algorithm workflow is divided into levels and scheduling is performed on each level. It uses the concept of sub-deadlines as well. That helps in finding the best resources in public cloud in terms of cost while keeping in view that the workflows are executed within the deadlines. Although the make span of level based approach is 1.55 times higher than the non level based approach, its cost is three times lower. In comparison with min-min, its make span is double but it costs three times lesser. This makes the proposed level based approach better as it costs less and meets the deadlines too although its make span is higher but it finishes the assigned tasks within the deadline.

Conclusion

Cloud computing is a utility to deliver services and resources to the users through high speed internet. It has a number of types and hybrid cloud is one of them. As one part of it is private, it is considered to be more secure but designing a hybrid cloud is a challenging job because of the complexities involved. Some benefits of hybrid clouds are optimal resource utilization, risk transfer, availability, reduction in hardware cost and better QoS. However, many challenges are also associated with hybrid clouds as elaborated. Some of them are interoperability and portability, cost, security, reliability, monitoring, denial of service, load balancing.

Load balancing algorithms can be broadly categorized into static and dynamic load balancing algorithms. A comparative study of different load balancing algorithms is presented. Load balancing is not only required for meeting users' satisfaction but it also helps in proper utilization of the resources available. The metrics that are used for evaluating different load balancing technologies are: throughput, overhead associated, fault tolerance, migration time, response time, resource utilization, scalability, and performance. According to this study, in honeybee foraging algorithm, throughput does not increase with the increase in system size. Different load balancing strategies in hybrid cloud are also discussed. A concept of federated cloud environment is proposed to maintain the promised QoS even when the load shows a sudden variation. Task scheduling plays a vital role in solving the optimization Problem in hybrid clouds. Another algorithm, adaptive-scheduling-with-QoS-satisfaction (AsQ) for the hybrid cloud is proposed that basically reduces the response time and helps increase the resource utilization.

References

1. Cisco (2009) Cisco visual networking index: Forecast and methodology, 2009-2014.White paper.

2. Weiss A (2007) Computing in the clouds. Networker 11: 16-25.

3. Hayes B (2008) Cloud computing. Commun ACM 51: 9-11.

4. Mell P, Grance T (2009) Draft NIST Working Definition of Cloud Computing. Nat Inst Standards Technol.

5. Tao Z, Long J (2011) The Research and Application of Network Teaching Platform Based on Cloud Computing. Inter J Info Edu Tech 1.

6. Aditya S (2015) Top 5 Best Web Hosting Service Providers in 2015. Open Cloud Manifesto.

7. Armbrust M, Fox A, Griffith R, Joseph A D, Katz R H, A et al. (2009) Above the clouds: A Berkeleyview of cloud computing. Electr Eng Comput Sci Dept Univ California, Berkeley CA Tech.

8. Zhang Q, Cheng L, Boutaba R (2010) Cloud computing: state-of-the-art and research challenges. Journal of Internet Services and Applications 1: 7-18.

9. https://www.google.co.in/docs/

10. Azure Services Platform.

11. Amazon Web Services.

12. IBM Smart Business Services.

13. Dillon T, Wu C, Chang E (2010) Cloud Computing: Issues and Challenges. International Conference on Advance Information Networking and Applications IEEE.

14. Adler B (2012) Designing Private and Hybrid Clouds. Architectural Best Practices.

15. M Armbrust, A Fox, R Griffith, AD Joseph, R Katz, et al. (2009) Above the Clouds: A Berkeley View of Cloud Computing. Technical Report.

16. Heckel PC (2010) Hybrid Clouds: Comparing Cloud Toolkits. Seminar Paper Business Informatics, University of Mannheim.

17. Aubert BA, Patry M, Rivard S (2005) A Framework for Information Technology Outsourcing Risk Management. Database for Advances In Information Systems 36: 9- 28.

18. Tripathi A, Jalil MS (2013) Data Access and Integrity with authentication in Hybrid Cloud. Oriental International Journal of Innovative Engineering Research.

19. Rimal, Prasad B, Choi E, Lumb V (2009) A taxonomy and surveyof cloud computing systems. Proceedings of 5th International Joint Conference on INC, IMS and IDC, IEEE .

20. Sinha PK (1997) Distributed operating Systems Concepts andDesign. IEEE Computer Society Press.

21. Toledo RM, Gupta P (2010) Green data center: howgreen can we perform. Journal of Technology Research, Academic and Business Research Institute 2: 1-8.

22. Alakeel AM (2010) A Guide to dynamic Load balancing in Distributed Computer Systems. International Journal of Computer Science and Network Security 10: 153-160.

23. Khan Z, Singh R, Alam J, Saxena S (2011) Classification of Load Balancing Conditions for parallel and distributed systems. International Journal of Computer Science Issue 8: 411- 419.

24. Gulati A, Chopra RK (2013) Dynamic Round Robin for Load Balancing in a Cloud Computing, International Journal of Computer Science and Mobile Computing 2: 274-278.

25. Wang SC, Chen CW, Yan KQ, Wang SS (2013) The Anatomy Study of Load Balancing in Cloud Computing Environment. The Eighth International Conference on Internet and Web Applications and Services 230-235.

26. Nishant K, Sharma P, Krishna V, Gupta C, Singh KP, et al. (2012) Load Balancing of Nodes in Cloud Using Ant Colony Optimization. Computer Modelling and Simulation 3-8.

27. Whitley D (1994) A generic algorithm tutorial. Statistics and Computing 4: 65-68.

28. Pop F, Cristea V, Bessis N, Sotiriadis S (2013) Reputation guided Genetic Scheduling Algorithm for Independent Tasks in Inter-Clouds Environments. Advanced Information Networking and Applications Workshops.

29. Bitam S (2012) Bees Life Algorithm for Job Scheduling in Cloud Computing. International Conference on Communications and Information Technology 186-191.

30. Babu LD D, Krishna VP (2013) Honey bee behavior inspired load balancing of tasks in cloud computing environments. Applied Soft Computing 13: 2292-2303.

31. Suresh M, Ullah Z S, Kumar S (2013) An Analysis of Load Balancing in Cloud Computing. International Journal of Engineering Research and Technology 2: 428-433.

32. Sran N, Kaur N (2013) Comparative Analysis of Existing Load Balancing Techniques in Cloud Computing. International Journal of Engineering Science Invention 2: 60-63.

33. Daryapurkar A, Deshmukh MV (2013) Efficient Load Balancing Algorithm in Cloud Environment. International Journal of Computer Science and Applications 6: 308-312.

34. Rajguru AA, Apte SS (2012) A Comparative Performance Analysis of Load Balancing Algorithms in Distributed System using Qualitative Parameters. International Journal of Engineering Research and Technology 1: 175-179.

35. Bittencourt LF, Madeira ERM, Fonseca N (2012) Scheduling in hybrid clouds. Communications Magazine, IEEE.

36. Zhang H, Jiang G, Yoshihira K, Chen H, Saxena A (2009) Intelligent Workload Factoring for A Hybrid Cloud Computing Model. Services World Conference.

37. Buyya R, Ranjan R, Calheiros RN (2010) Inter Cloud: Utility-Oriented Federation of Cloud Computing Environments for Scaling of Application Services. Algorithms and Architectures for Parallel Processing 1: 13-31.

38. Jiang WZ, sheng ZQ (2012) A New Task Scheduling Algorithm in Hybrid Cloud Environment. Cloud and Service Computing IEEE 45-49.

39. Wang WJ, Chang YS, Lo WT, Lee YK (2013) Adaptive scheduling for parallel tasks with QoS satisfaction for hybrid cloud environments. The journal of Super-Computing 66: 783-811.

40. Bittencourt LF, Madeira ERM (2011) HCOC: A Cost Optimization Algorithm for Workflow Scheduling in Hybrid Clouds. Journal of Internet Services and Applications, Springer 2: 207-227.

41. Genez TAL, Bittencourt LF, Madeira ERM (2012) Workflow Scheduling for SaaS /PaaS Cloud Providers Considering Two SLA Levels. Network Operations and Management Symposium 906-912.

42. Gupta P, Goyal MK, Kumar P (2013) Trust and Reliability based Load Balancing Algorithm for Cloud IaaS. Advance Computing Conference IEEE.

43. Hoecke SV, Waterbley T, Deneut JDT, Gelas JD (2011) Efficient Management of Hybrid Clouds. The Second International Conference on Cloud Computing, GRIDs, and Virtualization 167-172.

44. Chopra N, Singh S (2013) Deadline and Cost based Workflow Scheduling in Hybrid Cloud, International Conference on Advances in Computing. Communications and Informatics, IEEE.

9

Multiple Solutions for Elliptic Problem with Singular Cylindrical Potential and Critical Exponent

Mohammed El Mokhtar Ould El Mokhtar*

Qassim University, College of Science, Departement of Mathematics, BO 6644, Bu- raidah: 51452, Kingdom of Saudi Arabia

Abstract

In the present paper, a quasilinear elliptic problem with singular cylindrical potential and critical exponent, is considered. By using the Nehari manifold and mountain pass theorem, the existence of at least four distinct solutions is obtained. The result depends crucially on the parameters a, b, m, s, λ and μ.

Keywords: Singular cylindrical potential; Concave term; Critical exponent; Nehari manifold; Mountain pass theorem

Introduction

In this paper, we consider the multiplicity results of nontrivial nonnegative solutions of the following problem $\left(\mathcal{P}_{\lambda,\mu}\right)$

$$\begin{cases} -div\left(|y|^{-2a}\nabla u\right)-\mu|y|^{-2(a+1)}u = p|y|^{-bp}|u|^{p-2}u+\lambda|y|^{-c}|u|^{s-2}u, \text{in} \mathbb{R}^N, y\neq 0 \\ u \in \mathcal{D}_a^{1,2} \end{cases}$$

where each point x in $\mathbb{R}^N$ is written as a pair $(y,z)\in\mathbb{R}^m\times\mathbb{R}^{N-m}$ where m and N are integers such that $N\geq 3$ and m belongs to $\{1,...,N\}$, $-\infty < a < \sqrt{\bar{\mu}_m}$ with $\bar{\mu}_m=(m-2)^2/4$, $a\leq b<a+1, 1<s<2$, $p=2N/(N-2+2(b-a))$ is the critical Caffarelli-Kohn-Nirenberg exponent, $0<c=s(a+1)+N(1-s/2)$, $-\infty<\mu<\left(\sqrt{\bar{\mu}_m}-a\right)^2$, λ is a real parameter.

In recent years, many auteurs have paid much attention to the following singular elliptic problem, i.e., the case a=b=c=0,s=2 in $\left(\mathcal{P}_{\lambda,\mu}\right)$,

$$\begin{cases} -\Delta u-\mu|x|^{-2}u = |u|^{p-2}u+\lambda u, \text{in}\Omega \\ u = 0 \qquad\qquad \partial\Omega, \end{cases}$$

where Ω is a smooth bounded domain in $\mathbb{R}^N$ $(N\geq 3)$, $0\in\Omega, \lambda>0, 0\leq\mu<\bar{\mu}_N:=(N-2)^2/4$ and $2^*=2N/(N-2)$ is the critical Sobolev exponent, see [1-3] and references therein. The quasilinear form of (1.2) is discussed in [4]. Some results are already available for $\left(\mathcal{P}_{\lambda,\mu}\right)$ in the case m=N. Wang and Zhou [5] proved that there exist at least two solutions for $\left(\mathcal{P}_{\lambda,\mu}\right)$ with a=0, $0<\mu\leq\bar{\mu}_N=(N-2)^2/4$, Bouchekif and Matallah [6] showed the existence of two solutions of $\left(\mathcal{P}_{\lambda,\mu}\right)$ under certain conditions on a weighted function h, when $0<\mu\leq\bar{\mu}_N$, $\lambda\in(0,\Lambda_*)$, $-\infty<a<(N-2)/2$ and $a\leq b<a+1$, with Λ_* a positive constant.

Concerning existence results in the case $m<N$, we cite [7-9] and the references therein. Musina [9] considered $\left(\mathcal{P}_{\lambda,\mu}\right)$ with $-a/2$ instead of a and $\lambda=0$, also $\left(\mathcal{P}_{\lambda,\mu}\right)$ with a=0, b=0,λ=0 and $a\neq 2-m$. She established the existence of a ground state solution when $2<m\leq N$ and $0<\mu<\bar{\mu}_{a,m}=\left((m-2+a)/2\right)^2$ for $\left(\mathcal{P}_{\lambda,\mu}\right)$ with $-a/2$ instead of a and λ=0. She also showed that $\left(\mathcal{P}_{\lambda,\mu}\right)$ with a=0, b=0,λ=0 does not admit ground state solutions. Badiale et al. [10] studied $\left(\mathcal{P}_{\lambda,\mu}\right)$ with a=0, b=0,λ=0. They proved the existence of at least a nonzero nonnegative weak solution μ, satisfying $u(y,z)=u(|y|,z)$ when $2\leq m<N$ and $\mu<0$ Bouchekif and El Mokhtar [11] proved that $\left(\mathcal{P}_{\lambda,\mu}\right)$ admits two distinct solutions when $2<m\leq N$, $b=N-p(N-2)/2$ with $p\in(2,2^*]$, $\mu<\bar{\mu}_{0,m}$, and $\lambda\in(0,\Lambda_*)$ where Λ_* is a positive constant. Terracini [12] proved that there is no positive solutions of $\left(\mathcal{P}_{\lambda,\mu}\right)$ with b=0, λ=0 when $a\neq 0$ and $\mu<0$. The regular problem corresponding to a= b=μ=0 has been considered on a regular bounded domain Ω by Tarantello [13]. She proved that, with a nonhomogeneous term $f\in H^{-1}(\Omega)$, the

dual of $H_0^1(\Omega)$, not identically zero and satisfying a suitable condition, the problem considered admits two distinct solutions.

Before formulating our results, we give some definitions and notations.

We denote by $\mathcal{D}_a^{1,2}=\mathcal{D}_a^{1,2}\left(\mathbb{R}^m\setminus\{0\}\times\mathbb{R}^{N-m}\right)$ and $\mathcal{H}_\mu=\mathcal{H}_\mu\left(\mathbb{R}^m\setminus\{0\}\times\mathbb{R}^{N-m}\right)$, the closure of $C_0^\infty\left(\mathbb{R}^m\setminus\{0\}\times\mathbb{R}^{N-m}\right)$ with respect to the norms

$$\|u\|_{a,0}=\left(\int_{\mathbb{R}^N}|y|^{-2a}|\nabla u|^2\,dx\right)^{1/2}$$

and

$$\|u\|_{a,\mu}=\left(\int_{\mathbb{R}^N}\left(|y|^{-2a}|\nabla u|^2-\mu|y|^{-2(a+1)}|u|^2\right)dx\right)^{1/2},$$

respectively, with $\mu<\left(\sqrt{\bar{\mu}_m}-a\right)^2=\left((m-2(a+1))/2\right)^2$ for $m\neq 2(a+1)$.

From the Hardy-Sobolev-Maz'ya inequality, it is easy to see that the norm $\|u\|_{a,\mu}$ is equivalent to $\|u\|_{a,0}$. More explicitly, we have

$$\left(1-\left(\sqrt{\bar{\mu}_m}-a\right)^{-2}\mu^+\right)^{1/2}\|u\|_{0,a}\leq\|u\|_{\mu,a}\leq\left(1-\left(\sqrt{\bar{\mu}_m}-a\right)^{-2}\mu^-\right)^{1/2}\|u\|_{0,a},$$

with $\mu^+=\max(\mu,0)$ and $\mu^-=\min(\mu,0)$ for all $u\in\mathcal{H}_\mu$.

We list here a few integral inequalities.

The starting point for studying $\left(\mathcal{P}_{\lambda,\mu}\right)$, is the Hardy-Sobolev-Maz'ya inequality that is particular to the cylindrical case $m<N$ and that was proved by Maz'ya in [8]. It states that there exists positive constant $C_{a,p}$ such that

$$C_{a,p}\left(\int_{\mathbb{R}^N}|y|^{-bp}|v|^p\,dx\right)^{2/p}\leq\int_{\mathbb{R}^N}\left(|y|^{-2a}|\nabla v|^2-\mu|y|^{-2(a+1)}v^2\right)dx, \qquad (1)$$

for any $v\in C_c^\infty\left((\mathbb{R}^m\setminus\{0\})\times\mathbb{R}^{N-m}\right)$.

The second one that we need is the Hardy inequality with cylindrical weights [9]. It states that

$$\left(\sqrt{\bar{\mu}_m}-a\right)^2\int_{\mathbb{R}^N}|y|^{-2(a+1)}v^2\,dx\leq\int_{\mathbb{R}^N}|y|^{-2a}|\nabla v|^2\,dx, \text{for all}\, v\in\mathcal{H}_\mu, \qquad (2)$$

It is easy to see that (1) hold for any $u\in\mathcal{H}_\mu$ in the sense

---

*Corresponding author: Mohammed El Mokhtar Ould El Mokhtar, Qassim University, College of Science, Departement of Mathematics, BO 6644, Bu- raidah: 51452, Kingdom of Saudi Arabia, E-mail: med.mokhtar66@yahoo.fr

$$\left(\int_{\mathbb{R}^N} |y|^{-c} |u|^r \, dx\right)^{1/r} \le C_{a,r} \left(\int_{\mathbb{R}^N} |y|^{-2a} |\nabla v|^2 \, dx\right)^{1/2}, \tag{3}$$

where $C_{a,r}$ positive constant, $1 \le r \le 2N/(N-2)$, $c \le r(a+1) + N(1-r/2)$, and in [14], if $r < 2N/(N-2)$ the embedding $\mathcal{H}_\mu \hookrightarrow L_r\left(\mathbb{R}^N, |y|^{-c}\right)$ is compact, where $L_r\left(\mathbb{R}^N, |y|^{-c}\right)$ is the weighted L_r space with norm

$$|u|_{r,c} = \left(\int_{\mathbb{R}^N} |y|^{-c} |u|^r \, dx\right)^{1/r}.$$

Since our approach is variational, we define the functional J on $\mathcal{H}_\mu$ by

$$J(u) := (1/2)\|u\|_{\mu,a}^2 - F(u) - G(u),$$

with

$$F(u) := \int_{\mathbb{R}^N} |y|^{-bp} |u|^p \, dx, G(u) := (1/s)\int_{\mathbb{R}^N} |y|^{-c} \lambda |u|^s \, dx.$$

A point $u \in \mathcal{H}_\mu$ is a weak solution of the equation $\left(\mathcal{P}_{\lambda,\mu}\right)$ if it satisfies

$$\left\langle J'(u), \varphi \right\rangle := R(u)\varphi - S(u)\varphi - T(u)\varphi = 0, \text{for all } \varphi \in \mathcal{H}_\mu$$

with

$$R(u)\varphi := \int_{\mathbb{R}^N} \left(|y|^{-2a} (\nabla u \nabla \varphi) - \mu |y|^{-2(a+1)} (u\varphi)\right)$$

$$S(u)\varphi := p\int_{\mathbb{R}^N} |y|^{-bp} |u|^{p-1} \varphi$$

$$T(u)\varphi := \int_{\mathbb{R}^N} |y|^{-c} \lambda |u|^{s-1} \varphi.$$

Here $\langle \cdot, \cdot \rangle$ denotes the product in the duality $\mathcal{H}_\mu'$, $\mathcal{H}_\mu \left(\mathcal{H}_\mu' \text{dual of} \mathcal{H}_\mu\right)$.

Let

$$S_\mu := \inf_{u \in \mathcal{H}_\mu \setminus \{0\}} \frac{\|u\|_{\mu,a}^2}{\left(\int_{\mathbb{R}^N} |y|^{-bp} |u|^p \, dx\right)^{2/p}}$$

From [15], S_μ is achieved.

In our work, we research the critical points as the minimizers of the energy functional associated to the problem $\left(\mathcal{P}_{\lambda,\mu}\right)$ on the constraint defined by the Nehari manifold, which are solutions of our system.

Let Λ_0 be positive number such that

$$\Lambda_0 := \left(C_{a,s}\right)^{-s} \left(S_\mu\right)^{p/2(p-2)} \left(\frac{p-2}{p-s}\right)^{1/(2-s)} \left[\left(\frac{2-s}{p(p-s)}\right)\right]^{1/(p-2)}.$$

Now we can state our main results.

Theorem 1

Assume that $-\infty < a < (m-2)/2$, $0 < c < s(a+1) + N(1-s/2)$, $-\infty < \mu < \left(\sqrt{\overline{\mu}_m} - a\right)^2$ and λ verifying $0 < \lambda < \Lambda_0$, then the system $\left(\mathcal{P}_{\lambda,\mu}\right)$ has at least one positive solution.

Theorem 2

In addition to the assumptions of the Theorem 1, if λ satisfying $0 < \lambda < (1/2)\Lambda_0$, then $\left(\mathcal{P}_{\lambda,\mu}\right)$ has at least two positive solutions.

Theorem 3

In addition to the assumptions of the Theorem 2, assuming $N \ge \max(3, 6(a-b+1))$, there exists a positive real Λ_1 such that, if λ satisfy $0 < \lambda < \min\left((1/2)\Lambda_0, \Lambda_1\right)$, then $\left(\mathcal{P}_{\lambda,\mu}\right)$ has at least two positive solution and two opposite solutions.

This paper is organized as follows. In Section 2, we give some preliminaries. Section 3 and 4 are devoted to the proofs of Theorems 1 and 2 In the last Section, we prove the Theorem 3.

Preliminaries

Definition 1 Let $c \in \mathbb{R}$, E a Banach space and $I \in C^1(E, \mathbb{R})$.

i) $(u_n)_n$ is a Palais-Smale sequence at level C (in short $(PS)_c$) in E for I if

$$I(u_n) = c + o_n(1) \text{ and } I'(u_n) = o_n(1),$$

where $o_n(1)$ tends to o as n goes at infinity.

ii) We say that I satisfies the $(PS)_c$ condition if any $(PS)_c$ sequence in E for I has a convergent subsequence.

Lemma 1 Let X Banach space, and $J \in C^1(X, \mathbb{R})$ verifying the Palais-Smale condition. Suppose that $J(0) = 0$ and that:

i) there exist $R > 0$, $r > 0$ such that if $\|u\| = R$, then $J(u) \ge r$;

ii) there exist $(u_0) \in X$ such that $\|u_0\| > R$ and $J(u_0) \le 0$;

let $c = \inf_{\gamma \in \Gamma} \max_{t \in [0,1]} \left(J(\gamma(t))\right)$ where

$$\Gamma = \left\{\gamma \in C([0,1]; X) \text{ such that } \gamma(0) = 0 \text{ et } \gamma(1) = u_0\right\},$$

then C is critical value of J such that $c \ge r$.

Nehari manifold

It is well known that J is of class C^1 in $\mathcal{H}_\mu$ and the solutions of $\left(\mathcal{P}_{\lambda,\mu}\right)$ are the critical points of J which is not bounded below on $\mathcal{H}_\mu$. Consider the following Nehari manifold

$$\mathcal{N} = \left\{u \in \mathcal{H}_\mu \setminus \{0\} : \left\langle J'(u), u \right\rangle = 0\right\},$$

Thus, $u \in \mathcal{N}$ if and only if

$$\|u\|_{\mu,a}^2 - F(u) - G(u) = 0. \tag{4}$$

Note that N contains every nontrivial solution of the problem $\left(\mathcal{P}_{\lambda,\mu}\right)$. Moreover, we have the following results.

Lemma 2 J is coercive and bounded from below on N.

Proof. If $u \in \mathcal{N}$, then by (4) and the Hölder inequality, we deduce that

$$J(u) = \left((p-2)/2p\right)\|u\|_{\mu,a}^2 - \left((p-s)/ps\right)G(u) \tag{5}$$

$$\ge \left((p-2)/2p\right)\|u\|_{\mu,a}^2$$

$$- \left(\frac{(p-s)}{ps}\right)\lambda^{1/(2-s)}\left(C_{a,p}\right)^s \|u\|_{\mu,a}^s.$$

Thus, J is coercive and bounded from below on N.

Define

$$\phi(u) = \left\langle J'(u), u \right\rangle.$$

Then, for $u \in \mathcal{N}$

$$\left\langle \phi'(u), u \right\rangle = 2\|u\|_{\mu,a}^2 - p^2 F(u) - sG(u) \tag{6}$$

$$= (2-s)\|u\|_{\mu,a}^2 - p(p-s)F(u)$$

$$= (p-s)G(u) - (p-2)\|u\|_{\mu,a}^2.$$

Now, we split N in three parts:

$$\mathcal{N}^+ = \left\{u \in \mathcal{N} : \left\langle \phi'(u), u \right\rangle > 0\right\}$$

$$\mathcal{N}^0 = \left\{ u \in \mathcal{N} : \left\langle \phi^{'}(u), u \right\rangle = 0 \right\}$$

$$\mathcal{N}^{-} = \left\{ u \in \mathcal{N} : \left\langle \phi^{'}(u), u \right\rangle < 0 \right\}.$$

We have the following results.

Lemma 3

Suppose that u_0 is a local minimizer for J on N. Then, if $u_0 \notin \mathcal{N}^0$, u_0 is a critical point of J.

Proof. If u_0 is a local minimizer for J on N, then u_0 is a solution of the optimization problem

$$\min_{\{u/\phi(u)=0\}} J(u).$$

Hence, there exists a Lagrange multipliers $\theta \in \mathbb{R}$ such that

$$J^{'}(u_0) = \theta \phi^{'}(u_0) \text{ in } \mathcal{H}^{'}$$

Thus,

$$\left\langle J^{'}(u_0), u_0 \right\rangle = \theta \left\langle \phi^{'}(u_0), u_0 \right\rangle.$$

But $\left\langle \phi^{'}(u_0), u_0 \right\rangle \neq 0$, since $u_0 \notin \mathcal{N}^0$. Hence $\theta = 0$. This completes the proof.

Lemma 4

There exists a positive number Λ_0 such that for all λ, verifying

$$0 < \lambda < \Lambda_0,$$

we have $\mathcal{N}^0 = \varnothing$.

Proof. Let us reason by contradiction.

Suppose $\mathcal{N}^0 \neq \varnothing$ such that $0 < \lambda < \Lambda_0$. Then, by (6) and for $u \in \mathcal{N}^0$, we have

$$\|u\|_{\mu,a}^2 = p(p-s)/(2-s)F(u) \tag{7}$$

$$= ((p-s)/(p-2))G(u)$$

Moreover, by the Hölder inequality and the Sobolev embedding theorem, we obtain

$$\|u\|_{\mu,a} \geq \left(S_\mu\right)^{p/2(p-2)} \left[(2-s)/p(p-s)\right]^{-1/(p-2)} \tag{8}$$

and

$$\|u\|_{\mu,a} \leq \left[\left(\frac{p-s}{p-2} \right)^{-1/(2-s)} \left(\lambda^{1/(2-s)} \right) \left(C_{a,s} \right)^s \right]. \tag{9}$$

From (8) and (9), we obtain $\lambda \geq \Lambda_0$, which contradicts an hypothesis.

Thus $\mathcal{N} = \mathcal{N}^{+} \cup \mathcal{N}^{-}$. Define

$$c := \inf_{u \in \mathcal{N}} J(u), c^{+} := \inf_{u \in \mathcal{N}^{+}} J(u) \text{ and } c^{-} := \inf_{u \in \mathcal{N}^{-}} J(u).$$

For the sequel, we need the following Lemma.

Lemma 5

i) For all λ such that $0 < \lambda < \Lambda_0$, one has $c \leq c^{+} < 0$.

ii) For all λ such that $0 < \lambda < (1/2)\Lambda_0$, one has

$$c^{-} > C_0 = C_0\left(\lambda, S_\mu\right)$$

$$= \left(\frac{(p-2)}{(p-s)} \right) \left[\frac{(2-s)}{p(p-s)} \right]^{2/(p-2)} \left(S_\mu\right)^{p/(p-2)} + $$
$$- \left(\frac{(p-s)}{ps} \right) \left(\lambda^{1/(2-s)} \right) \left(C_{a,s} \right)^s.$$

Proof. i) Let $u \in \mathcal{N}^{+}$. By (6), we have

$$\left[(2-s)/p(p-1)\right] \|u\|_{\mu,a}^2 > F(u)$$

and so

$$J(u) = (-1/2)\|u\|_{\mu,a}^2 + (p-1)F(u)$$

$$< -\left[\frac{p(p-s) - 2(p-1)(2-s)}{2p(p-s)} \right] \|u\|_{\mu,a}^2.$$

We conclude that $c \leq c^{+} < 0$.

ii) Let $u \in \mathcal{N}^{-}$. By (6), we get

$$\left[(2-s)/p(p-s)\right] \|u\|_{\mu,a}^2 < F(u).$$

Moreover, by Sobolev embedding theorem, we have

$$F(u) \leq \left(S_\mu\right)^{-p/2} \|u\|_{\mu,a}^p.$$

This implies

$$\|u\|_{\mu,a} > \left(S_\mu\right)^{p/2(p-2)} \left[\frac{(2-s)}{p(p-s)} \right]^{-1/(p-2)}, \text{ for all } u \in \mathcal{N}^{-}. \tag{10}$$

By (5), we get

$$J(u) \geq ((p-2)/2p)\|u\|_{\mu,a}^2 + $$
$$- \left(\frac{(p-s)}{ps} \right) \lambda^{1/(2-s)} \left(C_{a,p} \right)^s \|u\|_{\mu,a}^s.$$

Thus, for all λ such that $0 < \lambda < (1/2)\Lambda_0$, we have $J(u) \geq C_0$.

For each $u \in \mathcal{H}$ with $\int_{\mathbb{R}^N} |y|^{-bp} |u|^p \, dx \neq 0$, we write

$$t_M := t_{\max}(u) = \left[\frac{(2-s)\|u\|_{\mu,a}^2}{p(p-s)\int_{\mathbb{R}^N} |y|^{-bp} |u|^p \, dx} \right]^{(2-s)/p(p-s)} > 0.$$

Lemma 6

Let λ real parameters such that $0 < \lambda < \Lambda_0$. For each $u \in \mathcal{H}$ with $\int_{\mathbb{R}^N} |y|^{-bp} |u|^p \, dx \neq 0$, one has the following:

There exist unique t^{+} and t^{-} such that $0 < t^{+} < t_M < t^{-}$, $(t^{-}u) \in \mathcal{N}^{+}$, $t^{-}u \in \mathcal{N}^{-}$,

$$J(t^{+}u) = \inf_{0 \leq t \leq t_M} J(tu) \text{ and } J(t^{-}u) = \sup_{t \geq 0} J(tu).$$

Proof. With minor modifications, we refer to [16].

Proposition 1 [16]

i) For all λ such that $0 < \lambda < \Lambda_0$, there exists a $(PS)_{c^{+}}$ sequence in $\mathcal{N}^{+}$.

ii) For all λ such that $0 < \lambda < (1/2)\Lambda_0$, there exists a $(PS)_{c^{-}}$ sequence in $\mathcal{N}^{-}$.

Proof of Theorems 1

Now, taking as a starting point the work of Tarantello [13], we establish the existence of a local minimum for J on $\mathcal{N}^{+}$.

Proposition 2 *For all λ such that $0 < \lambda < \Lambda_0$, the functional J has a minimizer $^{+} \in \quad^{+}$ and it satisfies:*

(i) $J\left(u_0^+\right)=c=c^+$,

(ii) $\left(u_0^+\right)$ is a nontrivial solution of $\left(\mathcal{P}_{\lambda,\mu}\right)$.

Proof. If $0<\lambda<\Lambda_0$, then by Proposition 1(i) there exists a $(u_n)_n$ $(PS)_{c^+}$ sequence in $\mathcal{N}^+$, thus it bounded by Lemma 2. Then, there exists $u_0^+ \in \mathcal{H}$ and we can extract a subsequence which will denoted by $(u_n)_n$ such that

$$u_n \rightharpoonup u_0^+ \text{ weakly in } \mathcal{H} \tag{11}$$

$$u_n \rightharpoonup u_0^+ \text{ weakly in } L^p\left(\mathbb{R}^N,|y|^{-bp}\right)$$

$$u_n \to u_0^+ \text{ strongly in } L^s\left(\mathbb{R}^N,|y|^{-c}\right)$$

$$u_n \to u_0^+ \text{ a.e in } \mathbb{R}^N$$

Thus, by (11), u_0^+ is a weak nontrivial solution of $\left(\mathcal{P}_{\lambda,\mu}\right)$. Now, we show that u_n converges to u_0^+ strongly in $\mathcal{H}$. Suppose otherwise. By the lower semi-continuity of the norm, then either $\left\|u_0^+\right\|_{\mu,a} < \liminf_{n\to\infty}\left\|u_n\right\|_{\mu,a}$ and we obtain

$$c \leq J\left(u_0^+\right)=((p-2)/2p)\left\|u_0^+\right\|_{\mu,a}^2 -((p-s)/ps)G\left(u_0^+\right)$$

$$< \liminf_{n\to\infty}J\left(u_n\right)=c.$$

We get a contradiction. Therefore, u_n converge to u_0^+ strongly in $\mathcal{H}$. Moreover, we have $u_0^+ \subset \mathcal{N}^+$. If not, then by Lemma 6, there are two numbers t_0^+ and t_0^-, uniquely defined so that $\left(t_0^+u_0^+\right)\in\mathcal{N}^+$ and $\left(t^-u_0^+\right)\in\mathcal{N}^-$. In particular, we have $t_0^+ < t_0^- =1$. Since

$$\frac{d}{dt}J\left(tu_0^+\right)_{|t=t_0^+}=0 \text{ and } \frac{d^2}{dt^2}J\left(tu_0^+\right)_{|t=t_0^+}>0,$$

there exists $t_0^+ < t^- \leq t_0^-$ such that $J\left(t_0^+u_0^+\right)<J\left(t^-u_0^+\right)$. By Lemma 6, we get

$$J\left(t_0^+u_0^+\right)<J\left(t^-u_0^+\right)<J\left(t_0^-u_0^+\right)=J\left(u_0^+\right),$$

which contradicts the fact that $J\left(u_0^+\right)=c^+$. Since $J\left(u_0^+\right)=J\left(\left|u_0^+\right|\right)$ and $\left|u_0^+\right|\in\mathcal{N}^+$, then by Lemma [3], we may assume that u_0^+ is a nontrivial nonnegative solution of $\left(\mathcal{P}_{\lambda,\mu}\right)$. By the Harnack inequality, we conclude that $u_0^+>0$ and $v_0^+>0$, see for exanmple (7).

Proof of Theorem 2

Next, we establish the existence of a local minimum for J on $\mathcal{N}^-$. For this, we require the following Lemma.

Lemma 7

For all λ such that $0<\lambda<(1/2)\Lambda_0$, the functional J has a minimizer u_0^- in $\mathcal{N}^-$ and it satisfies:

(i) $J\left(u^-\right)=c^->0$,

(ii) u_0^- is a nontrivial solution of $\left(\mathcal{P}_{\lambda,\mu}\right)$ in $\mathcal{H}$.

Proof. If $0<\lambda<(1/2)\Lambda_0$, then by Proposition 1 i) there exists a $(u_n)_n$, $(PS)_{c^-}$ sequence in $\mathcal{N}^-$, thus it bounded by Lemma 2. Then, there exists $u_0^-\in\mathcal{H}$ and we can extract a subsequence which will denoted by $(u_n)_n$ such that

$$u_n \rightharpoonup u_0^- \text{ weakly in } \mathcal{H}$$

$$u_n \rightharpoonup u_0^- \text{ weakly in } L^p\left(\mathbb{R}^N,|y|^{-bp}\right)$$

$$u_n \to u_0^- \text{ strongly in } L^s\left(\mathbb{R}^N,|y|^{-c}\right)$$

$$u_n \to u_0^- \text{ a.e in } \mathbb{R}^N$$

This implies

$$F\left(u_n\right)\to F\left(u_0^-\right), \text{ as } n \text{ goes to } \infty.$$

Moreover, by (6) we obtain

$$F\left(u_n\right)>A(p,s)\left\|u_n\right\|_{\mu,a}^2, \tag{12}$$

where, $A(p,s):=(2-s)/p(p-s)$. By (8) and (12) there exists a positive number

$$C_1:=\left[A(p,s)\right]^{p/(p-2)}\left(S_\mu\right)^{p/(p-2)},$$

such that

$$F\left(u_n\right)>C_1. \tag{13}$$

This implies that

$$F\left(u_0^-\right)\geq C_1.$$

Now, we prove that $(u_n)_n$ converges to u_0^- strongly in $\mathcal{H}$. Suppose otherwise. Then, either $\left\|u_0^-\right\|_{\mu,a} < \liminf_{n\to\infty}\left\|u_n\right\|_{\mu,a}$. By Lemma (6) there is a unique t_0^- such that $\left(t_0^-u_0^-\right)\in\mathcal{N}^-$. Since

$$u_n\in\mathcal{N}^-, J\left(u_n\right)\geq J\left(tu_n\right), \text{ for all } t\geq 0,$$

we have

$$J\left(t_0^-u_0^-\right)<\lim_{n\to\infty}J\left(t_0^-u_n\right)\leq\lim_{n\to\infty}J\left(u_n\right)=c^-,$$

and this is a contradiction. Hence,

$$(u_n)_n \to u_0^- \text{ strongly in } \mathcal{H}.$$

Thus,

$$J\left(u_n\right) \text{ converges to } J\left(u_0^-\right)=c^- \text{ as } n \text{ tends to } +\infty.$$

Since $J\left(u_0^-\right)=J\left(\left|u_0^-\right|\right)$ and $u_0^-\in\mathcal{N}^-$, then by (13) and Lemma 3, we may assume that u_0^- is a nontrivial nonnegative solution of $\left(\mathcal{P}_{\lambda,\mu}\right)$. By the maximum principle, we conclude that $u_0^->0$.

Now, we complete the proof of Theorem 2. By Propositions 2 and Lemma 7, we obtain that $\left(\mathcal{P}_{\lambda,\mu}\right)$ has two positive solutions $u_0^+\in\mathcal{N}^+$ and $u_0^-\in\mathcal{N}^-$. Since $\mathcal{N}^+\cap\mathcal{N}^-=\varnothing$, this implies that u_0^+ and u_0^- are distinct [17,18].

Proof of Theorem 3

In this section, we consider the following Nehari submanifold of $\mathcal{N}$

$$\mathcal{N}_\rho=\left\{u\in\mathcal{H}\setminus\{0\}:\left\langle J^{'}(u),u\right\rangle=0 \text{ and } \|u\|_{\mu,a}\geq\rho>0\right\}.$$

Thus, $u\in\mathcal{N}_\rho$ if and only if

$$\|u\|_{\mu,a}^2-pF(u)-G(u)=0 \text{ and } \|u\|_{\mu,a}\geq\rho>0.$$

Firstly, we need the following Lemmas

Lemma 8

Under the hypothesis of theorem 3, there exist ρ_0, $\Lambda_2>0$ such that $\mathcal{N}_\rho$ is nonempty for any $\lambda\in(0,\Lambda_2)$ and $\rho\in(0,\rho_0)$.

Proof. Fix $u_0\in\mathcal{H}\setminus\{0\}$ and let

$$g(t)=\left\langle J^{'}(tu_0),tu_0\right\rangle$$

$$=t^2\|u_0\|_{\mu,a}^2-pt^pF(u_0)-tG(u_0).$$

Clearly $g(0)=0$ and $g(t)\to-\infty$ as $n\to+\infty$. Moreover, we have

$$g(1)=\|u_0\|_{\mu,a}^2-pF(u_0)-G(u_0)$$

$$\geq\left[\|u_0\|_{\mu,a}^2-p(S_\mu)^{-p/2}\|u_0\|_{\mu,a}^p\right]+$$

$$-\left(\lambda^{1/(2-s)}\right)\|u_0\|_{\mu,a}.$$

If $\|u_0\|_{\mu,a}\geq\rho>0$ for $0<\rho<\rho_0=(p(p-1))^{-1/(p-2)}(S_\mu)^{p/2(p-2)}$, then there exists

$$\Lambda_2:=\left[(p(p-1))(S_\mu)^{-p/2}\right]^{-1/(p-2)}-\Theta\times\Phi,$$

where

$$\Theta:=(p(p-1))^{p-1}(S_\mu)^{-(p)^2/2}$$

and

$$\Phi:=\left[(p(p-1))(S_\mu)^{-p/2}\right]^{-1/(p-2)}.$$

and there exists $t_0>0$ such that $g(t_0)=0$. Thus, $(t_0u_0)\in\mathcal{N}_\rho$ and $\mathcal{N}_\rho$ is nonempty for any $\lambda\in(0,\Lambda_2)$.

Lemma 9

There exist V, Λ_1 positive reals such that

$$\langle\phi'(u),u\rangle<-V<0,\text{for}\,u\in\mathcal{N}_\rho,$$

and any λ verifying

$$0<\lambda<\min((1/2)\Lambda_0,\Lambda_1).$$

Proof. Let $u\in\mathcal{N}_\rho$, then by (4), (6) and the Holder inequality, allows us to write

$$\langle\phi'(u),u\rangle$$

$$\leq\|u_n\|_{\mu,a}^2\left[\left(\lambda^{1/(2-s)}\right)B(\rho,s)-(p-2)\right],$$

where $B(\rho,s):=(p-1)(C_{a,p})^s\rho^{s-2}$. Thus, if

$$0<\lambda<\Lambda_3=\left[(p-2)/B(\rho,s)\right],$$

and choosing $\Lambda_1:=\min(\Lambda_2,\Lambda_3)$ with Λ_2 defined in Lemma 8, then we obtain that

$$\langle\phi'(u),u\rangle<0,\text{for any}\,u\in\mathcal{N}_\rho. \tag{14}$$

Lemma 10

Suppose $N\geq\max(3,6(a-b+1))$ and $\int_{\mathbb{R}^N}|y|^{-bp}|u|^p\,dx>0$. Then, there exist r and η positive constants such that

i) we have

$$J(u)\geq\eta>0\text{ for }\|u\|_{\mu,a}=r.$$

ii) there exists $\sigma\in\mathcal{N}_\rho$ when $\|\sigma\|_{\mu,a}>r$, with $r=\|u\|_{\mu,a}$, such that $J(\sigma)\leq0$.

Proof. We can suppose that the minima of J are realized by (u_0^+) and u_0^-. The geometric conditions of the mountain pass theorem are satisfied. Indeed, we have

i) By (6), (14) and the fact that $F(u)\leq(S_\mu)^{-p/2}\|u\|_{\mu,a}^p$, we get

$$J(u)\geq\left[(1/2)-(p-2)/(p-s)s\right]\|u\|_{\mu,a}^2-(S_\mu)^{-p/2}\|u\|_{\mu,a}^p,$$

Exploiting the function $l(x)=x(p-x)$ and if $N\geq\max(3,6(a-b+1))$, we obtain that $\left[(1/2)-(p-2)/(p-s)s\right]>0$ for $1<s<2$. Thus, there exist η,

$r>0$ such that

$$J(u)\geq\eta>0\text{ when}\,r=\|u\|_{\mu,a}\text{ small}.$$

ii) Let $t>0$, then we have for all $\phi\in\mathcal{N}_\rho$

$$J(t\phi):=(t^2/2)\|\phi\|_\mu^2-(t^p)F(\phi)-(t^s/s)G(\phi).$$

Letting $\sigma=t\phi$ for t large enough. Since

$$F(\phi):=\int_\Omega|y|^{-bp}|\phi|^p\,dx>0,$$

we obtain $J(\sigma)\leq0$. For t large enough we can ensure $\|\sigma\|_{\mu,a}>r$.

Let Γ and c defined by

$$\Gamma:=\left\{\gamma:[0,1]\to\mathcal{N}_\rho:\gamma(0)=u_0^-\text{and}\gamma(1)=u_0^+\right\}$$

and

$$c:=\inf_{\gamma\in\Gamma}\max_{t\in[0,1]}\left(J(\gamma(t))\right).$$

Proof of Theorem 4

If

$$\lambda<\min((1/2)\Lambda_0,\Lambda_1),$$

then, by the Lemmas 2 and Proposition 1 (ii), J verifying the Palais-Smale condition in $\mathcal{N}_\rho$. Moreover, from the Lemmas 3, 9 and 10, there exists u_c such that

$$J(u_c)=c\text{and}u_c\in\mathcal{N}_\rho.$$

Thus u_c is the third solution of our system such that $u_c\neq u_0^+$ and $u_c\neq u_0^-$. Since $(\mathcal{P}_{\lambda,\mu})$ is odd with respect u, we obtain that $-u_c$ is also a solution of $(\mathcal{P}_{\lambda,\mu})$.

References

1. Cao D, Peng S (2003) A note on the sign-changing solutions to elliptic problems with critical Sobolev exponent and Hardy terms, J Differential Equations 193: 424-434.

2. Chen J (2003) Existence of solutions for a nonlinear PDE with an inverse square potential. J Differential Equations 195: 497-519.

3. Ekeland I, Ghoussoub N (2002) Selected new aspects of the calculus of variations in the large. Bull Amer Math Soc 39: 207-265.

4. Kang D (2007) On the elliptic problems with critical weighted Sobolev-Hardy exponents. Nonlinear Anal 66:1037-1050.

5. WangZ, Zhou H (2006) Solutions for a nonhomogeneous elliptic problem involving critical Sobolev-Hardy exponent in R^N. Acta Math Sci 26: 525-536.

6. Bouchekif M, Matallah A (2009) On singular nonhomogeneous elliptic equations involving critical Caffarelli-Kohn-Nirenberg exponent. Ric Mat 58: 207-218.

7. Mokhtar MEOR (2015) Five nontrivial solutions of p-Laplacian problems involving critical exposants and singular cylindrical potential. J of Physical Science and Application 5: 163-172.

8. Gazzini M, Musina R (2009) On the Hardy-Sobolev-Maz'ja inequalities: symmetry and breaking symmetry of extremal functions. Commun Contemp Math 11: 993-1007.

9. Musina R (2008) Ground state solutions of a critical problem involving cylindrical weights. Nonlinear Anal 68: 3972-3986.

10. Badiale M, Guida M, Rolando S (2007) Elliptic equations with decaying cylindrical potentials and power-type nonlinearities. Adv Differential Equations 12: 1321-1362.

11. Bouchekif M, Mokhtar MEMO (2012) On nonhomogeneous singular elliptic equations with cylindrical weight. Ric Mat 61: 147-156.

12. Terracini S (1996) On positive entire solutions to a class of equations with singular coefficient and critical exponent. Adv Differential Equations 1: 241-264.

13. Tarantello G (1992) On nonhomogeneous elliptic equations involving critical

Sobolev exponent. Ann Inst H Poincaré Anal Non Linéaire 9: 281-304.

14. Wu T-F (2008) The Nehari manifold for a semilinear elliptic system involving sign-changing weight functions. Nonlinear Anal 68: 1733-1745.

15. Kang D, Peng S (2004) Positive solutions for singular elliptic problems. Appl Math Lett 17:411-416.

16. BrownKJ, Zhang Y(2003) The Nehari manifold for a semilinear elliptic equation with a sign changing weight function. J Differential Equations 2: 481-499.

17. Drabek P, Kufner A, Nicolosi F (1997) Quasilinear Elliptic Equations with Degenerations and Singularities. Walter de Gruyter Series in Nonlinear Analysis and Applications, New York.

18. Liu Z, Han P (2008) Existence of solutions for singular elliptic systems with critical exponents. Nonlinear Anal 69: 2968-2983.

10

A Dynamic Service Composition on Social Networks

Pravin BR* and Geetha

P M.E Computer Science Engineering, DhanalaksmiSrinivasan College of Engineering and Technology, Chennai.

Abstract

To propose an algorithm based on semantic description to compose multiple composite services dynamically and give it to the user and allow the user to select an optimized composition based on his comfort. In today's world, web services are highly essential as they required for accomplishing tasks in a matter of second. Web services offer features such as e-Booking, e-Shopping, e-Banking that helps users to acquire everything from where they are. Currently the web developers use semantic based descriptions of web services to select and compose them and offer a single composition plan to the users. In certain cases providing a single plan to the users may not allow them to explore other good options that are available. Hence, giving multiple options to the user's request would help them select a plan according to their desire and comfort.

Keywords: Service composition; Social network; QoS

Introduction

In a large market place, many services are available, so selecting the services based on performance and efficiency is a hard task. So QoS used to select the service and used for service composition. The tradition approach in such marketplace use predefined business process. This restricts other schemes and services. The method of using predefined business process limit optimization of service composition and the user or the system only gets limited optimal solutions or cannot get globally correct or acceptable solutions. However by combining path planning with QoS service composition can overcome this problem of flexibility and it drastically increase the search space, as these Service composition used in the Big Data environment ,the search space is hauntingly large and efficiency of such methods create serious issues. To cut such a large search space social network based user centric dynamic composition with combined path planning used and return the composition to users and give them option of selecting the service which is efficient, in terms of cost, time and performance.

This paper provides optimized solutions from QoS, social networks and provides the user with option of selecting desired services based on the needs, efficiency and performance by seeing real-time data.

Related Work

This part gives a small literature survey on user centric social network analytic, QoS based service composition and combined path planning.

User centric social network analysis

The study about social networks brings the concept of strength between the relationships, the strength is generally strong or weak .In the strong relationship important messages transferred and only between certain individuals. General or not so important messages exchanged between the weak relationships [13]. In a business to business (B2B) model, a good long-term cooperating relationship increases authority. The reason behind using social network is to calculate QoS based on information transferred between two strong relationships and for authority.

Qos based service composition

This is to select the suitable and perfect service using the predefined business model and associate with the suitable Qos. By using ACAGA_WSC algorithm which is a combination Ant and Genetic algorithm the QoS values gets calculated. The reason behind using this algorithm is to overcome the shortcomings of Ant and Genetic algorithm. The data

generated from this algorithm combined with the user centric data from social network to get optimized and suitable service for the user.

QoS service selection with complex structures: This is to provide the user to select the suitable service based on queries. Here a proper planned method developed to find the Qos for the service with complex patterns. By taking into account of the probability and conditions of each complex structure, four types of composition patterns for composite services introduced. These are sequential, parallel, loop, and conditional patterns [14]. These patterns selected based on the results from QoS calculation.

Path planning

Path planning is a method to form service path that provides an analysis existing planning approach [3] [10]. The path planning proposes Xplan to build automatically the service progress or venture and provides re-planning [15] of web services.

Problem Modeling

In this section, the problem is modeled as online shopping website. It is consists of two parts shopping and shipping. In shopping the website consists of number of items and has to select as per the user needs. Consider a shopping site to purchase a book and after purchase select the way to ship the book. Suppose the shipping destination is Chennai and the product is in Bangalore. The user enters the query to search for the possible way between Chennai to Bangalore. The systems show four routes which is system predefined routes. The user needs to select any one route to begin the shipping. These four routes are generated based on various service composition algorithm such as Genetic or Ant Algorithm. The results generated by the system doesn't mean that the best solution or shortest distance as per the problem. Because there might be several other routes by which the shipping can be made quickly and easily. So the system need to provide all the possible routes so that user can select the best one (Figure 1).

*Corresponding author: Pravin BR, P.M.E Computer Science Engineering, Dhanalaksmi Srinivasan College of Engineering and Technology, Chennai
Email: pravin_babu@outlook.com

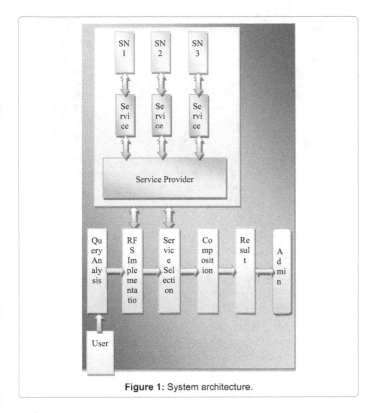

Figure 1: System architecture.

Solution

Consider there are four services; the user has to select any service for the purchase. The best service is provided by QoS calculating based on results by ACAGA_WSC algorithm and combining path planning with user centric Social Network Analysis. Also provide user with four types of composition patterns to select Complex composite service and similar process is done for shipping also.

Implementation

Based on this model is basically consists of five primary stages. The system architecture gives the outline of this model. The algorithm ACAGA_WSC algorithm, path planning, and social network analysis to calculate QoS all comes within this five states.

Query analysis

A user enters a word into to search engine to find want the user wants in the web, the search queries are of different forms such as normal text or hypertext such as each words are separated by "and", "or" and "-" to exclude. If a user is searching for certain information on different social networks that includes several area or facts and intended to describe every one of them by a disjunction. For example Android OR Smartphone OR Big Screen the user gets three types of results and takes disjunction query such as Android "and" Smartphone "and" Big Screen, the user gets specific results. By doing so the user is likely to get results from different social networks.

Rfs implementation

In the request for service phase, the needs of the user such as functional and non-functional specification of the consumer's needs to be fulfilled. The non-functional specification include involvement of human agent who acts as broker in providing the service, must has good reputation and has to provide good quality of service .The functional or technical specification include platforms such as hardware or software

and has to adhere strictly to the standard policies. If the consumer is satisfied with the certain service the consumer can request for service (RFS). The RFS is done in machine readable form by semantic web technologies. Suppose the requested service does not satisfy the user needs, the user always has the option of change of request by increasing or decreasing the Functional or Non-functional Requirements and the user can restart the discovery phase a RFS.

Service composition

The discovered service is taken the selected service is carried by technical and non-functional attributes and also by the budget, security and attitude of the consumer. The various service composition algorithm searches for best service. The service composition as discussed already by QoS calculation by combining path planning and results from social networks.

Pattern selection: In this section the calculation of QoS for composite services with complex structures are processed, taking into consideration of the probability and conditions of each execution path. There are various patterns, each pattern is given with QoS results and this generates a composition plan that meets the requirements. After getting the results from Pattern selection it is compared with results generated from QoS.

Composition environment: By having the results of above modules composition environment was created where the results of selected services are collected then composed so the ultimate user requested composed result was provided by this environment

Experiment

This section explains how this paper is executed in the small environment. Consider a shopping website, the consumer specifies requirements, the website has to deliver services based on the requirements. The shopping website service provider, cooperation network is created based on the history of cooperation of the service providers.

A social network consists of real persons and relation between them, as said earlier it might be strong or weak. These real people are called as Actor. These actors can be single, group or a part of organization. The actors of common history or strong relationship or part of a particular organization are becomes part of a Cooperation network. The relationship between the actors in common cooperation is strong and produces positive results. These results are used to calculate QoS.

The concept of partner circle is used, suppose an actor searches for a particular service, the partner circle algorithm searches for actors who belongs to any cooperation network, if the actor belongs to any cooperation network, the history of cooperation network members taken into account for providing service for similar specification. If not the system also searches for services with similar specification outside Partner Circle [1]. Also ACAGA_WS algorithm with the results from above is used to calculate QoS and services are provided. The actor has the option of selecting listed service or can reset it for new service. If the actor is not satisfied from QoS, the user cans it manually from the pattern selection [14]. Consider an e-Shopping where the actor needs to purchase a book, there are four services available first is author as a service, publication as a service, cost as service and lastly title as a service. Based on query best services are provided via QoS. If the actor is not satisfied from the service, actor can reset it and discovery new service or can select manually through pattern selection and can compare with QoS result for the efficiency.

The basic patterns are as follows (Figure 2) [8]:

This is condition pattern selection where Price as a Service is selected under conditional pattern. The minimum and maximum prize is set; the service within this price range comes from this (Figure 3).

In Loop Pattern selection, all the services will be present, the actor needs to select a service first, and based on the services selection other services will be appearing. Consider if the actor first selects any Author (Service) the results will appear based on the author selected and next the actor need to select Book Title (Service) based on that results will appear and so on (Figure 4).

In Parallel Pattern selection, the actor can search between the services. Actor searches for author as a service with Title as service .If it matches the results are shown other not (Figure 5).

Here all the services available are provided; the user needs to select it based on the specification.

These results from the pattern selections are compared with the QoS results and right service are selected.

Future Enhancement

This work can be enhanced with the dynamic QoS of a web service composition can be calculated based on the assumption that each task has a dynamic QoS. The dynamic QoS of each task is more

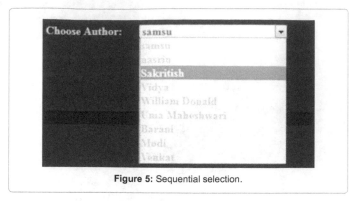

Figure 5: Sequential selection.

likely to be a probability distribution in reality. For future research, it is to study dynamic QoS calculation method for a composite service with component dynamic QoS modeled as general QoS probability distributions. It would be even challenging to estimate the probability distributions for services with short life cycle or less frequent use.

Conclusion

A systematic QoS analysis approach for dynamic composition is able to provide comprehensive QoS information for a composite service even with the existence of complex composition structures such as unstructured conditional patterns .The QoS information generated by the proposed QoS analysis approach includes not only the QoS of the web service composition but also the QoS and probability of the execution paths with the help of logistic services.

References

1. chen J, lin S, wang Y (2014) A Dynamic qos-aware logistics service composition algorithm based on social network .emerging topics in computing 2: 399-410.

2. Kouicem A, Chibani A, Abdelkamel T, Yacine A, Zahir T (2014) Dynamic Services Selection Approach For The Composition Of Complex Services In The Web Of Objects. Internet of Things (Wf-Iot), pp. 298-303.

3. Guobing Zou, Qiang Lu, YixinChen, Ruoyun Huang, You Xu, et al. (2012) QoS-AwareDynamic Composition of Web Services using Numerical Temporal Planning. IEEE Transactions on Services Computing 5: 18-31.

4. Hassan M, Sofien G, Mutaz B (2012) Web Service Composition: Models and Approaches. Multimedia Computing and Syst, pp. 718-723.

5. Liyuan X, Carl KC, HenlY, Kai-Shin L, Hsin-y (2012) Automated Web Service Composition using Genetic Programming. IEEE 36th International Conference on Computer Software and Applications Workshops, Izmir, pp. 7-12.

6. Liping C, Guojun Z (2013) A Petri Net Approach to Reliable Execution for Web Service Composition. Ninth International Conference on Computational Intelligence and Security, Leshan, pp. 105-109.

7. Mahmood A, Hadi S (2012) Effective Web Service Composition using Particle Swarm Optimization Algorithm. 6'th International Symposium on Telecommunications, Tehran, pp. 1190-1194.

8. Shanfeng Q, Xinhuai T, Delai C (2012) An Automated Web Services Composition System Based on Service Classification and AI Planning. Second International Conference on Cloud and Green Computing, Xiangtan, pp. 537-540.

9. Tarek Z, Chouki T, Foudil C (2014) Processing the Evolution of Quality Requirements of Web Service Orchestrations: a Pattern based Approach. IEEE/IFIP Conference on Software Architecture, Sydney, NSW, pp. 139-142.

10. Xinhuai T ,Feilong T , Liu B, Delai C (2013) Dynamic Web Service Composition Based on Service Integration and HTN Planning. Seventh International Conference on Innovative Mobile and Internet Services in Ubiquitous Computing, Taichung, pp. 307-312.

11. Liu G, Ramakrishnan KG (2001) A *Prune: an algorithm for finding K shortest paths subject to multiple constraints. Twentieth Annual Joint Conference of the IEEE Computer and Communications Societies. Proceedings. Anchorage, AK 2: 743-749.

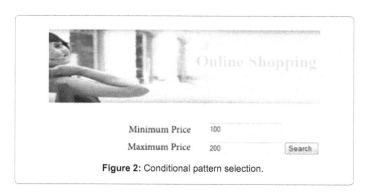

Figure 2: Conditional pattern selection.

Figure 3: Loop pattern selection.

Figure 4: Parallel pattern selection.

12. Travers J, Milgram S (1969) An experimental study of the small world problem. Sociometry 32: 425-443.

13. Zongkai Y, Chaowang S, Qingtang L, Chengling Z (2010) A Dynamic Web Services Composition Algorithm Based on the Combination of Ant Colony Algorithm and Genetic Algorithm. Jofcis 8: 2617-2622.

14. Weiliang Z, Jian Y, Bouguettaya A (2013) QoS Analysis for Web Service Compositions with Complex Structures Services Computing. IEEE Transactions on Serice Computing, pp. 373-386.

15. Matthias K, Andreas G (2005) Semantic Web Service Composition Planning with OWLS-Xplan. AAAI

11

Evaluation Report on e-Government Programme Focusing on Infrastructure/ Internet Gateway and Messaging System

Odewale OA*

Ondo State Information Technology Development Centre (SITDEC), 1, Farm House Aguda Close, Ondo Road Akure, Ondo State, Nigeria

Abstract

The revolutionary advances in Information and Communication Technologies (ICTs) are ushering in change in every aspect of life. Everything from business to governance is undergoing change. This report focuses on the deployment of Information Technology infrastructure in Ondo State, Nigeria as the nexus of the state e-Government programme with focus on (1) Central Base Station set up (2) Structured Local Area Network of Key Governmnet Offices (3) Fibre Optic Interconnectivity between central base station and governor's office complex plus allied locations (4) Installation and configuration of servers in the main Data Center (5) Installation and configuration of servers in the Disaster Recovery Centre (6) Installation and Configuration of Secured Wireless Network for remote Ministries, Departments and Agencies (MDAs) (7) Installation and Configuration of State Surveillance System (8) Training of users, technicians and other personnel (9) Provision of second layer support services for users and first layer support-technicians, and; (10) Provision of hardware and infrastructure support services to content providers like Oracle Financials, the state Electronic Personnel Administration and Salary System (ePASS) and the state Automated Revenue-generation, Collection-administration and Accounting System (ARCAS).

Keywords: e-government; Accounting system; Surveillance system

Introduction

Ondo State, Nigeria was established on 3rd of February 1976. According to the 2006 population census, the state has a population of 3,441,024 people disambiguated as 1,679,761 females and 1,761,263 males. The state has the reputation of a high literacy level relative to other states of the Nigerian federation. In 2004, few months after the new government had taken over; the State Executive Council adopted a policy classifying Information Communication Technology as an effective policy of state for the driving of the institution of governance as well as a tool for the promotion of efficiency, accuracy and speed of service delivery. To accomplish this, the state which hitherto was noted for being conservative veered off this traditional path and frontally adopt e-Governance as its core programme and thus become one of the leading lights amongst states of the federation that have taken the giant leap towards the adoption of information technology.

Objective and scope

1. The objective of this report is to itemize the functional steps taken in the deployment of a robust information technology platform in Ondo State

2. To itemize the gains resulting from this effort

3. To provide the adjusted design of the central data centre and main base station

4. To enumerate the roles and the reciprocal contribution to knowledge that resulted from the active participation of engineers-in-training as part of the deliberate local content initiative adopted by the government of Ondo State as at that time. The author of this work was privileged to be part of the young engineers in training who actively participated as a team member, sub-unit leader and measurement group leader throughout the duration of the deployment of the information technology tools. The author was also a participant in the train the trainer scheme designed to spread technical knowledge amongst the officials of the state's civil service. A technical team was setup by the coordinator in which I was the sub-unit leader and I worked as a Network Administrator after the various installations on daily bases.

Definition of core terms

e-Government: The term "e-government" focuses on the use of new information and communication technologies (ICTs) by governments as applied to the full range of government functions. In particular, the networking potential offered by the Internet and related technologies has the potential to transform the structures and operation of government [1]. The World Bank defines e-Government as "the use by government agencies of information technologies (such as Wide Area Networks, the Internet, and mobile computing) that have the ability to transform relations with citizens, businesses, and other arms of government" [2]. e-Government is thus the application of modern computing technology in driving all facets of governance in order to enhance government to citizen (G-2-C), government to business (G-2-B) and government to government (G-2-G) interactions, promote transparency, eliminate barriers with respect to space and time and make life better for the people by enhancing book keeping, record warehousing and safety and access to government and governance [3]. In the case of Ondo State, this would imply a total change in processes and system which in itself would require ultimately a specialized way to manage such changes.

Core Technology Application in Ondo State

The core areas of technology application in Ondo State are in which the author participated included:

1. Central base station set up

2. Structured Local Area Networking of Key Government Offices

*Corresponding author: Odewale OA, Ondo State Information Technology Development Centre (SITDEC), 1, Farm House Aguda Close, Ondo Road Akure, Ondo State, Nigeria, E-mail: ayoogundare@gmail.com

3. Fibre Optic Interconnectivity between central base station and governor's office complex plus allied locations

4. Installation and configuration of servers in the main Data Center

5. Installation and configuration of servers in the Disaster Recovery Centre

6. Installation and Configuration of Secured Wireless Network for remote Ministries, Departments and Agencies (MDAs)

7. Installation and Configuration of State Surveillance System

8. Training of users, technicians and other personnel

9. Provision of second layer support services for users and first layer support-technicians, and;

10. Provision of hardware and infrastructure support services to content providers like Oracle Financials, the state Electronic Personnel Administration and Salary System (ePASS) and the state Automated Revenue-generation, Collection-administration and Accounting System (ARCAS).Few of these will be explained in greater details.

Networking of the different government ministries, departments and agencies

This was to ensure every department can have access to records and make such available in a central pool accessible to authorized officials of government irrespective of their location. It was to enhance centralization while allowing for decentralization at the same time-a sort of dialectic (i.e., making sure all data or information units are available - as if such information are available at a central source) while at the same time allowing for such information to be accessible to myriads of people outside or in different workstations [4].

Satellite earth stations

As illustrated on the (Figure 1) two satellite earth stations were installed at the ICT center SITDEC. A 3.8m dish was installed to serve as the main circuit to the Internet while a 1.8m earth station provides backup. For optimal use of both circuits, load sharing at approximately ratio 7:3 is implemented. To provide diversity in technology, the 3.8

m Earth station uses *C-Band technology* while the 1.8 m earth station provides services using the *KU-Band technology* [5]. Also, the satellite providers are in different continents with one in Israel while the other is in Canada. This is to reduce the effect of disruption by sharing the risk.

Structured local area network

The entire cabling of the government offices and ministries was achieved using Ethernet cables in a structured fashion. All cables were well terminated on patch panel located in a rack at each ministry. The number of patch panel or size of rack was determined by the total number of points installed. From the patch panel, points were patched on to a Cisco catalyst switch which then connects to the backbone either through fibre or radio. All points were well labelled as indicated in the diagrams (Figures 2 and 3).

Fibre optic interconnectivity

Fibre Optic Cables were installed with SITDEC as the central point in a star topology format. Multimode optic fibre cable was installed to connect the Governor's office complex, the State Government Secretariate, and other ministries, department and agencies within the vicinity. Fibre optic has large bandwidth capacity and can accommodate the bandwidth requirements of the large ministries around the SITDEC. It also has spare capacity for future expansion. To provide redundancy, protection and long haul capacity, four core, armoured optic fibre cables were installed using direct burial methods. In laying the fibre, adequate care was taken to ensure protection. Fibre was laid at depth of 1 m below the top soil. At cross roads, galvanized pipes was used and manholes was installed at junction's necessary points along the fibre route each fibre was well terminated using fusion splicing techniques, and arranged in a fibre patch panel/cartridge at both ends. Single mode optic fibre cable was also used to interconnect the data recovery centre (DRC) and SITDEC. From the DRC, interconnectivity of the Government house is achieved using Ethernet cable and multimode fibre optic cable [6]. The total length of the fibre metro ring was 5.2 km (Figure 4).

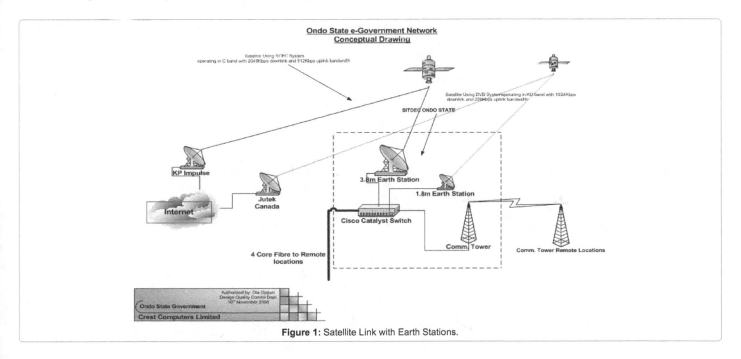

Figure 1: Satellite Link with Earth Stations.

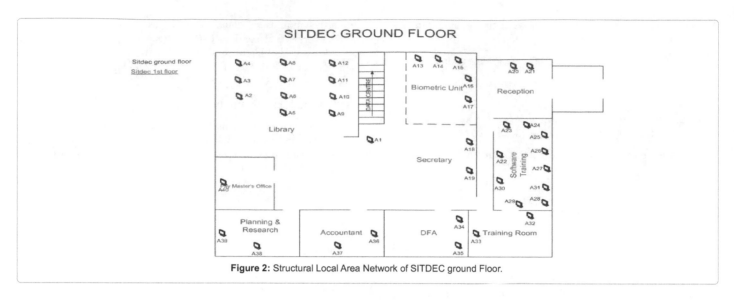

Figure 2: Structural Local Area Network of SITDEC ground Floor.

Figure 3: Structural Local Area Network of SITDEC First Floor.

Data center

In addition to the main communication network. The data center is used to house computer systems and associated components, such as telecommunications and other storage systems. It generally includes redundant or backup power supplies, redundant data communications connections, environmental controls (e.g., air conditioning, fire suppression) and security devices. The state governments seeing the challenges ahead repairs were made to SITDEC building, a 60 metre tower constructed and provisions made for following:

1. Installation of raised floors at SITDEC and the Data Recovery Centre.

2. Electrical works at both SITDEC and the Data recovery Centre.

3. Earthen (Grounding) of all electrical equipment.

4. Improvement or repair to buildings that accommodate Communication equipment including partition, painting etc as directed by SITDEC.

Wireless local area network

The wireless LAN operating on the 2.4 GHz frequency range consist

of the following networks provided by Mikrotik radio, SITDEC-1 or SITDEC, SITDEC-2 and SITDEC-WAP-1. SITDEC-WAP-1 is located in SITDEC building to provide wireless access within the building (Figure 5).

SITDEC-1 provides wireless access from the tower located at SITDEC to a distance of approximately 2 miles omni directionally (Laptop Wilan) and approximately 6 miles using an external antenna (topology considered).

SITDEC-2 is located on the former OSRC tower at Oke Eda. The choice of the location is to provide further coverage. Traffic from the station is backhauled to the network centre at SITDEC using Motorola point-to-point Backhaul radios. The backhaul radio operates at 5.8GHz. Frequency diversity is implemented on the Wireless LAN to avoid frequency interference.

Broadband radio network

The Motorola broadband radio network implemented operates at 5.8GHz frequency range. Three access points are located on the tower at SITDEC, while another two are on the tower at Oke Eda. The choice of the locations is strategic taking into consideration the topology and foliage around the installation environment (Figure 6).

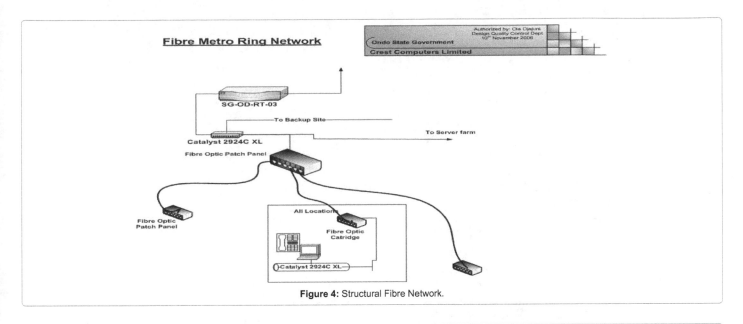

Figure 4: Structural Fibre Network.

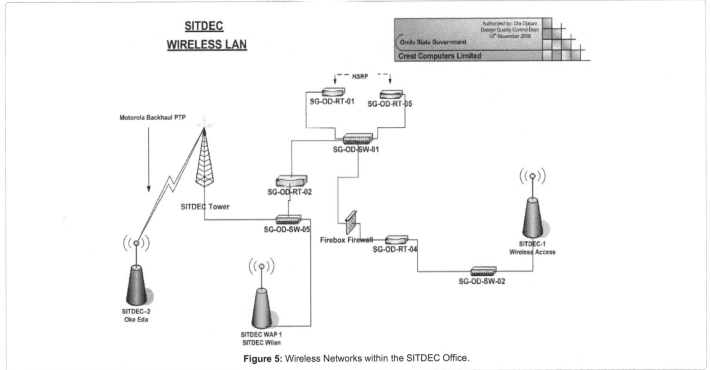

Figure 5: Wireless Networks within the SITDEC Office.

Subscriber modules are then installed at remote locations to provide access the State Government network. Security is provided by encrypting transmitted data between the subscriber modules and the access points. Interconnectivity of the State house of Assembly is achieved by using the Motorola point-to-point radio as indicated in the diagram.

State Surveillance System

A state wide surveillance system was also installed. To provide a real time view of places and locations in Ondo State for the purpose of monitoring events – movements, activities, civil disturbances, riots etc. In addition, a real time recording of activities for the purpose of providing intelligence materials for law enforcement agencies in

tracking criminals and criminal activities within the state capital. The cameras are so intelligent to track every visual activity even in night mode. In addition, the cameras can be integrated to an existing intranet or extranet network because of its capability as TCP/IP based design. Therefore more than of the cameras can be viewed at the same time. Below are demo pictures illustrating the capability of the surveillance security camera systems.

Training of personnel

People can be ignorant in any field, hence the idea of being "computer literate" cannot be over emphasize. The government took a bold step to make sure that all Ondo state staff was trained in ICT including the civil servant in the state. Once the people are trained,

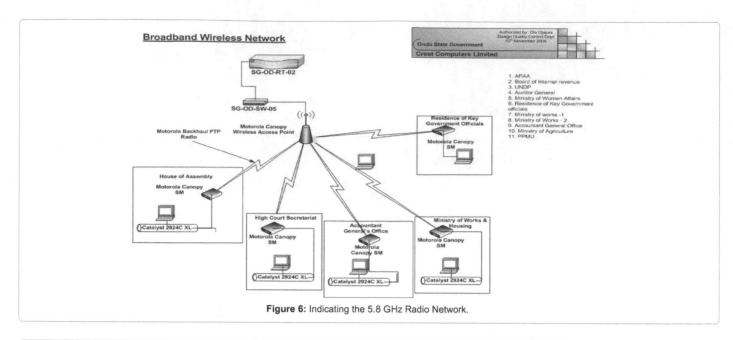

Figure 6: Indicating the 5.8 GHz Radio Network.

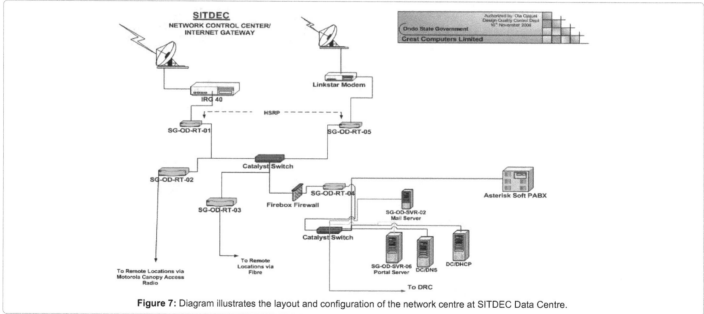

Figure 7: Diagram illustrates the layout and configuration of the network centre at SITDEC Data Centre.

then the first step towards e-governance has been taken. Training of assigned personnel was conducted by our instructors. Over eighty SITDEC administrators, Engineers and Youth Corpers took part in the training. This was conducted during and after the installations as part of technology transfer.

Network control centre/internet gateway

Internet services are provided using two modems, a Shiron IRG40, and a Linkstar .The Shiron gateway provides the main access to the Internet while the Linkstar provides redundancy. As indicated earlier, load sharing is achieved by using both modems at ratio 7:3. The first router (SG-OD-RT-01) connects to the Shiron satellite modem and the first catalyst switch while router five (SG-OD-RT-05) connects to the Linkstar modem. All other routers also connect to switch one (SG-OD-SW-01). The routing protocol in use throughout the network is Enhanced gateway Internet Routing Protocol (EIGRP) (Figure 7).

A Watch Guard firewall (SG-OD-FW-01) is installed right before router 4 (SG-OD-RT-04). This is to provide maximum security to critical application servers and the some wings of the State government networks. Security to other parts of the network is provided using Cisco IOS security.SG-OD-RT-01 and SG-OD-RT-05 runs Cisco proprietary HSRP to provide redundancy to the Internet. Router 2 (SG-OD-RT-02) segments the broadband radio network and wireless LAN while router 3 segments the fibre network (for load balancing, part of the fibre network and SITDEC-01 are segmented behind SG-OD-RT-02). Asterisk voice box provides PBX functions to all IP phone users irrespective on location on the state government network.

Services

Services which are capable of delivering Voice, Video and Data services in line with the requirements of Ondo State Government Project Team were also provided.

Telephony

This service is to be in the form of packetized voice over IP.

Data

The data services also provide a Broadband type access to IP based multimedia such as: - Video streaming (not to be confused with TV channel Broadcast/Streaming over IP).

Internet Access - provides connectivity to an ISP who delivers content-based services including email and WEB access.

Intranet – Access to information on a "need–to–know" basis, and information sharing and dissemination within the government establishment.

Microsoft operating system and back-end-servers

Microsoft windows 2003 server operating system was installed on all the servers' hardware. While Active Directory provides a single point of network resources management allowing administrators to add delete or relocate users and easily. This was installed and configured on the system and a limited amount of users and resources were configured for test purposes. Microsoft Portal services was installed and configured on SG-OD-SVR-06. Microsoft Exchange server 2003 was installed and configured on SG-OD-SVR-05. The following were verified among other things after the installation of the mail server.

1. Web access to e-mail boxes were provided for users.

2. User mailboxes were tested and verified to be available on the mail server.

3. E-mail profiles were configured such that certain defaults (i.e., automatically signed and/or encrypted) are applied based on the user profile.

4. E-mail management at all levels (SITDEC & branch) can be subject to policy- based profiles, including taking into consideration such criteria as business priority, bandwidth availability, and scheduled synchronization.

5. Standard security process standards (i.e., no external relaying) are applied to all e-mail servers. (These must be audited on a regular basis).

6. E-mail anti-virus services are installed on all e-mail servers, and will update automatically.

7. E-mail profiles (location of local e-mail server, size of mailbox, usage profiles) can be defined for all users based on their functional groups.

8. All outgoing e-mails can be tagged with an appropriate recipient/usage clause.

9. All e-mails going to/or coming from the Internet/Extranet are be filtered through a central email content management system.

10. The central e-mail content management system filters all incoming/outgoing mail for viruses and attachments. It quarantines suspected e-mails and/or their attachments. Alerts is be forwarded to the appropriate administrators/admin systems.

11. The e-mail content management system can filter the contents of all mails for policy-guided e-mail content. It is able to quarantine suspected e-mails and/or their attachments. Alerts, (including notifications of non-policy guided encryption of mails), must be forwarded to the appropriate administrators/admin systems.

12. Performance monitoring for the e-mail system can be integrated into the enterprise management.

Bill of engineering measurement and evaluation of e-Government project in Ondo State

Preliminary studies: A need assessment study was initially carried out by a team of experts to estimate the situation on ground in Ondo State before the commencement of e-Government programme. The discovery amongst others included:

1. Most government agencies still depended on typewriters for word processing. This impacted negatively on efficiency.

2. Computer to personnel ratio was very low while an entire Ministry comprising of about 2,000 workers had in certain instances just 2 computers.

3. It took an average of 22 days for the processing of monthly payroll of workers while cases of ghost workers were rampant.

4. Access to the internet was only possible in one point in the entire Ondo State government service.

5. Reports on the Ondo State Internally Generated revenue was only possible after 3 months thereby enabling banks to hold on perpetually to government money which in turn inhibited the government from being able to generate adequate funds.

Impact assessment: It was envisaged from the onset that the deployment of e-Government in Ondo State would have the following immediate impacts on governance:

1. Increase tremendously the computer to personnel ratio

2. Increase computer awareness and literacy

3. Each office in any Ministry would require being equipped with a computer and all computers would be on the same network to promote information sharing and sharing of common access to the internet.

4. Because of envisaged impacts on the existing system and processes, there would be needed to manage such changes through structured training and deliberate awareness campaigns targeted at the civil servants.

5. There would be need to put in place a computer training laboratory that could accommodate civil servants on a one year training programme and which would later serve as a permanent training location and refresher training center for workers.

6. Parts of the content to be placed on the infrastructure when completed would directly address monthly nominal and payroll management while effort would be made to also place a content that could help the state manage its internally fund generation stream.

7. Provide several nodes that could serve as points of access to the internet.

Bill of Engineering Measurement and Evaluation (BEME): Bill of engineering measurement and evaluation was shown in the Table 1.

Benefits

Some of the benefits recorded after the deployment of the e-Government programmes are:

1. Increased computer to personnel ratio

2. Increased core ICT manpower support technologist and engineers. The State was able to get 6 (six) of its workers certified in

J8131A	Curve Wireless Access Point	Pcs	4	25,000.00	100,000.00
J8443A	Curve ext AP 6 dBi direct antenna	Pcs	4	15,000.00	60,000.00
J8136A	Curve 802.11b AP Card 150wl 13CH	Pcs	4	5,000.00	20,000.00
5700BHRF20	5.7 GHz 20 Mbps Backhaul Kit with Reflector	Pcs	5	140,000.00	700,000.00
ACPSSW-02	90-230VAC/50-60HZ Power supply - includes Europlug (CEE 7/	Pcs	5	2,500.00	12,500.00
300SS	Surge Suppressor	Pcs	5	3,850.00	19,250.00
	Access Cards				
XBS-PCMCI-1	802.11b PCMCIA Access card	Pcs	1	3,000.00	3,000.00
XBS-PC-1	802.11b PCI card	Pcs	1		
	FIBRE-CABLE				
ARSMFibre	4 Core Single Mode Fibre 6 km	Lot	6000m		180,000.00
	Fibre Patch Panel - 12 Port	Pcs	8	10,000.00	80,000.00
	Fibre Fusion Splice tray	Pcs	8	5,380.00	43,040.00
	Fibre Pigtails	Pcs	44	2,500.00	110,000.00
	Terminating Kits		4	1,500.00	6,000.00
	Fibre Enclosures	Pcs	5	2,000.00	10,000.00
	MEDIA CONVERTER				
10/100bt-SM15	10/100base-T/100base-fl singlemode fiber converter 15km	Pcs	10	12,000.00	120,000.00
	CISCO SWITCHES AND ROUTERS				
WS-C2924C-XL-EN	10/100 Autosensing Fast Ethernet Switch	Pcs	25	25,000.00	625,000.00
WS-C2621	c2621 router	Pcs	6	100,000.00	600,000.00
WS-2960G	[2960G-24TC-L] 20 Ethernet 10/100/1000 ports, and 4 dual-purpose Gigabit Ethernet uplinks with LAN Base software	Pcs	2	40,000.00	80,000.00
Pix525	Cisco IOS Firewall Unrestricted	Pcs	1	150,000.00	150,000.00
	CANOPY SYSTEM				
TK1017	5.7 GHZ ACCESS POINT Cluster with 30 subcriber base modules	Pcs	1	120,000.00	120,000.00
27RD	Reflector Hardware Kit	Pcs	15	7,000.00	105,000.00
BAM02CD	BACM 2.0 Authentication Server Software CD	Pcs	1	25,600.00	25,600.00
BAMAP02	BACM 2.0 Software License Activation Key for AP Authentication	Pcs	6	5,000.00	30,000.00
S3	CAT 5 CABLE TESTER	Pcs	1	1,500.00	1,500.00
	LAN MATERIALS				
	Patch Panels	Pcs	80	8,000.00	64,000.00
	RJ 45	Pcs	4000	10.00	40,000
	Cat 5e Cables	Pcs	150	9,000.00	1,350,000.00
	Cable Ties	Pcs	100	500.00	50,000.00
	Trunkings	Pcs	500	350.00	175,000.00
	Face Plates & Accessories	Pcs	1000	550.00	550,000.00
	9U Racks		15	40,000.00	600,000.00
	22U Racks	Pcs	3	60,000.00	180,000.00
	48U Racks	Pcs	6	85,950.00	515,700.00
	Shielded Gigaplus Cable	Pcs	10	28,000.00	280,000.00
	60 metres Mast	Pcs	1	500,000.00	500,000.00
	Voice Over IP				
	Voice Business Edition	Pcs	1		
	5 hours pre-paid Technical Support & configuration	Pcs	1		
	Rack Server - Dual Intel Xeon processor, -3Ghz/1MB, - 4GB PC-2 3200 Memory, - 2 X HP 36.4GB Pluggable Ultra320 SCSI 15,000 rpm (1") Universal Hard Drive , - Dual GiGa Ethernet Port, - Redundant PSU, -Cd- Rom,	Pcs	1	400,000.00	400,000.00
	Hard IP Phones, - Omni-0104	Pcs	20		
	Wireless IP Phones - F1004	Pcs	5		
	Eyebeam Soft Phone, with v1.1, with Audio,Video+IM	Pcs	200		
	Video Conferencing Solution				
	3000 (NTSC) with Media Center Cart and one 34-inch (32 viewable) NTSC Display, IP as described in 2200-10800-001, English remote, NA power. Uses VSX built in speaker and subwoofer.	Pcs	3	250,000.00	750,000.00
	VSS Serial Network Module (V.35, RS449, RS530 with RS366 dialing), adapter cable, serial interface cable ordered separately	Pcs	3		
	VSS MultiPoint Software License Key	Pcs	3		
	CABLE - VSS Conference link cable, 50'	Pcs	3		
	Standard, 3 Yr, VSX7000, parts 30 day Return to Factory, telephone technical support during business hours, software updates & upgrades MSRP	Pcs	3		

	Surveillance Camera					
0221-002	Lexion 221 Day & Night Network Camera	Pcs	5			
0217-141	Verso Cool Outdoor Housing & Housing Fan HPV42K0A017	Pcs	5			
0217-091	Lexion Wall Bracket Adapter Plate WCPA	Pcs	5			
XPEBL	Milestone Xprotect Enterprise Base License	Pcs	1			
XPECL	Milestone Xprotect Enterprise Camera License	Pcs	1			
	Power Protection Systems					
	Digital Inverters	Pcs	5			
	Inverter Batteries	Pcs	5			
	10KVA Stabilizers	Pcs	5			
	Transtector Surge protection System	Pcs	1			
	20KVA UPS	Pcs	1			
	Blaxus Ring Earth & Lighting Protection System	Pcs	1			
	Internet Gateway Systems					
	3.8M Very Small Aperture System	Pcs	1			
	IPSAT or RG2000 Modem	Pcs	1			
	30794 5W C – Anacom	Pcs	1			
	Flexible Wave Guide (3ft)	Pcs	1			
	Mounting Kit Redundant	Pcs	1			
	MTx Reject Filter	Pcs	1			
	Cable 200ft	Pcs	1			
	IPSAT or RG2000 modem	Pcs	1			
	IBS Mux + reed Solomon Encoding	Pcs	1			
	Connector Kit	Pcs	1			
	Harmonic 501	Pcs	1			
	LNB	Pcs	1			
	Messaging System/Servers					
DELL	Rack Server - Dual Intel Xeon processor, 3Ghz/1MB, - 1GB PC-2 3200 Memory, - 2 X 76 GB Pluggable Ultra320 SCSI 15,000 rpm (1") Universal Hard Drive - Dual GiGa Ethernet Port, - Redundant PSU, -Cd- Rom,	Pcs	3			
DELL	Rack Server - Dual Intel Xeon processor, -3Ghz/1MB, - 1GB PC-2 3200 Memory, - 2 X 76 GB Pluggable Ultra320 SCSI 15,000 rpm (1") Universal Hard Drive - Dual GiGa Ethernet Port, - Redundant PSU, -Cd- Rom,	Pcs	4			
	Metadot Business Edition (World Class Web Portal)	LOT				
	LINUX BSD Mail	LOT				
	Cisco Secure ACS	LOT				
	Installations					
	LAN	LOT				
	WAN	LOT				
	Security	LOT				
	Video Conferencing	LOT				
	Softswitch VOIP	LOT				
	Surveillance Systems	LOT				
	Tower Erection/Painting	LOT				
	Server Installation and Configuration	LOT				
	Messaging and Collaboration Installation & configuration	LOT				
To be provided by client	Tower Foundation	LOT				
	VSAT	LOT				
	Freight and Duties	LOT	1			
	Contingencies 5% of Subtotal of Project Cost	LOT	1			
	Consultancy 10%	LOT	1			

Table 1: Showing list of equipment.

the following areas (networking, security, database administration etc.) with such qualifications as CCNA, CCNP, OCA, OCP etc.

3. In the first year of the state government putting software content to enhance internally generated revenue on the state ICT infrastructure, the state recorded total revenue of N4.4billion as against the previous N2.4 billion. This translated to a gain of N2.0 billion. This translated to an unprecedented increase of 83%. E-Government deployment

in Ondo State also reduced the time required to process reports for stakeholders from 3 months to a few minutes while searches on records took only a few seconds.

4. The State government was also able to increase its efficiency in the monthly payroll management by reducing the processing time required for the monthly preparation of payroll from about 22 days to about 2 hours. Access to previous records was also made possible

Description	₦ (-)	₦ (+)	In Kind
Total expenditure on e-Government in Ondo State	997,000,000		
Total direct financial gains accruable directly from e-Government in Ondo State during the same period		2,000,000,000	
Quantifiable savings from payroll preventive stuffing (traditional ghost worker syndrome)		400,000,000	
Gains from improved efficiency resulting from reduction in time required from processing assignments			Not directly measurable. Exempted from this work.
	997,000,000	2,400,000,000	
GAINS	1,403,000,000		

Table 2: Showing cost benefits and analysis.

within seconds as against endless time spent in ravaging files by civil servants before the advent of e-Government in Ondo State.

Cost benefit analysis

The cost and the benefit analysis shown in the Table 2.

Conclusion and Recommendation

It can be safely concluded that investing in modern technology and the deployment of same as have been done in Ondo State is profitable. Between 2004 and February 2009, the total investment of Ondo State government in ICT was N997 million whereas the corresponding gains to government totaled N2.4 billion during the same period. Of more importance however are the not-easily quantifiable gains that came into government during this same period. Such gains relate directly to the speed of service delivery that accompanied a shortened time e.g., bring the time required to process payroll from 22 days to about 2 hours would free civil servants time for other productive endeavors within the service. e-Government in Ondo State was not however without its own challenges. One of the core challenges is the distribution of internet access to ensure all civil servants could have access to the internet as originally envisaged. This has not been achieved. Other challenges are fear to embrace change and the problem of continuity. If these challenges can be tackled and overcome, the state would indeed be able to continue to benefit from the deployment of e-Government.

References

1. OECD (2002) Glossary of Statistical Terms.

2. World Bank (2009) e-Government. The World Bank.

3. Ariyomo O (2004) The e-Literacy-a simple guide to learning computer in 24 hours. Akure: African Pride Network.

4. Wright C (2008) The IT Regulatory and Standard Compliance Handbook.

5. Crest Computer Co. Limited (2006) As Built Documentation for Ondo State e Government Project.

6. Kocharians N (2009) Advance CCIE Routing and Switching 2.0.

12

Achieving Memory-saving Network Update

Jiyang Liu, Liang Zhu, Weiqiang Sun* and Weisheng Hu

State Key Laboratory of Advanced Optical Communication Systems and Networks, Shanghai Jiao Tong University, Shanghai 200240, China

Abstract

Software defined networking (SDN) offers opportunities to develop high-level abstractions for implementing network update, but current SDN controller platform lacks effect mechanisms for updating network configuration on the fly. There exist two main challenges for implementing network update: 1) network is a distributed system and 2) network controller can only update one network node at a time. Naïvely updating individual nodes may lead to incorrect network behaviors. Elegant solution based on two-phase update can guarantee that traffic will be processed consistently during network update, which means each packet can be routed based either on initial network configuration or target network configuration, but never a mixture of the two. Implementing consistent network update is expensive based on previous approach, and we present mechanisms for memory-saving two-phase network update. Our design addresses one major problem: how to delete the initial configuration effectively from network nodes when controller enforces the target configuration. We propose a hierarchical network metadata structure to accelerate the procedure of removing the initial configuration. Finally, we describe the results of some experiments demonstrating the effectiveness of configuration deletion and the effect of memory-saving for the network.

Keywords: Software defined networking; Network update; Network metadata structure

Introduction

Software defined networking

The Software Defined Networking architecture, based on separation of control and data plane in network elements, enables network programmability. In today's SDN solutions, controllers are able to provide open APIs through service abstractions. For instance, an application is able to invoke connectivity services across multiple domains through a single controller. It gets underlying connectivity, by deploying a series of flow table entries to physical network nodes though the controller, at the cost of switch memory resources such as ternary content-addressable memories (TCAM), which is expensive.

Network update

From network operators' perspective, network configuration need to be modified often in cases such as network topology changes, unexpected network node or link failures, transitions in network traffic and changes in network application's policy. The emergence of SDN allows transition of networks from initial state to target state by invoking the northbound APIs of SDN platform, the control-plane then issues a sequence of Open Flow commands to deploy the target configuration to networks. The SDN platform enables a centralized view of networks and forthright manner to perform network update for network operators.

Configuration changes of network update are a common source of instability in networks, it is error prone during a network update even the initial and target configurations are correct [1]. Networks are complex systems with many distributed network nodes, network operators cannot change the whole networks in a flash because it is not possible to modify numbers of network nodes at the very same time. The total time for network nodes to accept network forwarding rules differs. Hence, to perform a network update, network operators need to do a sequence of intermediate modifications on network nodes. Owing such sequence, it generates intermediate states for networks and may exhibit unexpected behaviors that would not arise in the initial and target configurations [2].

To address these problems, researchers have proposed a graceful update mechanism called two-phase update, which guarantees that each packet be routed based either on initial or target configuration.

More specifically, the idea is to pre-install the target configuration on the internal nodes, leaving the old version in place. Then, on ingress nodes, the controller sets idle timeouts, based on the Open Flow protocol, on the rules for the initial configuration and installs the target configuration at lower priority. When all flows matching a given rule finish, the rule automatically expires and the rules for the target configuration take effect [1]. However, to achieve such mechanism is expensive, it maintains forwarding rules on network nodes for both the initial and target network configurations simultaneously, and twice network memory resources consumption, during the period till the initial configuration has reached its timeout. Moreover, when multiple flows match the same rule, the rule may be artificially kept alive even though the "old" flows have all completed. If the old rules are too coarse in terms of the definition of their matching fields, then they may never die and keep consuming memory resources of the data-plane. In fact, there lack compact mechanisms to fully support efficient network update, especially in the SDN control-plane.

Our approach

From our perspective, we believe that, to achieve memory-saving network update, there need compact mechanisms to perform initial configurations deletion when networks have reached its target configurations. In order to delete the network configuration, it is necessary to locate the metadata such as network nodes and relevant flow table entries of the configuration on the control-plane. Only the relevant metadata on the control-plane get modified can the physical data-plane actually get manipulated [3,4]. Owing these, we have proposed an ideal hierarchical structure to organize metadata of configurations on the control-plane, which can accelerate the procedure of configuration retrieve and thus help to perform configuration

*Corresponding author: Weiqiang Sun, State Key Laboratory of Advanced Optical Communication Systems and Networks, Shanghai Jiao Tong University, Shanghai 200240, China, E-mail: sunwq@sjtu.edu.cn

deletion, which achieves memory-saving network update.

Related Work

Earlier research studied many distributed routing protocols [5-8] to minimize network disruptions during network routing changes. Kazemian et al. [9] proposed a graceful network abstraction model, and Reitblatt et al. [1] extended that model to well formalize network update problem. Research works in [1] introduce the notion of consistent network updates. For a given packet, the network forwarding path that a packet takes through networks, can only be in accordance with the initial configuration or the target configuration, but not a mixture of the two. It is not allowed that a packet be routed according to any intermediate state of networks during a consistent network update. And paper [1] also describes the Open Flow-compatible implementation for consistent network updates, which is called two-phase update. The basic idea of two-phase update is to explicitly tag packets upon perimeter switches, according to the version of configurations, and apply these tags as the matching fields of routing tables at each internal hop of the forwarding paths.

In the "Frenetic" project proposed in [10], two-phase update mechanisms are used to preserve consistency when performing network updates.

Based on the observation that sometimes consistency of network update can be achieved by choosing a correct order of switch updates, McClurg et al. [2] worked on ordering updates to preserve consistency during network updates. In the research, they proposed algorithms and optimizations to identify a sequence of commands to transition the network between different configurations without violating consistency invariants. Their work introduces "wait" operation for network control, to ensure that all in-flight packets of the forwarding paths based on old network configurations have left the network while the network reaches its new configurations.

Jin et al. [11] proposed a way to perform congestion-free network update. Instead of selecting one correct rule order to update networks, the paper [11] describes a new approach to dynamically select a rule order based on the update speeds of switches. They use a dependency graph to represent multiple valid orderings of rule updates, and propose algorithms to schedule updates based on the dependency graph.

The two-phase update is not always practical because that, during the transition, it consumes twice amount of switch memory resources, and it is heavy-weight. We help to eliminate the hard time for two-phase update, and we have proposed a well-defined hierarchical structure to record the relevant metadata of networks, which enables efficient transition between old and new network configurations.

This paper builds on our earlier conference paper [2], which did not include the discussion of network update. In our previous work, we proposed a network metadata structure which helps to retrieve forwarding behavior efficiently for individual network applications. It works in cases such as transitions in network traffic, changes in network application's policy, and unexpected network node or link failures. In the current paper, we move one step further by introducing the notion of network metadata into the network update problem in general.

Network Forwarding Model

To facilitate precise reasoning about network update and state our motivation in ways of formalization, this section describes the model of network forwarding behavior and the proposed metadata structure.

The network G consists of a set of nodes V and a set of links E. From the perspective of SDN, the switching function behaves as follows: (1) the first packet pk_1 of flow f is sent by the ingress node to the controller, (2) the forwarding path fp for flow f is computed by the controller, (3) the controller installs the appropriate flow table entries at each node along the forwarding path, and (4) all subsequent packets $\{pk_2, pk_3,...,pk_n\}$ in flow f or even different flows with matching attributes are forwarded in the data plane along the path and do not need any control plane action.

Definition 1 (Network forwarding path) As we can see from the above switching procedure of SDN, given a network flow f of some application, the network forwarding path fp_f is the designed switching tunnel chosen from the network topology by the controller and it consists of a set of nodes and a set of links. Formally,

$$fp_f = \{(ipt_{in}, N_{in}, ept_{in})^{tag},...,{}^{tag}(ipt_{out}, N_{out}, ept_{out})\} \tag{1}$$

where N_{in} and N_{out} are the ingress node and the egress node of the path respectively. When a packet is forwarded across a network node, ipt and ept repesent the ingress port and the egress port of the node to forward the packet. Three-tuple array such as $(ipt_{in}, N_{in}, ept_{in})^{tag}$ is a flow table entry for incoming flows on a network node. The tag label on the right side means the operation of pushing a tag on the headfield of incoming packets, while the tag label on the left side means performing packet matching based on the tag on packet's head. An orderedset of such three-tuple arraysfor a network flow forms the forwarding path.

The switching funtion of SDN behaves in ways much like the tunnel-based routing mechanisms such as MPLS. Forwarding pathsare settledin advanceforflows to be routed. Fixed network topology has limited number of forwarding elements, different forwarding paths may overlap. We thus introduce the notion of network forwarding route to represent physical forwarding tunnel for flows routed on the same tunnel.

Definition 2 (Network forwarding route) A flow traverses networks from ingress node to egress node, passing through a set of internal nodes. We organize the ordered set of nodes through which the flow passes, and define such ordered set as the forwarding route fr. Formally,

$$fr = \{N_{in}, N_1, N_2,..., N_{out}\} \tag{2}$$

As we can see from the definition, two or more forwarding paths may be placed on the same forwarding route. The forwarding route is actually a physical processing pipeline in the network.

Definition 3 (Consistent network update) In a network update, the switching function of networks is updated with new rules. The controller changes the forwarding rules by issuing commands to nodes. Intuitively, once the forwarding behaviors of network nodes have been changed, the network is actually updated. The forwarding path is the granularity of updates in practice. The controller pushes forwarding rules to network nodes to form forwarding paths and changes forwarding paths by issuing commands according to Open Flow protocol, which we write as $fp \xrightarrow{cmds} fp'$. From the controller's perspective, the network state S is the whole set of all forwarding paths. Formally,

$$S = \{fp_i \mid i = 1,...,k\} \tag{3}$$

$$S' = \{fp_i' \mid i = 1,...,k\} \cup \{fp_i'' \mid i = k+1,...\} \tag{4}$$

and we write $S \xrightarrow{u} S'$ to represent a network update u. Some fp in S may be null according to the path deletion command, and fp' in S' represents a newly added path. We call S stable if all nodes along with the forwarding paths are installed with new forwarding rules. And both the initial state S and the target state S' are stable. A consistent network update regulates that flows can only be processed according to forwarding paths either in the initial state S or in the target state S'during a network update.

Definition 4 (Two-phase update) In terms of the two-phase update, in the first phase, it populates the nodes in the middle of the forwarding paths with new configurations which have the tags, indicating the version of new configurations, in the matching fields. In the second phase, it enables the new configurations by installing rules at the ingress of networks and performs additional action that explicitly stamps packets with tags according to the version of configurations. Formally, suppose the initial forwarding path is

$$fp_{initial} = \{(ipt_{in}, N_{in}, ept_{in})^{tag}, {}^{tag}(ipt_1, N_1, ept_1), ..., {}^{tag}(ipt_{out}, N_{out}, ept_{out})\} \quad (5)$$

On the first phase, the forwarding path has been changed as

$$fp_{phase1} = \{(ipt_{in}, N_{in}, ept_{in})^{tag}, {}^{tag'}(ipt_1', N_1', ept_1'), ..., {}^{tag'}(ipt_{out}', N_{out}, ept_{out})\} \quad (6)$$

On the second phase, it goes like

$$fp_{phase2} = \{(ipt_{in}, N_{in}, ept_{in}')^{tag'}, {}^{tag'}(ipt_1', N_1', ept_1'), ..., {}^{tag'}(ipt_{out}', N_{out}, ept_{out})\} \quad (7)$$

During the first phase, the intermediate nodes may have been changed. The matching tag of flow table entries onboth the intermediate nodes and the egress node may have been modified. The ingress port of the egress node for coming packets may hasbeenshifted as well. When it comes to the second phase, The controller modifies boththe egress port of the ingress node for packets and the tags to push to packets' head.

To release networks from the aforementioned memory pressure during two-phase update, we perform fast process of forwarding path retrieve and deletion during the transition. We think thecontroller should remove the initialnetworkconfigurations in $fp_{initial}$ imediately after rules in fp_{phase2} have been installed on network nodes during a consistent network update.

Hierarchical Network Metadata Structure

To delete the initial network configurations after networks have deployed the target configurations, the relevant network metadata need to be located. For example, in the topology shown in Figure 1, a flow of video on demand (VOD) [12] type requests connection from node 1 to node 4. Suppose the controller deploys a forwarding path as shown below,

$$fp_{VOD} = \{(ipt_1, N_1, ept_1)^{tag}, {}^{tag}(ipt_2, N_2, ept_2), {}^{tag}(ipt_4, N_4, ept_4)\} \quad (8)$$

for the VOD flow initially. Then, after a peroid of time, the controller performs network update based on policy change, and the new forwarding path of the VOD flow is

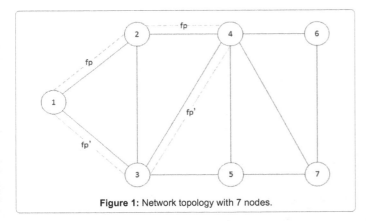

Figure 1: Network topology with 7 nodes.

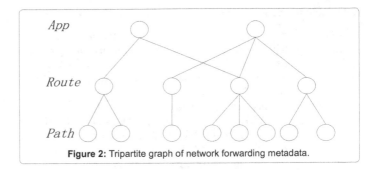

Figure 2: Tripartite graph of network forwarding metadata.

$$fp_{VOD}' = \{(ipt_1, N_1, ept_1)^{tag'}, {}^{tag'}(ipt_3, N_3, ept_3), {}^{tag'}(ipt_4, N_4, ept_4)\} \quad (9)$$

Ifthe controller wants to delete the configuration in fp_{VOD}, it first need to locate the target nodes and the corresponding flow table entries that should be removed from the network. So it is necessary for the controller to recored the information of fp_{VOD} which enables locatingthe target network metadata. In both wide area and data center networks, which deployed with many applications, the amount of forwarding paths for network flows may be tremendous large and the compact structure to organize the information of this many paths in the control-plane is a major challenge for configuration deletion.

We have proposed a structure to record network metadata such as forwarding paths and forwarding routes. In the SDN architecture, APIs are provided on the north bound, applications such as VOD can deploy policies such as bandwidth guarantee to the network control-plane through the north bound APIs. When a VOD flow requests routing through networks, the control-plane computes a forwarding path for the flow, according to the bandwidth guarantee policy as well as network conditions, and installs the forwarding path to the data-plane. The flow of VOD application then travels from an ingress node to an egress node along with the forwarding path settled by the control-plane. On account of that every forwarding path serves for its flows and each flow belongs to its network application, we introduce one more metadata of network forwarding, i.e. the network application (Figure 2).

To retrieve and remove forwarding paths efficiently, we organize forwarding paths in a hierarchical way. We abstract one potential common attribute for different forwarding paths, which is the forwarding route. Different forwarding paths may have the same physical nodes pipeline. In other words, these paths may be placed on the same forwarding route. There exists inner relation among network application, forwarding route and forwarding path.

We denote the relationship among application, route and path by tripartite graph $G= (V^{(1)}, V^{(2)}, V^{(3)} ; E)$, as shown in Figure 2. We define $V^{(1)}$, $V^{(2)}$ and $V^{(3)}$ and as three partition sets of G.

$$V^{(1)} = \{app_1, ..., app_l\} \quad (10)$$

$$V^{(2)} = \{route_1, ..., route_m\} \quad (11)$$

$$V^{(3)} = \{path_1, ..., path_n\} \quad (12)$$

Vertices in $V^{(1)}$, $V^{(2)}$ and $V^{(3)}$ represent applications, routes and paths respectively. There is no adjacent vertices between $V^{(1)}$ and $V^{(3)}$. Vertices in $V^{(2)}$ may have more than one adjacent vertices in $V^{(1)}$, while vertices in $V^{(3)}$ can only get one adjacent vertices in $V^{(2)}$. One vertices in $V^{(1)}$ may have multiple adjacent vertices in $V^{(2)}$. Two or more vertices in $V^{(1)}$ can share the same one adjacent vertices in $V^{(2)}$ because that one route can be shared with multiple applications. Vertices in $V^{(2)}$ cannot have multiple adjacent vertices in $V^{(3)}$ because the path is the connection which only locate in one specific route.

Once the network triggers a network update, after the target forwarding path get computed and deployed to the network, given the app tag of the new forwarding path, we can provide our first level of reference to the intial forwarding path, which is the app type of the forwarding path. Based on the reality that the initial and the target forwarding paths share the same ingress and egress nodes, given the ingress and egress nodes of the new computed path, we can provide our second level reference to the intial forwarding path to locate the route on the structure. At the third level, we get a small set of our candidate paths based on the first and second level references, and we can look upthe initial forwarding path based on the matching field on the ingress node, knowing that the intial and the target forwarding paths have the same matching field on their ingress nodes. After we retrievethe initial forwarding path, the controller can perform a sequence of Open Flow commands to delete the corresponding flow table entries on the nodes inthe data-planeaccording to the information of the initial forwarding path. The above mechanism is listed in Figure 3.

The hierarchical structure of network metadata accelerates the retrieve procedure for a specific forwarding path. Based on the multi level of references, we can locate the candidate set of forwarding paths quickly. And the amount of the candidatesis reduced enormously. After the procedure of multi level reference, we only need to check the matching field of the candidates to retrieve the desired initial forwarding path.

From our study, Onix [13] and PANE [14] matain the network metadata as the network information base (NIB), which is a database storing hosts, switches, ports queues, forwarding tables, links and their capabilities. NIB is responsble for holding network information and translating logcial actions of control to physical configurations. Modern SDN platform, such as Open Daylight [15], uses the concept of

NIB to build its service abstraction layer (SAL), which is the backbone of its architecture. We argue that the forwarding path of different network applications should be maintained as a meta element in NIB. Network update, which is one of the major events of SDN environment, deals with the forwarding paths. When network condition or applicationstate changes, the actionsfor forwaring paths need to be translated to network configurations. And a hirarchical way to maintain forwarding path would actually accerlerate network update operation and reduce overhead.

Implementation and Evaluation

In order to investigate the performance of forwarding path retrieve and the effect of reducing network memory overhead, both real network testbed experiments and simulations have been conducted.

Testbed experiments

We have built a prototype implementation of the hirarchical metadata structure. Open Day light is used as the controller software and we implement the proposed hierarchical structure as a plug in of Open Day light. The plugin maintains data of the structure and provides APIs to manipulate. The Mini net [2] environment is used to build the test bed network topology. A HP ProLiant ML350 Gen9 server is used as the controller host and is also connected to a set of DELL Inspiron 560 pcs running Mininet. We have designed two test cases. In both cases, a client connection reaching one of the pre-installed application servers is built randomly. We retrieve all the flow table entries of the corresponding forwarding paths in situations with and without the plugin respectively. The corresponding time cost is recorded.

In case 1, we build a test network topology with 100 network devices initially. There are 20 network applications deployed in the network. Each network node may have flow table entries related to the application's flow. We differentiate the application information of flow

---

Procedure: CONFIGURATIONDELETE (fp_{target} , T)

Input: forwarding path fp_{target} , hierarchical metadatatree structure T

Output: Remove $fp_{initial}$ from the network and return $fp_{initial}$

1: $app = getApp(fp_{target})$ //get the application type of the flow on fp_{target}

2: $src = getIngress(fp_{target})$ //get the ingress node of fp_{target}

3: $dst = getEgress(fp_{target})$ //get the egress node of fp_{target}

4: $mf_{target} = getMatchField(fp_{target})$ //get the matching field on the ingress node of fp_{target}

5: $T_{app} = getSubtree(T, app)$ //return a sub tree with the root node of app

6: $Set_{route} = getLayer(T_{app}, 2)$ //get all the elements on the second layer of the sub tree

7: **for all** $r \in Set_{route}$ **do**

8: $\quad src_r = getIngress(r)$

9: $\quad dst_r = getEgress(r)$

10: $\quad$ **if** $src = src_r$ **and** $dst = dst_r$ **then**

11: $\quad\quad T_r = getLayer(T_{app}, r)$

12: $\quad\quad Set_{fp} = getLayer(T_r, 2)$ //get all the forwarding paths on the route r

13: $\quad\quad$ **for all** $fp \in Set_{fp}$ **do**

14: $\quad\quad\quad mf = getMatchField(fp)$

15: $\quad\quad\quad$ **if** $mf = mf_{target}$ **then**

16: $\quad\quad\quad\quad fp_{initial} = fp$

17: $\quad\quad\quad\quad delete(fp_{initial})$ //remove $fp_{initial}$ from the data-plane

18: $\quad\quad\quad\quad$ **return** $fp_{initial}$

Figure 3: Configuration delete procedure.

table entries by their destination IP in the matching fields on the ingress nodes. We initially assign 10 nodes along the forwarding path carrying the randomly built connection. Consequently, there are 10 flow table entries constructing such a connection. Then we increase the total number of network nodes and also the number of nodes in each path, to observe the time cost under different network scales. In situation with the plugin, we locate all the flow table entries in a forwarding path by iterating the structure from the top layer to the bottom layer. In situation without the plugin, we have to look up all the network nodes to find the desired flow table entries. As shown in Figure 4, situations with and without the plugin differ more than one order of magnitude in time cost.

In case 2, 20 applications are deployed in the network. We change the number of network nodes both in a path and in the whole test network to observe the time cost. The increasing number of network nodes in a path would bring more flow table entries on the path. It takes more time to retrieve a specific path consequently. On the other hand, in situation without the plugin, the time cost is affected mostly by the network scale, as listed in Figure 5. We traverse all the network nodes to find the desired flow table entries in such situation. Therefore,

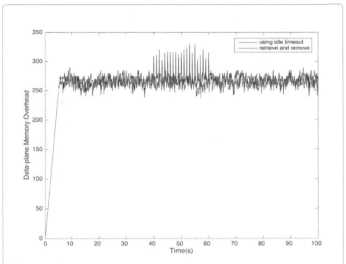

Figure 6: Data-plane memory overhead with 10 paths updated in a network update cycle.

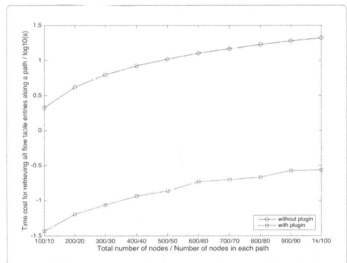

Figure 4: Time cost of retrieving flow table entries under different network scale.

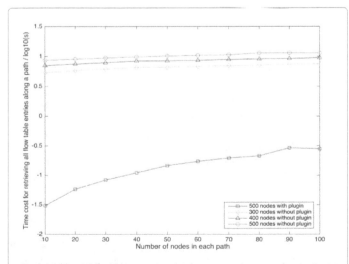

Figure 5: Time cost of retrieving flow table entries for fixed network scale with changing scale of path.

it takes more time to locate flow table entries of an application in a larger scale of network.

Simulations

In the simulation, we use random substrate topology. According to investigations of Albert et al. [4], given two arbitrary nodes, the number of intermediate nodes are generated by using the equation below:

$$l_{rand} \sim \frac{\ln(N)}{\ln(k)} \tag{13}$$

In Eq. (13), parameters N and k represent the whole number of nodes in a network and the average degree of network nodes respectively. In the simulation, we set $K=2.66$ according to [16]. The average number of nodes in a path, connecting two randomly selected nodes, is approximately equate to the right part of Eq. (13). In the simulated network topology, it is interconnected between each node. Periodically, the simulated network receives a fresh flow per 0.1 second. The idle timeout of a flow table entry is 5 second. We observe network behavior during time period of 100 seconds under different conditions.

We firstly set the scale of substrate network as 100 nodes and the average node number of forwarding paths is five, according to Eq.(13). During the time interval between the 40th second and the 60th second, we update the simulated network at each second. In Figure 6, we update 10 forwarding paths in an update cycle and record the data-plane memory overhead at different time points. Data-plane memory overhead is understood as the total amount of flow table entries in the substrate network. It is observed that the two-phase update, using idle timeout to uninstall configurations, leads to a sharp increase of memory overhead, while our proposed mechanism to remove configurations performs a stationary update process. In Figure 7, we increase the number of forwarding paths to be transformed to 20 in an update cycle. As we can see between Figures 6 and 7, the data-plane memory overhead rises as the scale of network update increases under the condition using idle timeout. While in situation with our mechanism, the update process keeps stationary at a coarse granularity. With the increasing scale of network update, mechanism of idle timeout for two-phase update brings more and more pressure to data-plane memory. Network traffic behavior differs a lot between day and night, and at some points of time, the network need to deploy large scale update to meet traffic

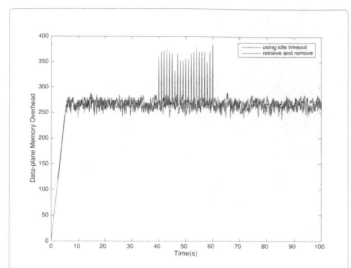

Figure 7: Data-plane overhead with 20 paths updated in a network update cycle.

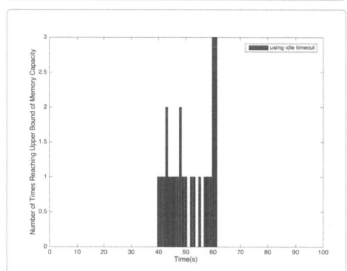

Figure 8: Number of times reaching upper bound of memory capacity of a node in two-phase update case using idle timeout.

characteristic. The two-phase update with our proposed mechanism can apply well to such scenario.

Next, we investigate the memory overhead of key nodes under a fixed topology as shown in Figure 1. There are 7 nodes totally and node 4 has the highest degree. In the simulation, since each node has the same probability to receive new flows, we think node 4 holds more traffic than others. We update the network at each second during the time period between the 40th second and the 60th second, and 10 forwarding paths are changed in every update process. We set the upper bound capacity of memory for each node to hold flow table entries as 25 and record the number of times for a specific node to reach its memory capacity in the span of one second. It is obvious from Figures 8 and 9 that our mechanism can help to ease off the memory overhead of network key node.

Now that we investigate the impact of network scales. We observe the memory overhead under different network scales with 100, 200 and 300 nodes respectively, and the corresponding number of nodes along a forwarding path is set as 5, 6 and 7. The simulation process updates the network at each second between time period from the 10th second

to the 30th second for the 300 nodes network, from the 40th second to the 60th second for the 200 nodes network, and from the 70th second to the 90th second for the 100 nodes network. 20 paths, 40 paths and 60 paths are updated in an update process for network scales of 100 nodes, 200 nodes and 300 nodes, respectively. The results in Figures 10 and 11 show that the memory overhead increases as the network scale grows, during the update process using idle timeout mechanism. In contrast, with the increasing network scale, the retrieve and remove mechanism using a hierarchical structure brings little impact to the memory overhead during the network update (Table 1).

Conclusion

In this work, we are interested in the memory overheadduringthe two-phase network update process. We provide a solution based on configuration deletion. We argue that the challenge is to realize efficient configuration retrieve, and we show that a network metadata structure to organize information of forwarding path in a hirarchical way which could accelrate the retrieve process, and should be designed as a meta

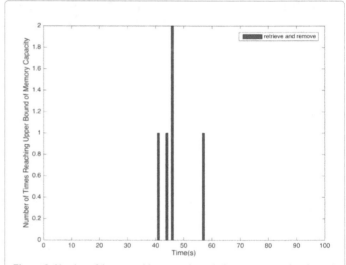

Figure 9: Number of times reaching upper bound of memory capacity of a node in two-phase update case using proposedmechanism.

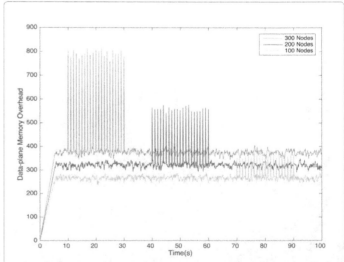

Figure 10: Data-plane memory overhead under different network scale in two-phase update case using idle timeout.

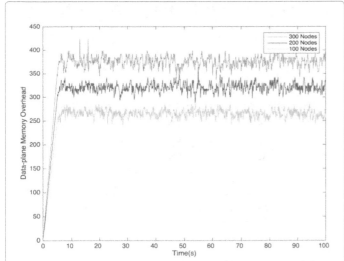

Figure 11: Data-plane memory overhead under different network scale in two-phase update case using proposed mechanism.

Symbol	Meaning
G	Physical network
V	Set of network nodes
E	Set of network links
pk	Packet
f	Flow
fp	Forwarding path
fr	Forwarding route
N	Network node
ipt	Ingress port of nodes for a packet
ept	Egress port of nodes for a packet
S	Network state

Table 1: Network forwarding Notations.

component in the network information base. We investigate the performance in both simulation and testbed environments [17]. The results show that the proposed mechanism outperforms the original one and brings performance enhancementin time cost for retrieving a forwarding path and in memory overhead under different scenarios.

Acknowledgement

This work is supported by NSFC (61433009, 61431009,61271217), and Ministry of Education (20110073130006).

References

1. Reitblatt M, Foster N, Rexford J, Schlesinger C, Walker D (2012) Abstractions for network update. In Proceedings of the ACM SIGCOMM 2012 conference on Applications, technologies, architectures, and protocols for computer communication. USA.

2. McClurg J, Hojjat H, Cerny P, Foster N (2014) Efficient synthesis of network updates. arXiv preprint arXiv.

3. www.mininet.org

4. Albert R, Barabási AL (2002) Statistical mechanics of complex networks. Reviews of modern physics, Indiana.

5. Liu J, Zhu L, Sun W, Hu W (2015) Scalable application-aware resource management in software defined networking. In Transparent Optical Networks (ICTON), 2015 17th International Conference on, Budapest.

6. Francois P, Shand M, Bonaventure O (2007) Disruption free topology reconfiguration in OSPF networks. In INFOCOM 2007, 26th IEEE International Conference on Computer Communications,Anchorage, AK.

7. Francois P, Bonaventure O, Decraene B, Coste P A (2007) Avoiding disruptions during maintenance operations on BGP sessions. Network and Service Management, IEEE Transactions on.

8. Raza S, Zhu Y, Chuah CN (2011) Graceful network state migrations. IEEE/ACM Transactions on Networking (TON), USA.

9. Kazemian P, Varghese G, McKeown N (2012) Header Space Analysis: Static Checking for Networks. In Networked Systems Design and Implementation (NSDI), USA.

10. Vanbever L, Vissicchio S, Pelsser C, Francois P, Bonaventure O (2011) Seamless network-wide IGP migrations. ACM SIGCOMM Computer Communication Review, USA.

11. Jin X, Liu HH, Gandhi R, Kandula S, Mahajan R, et al. (2014) Dynamic scheduling of network updates. In Proceedings of the 2014 ACM conference on SIGCOMM, USA.

12. Foster N, Guha A, Reitblatt M, Story A, Freedman MJ, et al. (2013) Languages for software-defined networks. Communications Magazine, IEEE 51: 128-134.

13. Koponen T, Casado M, Gude N, Stribling J, Poutievski L, et al. (2010) Onix: A Distributed Control Platform for Large-scale Production Networks. InOperating Systems Design and Implementation (OSDI), USA.

14. Ferguson AD, Guha A, Liang C, Fonseca R, Krishnamurthi S (2013) Participatory networking: An API for application control of SDNs. In ACM SIGCOMM Computer Communication Review, USA.

15. Jarschel M, Wamser F, Hohn T, Zinner T, Tran-Gia P (2013) Sdn-based application-aware networking on the example of youtube video streaming. In Software Defined Networks (EWSDN), 2013 Second European Workshop on, Berlin.

16. www.opendaylight.org

17. Govindan R, Tangmunarunkit H (2000) Heuristics for Internet map discovery. In INFOCOM 2000,19th Annual Joint Conference of the IEEE Computer and Communications Societies, USA.

13

An Efficient Task Scheduling of Multiprocessor Using Genetic Algorithm Based on Task Height

Ashish Sharma* and Mandeep Kaur

Department of Computer Science and Engineering , Guru Nanak Dev University, Regional Campus Jalandhar, India

Abstract

Static task scheduling in multiprocessor frameworks is one of the well-defined NP hard problem. Due to optimal utilization of processors and in addition investing less time, the scheduling of tasks in multiprocessor frameworks is of extraordinary significance. To solve NP hard problem using traditional strategies takes reasonable measures of time. Over the time, various heuristic procedures were presented for comprehending it. Therefore, heuristic methods such as genetic algorithms are appropriate methods for task scheduling in multiprocessor system. In this paper, a new GA for static task scheduling in multiprocessor systems has been presented whose priority of tasks' execution is based on the height of task in graph and other mentioned parameters and then scheduling is performed. This proposed method is simulated and then compared with basic genetic algorithm.

Keywords: Multi processor; Genetic algorithm; Schedule; Task graph; Distribute system; Task height; Make span; Schedule time

Introduction

It is difficult to execute a single big problem on a single processor in a reasonable time. Because of this, it is divided into number of tasks and the length of each schedule must be so that it results in appropriate scheduling in a multiprocessor system. The task scheduling [1,2] problem in multiprocessors is to allocate the set of tasks to processors such that optimal or sub optimal utilization of processors and minimum scheduling time are achieved.

For mathematical modeling if task assignment problem, direct acyclic graph (DAG) is used as each task is represented by its adjacent node in the graph [3]. The edge between task ti to task tj represents that task ti is not finished, task tj cannot start execution. The task assignment objective is to schedule the n tasks to m processors, while the priority of tasks is being taken care and the utilization is maximized. The communication delay between processors and the data volume transmitted between two tasks is also observed. Scheduling of tasks in a multiprocessor system is an NP hard problem [4]. It is expensive and time consuming to schedule tasks using traditional and dynamic approaches. However using heuristic methods we can have the optimal solution or nearly optimal solution for these problems. There are many heuristic methods which can be used such as: min–min, max min, duplex, minimum completion time (MCT), minimum execution time (MET) [5], simulated annealing (SA) [6], tabu search [7]. One of the heuristic method which is best for scheduling in multiprocessors system is genetic algorithm (GA).

Review of Genetic Algorithm Literature for Multiprocessors Task Scheduling

As scheduling is an NP-complete problem researchers try to apply heuristics or meta-heuristics to get optimum or near to optimum solution. People use a single heuristic or a combination of heuristics and meta-heuristics. It is called the hybrid meta-heuristics.

Ahmad et al. [8] have proposed performance effective genetic algorithm (PEGA). The PEGA efficiently finds the best solution from the search space; The reason why PEGA is performance effective is because of the effective utilization of genetic operators (crossover and mutation).

Agarwal and Colak [9], proposed a metaheuristic approach - called NeuroGenetic - which is a combination of an augmented neural

network and a genetic algorithm. The results showed that the neuro genetic approach performs better than either the augmented neural network or the genetic algorithms alone.

Parvan et al. [10], proposed a hybrid scheduling algorithm for solving the independent task scheduling problem in grid which comprises of GA with Firefly algorithm. It was indicated from the results that as compared to the best processed method, the proposed algorithm can decrease Makespan of 10%.

Mehrabi et al. [11], solved the task assignment problem by considering load balancing with the use of a new method, based on the genetic algorithms (GAs). GA uses a repair function to ensure valid assignments during the process of algorithm.

Devi and Anju [12], in their study emphasize on development of a multi objective scheduling algorithm using Evolutionary techniques for scheduling a set of dependent tasks in a multiprocessor environment which minimizes the makespan and reliability cost. NSGA-II is Elitist Evolutionary algorithm that takes the initial parental solution without any changes, in all iteration to remove the problem of loss of some pareto-optimal solutions.

Diana et al. [13], proposed improved genetic algorithm (IGA) based approach for the single mode resource constrained project scheduling problem (RCPSP) with makespan minimization as objective. The suggested way uses binary string based representations and operators for chromosomes.

Awadall et al. [14] highlights two new approaches, modified list scheduling heuristic (MLSH) and enhanced genetic algorithm by constructing promising chromosomes. The result after comparison shows that the proposed approaches works to enhance processor efficiency and decrease task makespan.

---

*Corresponding author: Ashish Sharma, Department of Computer Science and Engineering Guru Nanak Dev University, Regional Campus Jalandhar, India
E-mail: Iamashish90@gmail.com

Dhingra et al. [15], have proposed that Optimizing different parameters such as crossover, mutation, crossover probability, selection function etc. can lead to efficient and effective genetic algorithm.

Proposed Algorithm

We propose a genetic algorithm for scheduling tasks in multiprocessor environment. We have used the randomized height based approach. Below we have listed the steps of our proposed GA for tasks scheduling.

- Find height for each task in DAG
- Encoding chromosome
- Initial population
- Generate population
- Repeat (adjust height)
- Fitness Function
- Apply GA operators
- Update population
- Until stopping condition

Find height for each task in DAG

Height of each task can be calculated using DAG, if task is parent of other task then its height is 1- height of its child or height of child is 1+ height of its parent. Below is the equation that calculates the height of task.

Height [task]=0 (if task is root)

Otherwise

Height [task]=max (height (parents))+1

Calculation of height starts from entry node and ends at exit node (Figure 1 and Table 1).

Encoding chromosomes

Chromosome shows the possible state of scheduling. Each chromosome is represented by the tuple (T,P), where T is set of tasks and P is set processors in the framework. pi ∈ P is shown a processor that allocated to task ti ∈ T. Each chromosome represents the execution of tasks in the processor and also the sequence of tasks to processor [16]. In below table there are three processors and 7 tasks that are shown Table 2.

Generation of population

To generate population perform the steps shown below:

Repeat

Input number of tasks

Input number of processors

Check order of tasks

For i=0 to number_of_task

If (height [task[i]]=1)

Readytoexecute []=task[i]

end if

end for loop

Generate a random number x

Select readytoexecute[x]

Generate a random number y

Select machine [y]

adjust_height()

Repeat until there is no task with height 1

Adjust height

Tasks are queued in priority queue on the basis of their priorities. As it is mentioned above, task must be ready to execute and must have the higher priority and stand on priority queue. Adjust height function arranges tasks in all the possible ways. Using this method we update the task height which are dependent on the selected task. This change is just limited to this population only as it is the local height concept. In further populations global height parameter is considered.T1 is root and if selected first then suppose its height is updated to 0 then height of all children must be updated accordingly (Table 3).

After selecting each task for execution we update this table so that we can find the dependencies and arrange them in respective order. Scheduling is done based on tasks priority and in GA execution time, the sequence of tasks priority is not changed but the sequence of allocation of processors to the tasks is variant.

Task	T0	T1	T2	T3	T4	T5	T6
Height	1	2	2	2	2	3	4

Table 1: Tasks Height according to DAG.

Task	T0	T1	T2	T3	T4	T5	T6
Processor	1	3	2	3	1	2	1

Table 2: Sequence of tasks to processors.

Task	T0	T1	T2	T3	T4	T5	T6
Height	0	1	1	1	1	2	3

Table 3: Adjusted task height.

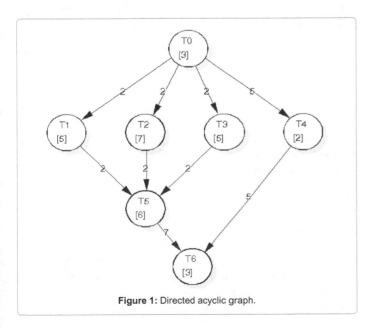

Figure 1: Directed acyclic graph.

Fitness function

The aim of the proposed scheduling algorithm is to minimize the schedule time of the parallel program. It is the measure which decides the fitness of function. It is calculated in terms of minimum schedule time so that utilization and speed up can be achieved [17]. We consider the computation cost [18], communication delay between processors and data volume transmitted between two tasks as well. We have calculated the starting time and finish time of tasks.

We derive a formula to calculate starting time (ST) of a task which is show below.

ST(task)=max (max[task at processor [id] [level order[task]], max time on machine)

The finish time (FT) of that task is summation of starting time and its execution time(ET). Its completion time is the available time for a machine on which it is executed.

FT(task)=ST (task)+ET(on particular machine)

Fitness=max(FT(Pj)

for j=1,2,...,n

Where n is the number of processors and *FT(Pj)* is the finish time of the final task in the processor *Pj*.

Reproduction

For reproduction, the pair of available solution is selected and then the reproduction operators like crossover and mutation are applied. All operators are discussed below.

Selection: The selection phase has two steps:

1) Applying a roulette wheel to select two chromosomes: After chromosomes are ascend on the basis of their fitness, a roulette wheel series is constructed based on their fitness [17]. Hence, the chromosomes with low fitness, occupy more slots in the roulette wheel. In this way the possibility of selecting chromosomes with best fitness is higher. Then two chromosomes will be selected.

2) Applying a roulette wheel for selecting a task: A roulette wheel is constructed for tasks based on their number of children. A task with more sub tasks has more probability to be selected compared to a task with fewer ones. The genetic operators like crossover, mutation will be applied on the current generation to produce the next generation.

Crossover: Crossover operator is used to differ the analogy of chromosomes from one generation to another. Single point crossover is used in proposed algorithm. Crossover is applied on the chromosomes so as to produce the best fit chromosome which has the best fitness than its parent. The crossover starts with two parent chromosomes to exchange subparts of them to create two new children chromosomes.

Following conditions must be satisfied for the reproduction of legal chromosome:

1) The height of the tasks next to the crossover points should be different.

2) The height of all the tasks immediately in front of the crossover points should be equal.

Mutation: The mutation selects a chromosome and then randomly exchanges the two tasks with the same height [17]. The mutation is applied with a certain mutation rate (Mr) which is used to prevent the search process from converging to the local optima prematurely.

Scheduling Algorithm

The code of proposed scheduling algorithm is shown below.

1. Generate the population

2. While (finish time of each machine in chromosome are equal or generations number is no more than given number) do

For every chromosome in this population do

calculate fitness of every chromosome

End for

While next population is generated and complete do

choose chromosomes with best fitness values by roulette-selection

use single point crossover operator to create next generation children

use mutation operator

End while

End while

The exit condition in proposed algorithm determines the equal processing time for all processors and also the number of generations. By using it the optimal parallelism can be achieved, as all processors can have the equal or nearly equal processing time

Implementation and Experimental Results of Proposed Algorithm

Implementation environment

A set of simulation is performed using Java on Eclipse platform on a computer Pentium IV, having AMD processor 2.8 GHz, and 512 MB memory of RAM to evaluate our suggested algorithm. To load tasks and processors we used input file in which the number of tasks and number of machines are described. The communication delay between processors, computation cost(Execution time of tasks) and data volume between two tasks is also mentioned in input file. Create population method is used to create population of 1000 chromosomes. Height of Node (int) method is used to determine the height of each task and also adjusts the height. Fitness (int id) checks the fitness (makespan) [14] of each task. Schedule task class is used to define and manage tasks, processors, starting time and finish time of each task .procAvT defines the processor available time. The task group is J30 and all communication delays and costs are defined in this group.

Results and comparison

Following Figures shows the results achieved [19] (Figures 2-5). The speedup and utilization and schedule time using this technique are better than basic GA. Figure 3 shows the schedule time using our proposed algorithm and schedule time using basic genetic algorithm. It is clear that our algorithm is better than basic GA.

Conclusion

We proposed a height base GA to solve task scheduling problem of dependent tasks in multiprocessor architecture. In this algorithm priority of tasks is based on their height, children number and execution time [20]. The experimental simulations applied on our algorithm using various task graphs and number of generations and by comparing it with Basic GA shows that proposed algorithm has less schedule time than basic GA. Under the same the schedule length, finish time are

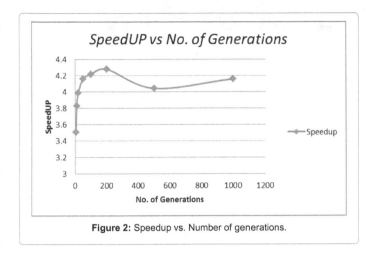

Figure 2: Speedup vs. Number of generations.

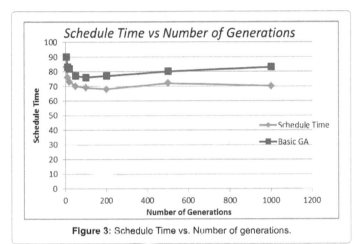

Figure 3: Schedule Time vs. Number of generations.

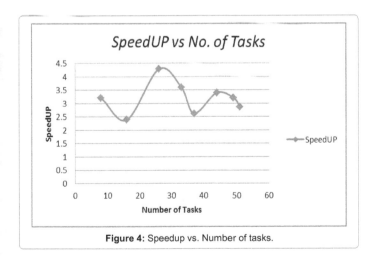

Figure 4: Speedup vs. Number of tasks.

also less. Therefore proposed algorithm can show effective behaviour and can be used as an efficient and better scheduling system in many applications.

References

1. Rewini HE, Lewis TG, Ali HH (1994) Task scheduling in parallel and distributed systems. Prentice Hall.

2. Kwok Y, Ahmad I (1999) Static scheduling algorithms for allocating directed

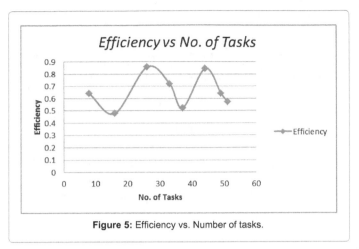

Figure 5: Efficiency vs. Number of tasks.

task graphs to multiprocessors. ACM Computing Surveys 31: 4406-4471.

3. Ahmad I, Kwok YK (1999) Benchmarking and comparison of the task graph scheduling algorithms. J Parallel Distributed Computing 95: 381-422.

4. Billionnet A, Costa MC, Sutter A (1992) An efficient algorithm for the task allocation problem. J ACM 39 : 502-518.

5. Braun TD, Siegel H J, Beck N, Boloni L, Maheswaran M, et al. (2001) A comparison of eleven static heuristic for mapping a class of independent tasks onto heterogeneous distributed computing systems. Journal of Parallel and Distributed Computing 61: 810-837.

6. Rahmani AM, Resvani M (2007) A novel static task scheduling in distributed systems by genetic algorithm using simulated annealing. 12th International CSI Conference, Iran 83.

7. Silva ML, Porto SCS (1999) An Object-Oriented Approach to a Parallel Tabu Search Algorithm for the Task Scheduling Problem. Proceedings of the 19th International Conference of the Chilean Computer Science Society 105-111.

8. Ahmad SG, Munir EU, Nisar W (2012) PEGA: A performance effective genetic algorithm for task scheduling in heterogeneous systems. IEEE 14th International Conference on High Performance Computing and Communications 1082-1087.

9. Agarwal A, Colak S (2014) The Task Scheduling Problem: A NeuroGenetic Approach. Journal of Business and Economics Research - Fourth Quarter 12.

10. Parvan H, Nejad EB, Alavi SE (2014) New hybrid algorithms for task scheduling in computational grids to decrease makespan. International journal of Computer Science and Network Solutions 2.

11. Mehrabi A, Mehrabi S, Mehrabi AD (2009) An adaptive genetic algorithm for multiprocessor task assignment problem with limited memory. Proceedings of the World Congress on Engineering and Computer Science 2.

12. Devi MR, Anju A (2014) Multiprocessor scheduling of dependent tasks to minimize makespan and reliability cost using NSGA-II. International Journal of Computer Science and Telecommunications 4.

13. Diana S, Ganapathy L, Pundir AK (2013) An improved genetic algorithm for resource constrained project scheduling problem. International Journal of Computer Applications 0975-8887 78.

14. Awadall M, Ahmad A, Al-Busaidi S (2013) Min–min GA Based Task Scheduling In Multiprocessor Systems International Journal of Engineering and Advanced Technology (IJEAT) ISSN 3: 2249-8958.

15. Dhingra S, Gupta SB, Biswas R (2014) Genetic algorithm parameters optimization for bi-criteria multiprocessor task scheduling using design of experiments. World Academy of Science, Engineering and Technology International Journal of Computer, Information, Systems and Control Engineering 8.

16. Sivanandam SN, Deepa SN (2008) Introduction to genetic algorithms. Springer Publishing Company, Incorporated.

17. Mitchell M (1998) An Introduction to Genetic algorithms. The MIT Press.

18. Bonyadi MR, Moghaddam ME (2009) A bipartite genetic algorithm for multi-processor task scheduling. International Journal of Parallel Programming 37: 462-487.

19. Chitra P, Venkatesh P, Rajaram R (2011) Comparison of evolutionary computation algorithms for solving bi-objective task scheduling problem on heterogeneous distributed computing systems. Sadhana 36: 167-180.

20. Hartmann S (1997) A competitive genetic algorithm for resource-constrained project scheduling. Naval Research Logistics 45: 733-750.

14

NAND Flash Memory Organization and Operations

Novotný R*, Kadlec J and Kuchta R

Brno University of Technology, Technická 3058/10, 616 00 Brno, The Czech Republic

Abstract

   NAND flash memories are well known for their uncomplicated structure, low cost, and high capacity. Their typical characteristics include architecture, sequential reading, and high density. NAND flash memory is a non-volatile type of memory and has low power consumption. The erasing of NAND Flash memory is based on a block-wise base. Since cells in a flash chip will fail after a limited number of writes, limited write endurance is a key characteristic of flash memory. There are many noise causes such as read or program disturbs, retention process, charge leakage, trapping generation, etc. Preferably, all errors in the storage would be adjusted by the ECC algorithm. The conclusion of all mentioned parasitic factors creates a set of external and internal influences which affects variable behaviour of memory in time. To prepare a review of all the important factors that affect the reliability and life-cycle endurance of NAND flash memories and was our main motivation for this paper.

Keywords: Flash memory; Non-volatile; Bit error rate; Error correction code; Architecture; Reliability

Introduction

   Flash memory has been an important driving force due to the increasing popularity of mobile devices with large storage requirements. Flash memory is respected in many applications as a storage media due to its high access speed, non-volatile type of storage (Figure 1), and low-power consumption. There is a wide range of non-volatile memories, and they all give various characteristics based on the complexity of array organization and structure of the selected cell type [1]. Flash memories are becoming widely deployed in many applications such as solid state drives (SSDs) for embedded controllers and traditional computing storage. NAND Flash memories are becoming more and more popular due to their usage as Solid-State Drives (SSDs) [2] and USB Flash drives which are in general called Flash storage devices. Another area of application is as the non-volatile memory in systems, which allow system reconfiguration, software updates, changing of stored identification codes, or frequent updating of stored information (i.e. smart cards). Electrically erasable and programmable read-only memories (EEPROM's), which are electrically erasable and programmable, will be produced only for specific applications, because they use larger chip areas and are more expensive (Figure 1). Flash memories as a type of memory device characterized by non-volatility. Following on from these advantages, the manufacturers of memories started to consider the role of flash memories for a new range of applications. These include hard disk caches, solid-state drives, mobile sensor networks, and data-centric computing. Many microcontrollers have integrated flash memory for non-volatile data storage. Flash memory is also used in many applications where data retention in power-off situations and reliability are crucial requirements, such as in embedded computers or wireless communication systems. Nowadays, flash memory is one of the most popular, reliable, and flexible non-volatile memories to store constant data values and software code. NAND Flash architecture and NOR Flash architecture (Figure 2) dominates the non-volatile Flash market [3] because NAND Flash is not byte addressable it is rarely used as the main memory of the system. As a result, there must be a controller to access data which is important in order to manage all the essential tasks of accessing NAND Flash device effectively [4]. The major differences between NAND and NOR flash memory (Table 1 and Figure 2). The cell structure of NOR and NAND Memory is shown in Figure 2. The structure of NAND Flash cell is depicted in (Figure 3). Bold lines in this figure capture current path (with or without wires). Depending on how memory cells are interconnected, it is possible to make a distinction between NAND and

NOR Flash memories. In NAND flash, cells are connected in series, resembling a NAND gate. In NOR flash, cells are connected in parallel to the bit lines. Due to the non-volatile nature of this storage media, there is a high demand for it in the mobile communication industry. Flash memory has become the most popular choice for mobile devices. NAND Flash memory is commonly found in portable or embedded memory for computers, digital cameras, mobile phones, MP3 players and other devices where data is generally written or read sequentially [5].

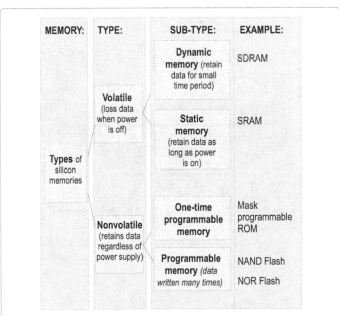

Figure 1: Flash memories as a type of memory device characterized by non-volatility.

*Corresponding author: Novotný R, Brno University of Technology, Technická 3058/10, 616 00 Brno, The Czech Republic, E-mail: novotnyr@feec.vutbr.cz.

	NAND	NOR
Memory cell arrangements (Figure 2)	Cells are arranged in series with the adjacent cells sharing source and drain.	Cells are arranged in parallel with all the source node of the cells connected to the bit line.
Capacity	Tens of Gbits, mass data storage.	Several Gbits, code storage.
Non-volatile	Yes, extremely high cell densities.	Yes, larger chip area per cell.
Interface	I/O interface	Full memory interface
High-speed access	Yes, random access.	Yes, serial access.
Access method	Sequential	Random byte level access
Page mode data access	Yes, organized into pages and erased on a block basis.	No, organized on a byte or word basis.
Performance	Fast read (serial access cycle) Fast write Fasted erase	Fast read (random access) Slow write Slow erase
Price	Lower cost per bit	Higher cost per bit
Life Span	10^5-10^6	10^4-10^5
Write cycles	10^6	10^6
Advantages	Fast programing and erasing	Random access, possible byte programing
Disadvantages	Slow random access, difficult byte programing	Slow programing, slow erasing
Typical uses and applications	Storage, file (disk) applications, voice, data, video recorder and any large sequential data archiving	Networking device memory, replacement of EPROM, applications executed directly from non-volatile memory

Table 1: The major differences between NAND and NOR flash memory.

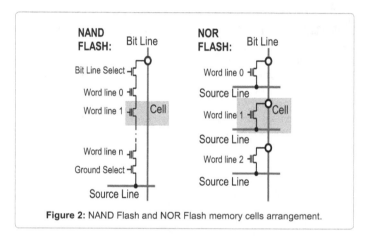

Figure 2: NAND Flash and NOR Flash memory cells arrangement.

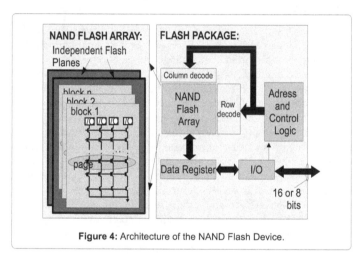

Figure 4: Architecture of the NAND Flash Device.

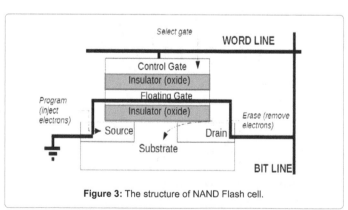

Figure 3: The structure of NAND Flash cell.

NAND Overview: Flash Array and Architecture

The overall architecture of the NAND flash device is shown in Figure 4. The figure shows the NAND Flash Controller which gives interface to application processors. The page register is a critical data holding area in NAND operations. The register is incorporated in order to receive new data while the data register simultaneously programs the NAND Flash array. Unlike most memory technologies, NAND flash is ordered in pages which are written and read as a unit. The elementary unit of operation for a NAND Flash device is one page of data with control commands of the whole block (multiple pages)

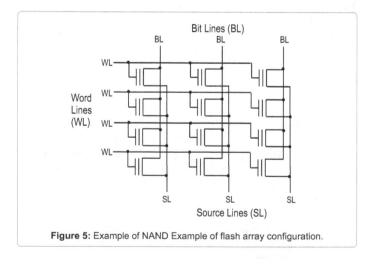

Figure 5: Example of NAND Example of flash array configuration.

or the whole chip [4]. Therefore data can be written only to one page at once. As shown in Figure 5, a page is defined as cells linked with the same word line. This is the smallest programmable unit physically made up of a row of cells. The page size is typically 2 or 4 Kbytes, while a block contains of 32 or 64 pages [6]. Figure 5 is an example of a flash array configuration. The word line (WL) is the horizontal line and the correspondent bit line (BL) is the vertical line. When a large number of a floating gate cells need to be operated in the NAND array it is necessary to consider that one floating gate cell is located at every crossing point of word lines and bit lines. Therefore on each NAND string, the bit lines are connected through the string select transistor to a number of memory transistors in series [7] Control gates are linked to the word line, where the decoded address is applied. The source line connects the sources to common grounds, and bit lines connect the drains together and represent data buses. The voltage concurrence applied to the bit line and word line determines an operation-reading, erasing or programming [8]. NAND Flash devices could be considered as large page and small page devices [4]. There are overall 528 bytes (264 words) per small page. For enormous capacities, typically 1 Gbit and more, a large page is used. A large page device usually has 2048 bytes of data and 64 bytes of spare data per page (Figure 6) while a small page device has 512 bytes of data and 16 bytes of spare data per page. Main stream devices today have 128/256 pages per block and 8 k/16 k bytes per page. The commands sequence for large page and small page devices are different so the controller must be aware of which kind of device is being used. As shown in (Figure 6), cells are organized in pages, and each page is divided into a data area, also named as a "Cell Array" page area, and a redundant area as a spare area for system overhead functions, also named as a "Spare Cell Array" page area. Spare blocks are set apart from the flash storage for remapping bad sectors. This solution prolongs the useful life and reliability of the flash storage device. The spare columns are fully addressable by the user and are typically used for storing Error Correction Code (ECC), wear-leveling, and other organization of information in order to improve data integrity. In operation, bytes from the spare area are equivalent to bytes from the data area and can be used to store the user's data. The spare area is not physically different from the rest of the page (Figure 6). The 2-Gbit NAND device is ordered as 2048 blocks, with 64 pages per block. Each page contains 2112 bytes total, covered of a 2048-byte data area and a 64-byte spare area [9]. Before programming, a page must be erased which sets all data bits to "1". Then only the value "0" can be programmed into each cell. An erased, blank page of NAND flash has no charges stored in any of its floating gates. Unlike block-oriented disk drives, nevertheless, pages must be erased in units of erase blocks including multiple pages (typically 32 to 128) before being re-written.

NAND Flash device: some aspects related to the page, block and plane

A NAND Flash device is composed by the memory array, which

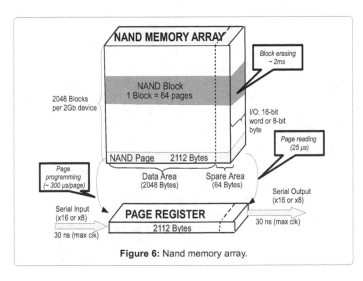

Figure 6: Nand memory array.

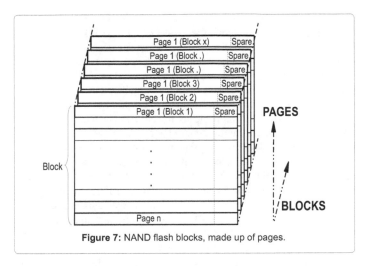

Figure 7: NAND flash blocks, made up of pages.

is separated into several blocks, where a block is the smallest erasable unit of storage (Figure 7) [10]. The reason for this is that all the NAND strings share the same group of word lines that are erased together. Each block involves a set of addressable pages, where MLC typically has 128 pages per block and SLC has 64 pages per block [11]. The basic unit of operation for a NAND Flash device is one page of data with some commands influencing the whole block. However, unlike block oriented disk drives, pages must be erased in units of erase blocks comprising many pages that have previously been re-written. In a block erase operation, a group of consecutive pages is erased in a particular operation. Erase operates on entire blocks and sets all the bits in the block to "1". Flash devices write in full blocks, which means, that in order to write to a block that may already hold some data the flash controller must move the existing data in the block and combine it with the new data and write all the data back to the flash memory. Read and write are both accomplished in two separate stages, containing the transfer of data over the bus to or from the data register, and the transfer between the data register and the flash array. In order to perform read, program, and erase further circuits are necessary (Figure 7). As the NAND die must be placed in a package with a defined size, it is essential to define a floor plan. The NAND Flash memory is composed of the blocks of pages, which could be grouped into a flash plane. Depending on the kind of device, planes are in principal mutually independent. A single plane covers local buffering for read and program data, and can process operations in parallel. Each plane, involves a set of blocks made up of 64 (SLC) or 128 (MLC) pages. NAND Flash devices can contain independent flash planes, characteristically for storing odd and even blocks, allowing concurrent operations for better performance. On the vertical direction a bit line is highlighted, while a word line is shown in the horizontal direction. All bit lines are linked to the sense amplifiers. The purpose of the sense amplifiers is to transform the current sank of the memory cell to a digital signal. The Row Decoder placed among the planes appropriately bias all the word lines belonging to the particular NAND string. In the peripheral part of the NAND Flash device there are voltage regulators and charge pumps, logic circuits, and redundancy structures [12].

Flash translation layer, wear leveling and garbage collection

Flash Translation Layer (FTL) is a software layer, which is between the NAND Flash storage physical media access layer and the File System layer. The FTL is the part of the NAND controller and performs a logical to physical address translation (data locations are represented by their physical addresses), a wear leveling mechanism to prevent the early wear out of block, bad block management, ECC and interleaving operations. The operating system can write to the memory on a page basis without worrying about the details of its physical address space [7]. Due to the nature of NAND flash, wear out is unavoidable when writing to a NAND flash. A related problem is to write to the same address space and create uneven wear of the memory block. The blocks keeping often-updated data are stressed with a large number of write/ erase cycles, while the blocks keeping data updated infrequently are much less stressed. The endurance of the NAND Flash memory can be significantly enhanced taking advantage of wear leveling mechanism which is able to distribute the memory usage uniformly over the memory blocks array [13]. Wear leveling is a process that spreads out the load of frequently rewritten memory blocks over the NAND Flash array as much as possible. When the host application needs an update of the same (logical) sector, the NAND controller dynamically maps the data into a different (physical) sector, keeping track of the mapping. With regard to the need to minimize the impact on performance, garbage collection process is executed in background [7]. There are two types of wear leveling algorithms: dynamic wear leveling and static wear leveling. In case of dynamic wear leveling algorithm the NAND controller internally maintains a map which links the logical block addresses with their corresponding physical Flash memory addresses. The NAND controller then assigns for every write operation a new empty page and links the new page to the original address. In static wear leveling mode, rarely updated static data are kept in "static" blocks while low usage cells are relocated to a new page what results to almost the same number of rewrite cycles [14]. Wear leveling techniques assume that there is the availability of free sectors. When the number of free sectors falls below a critical threshold value, there is an algorithm for sector back-up "compaction" and copying the last valid replication which allows that the obsolete copies can be deleted. Garbage collection prevents erasing a block with valid data and optimizes a process of cleaning the memory. Cleaning policies are set according to criteria used to pick up the block to be erased for garbage collection purposes [7]. NAND Flash memory is free from complex scheduling of the overhead like hard drive disk scheduling, but is affected by the garbage collection issue [15].

Program and Erase of NAND Memory Array

NAND Flash memory is controlled using set of commands, these sets of commands differ from memory to memory. There are many commands, some are universal to all NAND Flash manufacturers while some commands are manufacture specific and supported only by a few devices. According to the Open NAND Flash Interface (ONFI) Standard there is a list of the basic mandatory command set. The most common commands are ´program´, ´read data´, ´erase´, ´reset´, ´program confirmation´, ´read status´ and ´read ID´. Device specific commands contain ´random read´, ´page cache read´, ´random write´, ´page cache write´, ´internal data move´, ´two-planes write´, ´two planes read´, and some others [4]. NAND flash devices carry out three basic operations: program a page, erase a block, and read a page. In a NAND Flash device read and program operations take place on a page basis rather than on a byte or word basis like NOR Flash. This dictates the need to have the size of data I/O register equal to the page size.

Program a page

NAND Flash devices are programmed on a page by page basis. During the page program operation, a page is written into the data register and then programmed into the memory array. First the page address and the command word are moved into the device followed by the programming data. The programming steps of a NAND Flash device differ depending on whether it is a small block or a large block device and whether features such as a cache mode or two plane programming are applied. During programming, the ready/busy signal (R/B) is low to indicate that the device is in the busy state. The R/B- signal is low when the NAND chip operates a program, read or erase command and signalizes if the NAND flash device is ready for other operations.

Erase a block

Flash memory allows only two states: erased and non-erased. A given bit of data can only be written when the media is in an erase state. When data is written into, the bit is considered dirty and unusable for other write operations. A write operation in any type of flash device can only be accomplished on an erased unit and so a write operation must be preceded by an erase operation. In order to must be erased. During era recover the bit to the erase state, a meaningful large block of flash called an erase block, also called as an erase zone, sure operation all cells on the same bit string are erased. In the erase state, a byte can be either all zeroes or all ones depending on the kind of flash device. As a result, the flash technology does not allow the changing of individual bits or bytes from a non-erased state back to an erased state.

Read a page

Bits in a flash cell are read by changing the voltages on rows and columns of cells followed by assessing the results. In a page read operation, a page is moved from memory into the output data register. NAND Flash devices are read by shifting in the address and command. Once the command and address are shifted in, it requires a few tenths of a micro second to open a page. After a page is opened, data can be lifted out of the device by using the read (RD) command signal. Certain devices support cache read mode and some of them support random data read within a page functionality. NAND Flash memory reads and writes in high-speed, sequential mode, handling data in pages. Differences such as cache programming, random programming and two plane programming are enabled only by some NAND Flash devices.

Merging log blocks with blocks containing stale data

When units smaller than an erase block are mapped, stale data can remain there. Then the pages affected by the stale data are not accessible for new data. In the limited case of hybrid Flash Translation Layers (FTL), the used process consists of merging log blocks with blocks containing stale data, and programming the result into one or more free blocks [16]. Merge operation can be one of the following three types (full, partial, and switch merge) [17]. A switch merge is applied during sequential writing. The log block contains a sequence of pages precisely replacing an existing data block, and may replace it without any further operation. This means that the old block can then be erased. A partial merge duplicates valid pages from a data block to the log block, after which these two may be substituted. A full merge is desirable when data in the log block is out of order. Valid pages from the log block and the related data block are copied together into a different free block. The original data block and log block are then both erased [5].

NAND Flash Memory Characteristics

Development of NAND Flash memories has been driven by a gradual progress in novel cell structures and architectural solutions oriented to both reducing cell size and upgrading product functions. The NAND flash memory has become an indispensable component in embedded systems for its flexible features. Applications may need lesser or greater erase counts, different error correction capabilities, and a range of storage longevity requirements. NAND flash devices differs in many parameters and characteristics that include cell types, architectural, performance, timing parameters and command set. The following chapter provides an overview of the typical characteristics.

Architecture, Sequentially reading, and high density

NAND Flash architecture based on independent blocks was introduced by Toshiba in 1989. In the NAND-flash, unit cells are linked sequentially, where the cells resemble a NAND gate. This layout and architecture inhibits cells from being read and programmed independently. These cells must be read in series. Due to their excellent scalability and performances, NAND Flash has achieved very high density in terms of bits per mm^2 and feature size scaling.

Flash memory non-volatility and low power consumption

Flash memory is non-volatile, which implies that it retains data even without being powered-of. Non-volatility comes from the types of transistors used which are floating gate transistors. Since stored data stays even when the memory device is not electrically powered it does not need power to maintain its data. NAND flash is the only memory, which offers both GB density and non-volatility.

NAND Flash memory programming and erasing based on block-wise base

Flash memory has the ability to be programmed and erased electrically, hence combining the advantages of EPROMs and EEPROMs. They increased flexibility compared to electrically programmable read only memories (EPROM's), which are electrically programmable but erasable via ultraviolet (UV) radiation. The dissimilarity between the Flash Memory and EEPROM lies in the fact, that EEPROM erases and rewrites its content byte by byte. Since flash memory erases or writes its data in entire blocks, this makes it very fast in comparison with EEPROM. A single cell could be electrically programmable and a large amount of cells (block, sector, or page) are electrically erasable almost at the same time. Since NAND flash does not offer a random-access external address bus the required data are read on a block-wise basis (also termed as page access), where each block keeps hundreds to thousands of bits, similar to a kind of sequential data access.

Serial storage properties

From the system designer's perspective, the biggest difference is that the NAND Flash is a serial storage device whereas most other memories are random access memory (RAM). Serial storage device requires longer access times for obtaining data. The effect is that NAND flash as a serial storage device does not give a random-access external address bus and needs a special NAND Flash controller to access data and therefore is hardly ever used as the main memory of the system. System designers must reflect these differences when interfacing the end system with the NAND Flash device. Since most microprocessors and microcontrollers require byte-level random access this is one of the main explanations why NAND-flash is inappropriate to replace the RAM memory. The speed at which the DRAM or SRAM may access data and also their capability to address at byte level is incomparable with the Flash memory.

Noise in the reading process

In the NAND flash the only way to access the discrete cell for either reading or writing is across the other cells in its bit line. This enhances noise related to the read process [18], and also needs attention during writing to ensure that adjacent cells in the string are not disturbed. Many of the more difficult characteristics of NAND flash are due to this

organization, which removes much of the decoding overhead found in other memory technologies.

Restricted write endurance

Since cells in a flash chip will fail after a limited number of writes limited write endurance is a key characteristic of flash memory [19]. Infrequently cycled blocks will have longer retention and often cycled blocks will have shorter retention. It is highly important to employ a wear leveling mechanism, which ensures equal memory block load rather than cycling and potentially destroying the same block. Wear leveling is necessary on MLC (multi-level cell) devices where blocks can normally support less than 10,000 erase program cycles and offers additional advantages on SLC (single-level cell) devices where blocks can offer up to 100,000 erase-program cycles.

Some extended features

There are some extended features offered in addition to those basic ones:

- Device operation status read and manufacturer ID read,

- One-time-programmable area (OTP area) to keep vendor unique data such as serial number,

- Locking or unlocking the blocks to avert data loss on unintended software performance,

- Internal movement of the block into another memory location escaping time consuming data relocations from and back to chip (copy-back),

- Only a portion of a page may be programmed at a time and the rest may be programmed at some other time, avoiding block erasing (partial page programming),

- Boot-like feature, page 0 is loaded into data register automatically after reset or power-on,

- Supplementary cache register (cache operation) for read operation or pipe-lined program (Figure 8).

Error Correction Code in NAND Flash Memories

In digital communication, the quantity of bit errors is the number of received bits of a data stream sent over a communication channel that have been changed due to interference, noise, bit synchronization errors or distortion. The bit error rate or bit error ratio (BER) is the number of bits that have errors divided by the total quantity of

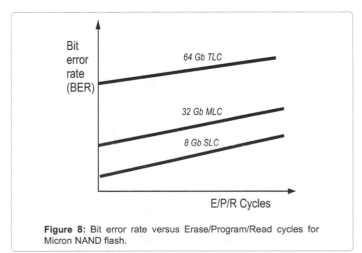

Figure 8: Bit error rate versus Erase/Program/Read cycles for Micron NAND flash.

transmitted bits throughout a given time interval. BER is a unit less measure, frequently formulated as a percentage. The raw bit error rate relates to the probability of a bit error occurring in an individual bit cell on a flash device [20]. Figure 8 shows that the bit error rate (BER) is much worse in parts that have consumed erase, program, read cycles, and is different for SLC, MLC and TLC NAND Flash technology.

Noise sources in NAND flash and the bit error rate (BER)

There are many noise causes existing in NAND flash, such as random noise, cell-to-cell interference (inter-cell interference), read or write disturb, programming errors, retention process (retention errors), random-telegraph noise, background-pattern noise, charge leakage and trapping generation, etc. [21]. Such noise sources considerably shrink the storage reliability of flash memory. Over time the quantity of affected cells increases (Figure 9). This figure shows that Read Disturb Error Rate is empirically much worse in devices that have consumed erase, program and read cycles than in uncycled devices [22]. Quality of data retention for uncycled or cycled devices is a natural consequence of the memory cell limited life (Figure 9). Bit errors are a natural consequence of uncertainty when executing any data storage and must be moderated by software or hardware so that the integrity of the original information is not compromised [20]. For NAND flash, this is implemented by using protecting groups of bits with a higher-level error correction algorithm. To reduce possible errors, Error Correcting Codes (ECC) are widely used in NAND memories. Through ECC it is possible to fill the discrepancy between the error probability offered by the memory and the desired error probability. ECC algorithm takes care of the failures during the life of the device and improves the reliability of the read operation in the customer final application [7]. Preferably, all errors in the storage would be adjusted [23]. In reality the algorithm protects against a range of errors that are probable to happen (Figure 10). The drawbacks of NAND scaling: decreasing endurance, increasing ECC [24]. Over time NAND flash has augmented storage density by storing more bits per cell and moving to smaller geometries. As NAND Flash memory moves towards more progressive process nodes, the cost of devices is decreasing, but the cells become more vulnerable [25]. The quantity of bits kept per cell is increasing, and bit values are represented by smaller voltage ranges, generating more uncertainty in the value stored in the bit cell due to more ambiguity in the amount of charge [20]. As the bit cells get smaller, the individual cells are more vulnerable to failure brought by high-voltage stress because fewer electrons can be trapped in the floating gates. The effect is to narrow the valid voltage ranges for a given value, increasing the probability for program and read disturbances. Since this solution requires higher levels of error correction mechanism in order to ensure

	SLC		MLC		
NAND Process	70/60/50 nm	40/30 nm	70/60 nm	50 nm	40/30 nm
ECC required	1-bit	4-bit	4-bit	4 ~ 8 bit	12 ~ 24 bit or more
Erase Cycle	100 K per block	100 K per block	10 K per block	5 K~ 10 K per block	3 K ~ 5 K per block
Data Retention	10 years	10 years	10 years	10 years	5 years

Table 2: Error correction for MLC flash and for SLC flash.

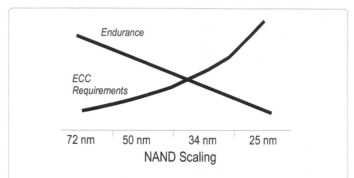

Figure 10: The drawbacks of NAND scaling: decreasing endurance, increasing ECC.

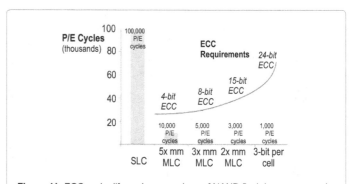

Figure 11: ECC and a life cycle comparison of NAND flash by process node.

the integrity of the data on the flash device, the new technology needs more Error Correction Code (Deal, Hamming, RS, BCH, LDPC) [26]. The accepted uncertainty upsurges the probability for data to be stored or read incorrectly, requiring higher levels of error correction for MLC flash than for SLC flash [20] (Table 2). Devices using NAND flash must integrate very high levels of error correction in order to guarantee support for next generation flash devices (Figure 10). A one-bit ECC algorithm is capable of correcting one failure bit per 512 bytes. SLC flash is able to work with single-bit correction over 512 byte sectors because the individual bit error rate is really low (Table 2) [24].

Multi-Level Cell (MLC) flash has required more powerful correction algorithms capable of correcting four to eight bits to manage the higher bit error rates arising from the greater uncertainty of charging and to detect the various voltage ranges in a single bit cell (Figure 11) [20]. For example the industry has started to deploy LDPC (low-density parity-check) in SSD controllers in order to improve error correction capability [27] (Figure 11). ECC and a life cycle comparison of NAND flash by process node: increase in correction capability is not enough to maintain endurance of the cell [28].

Error detection and correction in NAND Flash Memories

The error correction code (ECC) permits data that is being read or transmitted to be checked for errors and, when necessary, corrected.

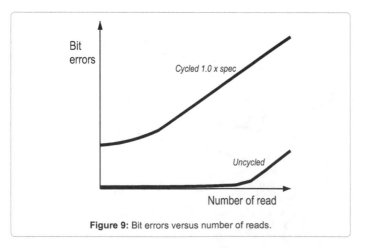

Figure 9: Bit errors versus number of reads.

ECC is a worthy way to recover the incorrect value from the residual good data bits [4]. Error detection and correction or error control includes techniques that permit reliable transfer of digital data by the detection of errors and reconstruction of the original, corrected error-free data. If the ECC cannot correct the error throughout read, it may still detect the error. The application of ECC is used with NAND flash parts to compensate bits that could fail during device operation. On-chip error correction code resolves many supposed complications of working with a NAND solution [29]. On chip ECC techniques have rarely been adopted [30], NAND controller includes a hardware that supports ECC calculations. Currently the error correction is an integral part of the NAND flash that guarantees data integrity. Up to now, more error correction has been required for MLC NAND technology, whereas SLC NAND has characteristically required only 1-bit ECC for densities up to 4 Gbits fabricated at 43 nm [25]. Current trends in the NAND flash market resulting to changes that must be made in the error correction algorithms to preserve the integrity of data stored in next-generation NAND flash devices [20]. The SLC NAND Flash devices, fabricated at 32 nm or 24 nm, require 4-bit or 8-bit ECC, respectively, per 512 bytes [25].

NAND Flash ECC Algorithms

NAND Flash devices need appropriate error correction algorithms to diminish errors that occur during the programming and read operations [20]. The Life span of NAND Flash could be prolonged without more ECC bits due to the especially proposed operation algorithm. Error detection is usually realized using an appropriate hash function or checksum algorithm. A hash function adds a fixed-length tag to a data, which can be whenever recalculated and verified (Table 3). The basic system of ECC theory is to enlarge some redundancy for protection. The redundancy permits the receiver to detect a limited number of errors that may happen anywhere in data, and usually to correct these errors without retransmission. Different ECC techniques are necessary in various types of flash memory. Error correction codes are typically divided into two classes: block codes and convolution codes. The difference between these codes is the encoding principle [31]. Block coding works with messages of fixed length. In the block codes, the information bits are followed by the parity bits.

In convolutional codes the information bits are spread along the sequence [32] Hamming codes, Bose-Chaudur-Hocquenghem (BCH) codes [33], Reed-Solomon (RS) codes, and Low-density parity check (LDPC) codes are most notable block codes and have been widely used in communication, optical, and other systems [22]. The choice of the most effective correction code is a compromise between the number of symbol errors that need to be corrected and the additional storage requests for the generated parity data. Early designs implementing SLC NAND used either no error correction or marginally correcting Hamming codes which offer single error correct and double error detect capabilities [20]. Given the low bit error rates of early flash, this was satisfactory to correct the sporadic bit error that arose. As bit error rates enlarged with each successive generation of both SLC and MLC flash, designers progressed to more complex cyclic codes such as Reed-Solomon (R/S) or Bose-Chaudhuri-Hocquenghem (BCH) algorithms to increase the correction capability [20]. While both of the algorithms are similar, R/S codes execute correction over multi-bit symbols while BCH makes correction over single-bit symbols (Table 4). Number of bits required for various ECC correction strengths [34]. Here is how it works for data storage: when any k-bit data is written to flash memory, an encoder circuit makes the parity bits, adds these parity bits to the k-bit data and creates an n-bit code-word [22] Parity bits form a code that refers to the bit sequence in the word and is stored along with the unit of data. The routinely computed ECC, i.e. the whole code-word, is kept in the spare area of the page to which it relates. Throughout the reading operation, a decoder circuit examines errors in a code-word, and corrects the mistaken bits within its error capability, thereby recovering the code-word [22]. When the unit of data is demanded for reading, a code for the stored and about-to-be-read word is calculated using the algorithm. ECC's are again calculated, and these values are compared to the ECC values held in the spare area. If the codes match, the data is free of errors. The outcome of this assessment yields an ECC "syndrome" that shows whether errors occurred, how many bits are in error, and, if the errors are recoverable, the bit position of incorrect bits. If the codes do not match, the missing or incorrect bits are determined through the code comparison and the bit or bits are corrected or supplied. The additional information represent redundancy added by the code is recycled by the receiver to recover the original data. The decoding phase can reduce read performance as well as the memory response time. A typical ECC will correct a one-bit error in each 2048 bits (256 bytes) using 22 bits of ECC code, or a one-bit error in each 4096 bits (512 bytes) using 24 bits of ECC code. However, as raw BER increases, 2-bit error correction BCH code becomes a desired level of ECC. Next generation flash devices will move to smaller geometries and increased number of bits per cell, features that will increase the underlying bit error rate [20].

NAND Type	SLC	MLC	TLC
Datasheet ECC Requirement	1-bit ECC per 528 bytes of data	12-bit ECC per 539 bytes of data	60-bit ECC per 1146 bytes of data
Bit Error Rate	0.02%	0.28%	0.65%
Suggested ECC	SEC/DEC Hamming Code or Reed-Solomon Code	BCH Algorithms	Low Density Parity Check (LDPC) Codes

Table 3: ECC recommendations.

Error Correction Level	Bits Required in the NAND Flash Spare Area		
	Hamming	Reed-Solomon	BCH
1	13	18	13
2	N/A	36	26
3	N/A	54	39
4	N/A	72	52
5	N/A	90	65
6	N/A	108	78
7	N/A	126	91
8	N/A	144	104
9	N/A	162	117
10	N/A	180	130

Table 4: Number of bits required for various ECC correction strengths.

Summary

Today, flash memory is one of the most popular, reliable, and flexible non-volatile devices to store data. NAND flash memory has become very popular for usage in various applications where a large amount of data has to be stored. This article discusses important aspects related to the NAND Flash memory, storage reliability and the actual bit error rate.

A NAND Flash device is composed by the memory array, which is separated into several blocks. In general it performs three basic operations: program a page, erase a block, and read a page. There are many noise sources that exist in NAND flash, which considerably shrink the storage reliability of flash memory [35]. The paper presents a preliminary technology review, which was conducted in connection with the preparation of an experiment for evaluating the reliability of

NAND flash memory. The purpose of this study was to summarize the theoretical background. The preliminary aim was to identify factors affecting the reliability for potential usage of the methodology of a statistical planned experiment (DOE, Design of Experiments) [36]. However, after considering all aspects, it has been realized that this approach is not possible. Therefore, further research will involve life-cycle and reliability testing using the Weibull analysis method [37].

Acknowledgement

This research has been supported by the European ARTEMIS Industry Association by the project 7H12002 "Interactive Power Devices for Efficiency in Automotive with Increased Reliability and Safety" and by the CZ.1.05/1.1.00/02.0068 project OP RDI "CEITEC-Central European Institute of Technology".

References

1. Pavan P, Bez R, Olivo P, Zanoni E (1997) Flash Memory Cells—An Overview. In Proceedings of the IEEE 85: 1248-1271.

2. Agrawal N, Prabhakaran V, Wobber T, Davis J, Manasse M, et al. (2008) Design Tradeoffs for SSD Performance. In USENIX Technical Conference, Boston, USA.

3. Gong Yi (2004) Testing Flash Memories. Available online.

4. NAND Flash FAQ (2013)

5. Boboila S, Desnoyers P (2010) Write endurance in flash drives: measurements and analysis. In Proceedings of the 8th USENIX conference on File and storage technologies, San Jose, USA 115-128.

6. Choi GS, Mankyu S (2014) Investigating Page Sizes in NAND Flash Memory. Proceedings 12: 377-379.

7. Micheloni R, Crippa L, Alessia M (2010) Inside NAND Flash Memories. Springer: New York, USA.

8. Paikin A (2004) Flash memory.Hitequest.com.

9. Nand Flash (2013) http://www.cheadledatarecovery.co.uk/wpcontent/uploads/2013/01/Nand.gif

10. Sandvido M, Chu F, Kulkarni A (2008) NAND Flash Memory and Its Role in Storage Architectures.

11. Cooke J (2014) The Inconvenient Truths of NAND Flash Memory.

12. Micheloni R, Marelli A, Commodaro S (2010) NAND overview: from memory to systems. Springer: Netherlands.

13. Campardo G, Tiziani F, Laculo M (2011) Memory Mass Storage. Springer: Heidelberg, Dordrecht, London, New York.

14. Joshi Y, Kumar P (2012) Energy Efficient Thermal Management of Data Center. Springer: New York, Dordrecht, Heidelberg, London.

15. Lim SH, Choi H, Kyo P (2007) Journal Remap-Based FTL for Journaling File System with Flash Memory. In High Performance Computing and Communications: Third International Conference, Houston, USA, HPCC, 192-203.

16. Gal E, Toledo S (2005) Mapping Structures for Flash Memories: Techniques and Open Problems. In Software-Science, Technology and Engineering. Proceedings. IEEE International Conference 83-92.

17. Gupta A, Kim Y, Urgaonkar B (2009) DFTL: A Flash Translation Layer Employing Demand-based Selective Caching of Page-level Address Mappings. In 14th international conference on Architectural support for programming languages and operating systems (ASPLOS'09), Washington, DC, USA, 229-240.

18. Aritome S, Shirota R , Hemink G, Endoh T , Masuoka F (1993) Reliability Issues of Flash Memory Cells. In Proceedings of the IEEE 81: 776 - 788.

19. Desnoyers P (2009) Empirical Evaluation of NAND Flash Memory Performance. In ACM SIGOPS Operating Systems Review 44: 50-54.

20. Deal E (2013) Trends of NAND Flash Memory Error Correction. Cyclic Design

21. Wang X, Dong G, Pan L, Zhou R (2013) Error Correction Codes and Signal Processing in Flash Memory.

22. Heidecker J (2012) NAND Flash Qualification Guideline. In 3rd NASA Electronic Parts and Packaging (NEPP) Program Electronic Technology Workshop USA.

23. Yang C, Emre Y, Chakrabarti C (2012) Product Code Schemes for Error Correction in MLC NAND Flash Memories. In Very Large Scale Integration (VLSI) Systems, IEEE Transactions on 20: 2302-2314.

24. How to handle the increasing ECC requirements of the latest NAND Flash memories in your Industrial Design (2013)

25. Deal E (2011) Hamming, RS, BCH LDPC-The Alphabet Soup of NAND ECC

26. Kuo W, Huang C, Chang H, Ko L, Hsueh W (2014) An Efficient Fault Detection Algorithm for NAND Flash Memory.

27. Shimpi LA (2010) Micron's Clear NAND: 25nm + ECC, Combats Increasing Error Rates.

28. Naftali S (2013) Signal processing and the evolution of NAND flash memory.

29. Serial NAND Flash Memory Flyer(2011) micron.com

30. Micheloni R, Marelli A, Ravasio R (2014) Error Correction Codes for Non-Volatile Memories. Springer: Netherlands.

31. Tomashevich V, Hanus P (2014) Convolutional Codes.

32. Micheloni R, Marelli A, Eshghi K (2012) Inside Solid State Drives (SSDs). Springer: London.

33. Carlo S, Fabiano M, Indaco M, Prinetto P (2013) Design and Optimization of Adaptable BCH Codecs for NAND Flash Memories. In Microprocessors and Microsystems 37: 407-419.

34. Micron Technology (2013)NAND Flash 101: An Introduction to NAND Flash and How to Design It In to Your Next Product.

35. Grupp L, Caulfield A, Coburn J, Swanson S, Yaakobi E, et al. (2009) In Characterizing Flash Memory: Anomalies, Observations, and Applications. MICRO'09, New York, USA.

36. Montgomery D (2012) Design and Analysis of Experiments, 8th Edition. John Wiley and Sons: New York.

37. Zhao K, Zhao W, Sun H, Zhang T, Zhang X (2013) LDPC-in SSD: Making Advanced Error Correction Codes Work Effectively in Solid State Drives.

15

A Comparative Analysis of Social Networking Analysis Tools

Hemant Agrawal, Ajay Thakur, Rajan Slathia, Sumangali K*

School of Information Technology and Engineering, VIT University, Vellore, Tamil Nadu, 632014, India

Abstract

Informal communities have known a vital improvement since the presence of web 2.0 stages. This prompts a developing requirement for informal community mining and Social Network Analysis (SNA) systems and instruments with a specific end goal to give more profound examination of the system additionally to distinguish groups in perspective of different applications. Thus, a ton of works have concentrated on chart portrayal or bunching and a few new SNA apparatuses have been created over these last years. The motivation behind this paper is to think about some of these instruments which actualize calculations devoted to informal community examination.

Keywords: Betweenness; Nearness; Social network analysis; Visualization; Vertices

Introduction

The blast of Web 2.0 (online journals, wikis, substance offering destinations, informal communities, and so forth.) opens up new viewpoints for imparting and overseeing data. In this setting, among a few developing exploration fields concerning "Web Intelligence", a standout amongst the most energizing is the improvement of utilizations spent significant time in the treatment of the social measurement of the Web. Especially, building and overseeing virtual groups for Virtual Enterprises require the improvement of another era of apparatuses incorporating interpersonal organization displaying and examination. A very long while back, the first deals with Social Networks Analysis (SNA) was done via specialists in Social Sciences who needed to comprehend the conduct and advancement of human systems. A few pointers were proposed to portray the on-screen characters and additionally the system itself. One of these indicators, for case, was the centrality that can be utilized as a part of showcasing to find the early adopters or the individuals whose action is prone to spread data to numerous individuals in a briefest manner. These days, the wide utilization of Internet around the globe permits to join quite a few people. As pointed in the Gartner study, this critical advancement of the systems offers ascend to a developing requirement for informal organization mining and informal community investigation strategies so as to give more profound perception of the system and to distinguish groups and study their development for applications in zones, for example, group advertising, social shopping, suggestion components and personalization sifting or graduated class management. For this reason, while numerous new advancements (wikis, social bookmarks and social labeling, and so on) and administrations (GData, Google Friend Connect, Open Social Face book Beacon) were proposed on web, a few new SNA devices have been created. These instruments are exceptionally valuable to dissect hypothetically an interpersonal organization additionally to speak to it graphically. They figure diverse markers which describe the system's structure, the connections between the performing artists and additionally the position of a specific performer. They additionally permit the examination of a few systems.

The motivation behind this paper is to present some genuine significant instruments and to depict some of their functionalities. A comparable examination has as of now been done in, however with a more measurable vision. Our relative review on the condition of- the-craftsmanship apparatuses for system visualization and investigation is centered on three fundamental focuses:

– Graph visualization;

– Computation of different pointers giving a neighborhood (i.e. at the hub level) or a worldwide portrayal (i.e. in general diagram);

– Community discovery

The hypothetical system for informal community investigation was presented in the 1960s. Taking after the fundamental thought of Moreno who proposed to speak to operators by focuses associated by lines. Therefore, they are considered as the organizers of the cutting edge diagram hypothesis for informal organization investigation. Two sorts of diagrams can be characterized to speak to an interpersonal organization: one-mode and two-mode charts.

One-mode graph

At the point when the connections between performing artists are viewed as, the interpersonal organization can be spoken to by a graph $G = (V, E)$ where V is the situated of hubs (or vertices) related to the performers, and $E \in V \times V$ is the situated of edges which compare to their connections. This is the case, for occurrence in a traditional dataset identified with a karate club where the hubs compare to the individuals from the club and where the edges are utilized to portray their fellowships. At the point when the connections are coordinated, edges arc supplanted by bends. Hubs and also edges can have traits. All things considered, we can speak then about named diagrams.

Two-mode diagram

At the point when the connections between two sorts of components are considered, for instance the individuals and the rivalries in the karate club, a two-mode diagram is most suited to speak to two sorts of vertices. The edges are permitted just between hubs of distinctive sorts. The most widely recognized approach to store two-mode information is a rectangular information network with the two hub sorts separately in columns and segments. Case in point, a 2 dimensional grid with the performing artists in lines and the occasions in sections can speak to a two-mode chart for the karate club. This representation is exceptionally regular in SNA. Two-modes diagrams can be changed in one-mode

*Corresponding author: Sumangali K, School of Information Technology and Engineering, VIT University, Vellore-632014, Tamil Nadu, India
E-mail: sumivenkata@gmail.com

charts utilizing a projection on one hub sort and making edges between these hubs utilizing distinctive conglomeration capacities. The idea of diagram can be summed up by a hypergraph, in which two arrangements of vertices can be associated by an edge.

Visualization

Visualization is a standout amongst the most needed functionalities in chart taking care of projects, and this stays valid for system examination programming. Numerous calculations comprise in pushing confined vertices toward unfilled spaces and in gathering contiguous hubs. These calculations are specifically roused by physical phenomena. Case in point, edges can be seen as springs and hubs can be taken care of as electrically charged particles. The area of every component is recalculated regulated. These techniques require a few cycles so as to give a decent result on extensive charts. Power based formats are easy to grow however are liable to poor neighborhood least results. Among these calculations, we can specify, Fruchterman and Reingold [1], which is an all-around utilized power based calculation for diagram visualization. An option is the calculation of Kamada and Kawai [2], which has a speedier union than Fruchterman and Reingold, yet, which regularly does not give so great results than this last one. It can be conceived to utilize Kamada and Kawai so as to ascertain a first position of the vertices. These two systems are among those called "spring calculations". Some different formats are distinctive in the way they give a perspective of the area for a hub (i.e. outspread design, hyperbolic format). 3d diagram visualization is the legitimate augmentation of planar representations. The majority of the systems proposed are versatile to 3d. Neighborhood zoom based, alleged fish-eye usefulness can be additionally intriguing to outwardly investigate extensive diagrams.

Pointer based system depiction

Numerous quantitative pointers have been characterized on systems. The descriptors at the system level are utilized to look at the extent of hubs versus edges, or to assess properties of the chart like the arbitrariness or little world appropriations. Then again, the descriptors at the hub level are helpful for recognizing the hubs deliberately put in the system or highlighting those that take a critical part in correspondence, for example, extensions or center points.

Vertex and edge scoring: The spot of a given performer in the system can be portrayed utilizing measures in view of vertex scoring. Regular sorts of vertex scoring are the centrality measures. For instance, to gauge how critical an individual is inside an interpersonal organization, Freeman [3] has recognized three principle centralities:

a) Degree centrality: The first and easiest measure is the degree centrality. It underlines hubs with the high degrees.

b) Closeness centrality: For associated charts, closeness centrality is the reverse of the normal separation to every other hub. This marker can be helpful for some applications in this present reality. Case in point, if edges were lanes, the intersection (vertex) with the most elevated closeness centrality would be the best place for crisis administrations.

c) Betweenness centrality: Betweenness centrality is another centrality measure of a vertex inside a chart. Vertices that happen on numerous briefest ways between different vertices have higher betweenness than those that don't.

d) Page rank: The score registered by Page Rank is higher for hubs that are exceedingly joined and associated with hubs that are very joined themselves.

e) HITS calculation: Hyperlink-induced topic search (HITS, otherwise called center points and powers) figures two scores: center point and power score. The more a vertex has active circular segments, the higher is its center point score. The more a vertex has approaching connections, the higher is its power score. Toward the starting each hub are considered as center and power scores are settled to a steady. At that point the scores are upgraded and they focalize after couple of cycles.

System scoring: System thickness is the rate of edges in the system over the quantity of edges that could exist in the system. This measure shows if the fundamental diagram is meager or thick. These markers have following been made an interpretation of in renditions relevant to coordinated charts, valuable in data dispersal hypothesis. This asymmetry prompts the idea of notoriety.

a) Dyad census: A dyad is a term obtained from social science used to portray a gathering of two individuals, i.e. the littlest conceivable social gathering. By expansion, it is utilized as a part of informal community investigation for outlining two associating hubs. Every dyad is arranged into one of the common, hilter kilter or invalid classes and the extent of each of these cases is given. These checks help to know whether the connections take after an irregular or a small world conveyance.

b) Triad census: with a specific end goal to augment the dyad check, Davis and Leinhardt [4] have proposed the triad number, with 16 particular cases (coordinated diagrams). Triadic examination performs the include of the triads every setup. Data gave is again valuable to contrasting a system and the irregular model.

Diagram and vertices closeness: In interpersonal organization investigation instruments, one can hope to discover capacities communicating likeness of hubs in a chart furthermore capacities to gauge the similitude between diagrams themselves. A few samples of similitude measures accessible in virtual products are the Jaccard, Dice or Tanimoto likeness.

Grouping or group location

The point of grouping is to identify gatherings of hubs with thick associations inside the gatherings and sparser associations between the gatherings. These gatherings are called groups by analysts and information mining experts while sociologists like to utilize the word groups. An extremely finish study on diagram grouping can be found in.

Fundamental methodologies of group discovery: Among the diverse systems proposed to distinguish groups, two primary methodologies can be recognized: from one perspective there is the progressive approach in which the hubs are totaled in a chain of importance of bunches from the discrete part to the entire system. This methodology assesses the vicinity between two hubs through a similitude measure and fabricates the gatherings utilizing an agglomerative procedure, similar to the single linkage calculation or the complete linkage calculation. Then again, there is the partition bunching which comprises in specifically isolating the system into a predefined number of gatherings. The base cut strategy is a case of this methodology in which the gatherings are characterized so as the quantity of edges between them is minimized. The virtual products considered in this benchmarking incorporate three grouping strategies. The first is the Newman [5] and Givan system. This is a progressive system, in view of the betweenness of the edges, which comprises in evacuating the edge with most astounding betweenness, and rehashing this procedure until no edge remains. The second strategy, called Walk trap is a partition calculation that uses an arbitrary stroll in the diagram keeping in mind the end goal to recognize the segments in which the walker has a tendency to remain. A progressive bunching is then performed to get the bunches. The last calculation is called spinglass. With various leveled techniques, a dendograms the best representation for picking the quantity of groups to hold. Another approach to focus the quantity of gatherings that must be held comprises in expanding a specific criteria, for example, measured quality.

Benchmarking

Numerous apparatuses have been made for system investigation and visualization purposes. An extensive rundown of devices is accessible on Wikipedia1, with altogether different methodologies. Numerous are absolutely scholarly programming. Some are situated toward visualization, other comprise in APIs permitting chart and hypergraph displaying with once in a while the likelihood of movement on vertices, for example, JUNG. A few apparatuses are enhanced for expansive information control. Others propose low level usage of particular calculations. Five instruments are considered: Pajek, Gephi,

Netlytic, GraphViz and Social Network Visualizer. The decision of them is taking into account:

– A harmony between settled devices and more up to date ones, in view of late advancement gauges (regarding ergonomics, measured quality and information convenience),

– A SNA perspective. The devices must give fundamental measurements to systems,

– The systems size can achieve countless hubs.

Pajek is a legacy programming, with its own chart situated methodology. Gephi speaks to a present day answer for diagram study with GUI (graphical client interface), open source logic and plugin introduction. Networkx and igraph are two key libraries for proficient huge chart taking care of. The accompanying segments portray the dataset and the criteria utilized as a part of the benchmark (Figures 1-5).

Dataset

The dataset considered in this overview is broadly utilized

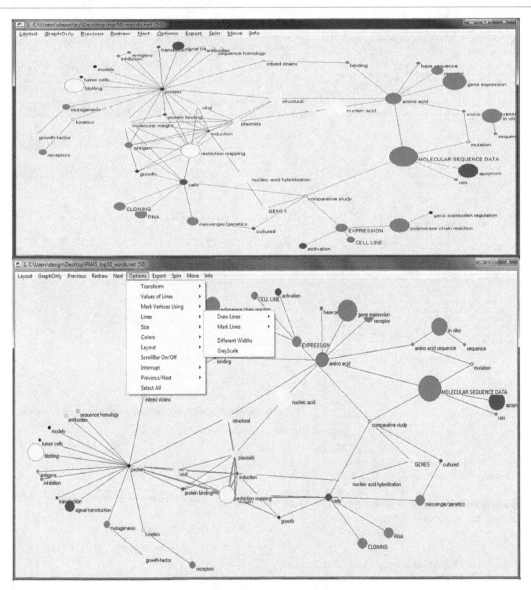

Figure 1: Pajekscreenshots.

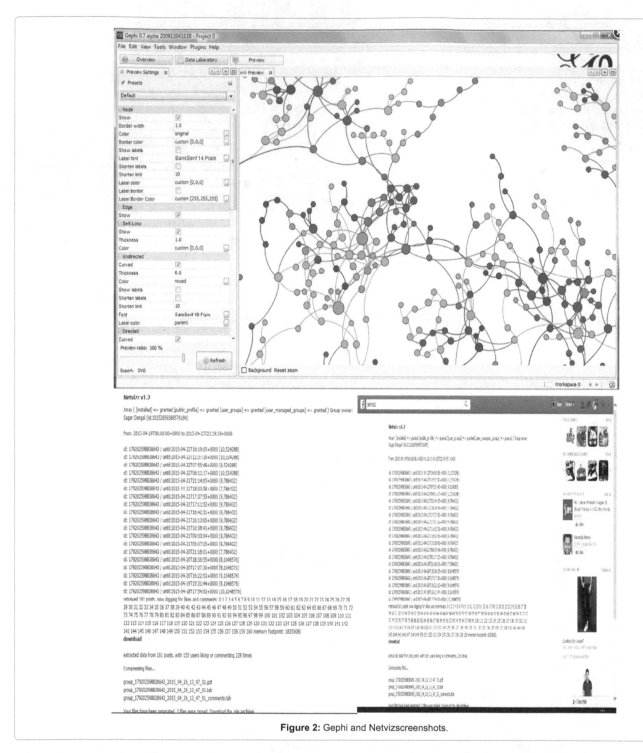

Figure 2: Gephi and Netvizscreenshots.

information set as a part of SNA writing. This dataset presents the connection diagram between 34 individuals from the karate club of a US college in 1970. Zachary's Karate Club2 has 34 vertex and 78 edges. Every vertex is numbered. An edge is available between two hubs when the two relating people "reliably connected.

Assessed criteria

In our benchmark, we have chosen an arrangement of assessment criteria. These criteria are the permit of the instrument, the information arrangement took care of, the diagram sorts upheld, the measure of

hubs that can be loaded in a sensible time, the accessible markers, the bunching calculations included and the visualization formats accessible. Every basis is itemized in the accompanying areas.

Document forms: There are primarily three approaches to express in a serial way the structure of a system:

– Nearness framework (square for coordinated charts, triangular for undirected ones)

– Nearness records (for coordinated diagrams), where the source hub is trailed by the rundown of the hubs that are the focuses of each

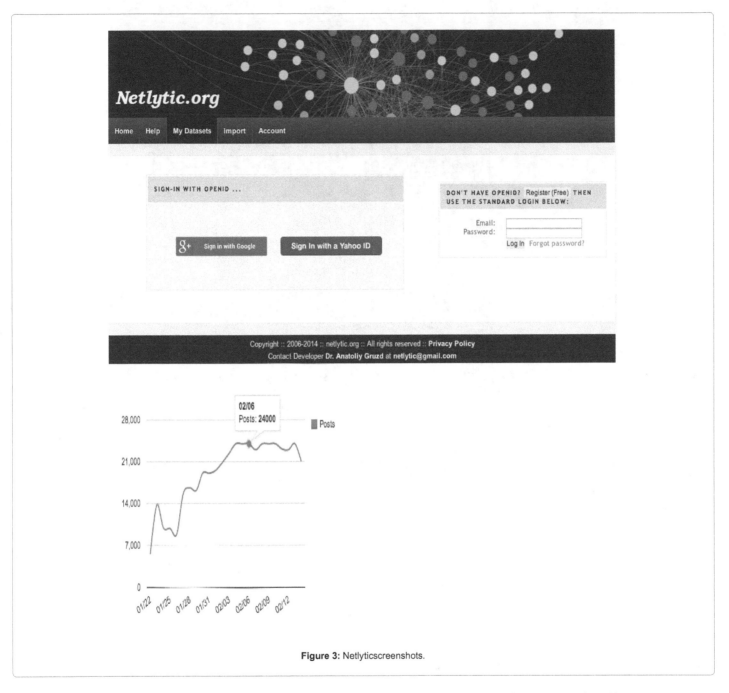

Figure 3: Netlyticscreenshots.

curves beginning from the hub

– Vertices sets. A few document configurations have been made keeping in mind the end goal to give diagram representations.

Here are the primary ones:

a. Pajek chart record configuration (.net augmentation), while not exceptionally very much archived, is extremely famous among interpersonal organization examination devices. It speaks to in a content document, first the vertices (one every line) and afterward the edges. This organization is not regularly taken care of in alternate usage aside from the Pajek program, which permits edge representation with a network or an edge rundown or curve list (for coordinated charts). Weighted systems are permitted. Weights in the discretionary third section are for the bends.

b. GML (Graph Modeling Language) is likewise a structures content document, where hubs and edges start with "node" and "edge" watchwords and their substance is between"["and"]". It permits annotations as content, such as directions for vertices.

GML bolsters:

– Coordinated and undirected diagrams

– Hub and edge names

– Graphical situation of hubs (directions)

– Different annotations

c. GraphML is a XML-based chart portrayal dialect

– coordinated, undirected, and blended charts,

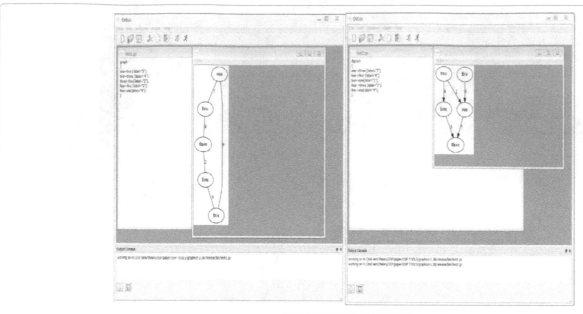

Figure 4: Graphviz screenshots.

Software	Pajek	Gephi	Social Network Visualizer	Netlytic	Graphviz
Version	1.26	0.7 alpha	1.56 Beta	Tier 1,2,3	2.38.0
Type	Stand-alone software	Stand-alone software	Stand-alone software	Stand-alone software	Stand-alone software
Platform	Windows	Java	Windows	Windows	Windows
License	Free	GNU GPL	Free	Tier 1,2 (Free) Tier 3 (CS)	Free
Expectable Computing Time	Fast(C)	Medium(JAVA)	Fast(C)	Medium(JAVA)	Fast(C)
Tractable number of nodes	500000 nodes	150000 nodes	100000 nodes	300000 nodes	1400000 nodes
Time to load 10^5 nodes and 10^6 edges	24 seconds	40 seconds	46 seconds	50 seconds	34 seconds
File formats					
GML	No	Yes	Yes	Yes	No
Pajek(.net)	No	Important Only	No	No	No
GraphML	Export only	Yes	Yes	Yes	No
DL	Yes	Yes	Yes	Yes	No
GEXF	No	Yes	Yes	Yes	No
Graph types					
Two-mode graphs	Yes	No	No	No	Yes
Multi-relational graphs	Yes	No	No	Yes	Yes
Temporality	Yes	No	No	Yes	Yes
Visualization layouts					
FruchtermanReingold	Yes	Yes	Yes	Yes	No
Kamada Kawai	Yes	Yes	No	No	Yes
Other spring layouts	No	Yes	Yes	No	Yes
Indicators					
Degree centrality	Yes	Yes	Yes	Yes	Yes
Betweenness centrality	Yes	Yes	Yes	Yes	Yes
Closeness centrality	Yes	Yes	Yes	Yes	Yes
Dyad census	No	No	No	No	No
Triad census	Yes	No	No	No	No
HITS	No	Yes	Yes	No	No
Page Rank	No	Yes	Yes	Yes	No
Clustering Algorithms					
Edge Betweenness	No	No	No	Yes	No
Walktrap	No	No	No	Yes	No
Spinglass	No	No	No	Yes	No
Dendogram Display	Yes	Yes	Yes	Yes	Yes

Table 1: Comparative analysis of Social Networking Analysis tools.

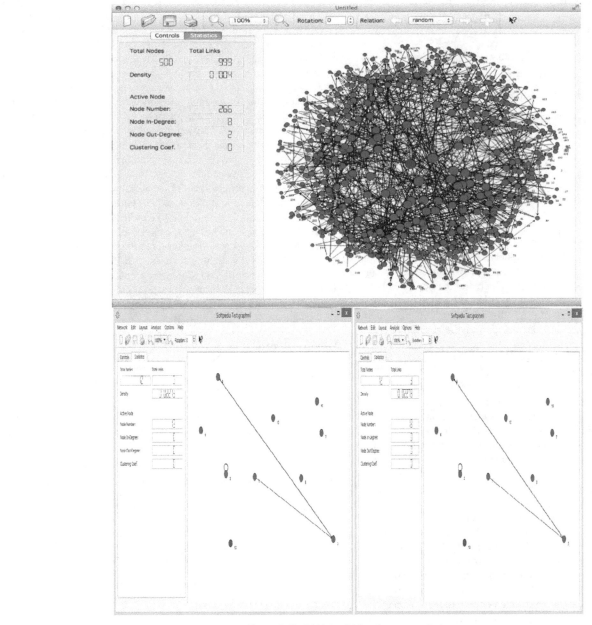

Figure 5: Social Network Visualizer screenshots.

– Hypergraphs,

– Various leveled charts,

– Graphical representations, and

– Application-particular characteristic information.

As all XML-based representation, it is very much a verbose one.

d. *DL* (Data Language) arrangement originates from the Ucinet program. The normal augmentation for this arrangement is .dat. A sample is given Figure

– Edge representation with a full grid, a halfmatrix, a bends rundown or an edges list,

– Record names,

– Rectangular networks for two-mode systems.

e. DOT is another famous chart depiction dialect, took care of mostly by Graphviz.

f. The Fruchterman-Reingold Algorithm is a force-directed layout algorithm. The idea of a force directed layout algorithm is to consider a force between any two nodes. In this algorithm, the nodes are represented by steel rings and the edges are springs between them.

g. A dendrogram (from Greek dendro "tree" and gramma "drawing") is a tree diagram frequently used to illustrate the arrangement of the clusters produced by hierarchical clustering. Dendrograms are often used in computational biology to illustrate the clustering of genes or samples.

h. Kamada and Kawai is a force directed layout algorithm. The idea of using only spring forces between all pairs of vertices, with ideal spring lengths equal to the vertices' graph-theoretic distance.

i. GEXF4 is a XML-based organization, from the GEXF Working Group. It supports

– Element diagrams,

– Application-particular property information, through the utilization of clients XML namespaces,

– Progressive structure (hubs can contain hubs)

– Visualization and situating data, for example, 3D directions, hues, shapes

Assessed instruments

Five instruments have been thought about: Pajek [6], Gephi [7], Netlytic [8], Social Network Visualizer [9] and Graphviz [10].

The benchmarking results are compressed in Table 1. They are point by point in this area, taking after the assessment criteria presented already: the permit of the instrument, the information organization took care of, the diagram sorts upheld, the accessible markers, the bunching calculations included and the visualization designs accessible. The main point is authorizing. It creates the impression that Social Network Visualizer [9] has the most lenient permit, permitting joining in exclusive programming. Both GraphViz [10] and Gephi have picked GNU GPL which does not permit the reconciliation in restrictive programming. Pajek [6] source code is undisclosed and the utilization of the product for business utilization is not free. In matter of information organization, Gephi handles all the organizations said here. GEXF is not accessible somewhere else predominantly in light of the fact that this arrangement began in the Gephi venture. DL accompanies UCINET; this last one being a task connected to Pajek, it is one of the favored configurations for this device. GML and GraphML are not upheld in Pajek, so you can lean toward the .net arrangement, which is widespread in our board. Concerning the bipartite charts study and their control, most devices propose a couple of primitives, for example, projection (change of a bipartite chart into a one-mode diagram), however we would not suggest Gephi [7] for that as two-mode diagrams is not entirely two-mode diagram empowered. Pajek can deal with connections from various types. The transience begins being considered in diverse undertakings. For the present, the information can be sifted in capacity of a year related to the hubs for instance, if the information organization is adjusted. The instrument showing up as the less proficient in matter of permitted vertices in memory is Gephi. After 200,000 hubs on our reference PC (Intel Core 2 Duo 2.5 GHz, 2 Go RAM, Windows), a few mistakes or messages welcome to expand the devoted memory for the virtual machine appear. The visualization sheet is an essential piece of Gephi, while alternate instruments can handle pointers autonomously of drawing the Graph. Such a structural engineering could punish the application for this standard. Pajek does not languish over this point and can stack 500,000 in 52 minutes. The igraph is quick for information stacking (22 seconds for 2.9 a huge number of hubs, however the dataset was sans characteristic (no name for hubs gave, as .net import is very confined for this apparatus). Gephi and Social Network Visualizer seem, by all accounts, to be restricted in their ability by the RAM utilization. Informal organization Visualizer is moderate for stacking 100,000 hubs, yet the stacking is sensible past. A few highlights, for example, administration of multi-diagrams can be the reason for debased execution. The five virtual products are suitable for figuring basic pointers, for example, chart measurements, degree centrality, closeness centrality and betweenness centrality (igraph and NetworkX executions of betweenness centrality are taking into account the calculation from Brandes [11]) Dyad and triad enumeration are accessible in igraph

and Pajek (for triad statistics). For HITS and files you cannot depend on Pajek which is not up and coming. In the event that you have to make your own pointers, the two libraries and Gephi are valuable. Group identification is exploratory in Gephi with a beta rendition of Markov bunch calculation (MCL) while couple of calculations is accessible in igraph. Pajek offers progressive grouping abilities. It can give a dendogram representation of a progressive bunching, as an EPS (PostScript) picture. The igraph offers the dendogram plotting abilities of R. On the off chance that you need propelled visualization, you need to change your information to another stage. The three different apparatuses perform the Fruchterman Reingold and Kamada and Kawai well known power based calculations. Be that as it may, the bunching calculations are missing. Hubs and edges can be any sort of articles (the main condition is to give a hash capacity to it). Utilizing programming dialects it makes simple to rethink protests, for example, hubs keeping in mind the end goal to handle them as subjective items. It has likewise some intriguing capacities on the off chance that you utilize bipartite diagrams. The igraph offers numerous calculations among which some bunching focused ones. It is accessible for both Python and R situations, and C libraries are accessible also. With R, it is anything but difficult to incorporate igraph schedules in a measurable methodology. Numerous functionalities are as of now upheld, however a few calculations are missing [12].

Other intriguing programming for interpersonal organization investigation

There are numerous other SNA apparatuses accessible, in this paper some of them were tried, for example,

– Tulip can deal with more than 1 million vertices and 4 millions edges. It has visualization, grouping and augmentation by modules capacities.

– UCInetis not free. It utilizes Pajek and Netdraw for visualization. It is had practical experience in factual and material investigation. It computes markers, (for example, triad evaluation, Freeman betweenness) and performs various leveled bunching.

– JUNG, for Java Universal Network/Graph Framework, is basically created for making intuitive diagrams in Java client interfaces, JUNG has been stretched out with some SNA measurements.

– GUESS is committed to visualization purposes. It is distributed under the GPL permit. The reasons why different apparatuses haven't been definite above are:

– Their tight and specific functionalities centered on a solitary viewpoint, i.e. Figure on visualization,

– Truthfully supplanted by different devices with the same target highlights and gathering of people (Tulip with Gephi),

– Are not centered around a software engineering vision,

– Are not freely available.

Conclusion

The way that Social Network Analysis is arranged between a few areas (social science, software engineering, math and material science) has prompted various methodological methodologies and to a ton of apparatuses. That is the reason such a variety of projects has been made with a specific end goal to control. While a standalone programming is extremely helpful for diagram visualization (up to a greatest of couple of a great many hubs), information design change or pointers processing, libraries are more adjusted for undertakings including a huge number of hubs and for operations, for example, the union and the contrast between sets of hubs or for the grouping. A reasonable partition of the calculations, the client interface and the visualization sheet is critical. Gephi received this methodology with the late arrival of the Gephi tool compartment, a library made from the Gephi rationale and calculations. We can likewise say that today the uninhibitedly accessible apparatuses have the capacity to give an exceptionally rich arrangement of functionalities, however in the event that one needs particular investigation, a business programming or correlative code improvements may be required. At long last right now, the fundamental difficulties concerning the diagram investigation are arranged toward abnormal state visualization (i.e. progressive diagrams), while amongst the conceivable improvements of informal organization investigation devices, we can specify firstly the fleeting examination which ought to permit to study the advancement of systems over the long run, and furthermore social mining which at the same time misuses the qualities of hubs and the chart structure.

References

1. Fruchterman TMJ, Reingold EM (1991) Graph Drawing by Force-directed Placement. Software: Practice and Experience 21: 1129-1164.

2. Kamada T, Kawai S (1989) An algorithm for drawing general undirected graphs. Information processing letters 31: 7-15.

3. Freeman LC (1979) Centrality in social networks conceptual clarification. Social networks 1: 215-239.

4. Davis JA, Samuel L (1967) The Structure of Positive Interpersonal Relations in Small Groups. Sociological Theories in Progress 2: 1-52.

5. Newman MEJ, Girvan M (2004) Finding and evaluating communitystructure in networks. Physical review E 69.

6. http://vlado.fmf.uni-lj.si/pub/networks/pajek

7. http://gephi.github.io

8. https://netlytic.org/home

9. http://socnetv.sourceforge.net

10. http://www.graphviz.org

11. Brandes U (2001) A Faster algorithm for betweenness centrality. Journal of Mathematical Sociology 25: 163-177.

12. Combe D, Largeron C, Zsigmond EE, Gery M (2010) A comparative study of socialnetwork analysis tools. International Workshop on Web Intelligence and Virtual Enterprises 2.

A New Approach to Enhance Avalanche Effect in Aes to Improve Computer Security

Ajeet Singh*

Lecturer in Jagaran Lakecity University, SOET, Bhopal

Abstract

Cryptography is the technique or process by which information or message is sent by a person or users to other person or users so that only the authorized person or users can receive the message. In this research, an Enhanced Advanced Encryption Standard (E-AES) algorithm is proposed for transfer of data to achieve various security goals. This new algorithm is based on the symmetric key encryption Advanced Encryption Standard (AES). E-AES analyzes Advanced Encryption Standard (AES) in terms of security which is calculated by avalanche effect and subsequent memory requirement. It adds one more step by including logical XOR in the existing AES algorithm which ensures improvement in the encryption in terms of avalanche effect. Plaintext and encryption key are mapped in binary code before encryption process. Avalanche Effect is calculated by changing one bit in plaintext keeping the key constant. The implementation of both techniques has been realized for experimental purposes. Experimental results reflect that E-AES exhibits significant high Avalanche Effect after comparative study with existing encryption algorithm.

Keyword: Encryption; Decryption; Security; Algorithm; Internet: Code; Cryptography

Introduction

Overview

It is already known that the use of internet in this era is increasing very rapidly and many of the users are sharing public and personal information over internet. This gives rise to the need of security as the data and information is very sensitive as its transmission is needed all the time. Encryption technique is one of the key measures which can be very useful to secure confidential information. This encryption is implemented by using some traditional encryption techniques. But traditional encryption technique has some shortcomings in terms of security. This is why an Enhanced encryption algorithm is proposed in this dissertation. This Enhanced encryption algorithm has capacity to improve transmission security, through researching, improving, and arranging several famous data encryption algorithms in some order like Advance Encryption Standard (AES). In this, a new enhanced AES crypto [1-4] concept is proposed by analyzing the principle of the cryptography technique based on the symmetric cryptography function. Moreover, the security and performance of the proposed technique will also be estimated. One function is added in the proposed work that user can directly send encrypted information to another user through email functionality so that security can be increased, rather than encrypting it through another algorithm and then send this information from software. The experimental results based on this symmetric function will approve the effectiveness of the proposed technique, and the enhancement of existing AES will show high-level security. The cipher text generated by this method will be approximately same in size as the plaintext and will be suitable for practical use in the secure transmission of confidential information over the Internet. Basically Cryptography provides a way where we can communicate securely in adversarial environments. Cryptographic technique/method can be symmetric, if both the sender side user and the receiver side user of a information are using the same private/secrete key, as in the case of stream and block ciphers and message authentication codes. Hash functions are also another type of symmetric cryptography technique, where neither sender side user nor receiver side user need to know a private/secrete key at all. In contrast to this, cryptographic technique/method can be asymmetric, if sender side user and receiver side user are using different keys (Public and Private) [4]. Symmetric cryptography technique are very efficient in practically than asymmetric cryptography technique, most security applications use symmetric cryptography to ensure the privacy/confidentiality, the integrity and the authenticity of sensitive/secured data. Even most applications of such type cryptography are actually working in a hybrid manner by transmitting a cipher key with asymmetric techniques while symmetrically encrypting the payload data under the cipher key [5,6]. A cryptosystem is an algorithm or some predefine steps, which include all possible plaintexts/characters, cipher texts, and keys value. Encryption/decryption functions are represented as:

$$E_{Key}(Msg) = Cip$$

$$D_{Key}(Cip) = Msg$$

These functions have the property that:

$$D_{Key}(E_{Key}(Msg)) = Msg$$

Most often, to keep secrets Aes is used for being confidential [6]. Everyone has a need to keep some things secret or confidential. The operating system has secrets or confidential it needs to keep away from users, Many users want their credit card details kept with full secure and away from hackers or attacker, everyone wants their financial and health affairs should be confidential or secret, and, sadly, it appears that even today users still need and required to keep their religious persuasions secret or confidential. It is unfortunate, but the need to keep/secure a wide variety of information secret/confidentially also means that users can also use encryption/decryption to keep secret things that society has decided are unlawful, such as the plans to rob a bank. Encryption/decryption technologies also have other valuable capabilities. Any attempt to falsify the content/information of an encrypted message will cause failure during attempt of decryption. Basically there are three type of cryptography (Figure 1) [7].

***Corresponding author:** Ajeet Singh, Lecturer in Jagaran Lakecity University, SOET, Bhopal, Madhya Pradesh India, E-mail: ajitsingh17985@gmail.com

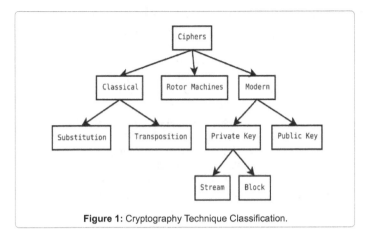

Figure 1: Cryptography Technique Classification.

- Classical cryptography
- Rotor Machine
- Modern Cryptography

In the proposed work we have concentrate on various binary codes, that mean plain text and corresponding key will convert in the selected binary code for the encryption [8,9]. At initial level we have describing existing AES algorithm shown in Figure 2 in brief. The algorithm begins with an Add round key stage followed by 9 rounds of four stages and a tenth round of three steps or stages. This applies for both encryption as well as decryption with the exception that each stage of a round the decryption algorithm is the inverse of its counterpart in the encryption algorithm. The four stages are as follows [10]:

1. Substitute bytes

2. Shift rows

3. Mix Columns

4. Add Round Key

The tenth round simply leaves out the Mix Columns stage or step. The 1st nine rounds of the decryption algorithm or technique consist of the following:

1. Inverse Shift rows

2. Inverse Substitute bytes

3. Inverse Add Round Key

4. Inverse Mix Columns

Again, the 10th round simply leaves out the Inverse Mix Columns stage [10]

Rest of the paper is organized as follow: section-II presents proposed work; Section-III presents results analysis and finally section four presents conclusion and references.

Proposed Work

Proposed architecture

Here an enhanced encryption algorithm for transfer of data is presented to achieve the various security goals i.e., Integrity, Availability, and Confidentiality. This new algorithm is based on the symmetric key encryption approach like AES. In this we analyze the Advanced Encryption Standard (AES), and add one more step which is including logical XOR operation to AES to ensure improving the encryption security in terms of avalanche effect. In the proposed algorithm we have applied post processing to standard AES Algorithm to increase the avalanche

Effect Figure 3 is showing general block diagram of E-AES. Here plain text and key both are converted into binary code. Then enhanced AES algorithm starts working for encryption which will finally produce cipher text. Detailed architecture is shown in Figure 3. In this all the steps are same except the last step which can be defined as:

- Take produced cipher text from AES and convert it into binary form. Then the output (128×N) bits of AES algorithm is produced as cipher text and is arranged in following way

B1	B2	B3	B4	B5	B6	B7	B8	...	Bn

Then apply XOR operation between each bit together. The last bit will be XOR with first bit.

For Example, B1 = B1 *EXOR* B2, B2 = B2 *EXOR* B3, Similarly, Bi = B (i) *EXOR* B (i+1), in decryption reverse processing of above steps takes place.

Results

For experiment purpose, proposed system has implemented AES

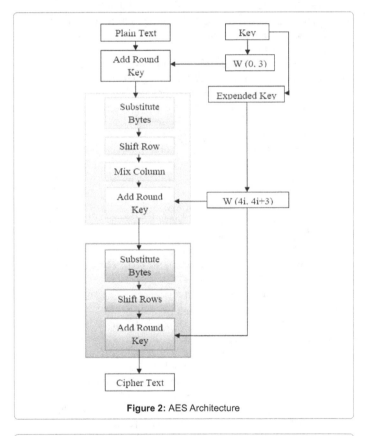

Figure 2: AES Architecture

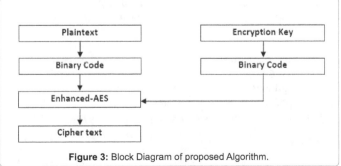

Figure 3: Block Diagram of proposed Algorithm.

and modify AES algorithm. Architecture of AES as shown in Figure 2 and modify AES architecture shown in Figure 4. Figures 2 and 4 has one step difference which is binary bit conversion with logical XOR operation in Figure 4. At the time of results calculation a desktop machine are using and the configuration of that machine is Intel Pentium Dual Core E3400 3.61 Ghz, 1 GB of RAM and Window-XP, in which performance data is collected. In the experiments, the system encrypts/decrypt with various binary code on various combinations of test message and fillied message. Each time, different plaintexts are respectively encrypted by AES and E-AES. Finally, the outputs of AES and E-AES are compared with each other in terms of avalanche effect, and it is measured in numeric form. Actually, for an encryption algorithm, the avalanche effect of encryption not only depends on the algorithm's complexity, but also the key and the plaintext have certain impact. Table 1 is demonstrates comparison between avalanche effect of AES and E-AES. In this table alphabets are converted into binary codes of seven types and then alphabet 'J' is flipped with alphabet 'A'. Here it can be seen that in each scenario of binary code, the avalanche effect of proposed algorithm is always greater than the existing AES. But highest avalanche effect in proposed algorithm is 75 which are achieved with binary code 5311 and second highest value is 67 with Gray binary code. It seems that both these binary codes will give us the desired result in terms of avalanche effect. The result produced in Table 1 is been graphicaly represented in Figure 5. It is clearly shown that result of avalanche effect is produced highest with binary code 5311. Moving further in result now in Table 2 alphabets are converted into binary codes of seven types and then alphabet 'A' is flipped with integer '5'. The motive here is to calculate the avalanche effect by flipping of character with integer. Here it can be seen that the binary code 5311 and the gray code that were producing the highest and the second highest result in the above table are now producing only 61 and 62 results respectively. Also the difference between the results of AES and E-AES is negligible that is one. Hence it can be concluded that the flipping of character with integer is not fruitful to achieve the target. But the surprising element is that the highest result produced in binary code 3321 is 77 which is not only highest in this table but is also higher than any other value produced in Table 1. In the same binary code i.e 3321 the difference between avalanche effect of AES and E-AES is 24 which is quite noticeable and therefore the research can be carried out in consideration with binary code 3321. The result produced in Table 2 is been graphically represented in Figure 6. So it can be concluded by above research that code 3321 is highly considerable. Now one of the characters in test sentence 'This is India', character 'd' is flipped one by one with integers ranging from 1 to 9. Maximum avalanche effect can be seen by flipping 'd' with integer '3' that is 228. Here the difference between AES and E-AES is maximum that is 38. From the Table 3 it can be seen that minimum difference from AES is 21 and it ranges up to 38. This is quite significant and noticeable. Result of Table 3 is graphically represented in below Figure 7. It clearly shows that the difference of avalanche effect between AES and E-AES is significant. The above discussion concludes that by using proposed algorithm that is E-AES we get maximum avalanche effect when plain text is firstly converted into 3321 binary code and any character in plain text is flipped by integer value. It is clear from Table 3, E-AES can produce avalanche effect above 200 with all possibility but flipping of character with special symbol is quite not acceptable because it can create confusion after decryption. On other hand flipping of character with integer is quite acceptable. For example we can write '0' zero as 'o' and '1' one as 'l'. In this type of flipping we also get significant avalanche effect.

Conclusion

In this dissertation enhancement in AES algorithm is proposed. In

the proposed algorithm that is E-AES, input plaintext and encryption key are mapped into various binary codes instead of giving plaintext and encryption key directly to the AES algorithm. E-AES includes two more steps to AES, which converts plain text into binary with logical and strong XOR operation. E-AES performs better when compared with the existing AES this is reflected by the corresponding is Avalanche Effect of both the existing and proposed E-AES due to one bit variation in plaintext (before being mapped in various binary codes) keeping encryption key constant in a binary code. Results and Analysis section indicates that the E-AES is definitely comparable with AES. The performance of E-AES is significantly better than AES algorithm. This result is achieved because the cipher produced by E-AES has strong bit level dependence. By result and analysis section it can be also concluded that E-AES can produce cipher with high avalanche effect in any binary code conversion as compared to AES.

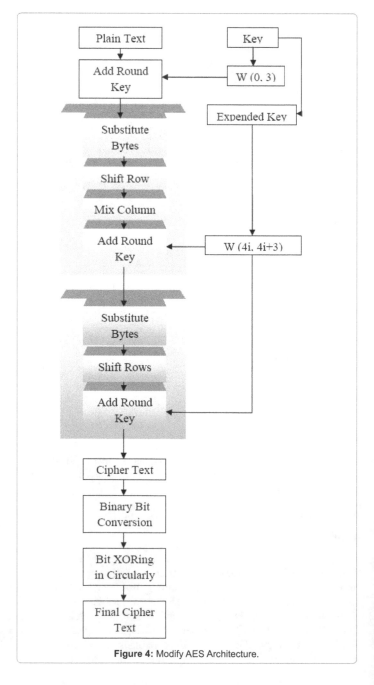

Figure 4: Modify AES Architecture.

CODE	STRING	C STRING	NUMBER OF BITS FLIPPED WITH AES	NUMBER OF BITS FLIPPED WITH E-AES	AVALANCHE % OF AES	AVALANCHE % OF E-AES	DIFFERENCE OF FLIPPED BITS (AES AND E-AES)
Gray Code	J	A	50	67	39.1	52.34	17
8421	J	A	56	66	43.8	51.56	10
7421	J	A	60	63	46.9	49.22	3
5421	J	A	62	62	48.4	48.44	0
5311	J	A	61	75	47.7	58.59	14
5211	J	A	65	65	50.8	50.8	0
4221	J	A	58	60	45.3	46.88	2
3321	J	A	57	64	44.5	50	7

Table 1: Avalanche effect comparison between AES and E-AES.

CODE	STRING	C STRING	NUMBER OF BITS FLIPPED WITH AES	NUMBER OF BITS FLIPPED WITH E-AES	AVALANCHE % OF AES	AVALANCHE % OF E-AES	DIFFERENCE OF FLIPPED BITS (AES AND E-AES)
Gray Code	A	5	61	62	47.7	48.4	1
8421	A	5	60	61	46.9	47.7	1
7421	A	5	61	65	47.7	50.8	4
5421	A	5	58	63	45.3	49.2	5
5311	A	5	62	63	48.4	49.2	1
5211	A	5	54	61	42.2	47.7	7
4221	A	5	66	68	51.6	53.1	2
3321	A	5	53	77	41.4	60.2	24

Table 2: Avalanche effect comparison between character and numeric by AES and E-AES.

S.NO	3321 CODE	ORIGINAL STRING	CHANGED STRING	BITS IN CIPHER TEXT	NUMBER OF BITS FLIPPED WITH AES	NUMBER OF BITS FLIPPED WITH E-AES	DIFFERENCE OF FLIPPED BITS (AES AND E-AES)
1	3321 Code	This is India	This is In1ia	1152	186	210	24
2	3321 Code	This is India	This is In2ia	1152	182	214	32
3	3321 Code	This is India	This is In3ia	1152	190	228	38
4	3321 Code	This is India	This is In4ia	1152	184	210	26
5	3321 Code	This is India	This is In5ia	1152	187	208	21
6	3321 Code	This is India	This is In6ia	1152	182	220	38
7	3321 Code	This is India	This is In7ia	1152	180	210	30
8	3321 Code	This Is India	This is In8ia	1152	181	218	37
9	3321 Code	This is India	This is In9ia	1152	188	216	28

Table 3: Result and Comparison of Avalanche Effect in a Sentence with 3321 code where character is flipped by Integer.

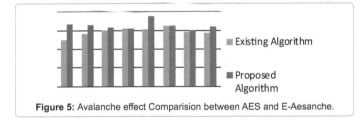

Figure 5: Avalanche effect Comparision between AES and E-Aesanche.

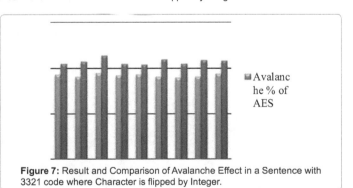

Figure 7: Result and Comparison of Avalanche Effect in a Sentence with 3321 code where Character is flipped by Integer.

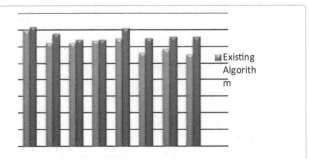

Figure 6: Avalanche Effect Comparison Between character and numeric by AES and E-AES.

Application

Enhanced AES algorithm can be applied in various systems like banking, defense, finance, government, educational, medical science and many more where confidential data are being stored in large manner and is being used in public network.

Limitation

Proposed algorithm is an enhancement to the AES algorithm so cryptanalysis is dependent on the AES architecture. If any dispense is found in AES then it will also reflect on proposed algorithm.

Future enhancement

In this dissertation algorithm used is E-AES works on post processing on cipher text generated by AES by which we achieve strong bit level dependence and improved avalanche effect. In future researches E-AES can be modified with both pre and post processing on AES to enhance security and efficiency of transmitting data.

References

1. Dewangan CP, Agrawal S, Mandal AK , Tiwari A (2012) Study of Avalanche Effect in AES Using Binary Codes. International Conference on Advanced Communication Control and Computing Technologies.

2. Mandal JK, Paul M (2012) A Bit Level Session Based Encryption Technique to Enhance Information Security. International Journal on Computer Science and Engineering 4: 321-326.

3. Landge I, Burhanuddin C, Patel A, Choudhary R (2012) Image encryption and decryption using blowfish algorithm.World Journal of Science and Technology 2: 151-156.

4. Prakash C, Dewangan, Agrawal S (2012) A Novel Approach to Improve Avalanche Effect of AES Algorithm. International Journal of Advanced Research in Computer Engineering & Technology 1: 248-252.

5. Sastry VUK, Murthy DSR, Bhavani SD (2010) A Block Cipher Having a Key on One Side of the Plain Text Matrix and its Inverse on the Other Side. International Journal of Computer Theory and Engineering 2: 805-808.

6. Mohit K, Mishra R, Pandey RK, Poonam Singh (2010) Comparing Classical Encryption With Modern Techniques 1: 49-54.

7. Sastry UV, Shanker NV, Bhavani SD (2009) A modified Playfair Cipher Involving Interweaving and Iteration International journal of Computer theory and Engineering 5: 597-601.

8. Elminaam DSA, Kader HMA, Hadhoud MM (2010) Evaluating the Performance of Symmetric Encryption Algorithms. International journal of network security 10: 216-222.

9. Hashim AT (2010) FPGA Simulation of Type-3 Feistel Network of The 128 bits Block Size Improved Blow fish Cryptographic Encryption. Eng & Tech .Journal 28: 115-119.

10. Landge IF (2011) Implementation of AES Encryption & Decryption using VHDL. International J of Engg. Research & Indu Appls 4: 395-406.

17

Design and Implementation of an Android Game: Duelling Phone

Alaa Hassan*

University of Kirkuk, Kirkuk, Iraq

Abstract

This paper presents the design and implementation of a unique two person Android game, called 'Duelling Phone'. To the Author's best knowledge, the reported game has never been implemented before.

The Model-View Controller (MVC) design pattern has been applied, as it represents a pattern for the Graphical User Interface. This particular design pattern has been used in order to separate the data from the visual representation, since it consists of three separate parts. The 'model' represents the actual data in the program, while the 'view' only illustrates the user interface. The 'controller', finally, controls the process of the communication between the view and the model.

The process that has been followed in order to implement this application is 'Rapid Application Development' (RAD), which represents the process where the development cycle of any application is accelerated. It allows for the application to be developed faster, helping to retain a valuable resource.

Two modes have been implemented successfully: 'Single Player' mode allows the player to play against the Android device, while the 'Two Player' mode allows two players to play against each other, passing one Android device between them. The results were established following testing on the emulator, and by using an actual Android device.

Keywords: Android; Mobile game; Mobile application; Software design

Introduction

Mobile applications represent a relatively new concept in today's market, and although Personal Digital Assistants (PDAs) were the first devices capable of handling mobile applications, these devices never became mainstream, tending to be used only by computer experts. Over time, the functionality of the mobile phone has engaged with PDAs, resulting in the generation of new devices, known as 'smartphones'.

Currently, three different smartphone developer platforms are available, represented by: the BlackBerry by RIM, which is not suitable to be utilized as a gaming platform, due to the small screen size; and two others representing the technological peak of industry operating systems- the iPhone Operating System (iOS) by Apple, and the Android by Google, both of which are ideal platform choices for game programming. However, unlike the iOS, Android applications can be programmed under an 'open source' license, and no special equipment is required to build a game. On the other hand, to build a game on Apple devices, both a developer license, and a Mac computer, are required to compile a gaming application [1]. The Android platform is one such platform whereby application writing is supported by Java programming languages [2], Eclipse, Free SDK and Emulator(SDK website), [3] (Eclipse website); in addition, Android devices have four different screen sizes making it possible to adapt the game for more than one screen size. In these circumstances, the Google Android seems to be the most logical platform to choose for the project proposed in this paper.

A 'mobile game' is a video game that can be played on the mobile phone, played by using the technologies installed within the device itself. The majority of smartphones are equipped with the hardware necessary for more advanced and complex games, which may be either a single or multiplayer game, the latter whereby consumers play the same game on their phones while connected to a shared network.

Games on Android are already soaring in popularity, and as the Android increases in computational power, the demand for more challenging games increases. Although Android games are programmed using the Java programming language, it doesn't use some of its core libraries, instead, its own libraries are utilized which are crafted for the specific needs of the platform. Consequently, it was necessary to study the specific details of the Android platform, and how to use its libraries. To write a good program and implement a game for the Android, it was necessary to gain a familiarity with the specific device that was used to run the application, in terms of the version of Android, and the resolution of the screen.

The objective of the project presented in this paper is to design, implement and test 'Duelling Phone', a two person Android game. It is not a difficult game to implement, but the extensions required to make it a practical, easy-to-use game with a variety of options, makes the project building challenging and results in an interesting, two persons, Android game.

Although the proposed game is similar to other Android games designed in the past(such as 'Tic Tac Toe', commonly known as 'Noughts and Crosses' in the UK) in the way that it is a two-persons game, based on an old pencil-and-paper game, the aim of this game, however, is quite different. It is also worth mentioning that the main focus of this project has been applied to implementing all requirements required to make the game playable, while artwork was kept minimal.

The rest of the paper is organized as follows: Section II presents the description of the implemented game. Section III is devoted to the design process of the game, represented by the Unified Modelling language (UML) diagrams and the wireframe of the application. Section IV discusses the implementation and testing of the Duelling Phone game. Finally, conclusions are given in Section V.

Game Description

As previously mentioned, the aim of this research is to design and

*Corresponding author: Alaa Hassan, University of Kirkuk, Kirkuk, Iraq
E-mail: eng.alaa.hassan@ieee.org

implement the 'Duelling Phone', two person Android game, and this section has been devoted to the description of what the formal elements and the challenges in the game as well as the balance in this game and how it works, by demonstrating a simple example.

- Formal Elements- the formal elements in this game are represented by the following elements: 1. Board; 2. Steps; 3. Coins; 4. Stack of chips; 5. Player side goal boundary

- Challenges - Beating the opponent by reaching the goal line on player's end.

- Balance- Both players have equal chance of losing and winning based on the value of the chips.

- There is no dominant strategy.

The game consists of two opposing sides, one side for each player, with three 'steps' on each side. A coin(or similar marker) will be on the middle line(denoted '0'), that separates the two sides. Whichever player manages to get to the end of their three steps first will be deemed the winner.

The game starts with each player have the same number of chips (50) in a stack, with each player wagering on a number. Whichever player wagered the most chips in that turn take one step towards their goal. If both players bet the same number of chips, the coin will remain in its place. On each turn, the number of each player's remaining chips is reduced from the stack by subtracting the amount bet. Subsequently, the game will continue until one of the players either reaches the end, or the game ceases (by neither player reaching the end before their pile of chips is reduced to 0). The following is an example of the 'Duelling Phone' game, won by the player on the right hand side. It shows the design of the game and how it works, step by step:

In this example, firstly, Figure 1 shows the game in its initial state;

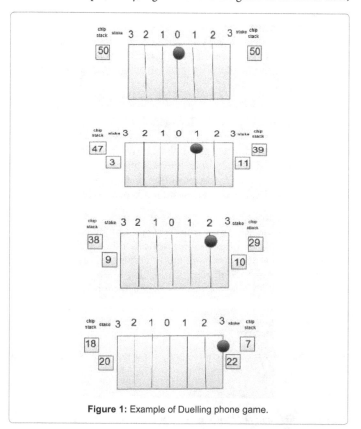

Figure 1: Example of Duelling phone game.

whereby no number has been bet, and the chip stacks contain the opening 50. The first turn of the game, in which the first player, located on the left hand side of the game boards, has bet 3 of their chips, so has 47 remaining in their chip stack (50-3 = 47). The second player, located on the right hand side of the game board, has bet 11 chips so has a remaining 39 in the chip stack (50-11). As a result, the coin (or other marker) moves one step forwards the goal of the second player, player 2 having bet a greater number than the first player. In the next turn, player 1 bets 9 of his/her 47 chips, so 38 now remain in the chip stack. Player 2, however, has bet 10 of 39 chips remaining leaving 29 in the chip stack, and, with a greater winning bet, again sees the marker moved another step towards his/her goal. In the next turn, the coin is in a critical position. In this situation, the player 1 should be aware, and critically think about choosing a number that will stop player 2 from winning, whether by a larger bet, or at a minimum, an equal bet to ensure the coin moves no nearer the goal of player 2. In our example, however, the first player chose only 20 for this bet, despite knowing that the second player could choose any number up to the 29 in their chip stack. In this situation, the player 2 chose to bet 22, ensuring the coin/marker moved the final step towards his/her goal, and in turn giving the win to the second player. In this turn, if the first player had thought more critically, and bet a larger number than the second player, the coin would have moved a step back towards the goal of player 1.

Functional Specifications and Technologies

Game specification

As mentioned earlier, the aim of this project is designing and implementing a Duelling phone-two person android game.

- The game should work perfectly with all the probabilities that may contain.

- The player of the Duelling phone game should be able to play the game either with the Android device (SinglePlayer mode) or with another player (TwoPlayer mode).

- In future, the developer should be able to extend the game and adding new feature and new forms of players without affecting the existing code of the game.

Technologies required for the implementation

These packages represent the software packages, chosen for the developing environment. Since it has been recommended by the official Android developer website, the game has been implemented using Eclipse. The available Android plugins simplify the building and running of the Android emulators also, making this choice preferable.

The Dalvik Debug Monitor Server (DDMS) is a tool which can be used for SMS and call spoofing. Boasting a plugin for Eclipse, it is able to access from within the IDE, and is used for debugging throughout the development process, finding any possible leaks in the memory usage and creating screenshots (these can then be posted on the Android market when marketing any application). On the other hand, Android Logcat shows information about user interactions, phone state, and the stack trace of any exceptions.

Quality assurance- lint warnings, emulators and test devices

There are many tools for testing: The Android Lint will be used to help minimize possible problems. This tool is capable of showing any warnings for any code in Eclipse that may cause accessibility problems, or fails to conform to best practice. The full list of checks that can be performed can be found on the Android Lint website.

Design

The functionality of the application (game), the way of using the interface, and how to play the game should be presented to the user in an easy-to-understand manner, while every player should be able to play the game without having to read the help guide first.

This section will discuss how the program was designed, represented by the use of a Case Diagram, an Activity Diagram, and the Wireframe that was used to design and understand the user flow of the application.

A design pattern

The design pattern is a template that shows the interactions between the program components, such as the classes and the objects. It is used as a reusable solution for software engineering problems.

Model-view-controller

The use of the MVC design pattern helped to separate the programming of the view and the model in two different classes, helping to extend and modify both much easier. The view provides a visual representation of the data model, while the controller links the model and the view, by 'listening' for events from the view, and carrying out the corresponding action on the model (Figure 2).

Design patterns in the duelling phone program design

The Model-View-Controller has been used in this program, where the Game.class represents the model containing all variables and methods employed in the game, and represented by the view. The work was started with a model class, Game.class, and one view class, 'DuellingPhone.class'. Following completion of this mode, which represents the SinglePlayer mode, the first extension of the game was made, represented by the Two Player mode. The first extension was implemented by adding another view for the Two Player mode, and the functions relating to the mode, simply added to the Game.class.

Use case diagram

One of the first steps in designing the game was to model it on its phases, where the Use case was designed first. Describing a set of actions the user can take while using the application, each use case should provide some valuable result to the users interacting with the system, but does not attempt to represent the number of times, nor the order, that the system's actions should be executed [4,5].

The following figure shows the Use Case diagram for the Duelling Phone game (Figure 3).

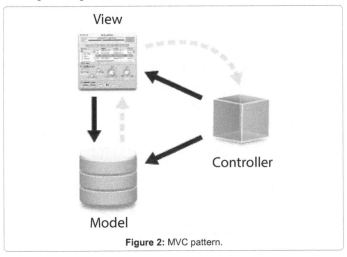

Figure 2: MVC pattern.

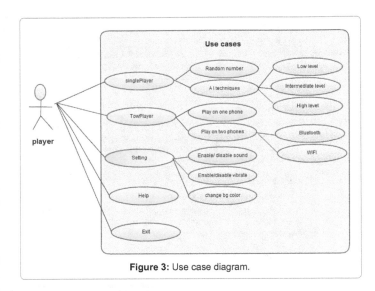

Figure 3: Use case diagram.

General use case description

The following are short descriptions of each use case illustrate in the use case diagram that will be used in the game (Table 1).

Activity diagrams

The Activity Diagram is an important UML diagram, describing how activities are coordinated. It essentially represents the flowchart showing the flow from one activity to another, whereby the activity can be represented as an operation of the system.

The activity diagram is potentially used for modeling the logic, captured by a single use case. With respect to the Duelling Phone game, the activity diagram has been designed for the first and second use cases.

The activity diagram shown in Figure 4 defines the basic structure of the SinglePlayer mode, and represents the realisation of the SinglePlayer Use case. When a player wishes to play on his own against the Android mobile device, it is performed, and after selecting the SinglePlayer mode from the Menu screen, the application proceeds to take the player to the screen showing the game itself. The game starts with 50 chips in the stack. When the player bets a number, this bet number must be less than the number of chips remaining in the chip stack, and after pressing the 'Go' button, a random number appears to represent the bet of the 'second player'-the Android device. The coin will then move one step toward the side of the player betting the larger number. If both numbers were the same, the coin's positional value will remain constant and will stay where it was. The number in the chip stack is reduced by the number of chips bet, and the game subsequently continues. It does so until either one of the players wins (reaches their end first), or both players end up with zero chips remaining in their stack.

The activity diagram for the Two Player mode is shown in Figure 5, and in this mode, this flow occurs also (Figure 6) presents a high-level design of the activity diagram, whereby the activity diagrams of the SinglePlayer and TwoPlayer modes were combined in one. By following this activity diagram, the player should choose either to play the SinglePlayer mode or the Two Player mode, and depending on what is chosen, the process in Figures 4 and 5 will commence.

Wireframe

The next step in designing the game was to design the Wireframe, which represents a visual representation of the interface, designed to

Use case:	Single Player
Goal	Start a new game in single player mode.
Description	In this mode, the player will play against the Android mobile device. The Android acts as the second player and here, there are two options. The device gives a random number as a bet number or uses AI techniques.

Use case:	Random number
Goal	Play the game in single player mode
Description	In this mode, the player will play against the Android mobile device. The Android acts as the second player and gives a random number as a bet number.

Use case:	AI techniques
Goal	Play the game in single player mode
Description	In this mode, the player will play against the Android mobile device. The Android acts as the second player and playing in an intelligent way using AI techniques.

Use case:	TwoPlayer
Goal	Start a new game in two player mode
Description	In this mode, two players will play against each other either on one Android device or on two Android devices.

Use case:	Play on one phone
Goal	Start a new game in two player mode
Description	In this mode, two players will play against each other on one Android device by pass the device between the two players.

Use case:	Play on two phones
Goal	Start a new game in two player mode
Description	In this mode, two players will play against each other on two Android devices. These devices connected to each other using via Bluetooth or WIFI.

Use case:	Setting
Goal	Show the setting screen
Description	Show the setting screen where the player can change the setting of the game like enabling or disabling the background music, changing the background color or enabling/disabling the vibration.

Use case:	Help
Goal	Show the Help screen.
Description	Shows an explanation of how the game works.

Use case:	Exit
Goal	Exit the game.
Description	Exit the playing screen and Finishing the game.

Table 1: Short descriptions of each use case illustrate in the use case diagram.

plan the functionality of each activity in the game. Used as a technical guide to specify the structure of the interface, before creating the actual UI for the game, it shows how the interface is compiled, its content, and how the data is organised. It also shows how the interface works, how the user interacts with the interface, and how it travels between the different states.

Implementation and Testing

Implementation

This application is made up of two, equally important parts- the user interface part, and the application logic part. It is worth noting that the programming environment of Android comes with great tools for localisation and internationalisation. All text, as a result, has been written to appear on the Android game's screen, and is originated from separate language files that make the game easily translatable. All activities, as well as the design for the (GUI), and the layouts, have been implemented in this application, and will be discussed in this Section.

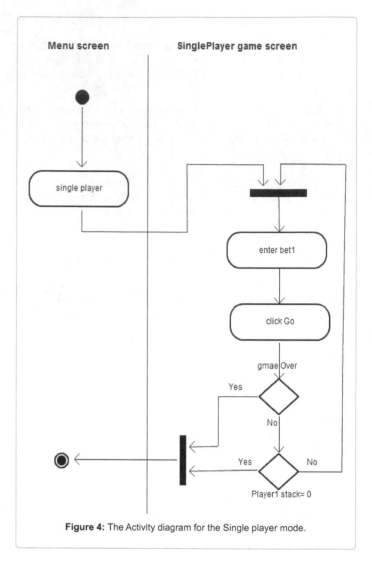

Figure 4: The Activity diagram for the Single player mode.

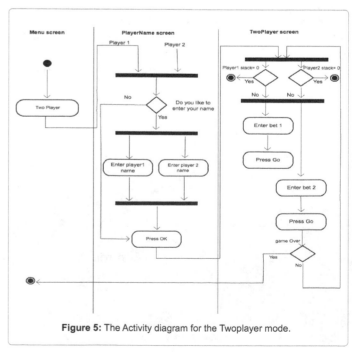

Figure 5: The Activity diagram for the Twoplayer mode.

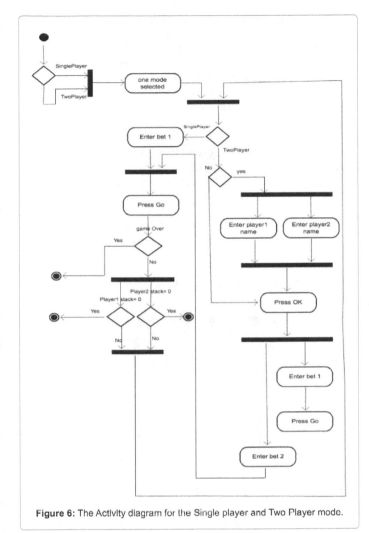

Figure 6: The Activity diagram for the Single player and Two Player mode.

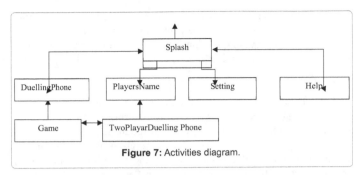

Figure 7: Activities diagram.

Implementing the activities

This section focuses on detailing the functions and methods that have been implemented in each activity. The following diagram shows all the activities that have been implemented to run this game (Figure 7).

Splash activity

The 'splash' is the first activity to start within the Duelling Phone game, and represents the launcher activity of the game. The activity is coded using a timer task to show the splash screen first, to display the Duelling Phone Logo to the user, and then to move on to the Menu activity of the application. The amount of time allocated to the display of the splash screen was 3 seconds. It is recommended in the literature that it would be good to have the splash screen display for a minimum of two seconds, as; anything shorter would not give the player a proper chance to view it. On the other hand, if it remains on the screen for more than 5 seconds, it violates the '5 second rule', which specifies that the interactive application should respond after a maximum of 5 seconds whenever possible [6]. Finally, this activity also uses a Media player object, in order to start the background music.

Menu activity

It represents the second activity that can be accessed in this game. Normally, the On Create() method was used to set the layout from the menu.xml file, and the activity also creates the button listeners that

are used to start the SinglePlayer mode, Two Player mode, the game Settings, the Help, and to Exit the game [7].

Duelling phone activity

This activity represents the view for the first mode the game, the SinglePlayer mode, which is devoted to playing against the device. The Duelling Phone activity includes all objects for initialising the Edit Text, Text View and buttons. It contains a listener for the 'Go' button, allowing state of the game to change after clicking it. The(Math.ceil(Math.random()*(game.PLAYER2STACKChIPS())*0.15) equation have been used to allow the mobile device gave a random number as a bet number. This random number multiplied by game.PLAYER2STACKChIPS() to allow the Android device bet a number of chips equal or less than the number of chips in his stack, while it multiplied by (0.15) to add simple level of intelligence to the game. From the equation, it is clear that a simple level of Artificial intelligence techniques have been applied. However, with more time available, more advanced artificial intelligent level can be implemented [8].

Players name activity

This activity includes the initialisations of buttons, the Text Views and the Edit Texts, which allow the players to enter their name. By pressing the OK button, a new intent will be called to start a new screen, the Two Player Duelling Phone screen.

Two player duelling phone activity

This activity represents the view for the second mode of the game, the Two Player mode, where two players play against each other using one Android device. The Two Player Duelling Phone activity includes all objects for initialising the Edit Text, Text View and buttons, and contains a listener for the 'Go' buttons to hide the first player's bet number and to change the state of the game in order to start another turn. After the player presses the first 'Go' button, the Edit Text for bet1 will be disabled until the second player finish their turn, meaning that the first player cannot play again before the second player finishes [9].

Game activity

Representing the backbone of this application, this activity contains the main methods needed to be implemented in order to run the game, since it represents the home to the model, and the controller, of this game. It contains the on Draw() method, which uses the bitmap Factory necessary to draw the image on the screen. Two other important methods have been created here- the CalculatePlayer1Stack() and the CalculatePlayer2Stack(), methods used in order to calculate the remaining numbers of chips in the stacks after each bet. For the Two player mode, similar methods were implemented. Correspondingly, the player1Stack_IsEmpty() and player2Stack_IsEmpty() were used to ensure that the stack is not empty, before allowing the player to bet a number. The Game Over() method is used to stop the game by returning a Boolean value= true, if both players stacks=0, and neither have reached the final step of the game. Other methods for checking the position, and changing the state, have been used to make the game work properly, with all probabilities that may be included [10].

Setting activity

This activity represents the standard style menu as seen throughout the operating system, which is familiar to Android users. The methods to change the settings of the game are included, such as the enabling and disabling of the sound, vibrations, alteration of the volume, and modifying the background colour, etc. In the case of this project, only the setting to enable/disable the sound has been implemented. In this case, the MediaPlayer object is used to start the background music, an object that can be controlled using a checkbox. A checkbox, rather than a wedge, was chosen, after reviewing a number of other Android applications, it became clear that the majority of them use this type of wedge to represent the sound on the Setting screen.

The get Preference object is used to help obtain the state of the checkbox, and whether it is checked or not. It can then save the state, using the Save() method, or loading the state using the Load() method, but, again due to lack of time, the other setting options were unfortunately left incomplete. For future development, the same methodology could be followed to apply them.

The 'Settings' activity also uses the 'Toast wedge' which allows a message to be shown, notify the player when the sound is being enabled or disabled [11].

Help activity

To display information to help the player during the game, and to give further information about the application (such as the version code), a standard Android activity initialises a text view.

Implementing the interface

The splash screen: This screen contains the logo that has been overwritten from iSmashPhone.com, after adding the name of the game (Duelling Phone) using PhotoShop software. The Logo was aimed at representing the application icon, and the splash screen. The reason for selecting this logo over others was that it was found to have some relationship to duelling, so the aim of the application and what it represented was made easier to understand (Figure 8).

The menu screen: It is the second screen of the game; a number of buttons used to perform different tasks are included. The first two buttons are the most important, as they take the player to the 'map' screen(the game screen) where the game itself begins. They represent the path to the game screen, where the user should choose one of two paths, either by deciding whether to play with the Android device, or to play with another person using the same handset (Figure 9).

The map screen for the SinglePlayer mode: This mode is the simplest mode of the game where the player plays against the Android phone. Two images are included: Board: that represents the board that represents the steps where the coin should move on and the Coin (a movable image), which should move to the left or to the right depending on the bet numbers (Figure 10).

The players name screen: This screen appears after choosing the Two Player mode from the Menu screen, showing two Edit Texts where the player can enter their name in order to appear on the main game screen. Otherwise, if the player does not wish to enter their name, player 1, player 2 is entered as a default name (Figure 11).

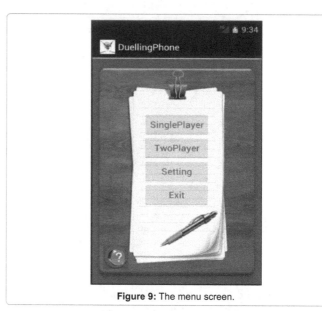

Figure 9: The menu screen.

Figure 8: The splash screen.

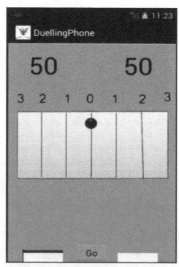

Figure 10: Single player mode screen.

The map screen for the two player mode: This interface has the same design as the one of the SinglePlayer mode except that the text view of player 2 bet is now an Edit text in order to allow the player to make the bet. In addition, another "Go" button has been added under the edit text of player 1. On clicking this "Go" button, the bet of player 1 will be hidden and the Edit Text will be disabled until player 2 places a bet. This is so that player 1 could not place two consecutive bets without player 2 having paced any [12] (Figure 12).

Testing

The Testing process was used to test any smaller divisions of the code, to ensure it is performing as expected. Two different types of tools have been used to test the Duelling Phone game: the emulator, and device testing.

The emulator, provided by Android for developing Android applications, has many benefits and drawbacks. Although it allows the

Figure 11: Player name screen.

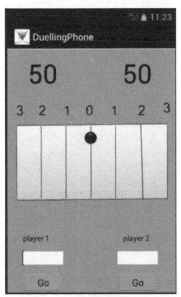

Figure 12: Two player mode screen.

Device	Android Version	Screen Size	Resolution	Processor	Memory
Samsung Galaxy Nexus	4.0.3	4.65-inch	720 x 1280 pixels	Dual-core 1.2 GHz	1 GB
Samsung Galaxy Nexus	4.0.4	4.65-inch	720 x 1280 pixels	Dual-core 1.2 GHz	1 GB
Samsung Galaxy Nexus	4.1.1	4.65-inch	720 x 1280 pixels	Dual-core 1.2 GHz	1 GB

Table 2: Various devices that have been used to test the application.

developer to test the application across a full range of devices (no extra hardware is required), it does not give a perfect representation of real world usage since there are many differences between the emulator and the actual hardware. There are differences in terms of security, network performance, and user experience, and while the button may be easily selected with the on screen cursor, it could be much more difficult to be selected using an actual touch event. Hence, it is of prime importance to test the application on an actual device. The following table shows the devices that have been used to test the application (Table 2).

It should be noted that in order to fix the problems found in the code, two main methods have been used to test each part of the code upon completion. The first method is represented by the Log class in Android.Util.Log. While running the game, this class creates and shows the log data, which represents the result of feedback from the code, while running it without any need to stop the program. On the other hand, the second method used for testing the project is by creating a breakpoint in the code. While running the program, the code stops at the breakpoint, going through the code, step by step. This provides many details about what the code is doing at any given line.

Conclusion

The goal of this research project was to design and implement the Duelling Phone game on open platforms for mobile devices. The Android has been chosen as the development platform for this game, since its API is open source, and its license is available free of charge which makes it accessible by commercial and experimental developers. Beside the SinglePlayer mode of the game, the game also provides a Two Player mode, whereby two people may compete against each other. The project works perfectly on Android devices with large screen sizes, which represents the vast majority of Android devices on the market.

It should be noted that as with most applications, there are updates and modifications to make the project even better. With new devices emerging in the electronics market every day, continuous support is an important issue to consider with Android applications, as, in the future, some changes may be required to support the different platforms. Although the project is not clear from several limitations, the objective of the project has been successfully achieved, with the creation and implementation of the Duelling Phone game in the SinglePlayer and the Two Player modes.

References

1. Charles A (2011) Nokia and RIM bleeding smartphone share while Android cleans up.

2. Virtual Technology Summit (2016).

3. Eclipse Homepage (2015).

4. Android Homepage (2015).

5. Siebers OP (2012) Object Oriented Modelling, Lecture 03. G64 Object Oriented System. The University of Nottingham.

6. Burnette Ed (2010) Hello, Android: Introducing Google's Mobile Development Platform. (3rdedtn), United States of America : Pragmatic Programmers.

7. Rogers R, Lobardo J, Mednieks Z, Meike G (2009) Android Application Development. O'Reilly Media. (1stedtn).

8. Cheng J (2007) iPhone in depth: the Ars review. Ars Technica.

9. Haselton T (2007) Rumor: 6G iPod manufacturing to begin in August. Ars technica.

10. Murphy Mark L (2009) The Busy Coder's Guide to Advanced Android Development. United States of America: CommonsWare.

11. Meier R (2010) Professional Android 2 Application Development. Wiley Publishing, Ed. Indianapolis, Indiana, US.

12. Application Fundamentals (2015) Android Developers.

18

Provenance Detection of Online News Article

Ruba Ali Alsuhaymi*

Department of Software Engineering, Prince Sultan University, Riyadh, Saudi Arabia

Abstract

At present, with the current wide spread of information on the social media, the recipient or the researcher needs more details about the received information or spread, including the provenance. With the current explosion of the news websites, there is a question of credibility of news articles on the internet. It is important to know whether the news is correct or not. This paper focuses on identifying the provenance of news articles. Also, trace the provenance of news articles often to see where did the first publication of such news appear. Is the news publication true (the credibility of the news), or is the news quoting from the provenance of the news on the news website or is plagiarism and redistributed on news websites on the Internet? In this paper, we will answer these questions through the design and implementation of two techniques Google Search API and Google Custom Search that will define the provenance of news articles through the technique Topic Detection and Tracking (TDT). Therefore, verifies the proposed technical quality in terms of performance metrics through several different experiments. Based on these experiments and tests it were discovered that the technique Google Search API is better performance than Google Custom Search in detecting the provenance of news articles. The Google Search API is the best technique, depending on the user satisfaction, the time it takes to view the results and the accuracy and validity. So, the result of the Google Search API is 90% while Google Custom Search 70%.

Keywords: Detection; News articles; Provenance; Plagiarism

Introduction

Nowadays, with the rapid growth of the Internet and the increasing amount of information on the Internet, and increase the number of news articles and news websites, huge amount of news articles that are published every day. So, the users need to know more details of information about the news articles published, including the provenance and the personal attributes of the user, like name, sex, education, location and race [1]. Thus, the challenges and the main purpose for the users is the capability for tracing and detecting the reliability and truth of information from among thousands of results. Through helping the readers to ensure the truthfulness of the news (the credibility of the news) through reading the news from news websites reliable. Also, check if the news website is plagiarized the news article and redistributed it on the news websites on the Internet or quoted the news article from the news website provenance. Finally, identify whether a news website is the first publication of such news. While the provenance is not limited to determining the news articles, the heritage of the artwork, archeology, paleontology, archives, manuscripts, printed books and computing science, is valid too many areas to find out their provenance facts.

Provenance is the history or chronology of the ownership of a valued object or work of arts or literature or location of historical objects. The provenance of an article can be defined as the information about the entities, activities and people involved in the production of a piece of data, and such can be used as information to evaluate the quality, reliability and confidence of the data [2]. Provenance (also referred to as lineage, pedigree, parentage, genealogy, and filiation) [3]. It can be described the provenance at different intervals depended on where it was used. Buneman et al. [4] definition the provenance of the data through the database systems, as well as describing the provenance of data and processes that reach into the database. Greenwood et al. [5] widen the definition of the provenance by recording workflow process through experience.

Plagiarism is theft of intellectual property, whether research or art or invention, etc. The reason of plagiarism is the easy access to web pages and databases, so the plagiarism is a big problem for publishers, researchers [6].

The benefit of this study is tracing and detecting the process of monitoring a stream of news articles in order to find those news articles that track (or discuss) the same event. The objective is to focus on detecting and organization the provenance of the news articles. As a result, the model will be developed to help individuals and organizing to define the provenance of news articles on any news websites also, support all languages such as Arabic and English etc. On the other hand, the research contributes to society by achieving the following objectives, help the reader to identify whether a news website is the first publication of such news, helping the reader to ensure the truthfulness of the news (the credibility of the news) through reading the news from news websites is reliable, or detect and determine whether the news article was quoting from the provenance or was plagiarism and redistributed on news websites on the Internet.

This paper describes the techniques that detect the provenance of news articles on the internet. The rest of this paper is organized as follows: Section 2 describes the related work. Section 3 describes the methods. Section 4 presents the experiments of the system and the results. Section 5 discusses the results of the system. Finally, give the conclusions and discussions of future work in section 6.

Related Work

Wylot et al. [7] the TripleProv is an approach used to collect data, storing, organizing, and tracking provenance information and then displaying the provenance. It can enter the provenance specification of the data one wants to use in order to reach the answer. Such as, if interest in the articles is about "Corona Virus" but you want the answer to come from provenance attributed to the "CNN News ".

Nallapati [8] presents a new approach to relate detection for Topic

---

*Corresponding author: Ruba Ali Alsuhaymi, Department of Software Engineering, Prince Sultan University, Rafha St, Salah Ad Din, Riyadh 12435 11586, Saudi Arabia, E-mail: ruba.alsuhaymi@gmail.com

Detection and Tracking (TDT) that will define the provenance of news articles. Topic Detection and Tracking (TDT) is a form of event-based information organization [9]. The goal of Topic Detection and Tracking (TDT) is gathering the news to groups to discuss a single topic.

Nies et al. [10] the resulting derivations are structured in the Provenance Data Model (PROV-DM), which is the discovery of provenance of news articles. With this approach, it was discovered that the provenance of news articles by 73% out of 410 news articles, and with 68% accuracy. The Provenance Data Model (PROV-DM), is being developed by the World Wide Web Consortium (W3C1) Provenance Working Group.

In Chang et al. [11] the focus is to design and implementation of an application that summarizes and tracks algorithms for Chinese news, and give lists of news that depends on the timestamp in orders to guarantee ease of understanding. Also, it has implemented Term Frequency- density (TF–density) algorithm work to weight the term list for each event. Also, it makes a word vector for each event by utilizing the term information table. Term Frequency- density (TF–density) algorithm that is proposed and compared with the algorithms Term Frequency– Inverse Document Frequency (TF-IDF) and Term Frequency– Inverse Word Frequency (TF-IWF).

The research provides an experimental analysis and focuses on improving means of summarizing a group of news articles to help readers to understand topics quicker. It is limited to tracking Chinese language news articles.

Bea and Claire [12] describes the Synergetic Content Creation and Communication (SYNC3) project for development of a system for tracking news articles. An event is defined in the news by using TDT techniques to know a particular time and place of event. The system tracks the provenance of news articles. Then these groups are handled by labeling and extracting the temporal and geographical relations between the events.

It is used to develop 12,547 documents from nine different news provenance "(AP, BBC, CNN, NYT, Reuters, Ria Novosti, USA TODAY, WP and Xinhua)" from the date 20 May to June 3, 2009 [12].

This study focused to labeling of the news article, with labeling the topic and the foundations of the temporal, spatial news articles, and provide some preliminary statistics on the data. This allows determining the suitability of the labels news articles as well as dates, locations, and adjust the accuracy of the labeling process [12].

Kamalpreet, Balkrishan [13] discussed a way to detect plagiarism through the crawl service provided by the custom search engine API using semantic technology. This approach is searching through a focus on keywords.

The verification of plagiarism in documents, through measuring the percentage of similarity and matching of a string of the document on number of n-grams participate between different documents. The results of the proposed method are a quick and efficient and accurate.

Methods

To detect the provenance of the news articles on the news websites on the Internet. The method proposed for detecting the provenance of news articles is Topic Detection and Tracking technique, through using Google Custom Search or Google Search API. Google Custom Search is a platform offered by Google that allows web developers to offer customized information in web search results. Also, classified and organize the queries and create customized search engines based on

Google search [14,15]. Google Search API is used to provide keywords for search engine Google and get the retrieval results from Google, and the combination of these two things can help users to find the information needed to better search [16].

The method consists of four interrelated phases. The first phase is search for the news articles on all the news websites, the second is printing the first published news article, the third is determined the type of news articles published by relying on the first news article published, and the final is displaying the results. These phases depend on each other.

In the first phase, enables the user to enter any news article, whether a word or several words or a phrase, or title of a news article, or even the full text of the news article in the text box; to search for all the similar news articles in the news websites. The second phase, displays the title of the news article and news websites link, date and time of the publication of the news article and the type of news article. Also, know the first publisher of the news, by searching for the oldest date among all publications of the same news article, considering the oldest date for each news article in the news website that is a first publisher the news article. The third phase, determined the type of news articles published, through compare the first news publication with other news articles, to detect if the news was quoted or plagiarized the news article, and it calculates the percentage of similarity and thus, printing "Plagiarism" if the percentage of copies and quote is great and not refer to the news provenance, but print "Quote this news article from the provenance of news website " when refer to the news provenance, or "Not related to this title" if this title not related to the title search, or print "This title written by this website" to tell the user this title copied from this website. Also, the search results are organized by the date and time.

Final phase, display the results and print the website name (link) that first news website published the news article, and the title of the news; to make it easier for the reader or researcher to find the provenance of news. Also, the user can compare the first news article enter with other news published on news websites, or compare the first news article was published with news articles published on other news websites, as shown in Figure 1.

On the other hand, are validated model proposed by experiment of two different techniques are Google Custom Search and Google Search API, in next section.

Experimental Results

In this section, will display the experiments and their results, by dividing the experience into two parts: the first experiment was applied Google Search API to detect the provenance of news articles in all the news websites in English and Arabic language. The second experiment was applied Google Custom Search service to detect the provenance of news articles to certain news websites in English and Arabic language.

In each experiment, will be the experiment the program by the 10 participants. To confirm and validate these experiments, it should be measured through using software metric factors, particularly factors that mean "how well does the tool run", factors of the product are Effectiveness, Efficiency and Satisfaction users [17,18]. So, after each experiment of the program, the participant will respond to the questions that display in Table 1 for first experiment and Table 2 for the second experiment. To determine the outcome or feedback of the experiment the program and how effective the program. In Tables 1 and 2 can show the usability standards during the user experiment this task. These standards are task, completion of the involved tasks, and the time to complete tasks, and satisfaction from the experiment. All these standards to measure based on user feedback. Thus, give the results of the completion of tasks or the time consumed to complete tasks from the user view which evaluates the experiment.

First experiment

In this experiment, we used the Google Search API to search in any news websites. The results of the questionnaire of the experiment are shown in Table 1. Also, the results of the experiment will show in Figures 1 and 2.

Advantages:

1. It allows to search in all the news websites only and support all languages.

2. The program arranged news articles by the date and time from the oldest to the newer and vice versa.

3. The software will also not allow the ads to appear in search results.

4. Allows viewing 100 results.

5. Can click on the link of news to read the full details.

Limitation:

1. Search in any news websites that may be no reliability for news articles.

Second experiment

In this experiment, we used Custom Search Google to search for news websites selected such as: BBC, CNN, CNBC, SPY, Aljazeera, Reuters, New York Times, Huffington Post, Al-Arabiya, Daily Mail. These websites were chosen based on a survey was published through social media. It received 73 responses, 43 responses by were female and 30 were male. Also, it ensures 3 people of PhDs and 13 Masters and 37 Bachelor's and 20 High school graduate. The results of the questionnaire of the experiment is shown in Table 2. Also, the results of the experiment will show in Figures 3 and 4.

Advantages:

1. It allows to search in any news websites selected before and support all languages.

2. The program arranged news articles by the date and time from the oldest to the newer and vice versa.

3. The software will also not allow the ads to appear in search results.

4. The websites that are being searched for news websites and has a reliable, professional standard for the news. Also, does not search in blog or any web pages on the Internet are not interested for the news articles and unreliable.

Usability Standards	Description				
Effectiveness	Task completion:				
	How describe the difficulty or easy to achieve these tasks?				
	Task	Completed successfully	Completed with difficulties	Failed	Not used used
	Enter the news article to be searched	100%			
	Click the search button	100%			
	Shows the results	90%	10%		
	Click compares button if the user wishes to compare the news article published with the first news article published	70%	10%		20%

Table 1: The usability results for the first experiment.

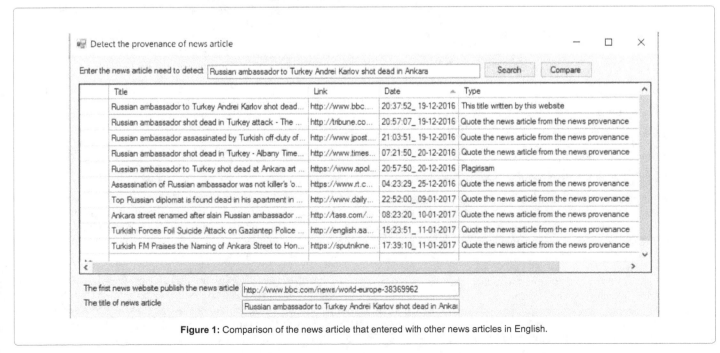

Figure 1: Comparison of the news article that entered with other news articles in English.

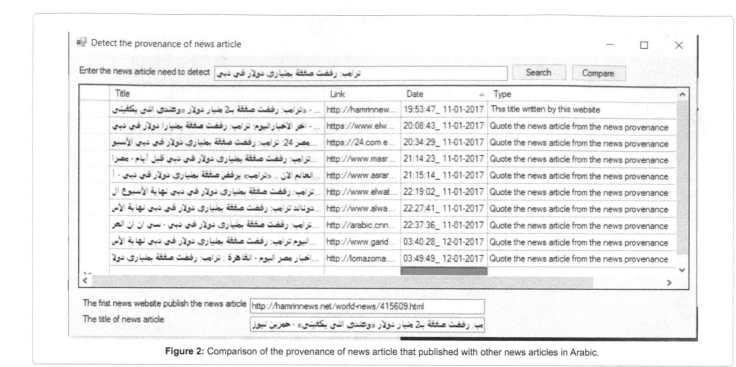

Figure 2: Comparison of the provenance of news article that published with other news articles in Arabic.

Efficiency	Consumed time:			
	What amount of time it took to achieve these tasks?			
	Task	**Very little time between (5-15 seconds)**	**Medium time between (16 seconds -1 minutes)**	**Too much time (more than one minutes)**	**Not used**
	Enter the news article to be searched	100%			
	Click the search button	100%			
	Shows the results	90%	10%		
	Click compares button if the user wishes to compare the news article published with the first news article published	70%	10%		20%
Satisfaction	Questions:			
	Questions	**Very satisfied**	**Normal satisfied**	**Unsatisfied**
	How satisfied while using this application for the detection the provenance of news articles?	90%	10%	

Table 2: The usability results for the second experiment.

5. Allows viewing 100 results.

6. Can click on the link of news to read the full details.

Limitations:

1. Sometimes it does not display the time and date.

2. Sometimes it does not display all the results accurately.

Finally, through two experiments using Google Search API and Google Custom Search. The results of the Google Search API are better than Google Custom Search to detect the provenance of news articles. The Google Search API best technique, depending on the user satisfaction and the time it takes to view the results and the accuracy and validity. Show in the figure each experiment is recorded and discussed. Therefore, the use of the program reduces the time and effort in the search for news articles and classified according to the older for the date and time and with accuracy and fast. Also, display the time and date of the news article and determine the type of news article is a plagiarism, or was excerpted the news article from the provenance of

the news on news website, or is it modified or not has any related to the title of the news article.

Discussion

There are two experiments involving 10 participants, and measured the usability to use and the time it takes for each task and finally the satisfaction the participant for the experiments. When looking at the results generally of experiments that presented in Tables 1 and 2, therefore, increased rate of satisfaction to achieve the desired usability of the terms: the ability to complete all tasks successfully, take a little time to finish the tasks, and satisfaction to use the program. In Table 3 show the usability results for different experiments.

Finally, through two experiments using the Google Search API and Google Custom Search. The results of Google Search API are better than Google Custom Search to detect the provenance of news articles. The Google Search API best technique, depending on the user satisfaction and the time it takes to view the results and the accuracy and validity.

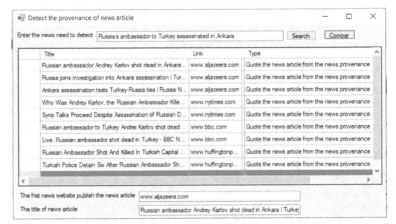

Figure 3: Comparison of the news article that entered with other news articles in English.

Figure 4: Comparison of the provenance of news article that published with other news articles In Arabic.

Task	Google Search API		Google Custom Search	
	Completed successfully	Completed in Very little time between (5-15 seconds)	Completed successfully	Completed in Very little time between (5-15 seconds)
Enter the news article to be searched	100%	100%	100%	100%
Click the search button	100%	100%	100%	100%
Shows the results	90%	90%	80%	80%
Click compares button if the user wishes to compare the news article published with the first news article	70%	70%	70%	70%

	published			
How satisfied while using this application for the detection the provenance of news articles	90%		70%	

Table 3: The usability results for different experiments.

As shown in Table 3.

Conclusion and Future Work

In this paper, we have investigated the detection of the provenance of news articles in various news websites on the Internet through developing a program for detection the first spread of the news article and the reliability of the news article. Also, determined if quotes the news article from the provenance of the news on the news website, or the news article has been plagiarized and redistributed on news website on the Internet, or not has any related to the news article. Finally, if the news websites where publication credible and correct a news article or not. They also discussed the relevant offering approaches, models and techniques related to the provenance in the literature review. As well as, display the projects, tools and theories about the provenance and that are related to the topic of the paper. It has been used Google Search API due to its efficacy in detecting the provenance of news articles. It involves detecting the provenance of news articles into four interrelated phases of the process. The first phase is search for the news articles on all the news websites, the second is printing the first published news article, the third is determined the type of news articles published by relying on the first news article published, and the final is displaying the results. These phases depend on each other. On the other hand, are validated model proposed by experiment of two different techniques are Google Custom Search and Google Search API. It has been the conclusion that the technique Google Search API is best through factor ease of use and user satisfaction with the results.

For the future works, will focus to enhance the results through increase the accuracy of the results. Furthermore, it can detect the provenance of the news articles through the inclusion of the photo or video or voice for news article.

References

1. Gundecha P, Ranganath S, Feng Z, Liu H (2013) A tool for collecting provenance data in social media. 19th ACM Special Interest Group on Knowledge Discovery in Data (SIGKDD), International Conference on Knowledge Discovery and Data Mining, KDD 2013, Chicago, Illinois, USA. pp: 1462-1465.

2. Groth P, Moreau L (2013) PROV-Overview An Overview of the PROV Family of Documents. World Wide Web Consortium.

3. Simmhan YL, Plale B, Gannon D (2005) A Survey of Data Provenance Techniques. Computer Science Department, Indiana University.

4. Buneman P, Khanna S, Tan WC (2001) Why and Where: A Characterization of Data Provenance. Lecture Notes in Computer Science, pp: 316-330.

5. Greenwood M, Goble CA, Stevens RD, Zhao J, Addis M, et al (2003). Provenance of e-Science Experiments-experience from Bioinformatics. UK e-Science All Hands Meeting 2003, East Midlands Conference Centre, Nottingham, pp: 223-226.

6. Maurer HA, Kappe F, Zaka B (2006) Plagiarism - A Survey. Journal of Universal Computer Science 12: 1050-1084.

7. Wylot M, Cudré-Mauroux P, Groth PT (2015) A Demonstration of TripleProv: Tracking and Querying Provenance over Web Data. International Conference on Very Large Data Bases (PVLDB) 8: 1992-2003.

8. Nallapati R (2003) Semantic Language Models for Topic Detection and Tracking. Conference of the North American Chapter of the Association for Computational Linguistics on Human Language Technology. Proceedings of the HLT-NAACL 2003 Student Research Workshop 3: 1-6.

9. Makkonen J, Ahonen-Myka H, Salmenkivi M (2003) Topic Detection and Tracking with Spatio-Temporal Evidence. ECIR'03 Proceedings of the 25th European conference on IR research ECIR, Pisa, Italy. pp: 251-265.

10. Nies TD, Coppens S, Deursen DV, Mannens E, De Walle RV (2012) Automatic Discovery of High-Level Provenance Using Semantic Similarity. Provenance and Annotation of Data and Processes - 4th International Provenance and Annotation Workshop. pp: 97-110.

11. Chang HT, Liu SW, Mishra N (2015) A Tracking and Summarization System for Online Chinese News Topics. Aslib Journal of Information Management. Emerald Group Publishing Limited 67: 687-699.

12. Alex B, Glaire C (2010) Labelling and Spatio - Temporal Grounding of News Events. Proceedings of the Workshop on Computational Linguistics in a World of Social Media at NAACL 2010, Los Angeles, USA. pp: 27-28.

13. Sharma K, Jindal B (2016) An improved Online Plagiarism Detection Approach for Semantic Analysis using Custom Search Engine. 3rd International Conference on Computing for Sustainable Global Development (INDIACom).

14. Gulli A, Signorini A (2005) The Indexable Web is More than 11.5 Billion Pages. WWW'05: Special Interest Tracks and Posters of the 14th International Conference on World Wide Web. pp: 902-903.

15. Allauddin M, Azam F (2011) Service Crawling using Google Custom Search API. International Journal of Computer Applications 34: 10-15.

16. Yunpeng C, Peng T, Shihong L, Sufen S (2010) Study of Agricultural Search Engine Based on FAO Agrovoc Ontology and Google API. Proceedings 2010 World Automation Congress (WAC), Japan. pp: 439-444.

17. Galin D (2004) Software Quality Assurance: From Theory to Practice. Pearson, England.

18. Cavano JP, McCall JA (1978) A Framework for the Measurement of Software Quality. ACM SIGMETRICS Special Interest Group on Performance Evaluation Review 7: 133-139.

19

Thermodynamic and Quantum Mechanical Limitations of Electronic Computation

Fayez Fok Al Adeh*

The Syrian Cosmological Society, Damascus, Syria

Abstract

The role of entropy and uncertainty in electronic computations is used to derive a fundamental thermodynamic equation. The thermodynamic limitations of electronic computations are expressed in terms of macroscopic disorder, while quantum mechanical limitations are formulated through uncertainty relationships. Electronic computations are described quantum-mechanically, and hence provide a reasonable argument in favour of the wave interpretation of quantum mechanics.

Keywords: Entropy; Electronic computations; Uncertainty; Quantum mechanics

Introduction

The second law of thermodynamics is a universal law. The galactic spiral structures, for example [1], arise in response to the interaction of that law and the law of gravitation. The second law states that some forms of transformation of one kind of energy to another do not occur in natural processes. The allowed transformations in a closed system are always characterized by a non-decreasing entropy (introduction of macroscopic disorder). In open systems where the entropy is kept constant [1], the allowed transformations are always characterized by a decrease in the amount of free energy available to do useful work.

Another profound principle of nature is worth mentioning here. The Heisenberg's uncertainty principle asserts that nature forbids knowledge beyond a certain limit [2]. This is not the result of the restricted abilities of the available tools or the contemporary theorizing methods.

I will now attempt to apply both the second law of thermodynamics and Heisenberg's uncertainty principle to electronic computations. I will conclude by giving a quantum mechanical description of these computations.

Floating - Point Numbers

$$0.1 < |m| < 1$$

By a normalized floating-decimal representation of a number a, we imply representation of the form:

$$a = mx \quad a = m \times 10^q$$

where q is an integer. Such a representation is possible for all numbers, and unique if $a \neq 0$ [3]. The variable m is the fractional part or mantissa and q is the exponent.

In a computer, the number of digits for q and m is limited. The number of digits characterizes a given computer. This means that only a finite set of numbers can be represented in the machine. The numbers in this set (for a given q and m) are called floating-point numbers. The limited number of digits in the exponent implies that a is limited to an interval which is called the machine's floating-point variable range.

In a computer, a is represented by the floating number $\overline{a} = \overline{m} \times 10^q$

Where $\overline{m}$ is the mantissa m, rounded off to t decimals. The precision of the machine is said then to be t decimal digits. Now suppose that the floating numbers in a machine have base B (ten for the decimal number system) and a mantissa with t digits. (The binary digit which gives the sign of the number is not counted) Then, every real number in the floating-point range in the machine can be represented by a relative error which does not exceed the machine unit (round-off unit) u which [3] is defined by:

$$u = \begin{cases} 0.5 \times B^{1-t} & \text{if rounding is used} \\ B^{1-t} & \text{if truncation is used} \end{cases}$$

The floating-point set of numbers is not a field. It is also not a ring. Besides, it is neither a group, nor a semi-group. The elementary operations in the real number system, are not well defined in this set. If we denote the result of addition in this set by fl(x + y), then associativity does not, in general, hold for floating addition. Consider floating addition using seven decimals in the mantissa,

$$a = 0.1234567 \times 10^0, \ b = 0.4711325 \times 10^4, \ c = -b$$

$$\text{fl } (b + c) = 0$$

$$\text{fl } (a + \text{fl } (b + c) = 0.1234567 \times 10^0$$

$$\text{fl } (a + b) = 0.4711448 \times 10^4$$

$$\text{fl}(\text{fl } (a + b) + c) = 0.0000123 \times 10^4 = 0.123 \times 10^0$$

Hence: $\text{fl}(\text{fl } (a + b) + c) \neq \text{fl}(a + \text{fl } (b + c))$

In general, the usual laws and operations of the real number system are not applicable to the floating-point set of numbers. Strictly speaking, we have to define special new laws and operations for each computer and each problem. Moving the problem to a new computer forces a redefinition of these laws and operations. Such a definition necessitates a premature prediction of the results obtained after solving the problem. This situation constrains us to a vicious circle; defining the aforementioned laws and operations is conditional, we must know beforehand the results based on using them. These results represent what we expect upon employing a given computer in solving a definite problem. Here we face a sort of a contradiction; it is the problem of formulating a definition and then reformulating a new one and then

*Corresponding author: Fayez Fok Al Adeh, President of The Syrian Cosmological Society, Damascus, Syria, E-mail: hayfa@scs-net.org

another one and so on ad infinitum. The task looks impossible, and the impossibility appears to be fundamental. It is not the result of a lack of abilities of a given machine, and it has nothing to do with the insufficiencies inherent in the chosen algorithm.

In real life, we seek a separate fundamental [4] algorithm and apply a suitable algorithm to each problem. The applied algorithm depends on the machine and the operating system used. An amalgamation of these two types of algorithms leads to a resultant program. I call this the resultant algorithm. The whole process is based on supplying concrete proofs assuring that the algorithms (fundamental, applied, and resultant) that are looked for will solve the problem during an acceptable period of time, using a given machine and a definite operating system.

The various sources of errors are important in formulating my results [5]. Among these are:

- errors due to rounding;

- errors due to the truncation of series; unjustified simplification of formulae;

- a complex of correct logical propositions resulting in a machine default; mathematical instability;

- catastrophic cancellation; and

- Exaggerated sensitivity of an algorithm.

It is a good programming practice, however, to seek a limit [3] for the relative error in the output data. Such a limit is given by:

$$\approx C_p(r + C_A u) \tag{1}$$

where: r is a bound for the relative error in the input data; u is the machine unit; C_p is the condition number for the problem p. With given input data, it is the largest relative change, measured with u as a unit, that the exact output data of the problem can have, if there is a relative disturbance in the input data of size u; C_A is the condition number for the algorithm A. By means of backward error analysis, the output data which the algorithm produces (under the influence of round-off error) is the exact output data of a problem of the same type in which the input data has been changed relatively by a few u. That change measured with u as a unit, is called the condition number of the algorithm. Hence, the condition number has a small value for a good algorithm and a large value for a poor algorithm.

Entropy

The equivalence of information and entropy [6] is no more surprising than the equivalence of mass and energy implied by Einstein's formula: $E = m c^2$, where $c = 3 \times 10^{10}$ cm s^{-1} is the velocity of light; 1 erg is equivalent to a mass of 10^{-21} g. Likewise, 1 bit of information is equivalent to $K ln\,2 = 10^{-16}$ erg/degree kelvin of entropy (where $K = 1.38 \times 10^{-16}$ erg/ degree Kelvin, is Boltzmann's constant).

In general, let W represent the number of different micro-states which correspond to the same macrostate. The entropy S of a macrostate is equal to [6]:

Boltzmann's constant K times the natural logarithm of W:

$$S = K \ln W \tag{2}$$

Since the natural logarithm is a monotonic function, S attains its maximum value when W does.

The equivalence of entropy and information means that new information is obtained at the price of increased entropy (in a different part of the system). In other words, some energy must be dissipated. The minimum energy consumption per one bit of information obtained is $K\,T$. In 2, where T is the absolute temperature. Suppose that we are running a moderate program, the output of which consists of 10000 decimal numbers. Assume also that to each one of these numbers there corresponds a set of configurations of the internal memory equivalent to 10 decimal numbers.

We would then have a total of 110 000 decimal numbers. An increase in accuracy of one decimal digit per number will entail a corresponding increase in global entropy given by:

$$10^{-16} \times 16 \times 11 \times 10^4 \times 300 \times 4 \approx 10^{-8}\,\text{erg}$$

assuming an absolute temperature of 300 K and four bits of information for the additional decimal digit. This is still a very small amount of entropy. In the next section, we will formulate a conclusion about the temperature of the memory and its role in the energy consumption for a computation.

I consider as a microstate, a set of real numbers representing a theoretical solution to a given problem. It is assumed that such a solution exists but is not necessarily attained. Any computerized solution of the problem is only an approximation of this set of real numbers. The microstate is the sequence of configurations of the internal memory of the computer leading to the approximate solution which can be included within the microstate. A program is executed by triggering a series of pulses [7]. Each pulse gives rise to a new configuration of the memory. The set of all these configurations constitute a microstate of the sought for theoretical solution. Trying to solve the same problem using another computer and a different algorithm provides a new microstate. Each pulse, in a sense, assigns the memory. Each assignment, in turn, can be translated into some set of floating-point numbers. In some programming languages (such as APL/360) [8], one can write a program using assignments only.

An increase in accuracy forces an extension of the mantissa. I can now introduce the notion of a dynamic computer. This is a computer whose set of floating-point numbers can be extended in response to any demand for more accuracy, and it must be ever developing. This is equivalent to the continuous employment of successive generations of computers.

In what follows, 'computer' will define a dynamic computer which is necessary to attain an increase in accuracy. A dynamic computer allows new microstates to develop and produce corresponding increases in global entropy. This is easily verified using Equation 2 which tells us that the continuous search for more accuracy entails a gradual increase in global entropy. Moreover, an indefinite search for accuracy will lead to infinite global entropy. If we refer to the formula [9]:

$$I = I_0\,e^{-S/K}$$

Here I and I_0 are the information content at ordinary temperatures, and at absolute zero respectively, of a closed local system. More accuracy means an increase of local informa-tion content and a corresponding decrease in local entropy. This is balanced by a parallel increase in global entropy.

Thermodynamic Equation

The second law of thermodynamics can be written in the form:

$$T ds \geq du + p dv + y dx \tag{3}$$

or by using equation (2)

$$TKdw/w \geq du + pdv + ydx \tag{4}$$

where T, is the absolute temperature; S, the entropy of the system; U, the internal energy of the system; P, the pressure within the system; V, the volume of the system; y, a generalized external force; and x, a generalized coordinate

The inequality corresponds to a nonequilibrium state of the system; when the system is still on the way to equilibrium, and the equality corresponds to a system already in equilibrium.

$$Tds = du + pdv + ydx \tag{5}$$

or again by using equation (2)

$$TKdw/w = du + pdv + ydx \tag{6}$$

The different components of a computer communicate with each other by signals. The reception and interpretation of a signal constitutes a physical measurement, which is assigned to a given location of the memory. The degree of assignment is characterized by the total sum per unit volume of the number of different assigned locations of the memory:

$$j = \frac{1}{V} \sum_{i-1}^{n} ji \tag{7}$$

where j_i refers to a distinct location of the memory, and V (the volume) is the total number of accessible locations of the memory.

If M is the mass of the memory, then:

$$j = A \; M \tag{8}$$

A is the mass specific degree of assignment, or the mass specific number of distinguishable messages. If the assignment is the outcome of a physical measurement, then the faster the measurement the larger is the energy that is required to make the signal readable with sufficiently small error probability. If the total signalling energy is limited, then there is a trade-off between the number of distinguishable signals that can be sent and the time required to identify them.

Let H denote the total signalling energy. It is expressed in units of energy. But H affects an assignment which is interpreted as information. Hence we can refer also to H in bits of information.

Now H changes j to $j + dj$. The work done in such a change is:

$$dL = -Hdj \tag{9}$$

The minus sign shows that when the number of assigned locations increases, work is expended on the memory.

Replacing y dx in equation (5) by $-H$ dj, and get:

$$Tds = du + pdv - Hdj \tag{10}$$

The enthalpy of the computer in this case is:

$$I = u + pV - Hj \tag{11}$$

Maxwell's thermodynamic equations give us:

$$\left(\frac{\partial j}{\partial T} \right) S,V = \left(\frac{\partial S}{\partial H} \right) j,v \tag{12}$$

$$\left(\frac{\partial j}{\partial S} \right) H,P = \left(\frac{\partial S}{\partial H} \right) S,P \tag{13}$$

$$\left(\frac{\partial j}{\partial S} \right) T,V = \left(\frac{\partial T}{\partial H} \right) J,V \tag{14}$$

$$\left(\frac{\partial j}{\partial T} \right) H,P = \left(\frac{\partial S}{\partial H} \right) T,P \tag{15}$$

From Equation 2 by taking differentials:

$$dS = K \frac{dW}{W} \tag{16}$$

substituting in Equation 10 from Equation 16 we get

$$TKdW = \left(du + pdV - Hdj \right) \tag{17}$$

By combining Equations 17 and 11 with Equations 12-15 it is easy to find the relation between the entropic properties of the memory (i.e. its macroscopic disorder properties), its internal energy and enthalpy, and j and H. Equation 17 is the fundamental thermo-dynamic equation of electronic computations.

In the case of the dynamic computer, we should rewrite Equation 17 in the form of an inequality:

$$TKdW \geq \left(du + pdV - Hdj \right) W \tag{18}$$

At absolute zero where $T = 0$, d $W = 0$, Equation 17 gives us:

$$Hdj = du + pdv \tag{19}$$

substituting in Equation 11, we deduce that the enthalpy of the memory remains constant at absolute zero. Equation 10 yields:

$$\left(\frac{\partial u}{\partial j} \right) T,V = \left(\frac{\partial S}{\partial j} \right) T,V + H \tag{20}$$

Using Equation 14 we find that:

$$\left(\frac{\partial u}{\partial j} \right) T,V = H - T \left(\frac{\partial H}{\partial T} \right) j,V \tag{21}$$

The physical meaning of the derivative shows how much H must be increased with increasing temperature of the memory so that the assignment j remains the same, regardless of the increase in temperature (which will affect the assignment).

Note that the memory's macroscopic disorder is not meant to be realistic in that it would be practically possible for such disorder to be attained. The entropy of the memory is merely a yardstick beyond which macroscopic disorder surely takes place. It is comparable to saying that astronauts cannot travel at speeds exceeding the velocity of light, though in practice their speeds are much more limited.

If a result is to be formulated, then it will be a sort of summary asserting that electronic computations are not out of the grasp of the second law of thermodynamics. A computer is only a limited ordering machine. Increasing its ordering tasks without bounds is impossible, for such an increase will end sooner or later in macroscopic disorder and chaos.

Heisenberg's Uncertainty Principle

According to quantum mechanics, the existence of a physical system is related to measurement. A measurement by definition, is any physical interaction, and physical interactions obey Heisenberg's uncertainty principle. The so-called energy [10] version of the principle states that if a limited time T is available for making the measurement, then the energy of the system cannot be determined better than to within an amount of order h / T.

This is equivalent to:

$$ET \geq \hbar \tag{22}$$

where: E is the energy of the system; T, the period or measurement; and $\hbar$ planck's constant divided by 2 .

In particular, if a system is unstable having a finite lifetime t, its energy cannot be measured to within an accuracy better than about $\hbar /t$.

Let the measurement in our case be a signalling process producing a bit of information. Denote by F the rate of signal flow in a computer (in bits per second). Then F and T would be reciprocals. We can deduce that no closed computer system, however constructed, can have F exceeding E/$\hbar$.

Let m be the total mass of the system: which includes the mass equivalent of the energy of signals employed in the computer, as well as the mass of the materials of which the computer and its power supply are made. In computers the structural mass outweighs the mass equivalent of the signal energy, However, the mass equivalent of the energy of signals can be computed by applying Einstein's formula: Energy = (mass) × (square of velocity of light).

In other words, the total mass equivalent of the energy that is invested in signals cannot exceed m, the total mass of the system.

We would have:

$$F \geq \frac{mc^2}{\hbar} \tag{23}$$

I now consider the electro weak theory which unifies electromagnetism and weak forces. It indicates that, during infinitesimal periods of time, huge amounts of energy can be created from nothing and even transformed into particles [11]. But before such periods end, everything created from nothing must vanish, and the situation must return to normal.

Imagine a hypothetical computer which accomplishes all of its tasks during an infinitesimal period. The result will not be transferred to the usual output devices, but they will be transmitted by telepathy to the mind of the operator. Such a hypothetical computer is called a quantum computer, and should be developed during the coming centuries. Remember, any concrete scientific model is based on stirring of the imagination!

Consider the momentum version of Heisenberg's uncertainty principle. It says that one cannot know both where something is and how fast it is moving. The uncertainty of the momentum and the uncertainty of the position are complementary and the product of the two is constant [12]. We can write the law as:

$$\Delta x \, \Delta p \geq \hbar \tag{24}$$

where: x is the uncertainty in the position; p, the uncertainty in momentum.

Let (x, t) be the wave function of an electron contributing to an assignment at a location of the memory given by the coordinate x. (We assume here a linear memory). This assignment takes place at the moment t.

If we assume a gaussian wave packet, then it is easy to verify that [13]:

$$\left(\Delta x \right)^2 = \frac{1}{4} a^2 + h^2 t^2 / m^2 a^2 \tag{25}$$

where a is a constant.

Equality 25 says that assignments occurring at later times are prone to higher uncertainties. Since x refers to a general location of the memory, we conclude that no closed computer system, however constructed, can run programs of infinite lengths (practically very long programs). Compare with the very long program that governs the lifetime of a human individual, perhaps it violates the principles of quantum mechanics?

Consider now the case in which the probability density at each location x of the memory is independent of time. It is called a stationary state, and is characterized by a definite energy.

If we substitute zero for t in Equation 25, we obtain:

$$\Delta x = \frac{a}{2} \tag{26}$$

Using Inequality 24 we arrive at:

$$\Delta p \geq \frac{2\hbar}{a} \tag{27}$$

Since uncertainty in momentum induces a corresponding uncertainty in assignment, a similar conclusion to the previous one can be drawn from Inequality 27.

As in the case of entropy in electronic computations, uncertainty limitations may not emerge in practical situations, yet they form another yardstick beyond which improvement cannot be made: improvements mean extending tlie memory, as well as increasing the lengths of programs.

Quantum Mechanical Description

This section is not strictly devoted to a quantum mechanical description of electronic computations, rather it looks at what such a description can provide in terms of the many-worlds interpretation of quantum mechanics [14].

The interpretations of quantum mechanics are, in brief:

1. The popular interpretation: here the wave function is regarded as objectively characterizing the single system, obeying a deterministic wave equation when the system is isolated but changing probabilistically and discontinuously under observation.

2. The Copenhagen interpretation.

3. The 'hidden variables' interpretation.

4. The stochastic process interpretation: this point of view holds that the fundamental processes of nature are stochastic.

5. The wave interpretation: this is the interpretation we are interested in. A correlation is established between the observer and the observed. In this situation, any borderline between the two disappears.

In our case the observer is the mind, and the observed is the computer.

A computer that is operated for a finite period of time, and a future computer will be equivalent in the sense that the fundamental characteristics of the floating-point set of numbers will be the same in both. This is because any computer has a limited space for the mantissa. This quantity is the precision of the machine t.

Suppose now that one of the following two scenarios occurs. In the first case, we partition a given problem and all the operations included therein, so that the available space for the mantissa is used iteratively so that all the input, intermediate, and output digits are accommodated without truncation. From a theoretical point of view, we will need an infinite period of time to process the whole problem. In the second case, we wait for an infinite period of time and use the computer that will be available afterwards to solve the same problem.

In both cases, the floating-point set of numbers will converge and coincide in the limit with the real number system. Besides, all of the aforementioned sources of errors will be eliminated. Specifically, we do not need simplification of formulae without justification. Also we can avoid use of algorithms with exaggerated sensitivity. Lastly, we will be in a position to choose the simplest possible logical propositions.

Under our assumptions, the bound for the relative error in the output data, given by Equation 1, should become independent of the machine unit.

Differentiating with respect to u, we get:

$$\Delta' = C_p' \left(r + C_A u \right) + C_p \left(r + C_A u \right)' \qquad (28)$$

$$\frac{\Delta'}{\Delta} = \frac{C_p'}{C_p} + \frac{\left(r + C_A u \right)'}{\left(r + C_A u \right)} \qquad (29)$$

putting $\Delta' = 0$ in Equation 29 gives:

$$\frac{C_p'}{C_p} + \frac{\left(r + C_A u \right)'}{\left(r + C_A u \right)} = 0 \qquad (30)$$

Integrating this differential equation, we obtain:

$$C_p \left(r + C_A u \right) = \Delta = \text{constant} \qquad (31)$$

Since r is arbitrary, Equation 31 cannot hold unless $u = 0$, and hence $C_p = C_A = 0$.

Since u is proportional to B^{1-t}, in both cases t will equal infinity. Hence, either of our proposed cases is equivalent to operating a computer built so that the space designed to hold the mantissa is of infinite size, i.e. the precision of the machine equals infinity. Such a computer will coincide exactly with the real number system.

Since the real number system is what the mind tries to test on observing the computer, we conclude that the borderline vanishes completely between the mind and the computer in the aforementioned situation. One of the main characteristics of the wave interpretation of quantum mechanics is its specific viewpoint of measurement. According to this interpretation, any interaction between two entities is a measurement. We might reasonably assert from this that either the first quantity measures the second, or vice-versa. For finite times of interaction the measurement is only approximate, approaching exactness as the time of interaction increases indefinitely. But through our mental experiment we have shown that this amounts to the same thing. Thus we have succeeded in providing a reasonable argument in favor of the wave interpretation of quantum mechanics.

References

1. Shu FH (1982) The Physical Universe, An Introduction to Astronomy. University Science Books.

2. d'Espagnat B (1976) Conceptual Foundations of Quantum Mechanics. Massachusetts: Benjamin, Inc.

3. Dahlquist G, Bjorck A (1974) Numerical Methods. New York: Prentice-Hall 43-59.

4. Rader R (1979) Advanced Software Design Techniques. New York: McGraw-Hill 105-110.

5. Rifai G (1977) Supreme Council of Sciences- SYRIA 17th Science Week Publications, pp: 324-54.

6. Makarov IM (1987) Cybernetics of Living Matter. Moscow: Mir Publishers 83-86.

7. Nashelsky L (1988) Introduction to Digital Computer Technology. New York: Wiley pp: 389-420.

8. Hellerman H, Smith IA (1976) APL/360 Programming and Applications. New York: McGraw-Hill pp: 35-122..

9. Stonier T (1990) Information and the Internal Structure of the Universe. Berlin: Sprin ger-Verlag pp: 37-41.

10. Tarasov L (1980) Basic Concepts of Quantum Mechanics. Moscow: Mir Publishers pp: 25-48.

11. Davies P (1984) Superforce. New York: Simon and Schuster pp: 117-124.

12. Landshoff P, Metherell A (1979) Simple Quantum Physics. Cambridge University Press pp: 1-40.

13. Feynman R, Leighton R, Sands M (1963) The Feynman Lectures on Physics. New York: Addison -Wesley pp: 6-7.

14. Dewitt BS, Graham N (1973) The Many-World Interpretation of Quantum Mechanics. Princeton University Press pp: 167-218.

20

Design and Simulation of a Linear Prolate Filter for a Baseband Receiver

Sagar Soman* and Michael Cada

Department of Electrical and Computer Engineering, Dalhousie University, Halifax, NS, Canada

Abstract

Digital signals transmitted over a communication channel are mostly affected by noise. To reduce the detrimental effects of noise, a band-limited filter is used at the receiver, which results a phenomenon known as Inter-Symbol Interference. To avoid Inter-Symbol Interference, filters with greater bandwidth can be used. However, this causes high frequency noise to interfere with the transmitted information signal. This paper illustrates an innovative way to reduce Inter-Symbol Interference in the received baseband signal. This is achieved by making use of the processing bandwidth of a special filter designed by using Linear Prolate Functions. The result of the signal reconstruction capabilities of a prolate filter are compared with those of an ideal low pass filter in this paper.

Keywords: Inter-symbol interference; Linear prolate functions; Prolate filter; Processing bandwidth; Baseband receiver

Introduction

The transmission of low frequency digital data pulses with sizeable power is known as Baseband transmission [1]. Common examples of channels used for baseband communication are optical fibers, twisted pair cables and co-axial cables [2]. Noise present in a communication channel causes distortion in the system, which can be detrimental to the information content. These undesirable effects can be reduced by using a band-limited low pass filter at the receiver. The band-limited frequency response of the filter at the receiver causes digital pulses to broaden outward leading to a phenomenon known as Inter-Symbol Interference (ISI). This affects the capability of the receiver to reproduce the original signal correctly after filtering.

The aim of this paper is to reduce ISI caused by a band-limited frequency response of the filter at the receiver. Raised cosine filters [2] can be used to optimise the response of the ideal low-pass filter by fluctuating the slope of the filter's roll off. This filter allows an excess bandwidth in the frequency domain to pass, keeping the amplitude of the side lobes of the signal in the time domain as small as possible. The smaller side lobe amplitude leads to reduced ISI interference after filtering. But, the excess amount of bandwidth transmitted with the information pulses increases the cost of the telecommunication system. This higher cost is undesirable for any telecommunication service provider. To remediate this problem, there is a need for a filtering technique that can provide an interference reducing capability with less bandwidth consumption. This paper intends to fulfill this need for a filtering technique by studying, designing and simulating a special filter termed as "prolate filter" using linear prolate functions.

In the past, researchers were not able to achieve a high precision of linear prolate functions due to limited processing power, inefficient algorithm techniques, and insufficient numerical precision. Therefore a practical exploitation of intriguing properties of linear prolate functions (see Sections II and III) in, for example, optical image and/ or signal processing applications was not feasible. We have developed a robust algorithm to evaluate linear prolate functions accurately, quickly and for all orders and frequency parameters [3]. A desirable feature of the prolate filter is that the bandwidth consumed by a prolate filter is same as the bandwidth used by a low pass filter while the interference reducing capability is similar to a raised cosine filter.

In this paper, section I introduces the problem of ISI and details the motivation behind using a prolate filter to solve this problem. Section II introduces the theory of linear prolate functions. Section III reviews various mathematical notations and properties of linear prolate functions. Section IV explains the mathematical concepts of a prolate filter. Section V describes some illustrative results of using a prolate filter as a receiver's filter in a baseband receiver, and compares the results with those obtained with using an ideal low-pass filter. It specifies some alterations that can be done to a prolate filter in order to change its response. Section VI offers concluding remarks that summarize the advantages and outcomes of the research.

Linear Prolate Functions

There is a reciprocal relationship between time and frequency. The Fourier transform of a small instant in time is equal to an infinitely wide band of frequencies in the frequency domain, and vice versa. Every physical device has a limited bandwidth response, which causes its output to undergo severe attenuation, if a high frequency signal is applied to its input. This band limiting nature of all devices prevents a successful reconstruction of any high frequency signals. For a single instant in both time and frequency domain, if a signal is confined to a specific interval or bandwidth, it can be exactly reconstructed at the receiver. However, there are no signals that can be confined in both time and frequency domain. This problem of simultaneously confining the signal and its amplitude spectrum has been present for a long time in digital communication systems [4].

Mathematically, a measure of concentration for a signal r (t) is a fraction of the signal's energy that lies in a particular time slot, T, which can be written as:

$$\alpha^2(T) = \frac{\int_{-T/2}^{T/2} r^2(\text{t})\,\text{dt}}{\int_{-\alpha}^{\alpha} r^2(\text{t})\,\text{dt}} \quad (1)$$

where r (t) is a bandlimited signal with unit energy such that [4]:

$$\int_{-\alpha}^{\alpha} r^2(\text{t})\,\text{dt} = \int_{-\alpha}^{\alpha} \left| R(f) \right|^2 df = 1 \quad (2)$$

If r (t) is time-limited to an interval (-T/2 to T/2), then $\alpha^2(\text{t})$ will have a maximum value of unity. Because of the inverse relationship between time and frequency, any band-limited signals cannot be

---

*Corresponding author: Sagar Soman, Department of Electrical and Computer Engineering, Dalhousie University, Halifax, NS, Canada
E-mail: sagar_soman1989@yahoo.co.in

time-limited. The issue of obtaining a unity value for $\alpha^2(t)$ while keeping r (t) band-limited, was undertaken by three scientists from Bell Laboratories, namely H Pollak, H Landau, and D Slepian. The issue was resolved by developing a set of band-limited functions that were maximally concentrated in a given time interval [5]. These functions are known as Prolate Spheroidal Wave Functions [6].

By solving the Helmholtz wave equation in spherical co-ordinates, two different kinds of solutions, i.e., angular and radial, can be obtained. Out of these solutions, the prolate spheroidal angular functions of the first order, which are denoted as $S_{0n}^1(c,t)$, can be used to derive a set of functions known as Linear Prolate Functions designated by $\psi_n(c,t)$. These functions have many advantageous properties over trigonometric functions [7]. Similarly, the prolate spheroidal radial functions of the first order $R_{0n}^1(c,1)$ can be used to determine the corresponding linear prolate eigenvalues designated by $\lambda_n(c)$ Mathematically, linear prolate functions and their corresponding eigenvalues are expressed as follows [5,8]:

$$\psi_n(c,t)=\frac{\sqrt{\lambda_n(c)/t_0}}{\sqrt{\int_{-1}^{1}(s_{0n}(c,t))^2\,dt}}*S_{0n}\left(c,\frac{t}{t_0}\right) \tag{3}$$

$$\lambda_n(c)=2c/\pi\left[R_{0n}(c,1)^2\right] \tag{4}$$

An application of linear prolate functions with high precision to numerical analysis and synthesis of signals was studied for the first time in [9].

Notations and Properties of Linear Prolate Functions

In this paper, the mathematical notations and normalizations used for the prolate spheroidal wave functions are similar to those used by Flammer [6] and Slepian [5] Linear prolate functions $\psi_n(c,t)$ are dependent on four factors [10]: the time parameter t, the time-limited interval t_0, the order of the function n, and the space bandwidth product parameter c with $c=t_0\Omega_0$, where Ω_0 is the finite bandwidth. Figure 1 illustrates some of these functions.

The properties of prolate functions were first studied by Slepian and Pollak in [5] and were analytically discussed in detail by Frieden in [8]. With regards to this paper, some of the important properties of linear prolate functions are as follows:

Invariance to fourier transform

Linear prolate functions are invariant to finite and infinite Fourier transform:

$$\int_{-x_0}^{x_0}\psi_n(x)e^{j\omega x}\,dx=j^n\left(2\pi\lambda_n x_0/\Omega\right)^{\frac{1}{2}}\psi_n\left(\omega x_0/\Omega\right) \tag{5}$$

$$\int_{-\infty}^{\infty}\psi_n(x)e^{-j\omega x}\,dx=\begin{cases} j^{-n}(2\pi x_0/\Omega\lambda_n)^{\frac{1}{2}}\psi_n\left(\frac{x_0\omega}{\Omega}\right), & \text{for } |\omega|\le\Omega \\ 0, & \text{for } |\omega|>\Omega \end{cases} \tag{6}$$

One can observe that the Fourier transform of linear prolate functions produces a scaled version of the same prolate function except for a scaling multiplier.

Eigenvalues λ_n of linear prolate functions

By performing a finite Fourier transform on (5) we obtain:

$$\int_{-x_0}^{x_0}\psi_n(x)\frac{\sin\Omega(y-x)}{\pi(y-x)}\,dx=\lambda_n\psi_n(y) \tag{7}$$

The general equation for eigenvalues and eigenfunctions is satisfied by (7), thus the eigenvalues for linear prolate functions are the same as eigenvalues of a sinc kernel function.

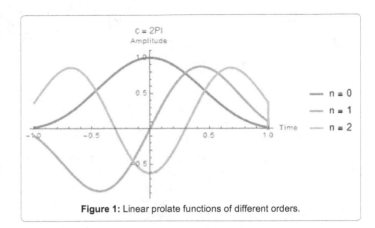

Figure 1: Linear prolate functions of different orders.

Orthogonality and orthonormality property

Linear prolate functions have many advantages over trignometric functions, one of which is that the prolate functions are not only orthonormal on an infinite interval but they are also orthogonal on a finite interval:

$$\int_{-\infty}^{\infty}\psi_m(x)*\psi_n(x)\,dx=\begin{cases} 0, & \text{for } m\neq n \\ 1, & \text{for } m=n \end{cases} \tag{8}$$

$$\int_{-x_0}^{x_0}\psi_m(x)*\psi_n(x)\,dx=\begin{cases} 0, & \text{for } m\neq n \\ \lambda_n, & \text{for } m=n \end{cases} \tag{9}$$

Implementation

In optical imaging systems, diffraction affects the resolving capability of a system. This diffraction problem is quite similar to the ISI problem present in digital communication systems. Hence, a solution for the diffraction issue in optics, can also be applied to resolve the interference problem in digital communication systems. Several researchers such as G. Toraldo Di Francia in [11], H. Osterberg and J. Wilkins in [12], J. Harris in [13] and C. Barnes in [14] have proposed various methodologies with different shortcomings, to overcome the diffraction problem in imaging systems. B. Frieden [8] proposed a theory which overcame the shortcomings of the methodologies proposed by these previous researchers. To solve the diffraction problem, Frieden used linear prolate functions to construct a point amplitude response whose side lobes do not increase in size even when the order 'n' of the prolate function is increased.

It is known that the Fourier transform of a unity function is a Dirac Delta function; but this statement is not true if a finite Fourier transform is considered, as there no functions available today whose finite Fourier transform is a Delta function. However, with the help of linear prolate functions one can obtain a function whose finite Fourier transform is a Dirac delta function over a finite extent. Mathematically, one desires a function as follows:

$$\int_{-\Omega}^{\Omega}d\omega U(\omega).e^{j\omega x}=\delta(x)\,for\,|x|\le x_0 \tag{10}$$

Since $U(\omega)$ is only defined over a finite interval $|\omega|\le\Omega$ (10) can also be written as:

$$U(\omega)=\sum_{n=0}^{\infty}a_n.\psi_n(\omega x_0/\Omega)\,for\,|\omega|\le\Omega\text{--} \tag{11}$$

Substituting (11) back into (10) one finds that coefficients a_n are needed to satisfy a condition:

$$(2\pi\Omega/x_0)^{1/2}\sum_{n=0}^{\infty}j^n\lambda_n^{1/2}a_n\psi_n(x)=\delta(x)\,for\,|x|\le x_0 \tag{12}$$

The completeness and orthogonality property of linear prolate functions as seen in (9) can also be written as follows:

$$\sum_{n=0}^{\infty} \lambda_n^{-1} \psi_n(0) \psi_n(x) = \delta(x) \ for \ |x| \leq x_0 \qquad (13)$$

By comparing (12) and (13) one can find coefficients a_n:

$$a_n = \left(x_0 / 2\pi\Omega\right)^{1/2} j^{-n} \lambda_n^{-3/2} \psi_n(0) \qquad (14)$$

Substituting a_n from (14) back into (11) yields:

$$U_M(\omega) = \left(x_0 2\pi\Omega\right)^{(1/2)} \sum_{n(even)=0}^{M} (-1)^{n/2} \lambda_n^{-3/2} \psi_n(0)\left(\omega x_0 / \Omega\right) \qquad (15)$$

In order to evaluate (15) in practice, the upper limit of the summation is changed from ∞ to M where M indicates the maximum number of terms required to obtain the required response. In this paper, M will be referred to as the threshold value. Solving (15) in Mathematical software and employing our original proprietary algorithm [3], the frequency response of a prolate filter is as seen in Figure 2.

The inverse Fourier transform of (15) provides the required Dirac delta function as seen in (16) below. Employing our proprietary algorithm [3], one obtains the time domain response for the prolate filter – illustrated in Figure 3.

$$\delta_M(x) = \sum_{n=0}^{M} \lambda_n^{-1} \psi_n(0) \psi_n(x) \qquad (16)$$

The width of the main lobe for the function as seen in Figure 3 is expressed analytically as [8].

$$\delta_M = \frac{3C}{M\pi} \qquad (17)$$

It should be noted that the function in Figure 3 is a true delta impulse on a finite interval. The fact that it shows a finite width is a result of the numerical limit of M=60 in this case; an infinite M does produce a true delta function.

Figure 4 compares the time domain response of a prolate filter with the time domain response obtained from an ideal low-pass filter with both filters having the same physical bandwidth:

As mentioned earlier there are no functions available today which can provide a delta response in the time domain for a finite interval. However, by increasing the threshold value M in (17), the width of the main lobe of the sinc signal can be reduced considerably such that a delta function is obtained in the time domain. Furthermore, if a Fourier transform is performed on such a function, then a filter response can be obtained in the frequency domain which has theoretically infinite bandwidth.

The most advantageous feature of a prolate filter is the concept of a virtual bandwidth which can be extended to an infinite value even

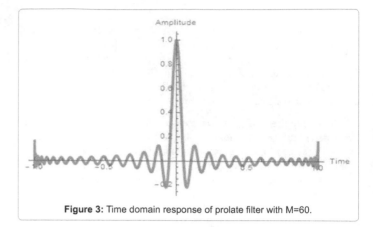

Figure 3: Time domain response of prolate filter with M=60.

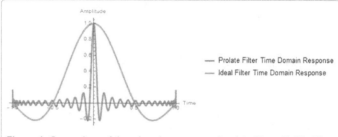

Figure 4: Comparison of time domain response of prolate filter with ideal low-pass filter.

when the physical bandwidth has only a certain finite value. In this paper, this virtually or synthetically extended bandwidth is termed as 'processing bandwidth'.

Results and Discussion

In digital communication systems, the baseband transmission of information pulses is severely affected by ISI. Generally, low-pass filters are used at the receiver to filter out the noise from the received signal. The band-limited frequency response of these filters causes the interference to occur. This problem can be avoided by using a prolate filter. Consider a digital ted in Figure 5.

In signal processing, for calculating communication system that transmits digital pulses 1001 to the receiver through a communication channel, as indicating the output of any system, the time domain analysis using convolution can be extremely complex and time consuming. Hence, in order to simplify the calculations, the frequency domain analysis is employed by performing a discrete Fourier transform operation on the input signal, which is shown in Figure 6.

We assume for the illustration purposes that this signal is transmitted through a channel with a bandwidth of $\pm 2\pi$ and is noiseless. At the receiver the signal is filtered by the receiver's filter. For a better understanding of the advantages of a prolate filter, initially consider the received signal be filtered by an ideal low-pass filter having a frequency response as shown in Figure 7.

In order to obtain the transmitted signal at the receiver the signal is converted back into the time domain by performing an inverse Fourier transform operation. Due to the band-limited nature of the ideal low-pass filter, valuable information needed for signal reconstruction is lost. The reconstruction of the transmitted signal at the receiver is severally affected by this problem, as seen in Figure 8.

The reconstruction of the transmitted signal is significantly

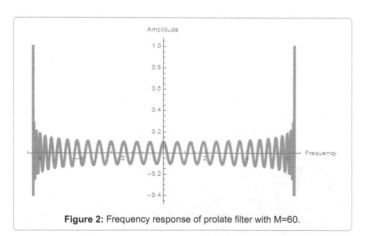

Figure 2: Frequency response of prolate filter with M=60.

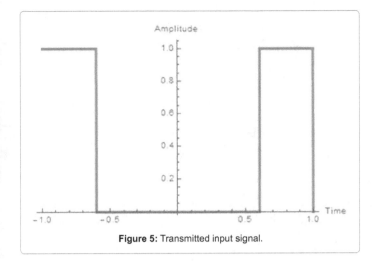

Figure 5: Transmitted input signal.

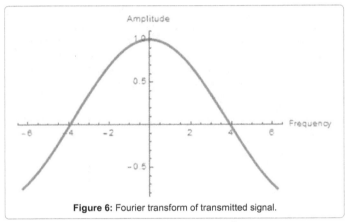

Figure 6: Fourier transform of transmitted signal.

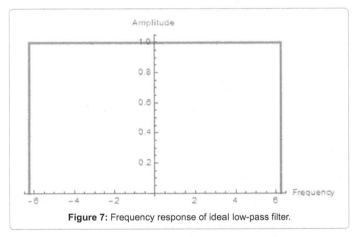

Figure 7: Frequency response of ideal low-pass filter.

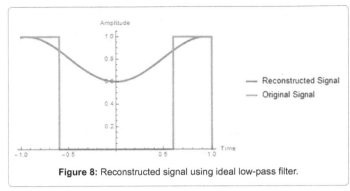

Figure 8: Reconstructed signal using ideal low-pass filter.

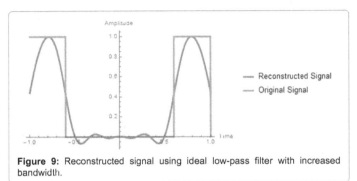

Figure 9: Reconstructed signal using ideal low-pass filter with increased bandwidth.

low pass filter.

The reconstructed signal obtained by using a prolate filter is illustrated in Figure 11. One observes that it is the same as the one obtained by physically increasing the bandwidth of an ideal low-pass filter in Figure 9.

The response in Figure 12 can be improved further by increasing the threshold value M.

The prolate filter operates efficiently even with the change in transmitted signal, as shown in Figure 13 with input signal 10101.

For the prolate filter to operate efficiently, the value of space bandwidth parameter c must be equal to or greater than the bandwidth of the channel under consideration. The major advantage in using prolate filters, in addition to their larger processing bandwidths, in place of low-pass filters is exactly this parameter c because it is a free parameter one can choose as necessary. In order to illustrate this, consider for comparison the use of prolate filters with $c = 2\pi$, $c = 10\pi$ and c 20π along with a channel bandwidth of $\pm 20\pi$. The time domain response obtained by using these variations of a prolate filter is illustrated in Figure 14.

The prolate filters with $c = 2\pi$ and $c = 10\pi$ both fail to operate properly and their signal reconstruction is unsatisfactory. On the other hand, the prolate filter with $c = 20\pi$ operates flawlessly.

Conclusions

This paper provides an innovative filtering technique, which can used to reduce ISI in a baseband communication system. Linear prolate functions numerically evaluated with a high precision for large orders were used in this technique for designing the prolate filter. The major advantage of using the prolate filter is that it can theoretically provide an infinitely large processing bandwidth and is only limited by the processing algorithm as it can only include a finite number of linear prolate functions in its calculations. By extending the bandwidth of a low pass filter, its interference reducing capabilities can be improved

improved by increasing the bandwidth of the ideal low-pass filter as seen in Figure 9.

This increase in bandwidth introduces high frequency noise into the system which defeats the major purpose of a filter and also increases the cost of hardware. Hence, in order to overcome the limitation of physically increasing the bandwidth of a low-pass filter, one can instead increase the bandwidth virtually by making use of a prolate filter's processing bandwidth. The equation for obtaining the frequency response of the prolate filter is in (15) and the response it generates is shown in Figure 10. The physical bandwidth the prolate filter in this case is from -2π to $+2\pi$ which is the same as the one used in the ideal-

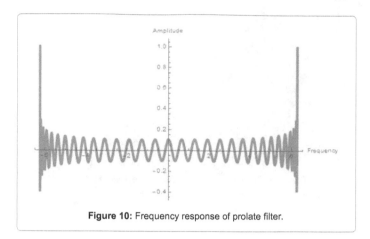

Figure 10: Frequency response of prolate filter.

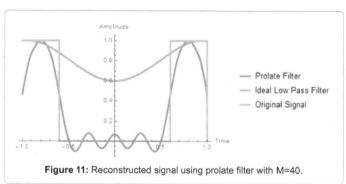

Figure 11: Reconstructed signal using prolate filter with M=40.

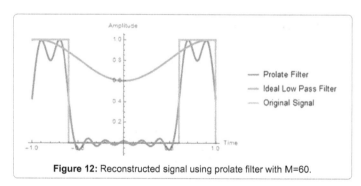

Figure 12: Reconstructed signal using prolate filter with M=60.

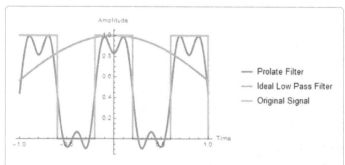

Figure 13: Reconstructed signal using prolate filter with input signal 10101 with M=60.

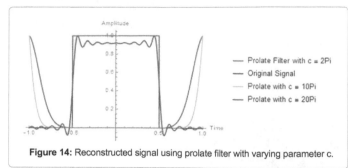

Figure 14: Reconstructed signal using prolate filter with varying parameter c.

The interference reducing capability of the prolate filter will be same as an ideal low-pass filter when the threshold value M is equal to $n_{critical}$ given by $\frac{2c}{\pi}$. It needs to be noted that the actual usable processing bandwidth of the prolate filter is obtained only when the threshold value 'M' is well above $n_{critical}$. This fact has caused insurmountable numerical problems in the past that in fact prevented a wider use of linear prolate functions in both, image and signal processing applications. The robust algorithms developed for the first time in is now available and thus overcomes these problems, as illustrated in this paper. It can also be noted that in order to obtain the best interference reduction capability of the prolate filter, the value of the space-bandwidth parameter 'c' should be equal to the bandwidth of the communication channel.

References

1. Haykin S (2008) Communication Systems. John Wiley & Sons Inc, US.

2. Sklar B (2001) Digital Communications, Fundamentals and Applications. Prentice Hall, US.

3. Cada M (2002) A robust algorithm for numerical evaluation of linear prolate functions with high precision and for arbitrary indices and arguments. IC Litewaves, Inc., Halifax.

4. Slepian D (1983) Some Comments on Fourier analysis, Uncertainty and Modeling. Society for Industrial and Applied Mathematics 25: 379-393.

5. Slepian D, Pollack H (1961) Prolate Spheroidal Wave Functions, Fourier Analysis and Uncertainty-I. Bell Systems Technical Journal 40: 43-63.

6. Flammer C (1957) Spheroidal Wave Functions. Stanford University Press.

7. Van BA, King B, Hanish S (1975) Tables of Angular Spheroidal Wave Functions. Prolate m =0. Defense Technical Information Center 1: 8-15.

8. Frieden RB (1971) Evaluation, Design and Extrapolation Methods for Optical Signals, Based on Use of the Prolate Functions. Progress in Optics 9: 311-407.

9. Moore IC, Cada M (2004) Prolate Spheroidal Wave Functions, An Introduction to the Slepian Series and its Properties. Applied and Computational Harmonic Analysis 16: 208-230.

10. Moore (2003) An Introduction to the Slepian series and its Applications. Halifax.

11. Di Francia GT (1952) Super Gain Antennas and Optical Resolving Power. Nuovo Cimento 9: 426-438.

12. Osterberg H, Wilkins J (1949) The Resolving Power of a Coated Objective I. Journal of the Optical Society of America 39: 553-557.

13. Harris JL (1964) Diffraction and Resolving Power. Journal of Optical Society of America 54: 931-936.

14. Barnes CW (1966) Object Restoration in a Diffraction Limited Imaging System. Journal of Optical Society of America 56: 575-578.

further. However, the excess bandwidth is undesirable. Hence, the prolate filter consumes a smaller bandwidth while utilizing its processing bandwidth, to provide an interference reducing capability similar to the low pass filter with an extended bandwidth. The interference reducing capability of the prolate filter can be further improved by increasing the threshold value M of the filter.

21

Root Causes for the Failure of Communication in GSD

Hassan Khalid*, Farhat-ul-ain and Kokab Khushboo

Department of Computer Science, Abdul Wali Khan University, Mardan, Pakistan

Abstract

At the moment majorly software development organizations tends to obtain common interest by implying software development using global approach. Global software development (GSD) is the essence of this global approach. In practical GSD faces several challenges in different software development organizations. The core issue is communication which becomes more complex while using requirement change management (RCM). The focus of this work is to figure out different factors which are effected by RCM for GSD. Hypotheses are constructed and a framework architecture is proposed on which a mathematical/statistical/quantitative is applied to analyze the data. Multi-regression technique is used to analyze the hypotheses saying whether they are supported or not supported according to the developers of several software development organizations.

Keywords: Global software development; Multi-regression technique; Framework; Communication; Distributed software developments

Introduction

Software developments using global concept is acquiring the interest of many researchers. Global software development outlaws the barriers of boundaries like time differences, cultural diversity and language [1]. Additionally, as open source software developments hit the web; the trend of using Distributed Software Developers (DSD) reinforces up the method. Multiplicity of aptitude pool and minor development cost and wider developments are the main reasons for the selection of GSD [1]. A software development process can be definite, accomplished and dignified. Any process development which follows the same can be achieved continuously. The worth of software system is reliant on the worth of process followed to develop it [2]. Agile principles and its applications combined with Global Software Development (GSD) appears to offer numerous benefits like inferior production cost, round the clock development, and closer time to market. It also gives the authority of comprising the most endowed developers around the world [3].

Basically, GSD is an essential outsourcing technique whereas Distributed software development is the replacement term used by some researchers instead of outsourcing. Which means developers employed at distant localities with different time zones deliver their facilities to the customers. The developers in GSD environment come having multiple nationalities, cultural and religious experiences [4]. The crucial reason for the admiration of Distributed software development jobs is that GSD deals with the number of benefits over the conservative techniques. The utmost importance of these benefits are the significant discount in the development cost caused by inconsistencies in wages of software engineers. Communication is one of the main issue in RCM process in GSD. The core addressed communication issues are weak communication, lack of face to face meetings, poor business language skills, lack of mutual understanding, delay in responses, lack of trust, lack of cultural awareness, less time overlapping and dependency on asynchronous communication. In GSD software development requirement tend to constantly change from software requirements stage to the maintenance stage. RCM is one of the utmost thoughtful action which carriages major problems with DSD teams. The privation of appropriate RCM may lead towards software failure. It is very challenging to accomplish change requirement due to communication and coordination issues.

This paper contains the following sections. Section 2 describe the problem formulation about the factors of communication issue. The Section 3 gives the construction of framework and hypothesis. We discuss the Research methodology to apply some techniques. Sections 5 discuss the result which we get from applied techniques. The potential future work to this research is described in section 6 and finally we conclude in the last section.

Problem Formulation

Haq S et al. [4] conducted a critical review on issues in GSD; they concluded a comparative metric for the benefits and challenges in GSD. They also highlighted communication as a major issue in GSD which effect the overall project life cycle. Khan RA and Khan SU [5] performed a systematic literature review to identify the communication and co-ordination challenges at vendor side in offshore development projects. In this study authors listed eighteen factors which are causing or caused by communication barrier. Factors which got more votes in this study were geographical, cultural and language diversity and lack of technological cohesion.

Social media is playing a vital role in every aspect of our daily life and we cannot ignore the role of social media in our everyday life. Teams and companies are adopting social media and using various social media channels in their day to day communication. As the GSD teams are adopting these channels for communication this opportunity created a new window for GSD researchers to examine the role of social media and its impact on communication and compare the results of the different social media platforms as a single one or multiple in combination. In this regard Manteli C et al. [6] conducted a study which reveals the importance of social media in GSD. Every communication channel and media has its own limitations. We need something that communicate instantly and more frequently on which we can reach to the person in offline hours. By offline hours here it is meant that if a resource is offline after his/her work hours and a bug in a production line happens to appear and it is urged to resolve immediately [7,8]. Another challenge is to keep track of all communications and discussions. Keeping in mind all these scenarios Media selection become a challenging decision. In this connection Gu R et al. [9] conducted a study on communication

*Corresponding author: Hassan Khalid, Department of Computer Science, Abdul Wali Khan University, Mardan, Pakistan, E-mail: malikhasankhalid@gmail.com

media selection. In this study they discussed about Media Richness Theory (MRT), Social Influence Perspectives (SIP), and Media Fitness Framework (MFF). These theories and techniques can help in taking the decision for media selection.

Construction of Framework and Hypothesis

A framework for the issues effecting communication in GSD is given in Figure 1. As discussed earlier there are nine issues of concern. These are shown as under:

In the above figure nine hypotheses are shown which the root cause for issues in communication [10]. We have taken two hypothesis for each factor the one is null hypothesis (H0) the other one is alternative hypothesis (H1).

The detail of the Figure 1 is defined below:

Poor communication

Poor communication basically occur due to geographical distance between software development teams. It is obvious to communicate at the initial level between the team members [11]. Therefore, poor communication may lead towards diverted communication issues. It is understood that due to poor communication the relationship between remote team members becomes poor causing repeated rework [11]. Therefore, we could suppose hypothesis as given below:

H0=Poor communication is not directly affect overall communication in GSD.

H1=Poor communication directly affect overall communication in GSD.

Delay in response

Delay in response occurs due to temporal distance. It is because of distance factor effected by different time zones giving issues to get fast response [11]. It may be a serious problem in distributed software development because delay in response make team members unable to discuss their overall development procedure [11]. Therefore, we could suppose hypothesis as given below:

H0: Delay in response is not directly affect overall communication in GSD.

H1: Delay in response directly affect overall communication in GSD.

Absence of face-face meetings

In GSD absence of face-face communication is always been a major

concern in GSD. Geographical locations always provide opportunity which could easily create misunderstanding in design patterns. Face-face meetings are mandatory to overcome these misunderstandings of the process requirements [12]. Therefore, we could suppose hypothesis as given below:

H0: Lack of face-face meeting is not directly affect overall communication in GSD.

H1: Lack of face-face meeting directly affect overall communication in GSD.

Absence of trust

Trust wordiness between team members is the core factor raised due to geographical locations in GSD. It is hard to establish trust among newly spread teams due to communication issues [11]. Absence of trust and absence of readiness are parallel factors occurring due to communication issue. Therefore, we could suppose hypothesis as given below:

H0: Lack of trust is not directly affect overall communication in GSD.

H1: Lack of trust directly affect overall communication in GSD.

Weak business language skills

In recent time, English has been used as a business language at national and international level, but still language is an issue for communication in GSD. Due to weak business language skills, communication hazards arise [13]. The understanding of such language depends upon organizational, cultural, circumstantial and occupational structures. Therefore, we could suppose hypothesis as given below:

H0: Weak business language skills is not directly affect overall communication in GSD.

H1: Poor business language skills directly affect overall communication in GSD.

Absence of cultural awareness

Transnational companies are hiring staff from various places across the globe. But, due to cultural multiplicity various challenges are faced. Individuals from different cultural circumstances have different behaviors, views and thinking's which leads towards issues in GSD [14]. In GSD, due to the increase in geographical and temporal locations, cultural distance becomes effected which can make the communication and development process more challenging. Therefore, we could suppose hypothesis as given below:

H0: Lack of cultural awareness is not directly affect overall communication in GSD.

H1: Lack of cultural awareness directly affect overall communication in GSD.

Absence of mutual understanding

Basically, lack of mutual understanding occur due to socio-culture differences. In GSD, software engineers come across from different cultural backgrounds having their own view and thinking's. Language is the basic part of communication and difference in languages may create misinterpretation between team members by which communication can be negatively affected in GSD [15]. So, due to absence of mutual understanding we could suppose hypothesis as given below:

H0: Absence of mutual understanding is not directly affect overall communication in GSD.

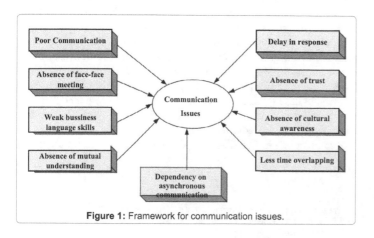

Figure 1: Framework for communication issues.

H1: Absence of mutual understanding directly affect overall communication in GSD.

Less time overlapping

Due to temporal distance less time overlapping occur. Between sites, the number of overlapping hours are reduced during a workday which may lead to miscommunication. So, in GSD less time overlapping is considered a positive stimulus issue for communication challenge [16]. Therefore, we could suppose hypothesis as given below:

H0: Less time overlapping is not directly affect overall communication in GSD.

H1: Less time overlapping directly affect overall communication in GSD.

Dependency on asynchronous communication

It can be risky to use asynchronous communication tools for communication and coordination purpose. Email may get lost or unnoticed. Therefore individual have doubt of whether or not a reply is coming and there is also a need to resend email after number of days. The chance of misunderstanding between team members is high due to asynchronous communication [17]. Therefore, we could suppose hypothesis as given below:

H0: Dependency on synchronous communication is not directly affect overall communication in GSD.

H1: Dependency on synchronous communication directly affect overall communication in GSD.

IF (α>0.05), where α= Significance level

Then H0 will be supported and our hypothesis will be not supported.

IF ($\alpha \leq 0.05$)

Then H1 will be supported and our hypothesis will also be supported.

Research Methodology

This quantitative study consist of two approaches. Web-based questionnaire and self-administered based questionnaire. The target population included developers from software houses at different locations in Pakistan. Total questionnaires distributed were 400 in which 196 responses came back, 166 responses were complete and hence are selected whereas the rest were discarded [18]. This respondent data was evaluated by keeping statistical, reliable and regression analysis for the hypothesis was done in SPSS version-19 (Table 1).

Model for data analysis β

Data analysis includes multiple linear regression analysis that attempts to model the relationship between two or more explanatory variables and a response variable by fitting a linear equation to the observed data [19]. The population regression line for 'p' explanatory variables x1, x2, xp is defined to be:

$$\mu_y = \beta 0 + \beta 1X1 + \beta 2X2 + ... + \beta 9X9. \quad (1)$$

As the mean response μ_y change with the explanatory variables therefore the observed values for 'y' vary about their means μ_y that have the same standard deviation σ. So for the variance of means μ_y, the multiple regression model includes term for its variation. This model is expressed in words as:

DATA = FIT + RESIDUAL (2)

Where 'FIT' is the term that represents the expression $\beta 0 + \beta 1X1 + \beta 2X2 + ... \beta 9X9$ and 'RESIDUAL' is the deviation of the observed values y from their means μ_y. Now formally, the model for the multiple linear regression for n observations is:

$$yi = \beta 0 + \beta 1xi1 + \beta 2xi2 + ... \beta 9xi9 + \varepsilon I$$

For $i = 1, 2 ... n$ (3)

Results and Discussion

Questionnaire result

The questionnaire results are represented in Graphs 1-12.

Reliability analysis

To analyze the reliability of the questionnaire Cronbach Alpha test has been used. As by [20], depending on the estimation procedure used, estimates of alpha value may take on any value less than or equal to 1 for reliable analysis. Using the fact of reliability test having value 0.812 near to 1 in positive direction show that 81.2% of the data is reliable (Table 2).

Hypothesis testing

In this section the results of the study obtained is presented. Multilinear regression analysis has been used to analyze the data and get the desired results in terms of relationship between several variables [21,22]. To determine the strength, direction and impact of relationship it is also very important to present the interpretation for different correlation and regression coefficients. To analyze the results different values of R, R2 and significance value P have been used (Table 3).

As we know the value of R shows the strength of the relationship between variables having ranges from +1 to -1. As the value of R approaches '+1', it shows the strength of the correlation relationship whereas a value of R closer to '0' shows a weaker or no correlation relationship [23,24]. For R having value below '0' means that there is negative correlation relationship. The direction of the relationship is determined by the positive or negative value. So a positive sign show direct relationship in which we have increase in 1 may also increase the other. To present the percentage of variance caused due to independent variable within the dependent variable is R2 value. P value is used for significance of the relationship in which if it is less than 0.05 then we may say that the relationship is significant [25]. The results in the significance value is shown in Table 4.

The significance of each hypothesis with clear verdict whether it is supported or not supported is illustrated in Table 5. When the significance value P is below 0.05 it show that hypothesis is supported whereas others values show that hypothesis is not supported [26]. The result for poor communication having significance value 0.016 illustrates a positive influence over communication issues and supports hypothesis of this research. The value for delay in response

Cities	No. ofRespondents	Developers Experience	
		3 year experience	More than 3 year experience
Islamabad	33	20	13
Mardan	57	40	17
Rawalpindi	26	15	11
Peshawar	20	13	7
Faisalabad	30	18	12
	166		

Table 1: Responses from different software houses.

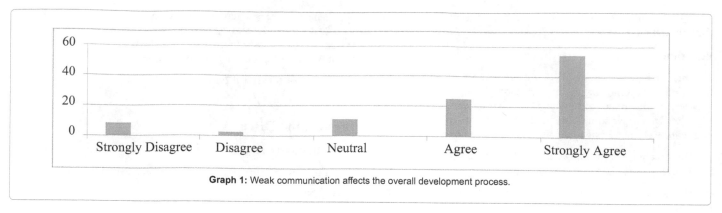

Graph 1: Weak communication affects the overall development process.

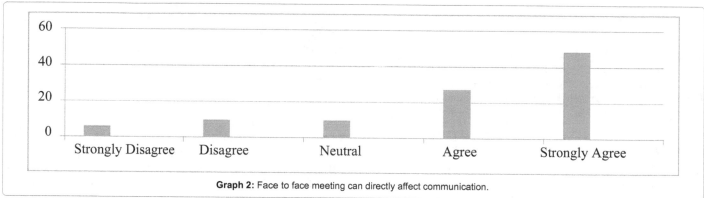

Graph 2: Face to face meeting can directly affect communication.

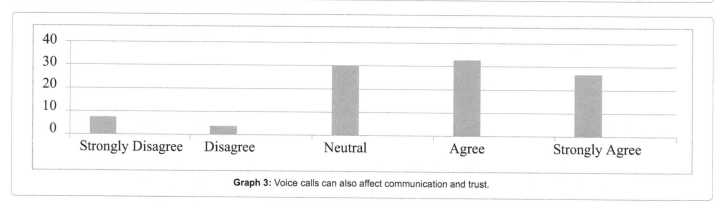

Graph 3: Voice calls can also affect communication and trust.

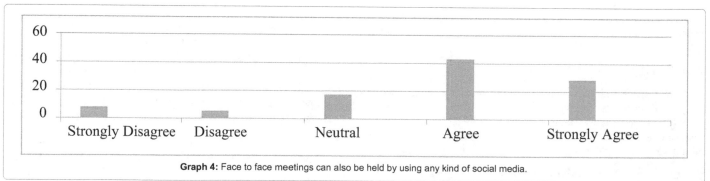

Graph 4: Face to face meetings can also be held by using any kind of social media.

is 0.028 which is less than 0.05, the hypothesis is supported and there is a positive relationship. From the Table 5 the significance value for absence of face-face meetings is 0.019 showing that the hypothesis for this research is supported. Here the factor 'absence of trust' is having a strong significance value of 0.019 hence supporting the hypothesis having value less than 0.05 [27].

In Table 5 we have results that do not support the hypothesis such as week business language skills that have beta value of -0.099. It shows a negative influence over communication issues. It is also noted that the value of significance P is 0.142 which is greater than 0.05 implies that there is no correlation between week business language skills and communication issues that is not supported at all [28,29]. The

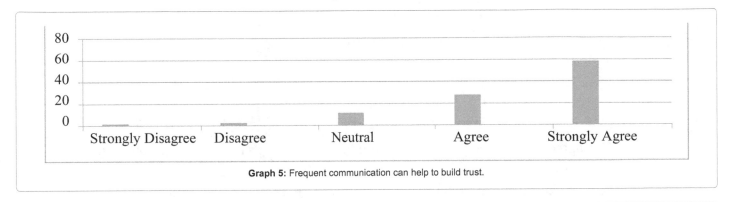

Graph 5: Frequent communication can help to build trust.

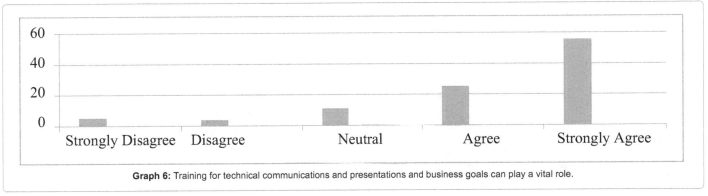

Graph 6: Training for technical communications and presentations and business goals can play a vital role.

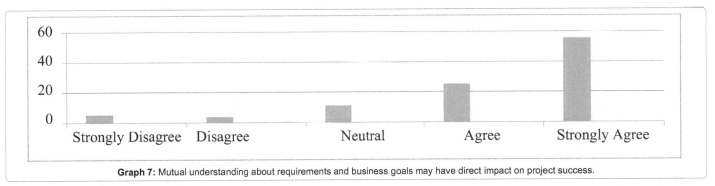

Graph 7: Mutual understanding about requirements and business goals may have direct impact on project success.

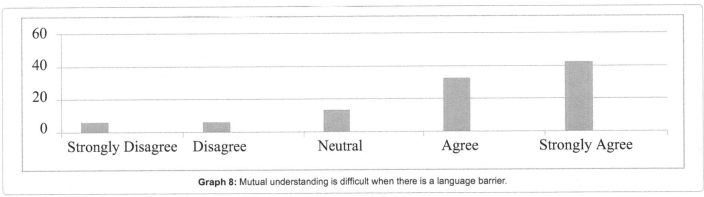

Graph 8: Mutual understanding is difficult when there is a language barrier.

significance value for absence of cultural awareness is 0.017 which is also a supported hypothesis that predicts the strong relationship for absence of cultural awareness with communication issues in GSD. The same is the case with the independent variable with absence of mutual understanding by having significance value equal to 0.05. Here we have another case that rejects the hypothesis for less time overlapping by having significance value 0.531 that is greater than 0.05. Finally, the last variable Dependency on asynchronous communication gets 0.008 significance value that helps the hypothesis to be supported for this research [30].

Directions for Future Research

Typical solutions for the research conducted in the area of GSD have mostly focused the issues related to the challenges faced by the

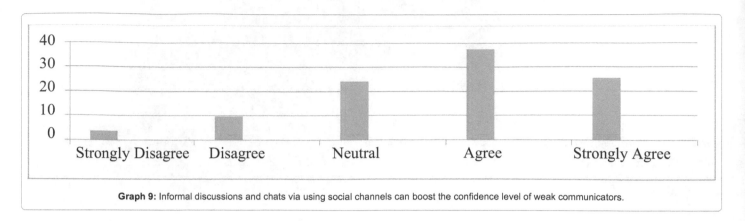

Graph 9: Informal discussions and chats via using social channels can boost the confidence level of weak communicators.

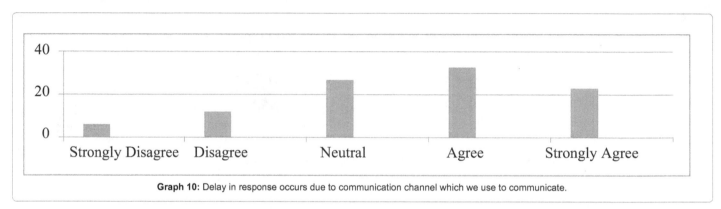

Graph 10: Delay in response occurs due to communication channel which we use to communicate.

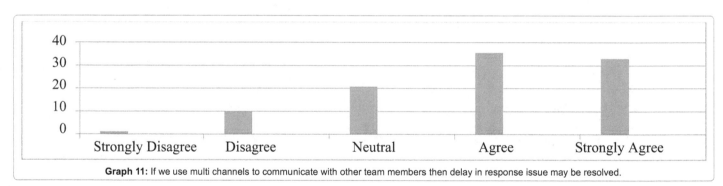

Graph 11: If we use multi channels to communicate with other team members then delay in response issue may be resolved.

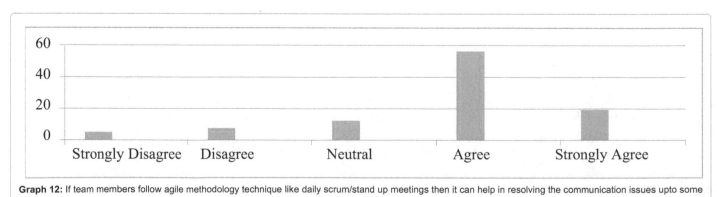

Graph 12: If team members follow agile methodology technique like daily scrum/stand up meetings then it can help in resolving the communication issues upto some extent.

Cronbach's Alpha	N of Items
0.812	14

Table 2: Reliability statistics.

Model	R	R Square	Adjusted R Square	Std. Error of the Estimate
1	0.633(a)	0.400	0.357	0.924

Table 3: Multilinear regression analysis.

Model	Sum of Squares	Df	Mean Square	F	Sig.
Regression	87.807	11	7.982	9.344	0.000(a)
Residual	131.566	154	0.854		
Total	219.373	165			

Table 4: ANOVA.

Model	Unstandardized Coefficients		Standardized Coefficients	T	Sig.	Hypothesis
	B	Std. Error	Beta			
Poor Communication	1.232	-0.044	-0.014	2.442	0.016	Supported
Delay in response	0.177	-0.107	-0.044	-0.389	0.028	Supported
Absence of face- face meetings	0.155	0.085	-0.107	-1.086	0.019	Supported
Absence of trust	0.086	0.136	0.085	1.020	0.049	Supported
Weak business language skills	-0.099	-0.014	0.136	1.474	0.142	Not Supported
Absence of cultural awareness	-0.019	0.297	0.297	2.407	0.017	Supported
Absence of mutual understanding	0.245	0.171	0.171	1.936	0.055	Supported
Less time overlapping	0.245	0.171	0.171	1.936	0.055	Supported
Dependency on asynchronous communication	0.280	0.265	0.265	2.679	0.008	Supported

Table 5: Coefficients (a) dependent variable: overall communication in GSD.

software developers at vendor organizations. However the stakeholder side have been overlooked. Keeping in view this fact, there is a need to conduct a survey to collect data from clients having information about the different problems faced while working on GSD projects. A new framework that duly provides the solution set to account for the issues faced by GSD clients is needed [31].

Conclusion

In this research study communication challenges in GSD with factors which effects the RCM process has been assessed. These are Poor communication, delay in response, absence of trust, absence of cultural awareness, absence of face-face meetings, weak business language skills, absence of mutual understanding, less time overlapping and dependency on asynchronous communication. This paper proposed a framework with 9 hypothesis which examined the effect of various factors. Out of these 9 hypothesis 7 are supported and 2 are not supported. It means that weak language skills and less time overlapping did not make any issue in communication while others 7 issues impacted the communication in one way or the other.

References

1. Haq SU, Khan NA, Tariq M (2011) The Context Of Global Software Development: Challenges, Best Practices And Benefits. Information Management and Business Review 3: 193-197.

2. Khan AS, Subhan Z (2014) Distributed Software Development Process, Initiatives and Key Factors: A Systematic Literature Review. International Journal of Multidisciplinary Sciences and Engineering 5: 7-21.

3. Alzoubi YI, Gill AQ (2014) Agile Global Software Development Communication Challenges: A Systematic Review. Pacific Asia Conference on Information Systems.

4. Haq SU, Raza M, Zia A, Khan AMN (2011) Issues in Global Software Development: A Critical Review. J Software Engineering & Applications 4: 590-595.

5. Khan RA, Khan SU (2014) Communication and Coordination Challenges in Offshore software Development Outsourcing Relationship from Vendors' perspective: Preliminary Results. International Symposium on Research in Innovation and Sustainabilityo 26: 1425-1429.

6. Rufadillah K, Mansor Z, Widyarto S, Lecthmunan S, Arshad NH (2013) Social Media: How it Ensures Effective Communication Among Project Team's. Recent Advances in Computer Science, pp: 222-227.

7. Kumar SA, Kumar TA (2011) Study the Impact of Requirements Management Characteristics in Global Software Development Projects: An Ontology Based Approach. International Journal of Software Engineering & Applications 2: 107-125.

8. Herbsleb JD, Mockus A, Finholt TA, Grinter RE (2001) An Empirical Study of Global Software Development: Distance and Speed. Software Engineering, Proceedings of the 23rd International Conference.

9. Rui GU, Higa K, Moodie DR (2011) A Study on Communication Media Selection: Comparing the Effectiveness of the Media Richness, Social Influence, and Media Fitness. Journal of Service Science and Management 4: 291-299.

10. Durranl R, Javed MA (2009) Agile Software Development Practices in Distributed Environments. IRCSE, pp: 1-7.

11. Khan AA, Basri S, Amin F (2014) A Survey Based Study on Factors Effecting Communication in GSD. Research Journal of Applied Sciences, Engineering and Technology 7: 1309-1317.

12. Curtis B, Krasner H, Iscoe N (1988) A Field Study of the Software Design Process for Large Systems. Commun ACM 31: 1268-1287.

13. Hossain E, Bannerman PL, Jeffery DR (2011) Scrum Practices in Global Software Development. Product-Focused Software Process Improvement, pp: 88-102.

14. Javed MA (2006) Cross-Cultural Management Strategies for Software Development in Global Environment.

15. Sengupta B, Chandra S, Sinha V (2006) A Research Agenda for Distributed Software Development. Proceedings of the 28th International Conference on Software Engineering, pp: 731-740.

16. Zada I, Shahzad S, Nazir S (2015) Issues and Implications of Scrum on Global Software Development. Bahria University Journal of Information & Communication Technologies 8: 81.

17. Raffo D, Setamanit SO (2007) A Software Process Simulation Model of Global Software Development (GSD) projects.

18. Ritter N (2010) Understanding a Widely Misunderstood Statistic: Cronbach's Alpha. Paper presented at Southwestern Educational Research Association (SERA).

19. Holmstrom H, Conchuir EO, Agerfalk PJ, Fitzgerald B (2006) Global Software Development Challenges: A Case Study on Temporal, Geographical and Socio-

Cultural Distance. International Conference on Global Software Engineering.

20. Jalali S, Wohlin C (2012) Global Software Engineering and Agile Practices: A Systematic Review. Journal of Software: Evolution and Process 24: 643-659.

21. Klimpke L (2011) Microblogging in Global Software Development. CEUR Proceedings.

22. Begel A, DeLine R, Zimmermann T (2010) Social Media for Software Engineering. Proceedings of the FSE/SDP Workshop on the Future of Software Engineering Research.

23. Pallant J (2010) A Step by Step Guide to Data Analysis using SPSS for Windows. Spss Survival Manual.

24. Sweet SA, Martin KG (2011) Data Analysis with Spss: A First Course in Applied Statistics.

25. Storey MA, Treude C, Deursen AV, Cheng LT (2010) The Impact of Social Media on Software Engineering Practices and Tools. Proceedings of the FSE/SDP workshop on Future of software engineering research, pp: 359-364.

26. Shah YH, Raza M, Haq SU (2012) Communication Issues in GSD. International Journal of Advanced Science and Technology 40: 69-76.

27. Mockus A, Herbsleb J (2001) Challenges of Global Software Development. Proceedings of the Seventh International Software Metrics Symposium 1: 1530-1435.

28. Rehman S, Khan SU (2014) Software Quality Attributes in Global Software Development: Initial Results. International Symposium on Research in Innovation and Sustainability 26: 1415-1419.

29. Rashid N, Khan SU (2015) Green Agility for Global Software Development Vendors: A Systematic Literature Review Protocol. Proceedings of the Pakistan Academy of Sciences 52: 301-313.

30. Manteli C, Vliet HV, Hooff BVD (2012) Adopting a Social Network Perspective in Global Software Development. IEEE Seventh International Conference on Global Software Engineering, pp: 124-133.

31. Begel A, Nagappan N (2008) Global Software Development: Who Does It? International Conference on Global Software Engineering.

22

A Critique of Museum's Web Presence in the Kingdom of Saudi Arabia: A Study of Selected Museums

Hamed M* and Higgett N

School of Art, Design and Humanities, De Montfort University, Leicester, UK

Abstract

This paper explores useful and practical utilisation of the theoretical concept of web-presence to increase museum audience in the Kingdom of Saudi Arabia (KSA). A qualitative and quantitative research methodology is adopted relying on critical review of literature on web-presence to provide justifications for web-presence as innovative means of managing museums in KSA. Currently, KSA uses traditional methods for museum promotion, which can be problematic. However, by adopting internet technology, KSA is fast becoming an information-based society and there is a need for a paradigm shift to correct the misguided notion that museums are just for children or keeping worn-out artefacts. Effective use of web-presence provides certain benefits: wider dissemination of information on the museums to visitors, promotion of e-museums, promotion of Saudi's heritage, faith and culture online, and improved visitors' satisfaction. The paper concludes with further research plan to build a theoretical framework for web-presence design for Saudi museums.

Keywords: Museums; e-marketing; Web-presence; Web design; Saudi Arabia

Introduction

It is now commonly accepted that the days of organisations, such as museums, advertising to market themselves whilst solely using old methods of magazine and printed posters, are past. While this is true, the modern ways of advertising brought about various challenges for museums. For example, as well as traditional media channels which still exist, museums are now further expected to use new and modern web media tools. The reason is that this provides more effective ways using which museums can advertise themselves to the public. This kind of advertising experience in which the museums can put themselves in the public domain is very important in an environment where market competition is ever increasing. The centrality of this challenging concept lays in the fact that the nature of the public's expectations is changing and people are now more than ever informed and technologically experienced. What this means is that this awareness and experience can be used to shape the activities which museums provide to their customers. As a result, economic, cultural and social changes that take place affect the methods in which museums functions and also how they view themselves as well as their audience.

The reaction to this can be observed in the rise of marketing as crucial component in the ways museums are managed. Such emphasis on this type of marketing means museums are actively and constantly seeking to communicate with potential visitors and customers and hence increase their profit and popularity. In order to do this, considering the changes and the dynamics that take place in the museums' marketplace, it becomes necessary to exploit electronic media 'within integrated marketing communication strategies' (Lehman, 2008). Lehman maintained that despite increasing need to go digital, this method as a marketing strategy has received little attention within the academic world.

Background

Currently, as stated by Reachlocal [1], the majority of people around the world spend more time with interactive online content than traditional media. As a result, many cultural organisations like museums use their websites and social media to promote themselves [2]. However, social media, the essence of web 2.0, require a change from unidirectional information to two way communication and user participation [3]. Designing an organisational web-presence is now

shifting from reaching customers to engaging them. "Everyone can now reach customers online; the challenge is about how to engage them" [4]. According to Villaespesa [5] and Nosen [6] many museums currently have or are developing a social media profiles to foster their online community. For example, in the US, an increasing number of museums are beginning to adopt social media [7]. While in the UK, many museums already utilise various social media to enhance their popularity [8]. On the other hand, museums in Saudi Arabia are far away from using the internet to promote themselves as there are just five museums that have a webpage out of 138 museums in the country (Appendix A).

The kingdom of Saudi Arabia (Background)

The Kingdom of Saudi Arabia (KSA) is the largest country in the Arabian Peninsula (Figure 1) [9]. It occupies an area of more than nine times the size of the UK. According to the 2013 census, Saudi Arabia's population reached over 29 million, including about 9 million foreign residents. The capital city of Saudi Arabia is Riyadh [10].

In the past, the Saudi people tended to live near wells and oases. Some were nomads who kept livestock and moved their animals to the limited pastures produced by infrequent rains. In addition, some Saudi people worked in trade which was limited primarily to the annual influx of pilgrims visiting the holy places in Makkah and Madinah [11].

Recently, Saudi Arabia was confronted with what many consider its greatest challenge: achieving modernity without surrendering its heritage, faith or culture. It is a nation marked by sophisticated political, legal, and financial systems, with a culture rich in history and deep in faith [10,11].

KSA is a religious country and the mother country of Islam.

---

*Corresponding author: Hamed M, School of Art, Design and Humanities, De Montfort University, Leicester, UK, E-mail: moneer97@gmail.com

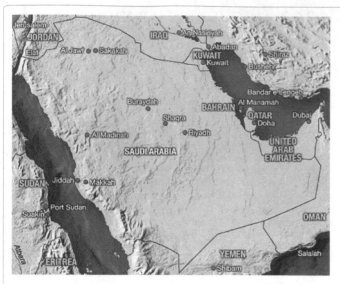

Figure 1: The geographical location of the Kingdom of Saudi Arabia.

The country is based on a strong relationship between the religious institution and the Al Saud kingship. However, it is not easy to distinguish between the religious establishment and the Al Saud as the religious institution seemingly has more impact on the regional domain, the state along with social life and culture [12].

The problem and motivation

Many museums in developed counties have or are developing a social media profiles to foster their online community. By contrast, museums in Saudi Arabia have a very limited web-presence. In any society, the internet and social media cause social changes and reflect social systems [13]. However, the National Museum of Saudi Arabia, Abdul Raouf Kalil's museum, is one of the major national museums in Saudi Arabia, and is the most visited museum in the country; still, the museum does not have a profile on any social media platforms. Moreover, Abdul Raouf Kalil's museum does not even have a webpage yet.

Aggad [14], Kaufman [15] and Solni [16] point out the importance of utilising social media by organisations to attract the public's attention. For instance, these authors explain that since the current economic downturn has affected many organisations, museums are one type of organisations that would particularly benefit from utilising cost-effective interactive elements of social media to increase engagement with the public, who are their main sources of income. Although a number of organisations have started utilising social media as part of their communication strategies, there is, as of yet, little research that investigates key questions regarding the effective implementation of communication strategies in social media [17]. This is because as museums are increasingly feeling the pressure to respond to new opportunities offered by social media for connecting with active audiences, it becomes crucial that more is understood about the impact of social media on organisations and how they should practically go about incorporating social media into museum programmes [18].

For this reason, this research addresses the possible barriers and opportunities to web2.0 technologies in museums. However, the research focuses on Saudi Arabia and explores innovative and culturally sensitive ways that can enhance museums' web-presence and improve their online marketing strategies.

Research aim and objectives

Research aim: The focus of this study is adapting the usage of web-presence for museums in Saudi Arabia in connecting with their online marketing strategy. The main aim is to develop a theoretical framework for the design of the web-presence and associated online marketing for museums in Saudi Arabia in order to develop their web usage to effectively promote themselves and to enhance their engagement with their target audience.

Research objectives: The objectives set to address this aim are:

- To examine the existing web-presence of museums in Saudi Arabia;

- To examine the perceptions of visitors on the existing web-presence of museums in Saudi Arabia;

- To develop a multimedia-based framework for web-presence and associated online marketing for museums in Saudi Arabia; and

- To assess the effectiveness of the designed multimedia-based framework for web presence and associated online marketing strategy for museums in Saudi Arabia.

Research methodology: According to the research aim, the study involved multidisciplinary area and needed the researcher to develop a multi-stage research methodology to fulfill the aim of this study.

The researcher produced a graphical representation of the proposed research methodology adapted in this study. Figure 2 gives a general overview of the methodology. The graph presents the methodology concatenation that was developed to curry out this research in an organised and orderly way in its different stages.

The research methodology for this study includes the following:

- An extensive and critical literature review conducted on using social media in museums, with the main focus on the nature of Saudi culture in a museum context, museum communication and promotion, interactive and social media technologies, traditional and online museum visitor behaviour and engagement and online marketing.

- Questionnaire collected from people who visit museums in Saudi Arabia. This is to determine how often they go to museums, how they get museum information, whether they engage with a museums' online presence and their use of museums' social media platforms.

- Semi-structured interviews carried out with key stakeholders (people who run museums in both the UK and Saudi Arabia).This is to gauge their views and understanding of their online marketing goals, what they want to achieve, how they reach their audience and engage with them and how they plan, manage and use their web-presence.

The findings from items 2 and 3 will be collected and critically analysed to enable the design of a conceptual web-presence framework and model for an online marketing strategy to be developed for museums in Saudi Arabia. A prototype based on the conceptual framework will be built to test and evaluate both the framework and strategy with experts and users.

A research framework defines the categories of outputs that research can produce. It also defines a set of different research activities. Moreover, it defines what kind of research can be used to produce specific outputs [19]. The research framework outlines all the developed five phases of the research process, as shown in Figure 2.

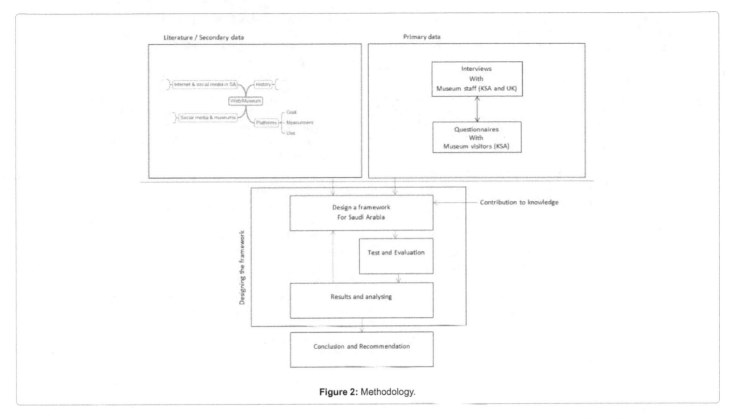

Figure 2: Methodology.

Research Findings

This research applied an initial survey to measure if the survey covers all aspects of the research questions or not. Also, this helps to test and measure data collected to ensure that the questions are measuring the research proposed as well as to test what the participants did not like and what they liked about the questions.

This initial survey was undertaken to ascertain the workability and reliability of the research instruments adopted for this research project. The initial survey was carried at Dar-Al-Madina Museum and Madina Media Museum from 13th to 24th April, 2014 at the Al-Madinah region in KSA.

A mixed method research strategy was selected as discussed in the methodology. Face-to-face interviews and a semi-structured questionnaire were the research instruments employed for the qualitative and quantitative methods respectively. Purposeful sampling technique was employed for the selection of all the survey participants. According to Walliman [20], purposeful sampling is a non-probability sampling that is most suitable for any specific research with target participants. The choice of this sampling technique would also enhance the overall authenticity of research findings.

The face-to-face interviews with people who run the museum

Number of interviewees: 2

Number of questions: 23

Type of questions: Semi-structured

Where: Al-Madinah, Saudi Arabia

When: May, 2014

Duration of each interview: about 20-30 minutes each

From this initial survey, the researcher found that:

Both interviewees agreed that the website and social media are important for the museum.

Both interviewees have websites and social media for their museums.

Both interviewees created or updated the webpage in 2014.

Both interviewees post pictures, links and museum's news on their social media.

Both interviewees have limited printed ad.

Neither of the interviewees have any particular target audience.

Both interviewees believe that these sites and tools reach their audiences.

Just one interviewee has an online marketing strategy, which is exchange advertising with other websites and having Friends of the Museum's society to use them as marketing advisors.

The questionnaire

Number of participants: 10

Number of questions: 20

Type of questions: closed-ended and open-ended.

Where: Al-Madinah, KSA

When: May, 2014

Duration of the survey: about 10 minutes each

The qualitative method employed the use of a questionnaire to collect quantitative data. This is because the questionnaire allows data to be collated from a large number of participants. The questionnaire was intended to address research objective 2. A total of 20 questionnaires were distributed and a total of ten questionnaires were returned, suggesting a 50% response rate.

In this questionnaire (Table 1), questions are listed in a pre-arranged order and respondents are told about the purpose of collecting the information. So, this is a structured non-designed questionnaire. Most questions are closed-ended with some open-ended questions. Participants are randomly sampled. Table 1 shows participants answers.

Analysis and Discussion

As obvious from the interviews above, the museums' stuff are aware of the importance of the internet and social media and they already created website and social media profiles. Also, they are not depending mainly on printed advertisements reflected by having limited printed advertisement.

Also, both interviewees agreed to all the interview statements except on the use of online marketing strategy, which was used by only one interviewee. Kotler et al. [21] mentioned that museum marketing strategy should look into the range of marketing tools and include the current data on branding, positioning and e-marketing. Kremer [22] added that the strategic plan should consider increasing the number of visitors, creating more engagement and driving the museum's loyalty.

All these strategies should be a part of the museum's practice [23]. According to Kotler et al. [21], "exchange advertising" with other web sites, having friends of the museum society to use them as "marketing advisors" are closer to being a marketing method than an online marketing strategy.

On the other hand, it is clear that most participants in the questionnaire use the internet and social media. However, only 10% of them heard about the museum online. At the same time, all participants believed that websites and social media are important for museums as they help museums to advertise and present more information.

By comparing the interviews and the questionnaires, it is clear that the museums' stuff think that their web-presence has a good response and results. However, 90% of visitors did not see any of the museums web-presence aspects and they came through friends or other people, which means that this research strongly recommends helping museums in Saudi Arabia to reach and engage with their audience online [24].

Anticipated Contribution to Knowledge

There are only few studies on museum marketing in KSA. Available studies are quite out-dated and not relevant to online marketing. This paper is an attempt to fill the gap in the design of museum's web-presence and associated online marketing in KSA.

#	Question	1	2	3	4	5	6	7	8	9	10
20	Which advertisement about this museum you have ever seen?	-	-	-	-	-	Inside it	-	-	-	-
19	Have you ever seen any advertisement about this museum?	N	N	N	N	N	Y	N	N	N	N
18	What information would you expect from a museum's social media?	N	-	I	I	I, share	Contact, offers	-	I	-	-
17	If yes, were they useful?	-	-	-	Y	-	-	-	-	-	-
16	Have you seen any social media posts for this museum?	N	N	N	Y	N	N	N	N	N	N
15	How could it be improved?	-	-	Audio guide	More info	More languages, organising	I, content and contact	-	languages	-	-
14	Was it useful?	-	-	-	Y	-	-	-	-	-	-
13	If yes, what did you use it for?	-	-	-	I	-	Not fined it	-	-*	-	-
12	Have you seen the website of this museum?	N	N	N	Y	N	N	N	N	N	N
11	Name some social media sites /tools that you think it may have no museum value?	-	N	0	0	t y L	L	-	0	y	L
10	Name some social media sites /tools that you think it may have strong museum value?	f,t,y	f,t	T	f,t,y,In	F	f,t,y	-	f,t,y	f,t,L	f,t,y
9	If so, Why?	Ad	spread	spread	spread	ad	Ad, communication	-	Benefit people	Ad, spread, share	info
8	Do you think social media is important for museums?	Y		Y	Y	Y	Y	-	Y	Y	Y
7	If so, Why?	I	I, ad	I, ad	I, ad	ad	I, events	-	Help who can't visit	Ad, spread	Ad, spread
6	Do you think website is important for museums?	Y	Y	Y	Y	Y	Y	-	Y	Y	Y
5	How did you hear about this museum?	Fr	Fr	Fr	Fr	Fr	Fr	-	Fr	Fr	Fr
4	Which social media tools/sites are you most comfortable with?	-	f t	t	-	f	f ,y	f	f, y	t	t
3	How long have you been using social media site?	-	5y	7y	-	2y	-	8y	4y	12y	9y
2	Do you have a personal social media account?	N	Y	Y	N	Y	Y	Y	Y	Y	Y
1	Do you have a personal Web site?	N		N	N	N	Y	Y	Y	-	N

Table Key

Symbol	Meaning	Symbol	Meaning	Symbol	Meaning
Y	Yes	f	Facebook	I	Information
N	No	t	Twitter	In	Instagram
Fr	Friends	y	YouTube	L	LinkedIn

Table 1: Questionnaire participants' answers.

The result of this research is a theoretical framework for the design of web-presence and associated marketing strategy for museums in KSA. This would offer museums in Saudi Arabia a chance to increase the number of visitors and to create more engagement with them and help increase the awareness of Saudi people about museums' culture.

Conclusion and Further Research

This paper reached an advanced stage of data collection and analysis. All secondary data required for analysis of the quantitative and qualitative research aspects of the research have been collected. The next stage is analysis of data. The findings of the mixed research methods will be followed by building a theoretical framework for the design of web-presence for museums in KSA.

Acknowledgements

The authors would like to acknowledge King Abdullah Foreign Scholarship Programme, KSA, for funding, Dr Abdul Aziz Kaki the owner of Dar Almadinah museum for participation, Dr Khaled Abualkhair the owner and manager of Almadinah Museum for his time, Hassan Taher the manager of Dar Almadinah museumfor his time and the visitors of Dar Almadinah museum for participating in the questionnaire.

References

1. Reachlocal (2012) 150 Smart Stats: Online Marketing.

2. Miller CC (2011) Social Media as Inspiration and Canvas. The New York Times.

3. Sanz MR (2012) Estrategia comunicativa digital en el museo. El Profesional de La Informacion 21: 391–396.

4. Baird CH, Parasnis G (2011) From Social Media to Social CRM. IBM Institute for Business Value.

5. Villaespesa E (2013) Diving into the Museum's Social Media Stream. Analysis of the Visitor Experience in 140 Characters. In The annual conference of Museums and the Web, Portland.

6. Nosen K (2009) Do you follow: Impacts and implications of social media in museums. A Master's Project, university of Oregon.

7. Barry F (2012) Using Social Media to Bring Museum Exhibits to Life.

8. Sounddelivery Social Media Guide.

9. Countrystudies.us. (1992) Saudi Arabia - Geography.

10. The Royal Embassy of Saudi Arabia Homepage.

11. Hamed M (2010) Advertising for the Web. University of Wolverhampton.

12. Diemen R (2012) Politics and Religion in Saudi Arabia.

13. Samin N (2012) Saudi Arabia, Egypt, and the Social Media Moment. Arab Media and Society.

14. Aggad K (2012) An Exploratory Study of the Use of Social Media by Al-Riyadh Bank, Saudi Arabia. Dublin Institute of Technology.

15. Kaufman, Edward J (2009) Museums make deep cuts in face of global financial crisis. The Art Newspaper 18.

16. Solnik C (2009) For museums, financial crisis is not a pretty picture.

17. Fletcher A, Lee M (2012) Current social media uses and evaluations in American museums. Museum Management and Curatorship 27: 505-521.

18. Fell G (2012) Going Social: A Case Study of the Use of Social Media Technologies by the Museum of New Zealand Te Papa Tongarewa. University of wellington.

19. Jokela T (2001) Assessment of User-Centred Design Processes as a Basis for Improvement Action. An Experimental Study in Industrial Settings, University of Oulu.

20. Walliman N (2010) Research methods.

21. Kotler N, Kotler P, Kotler W (2008) Museum marketing and strategy: designing missions, building audiences, generating revenue and resources. John Wiley and Sons.

22. Kremer HH (2013) Social Media.

23. Gu M (2012) Engaging Museum Visitors through Social Media : Multiple Case Studies of Social Media Implementation in Museums. Ohio state university.

24. Lehman K (2008) Museums and marketing in an electronic age. University of Tasmania.

23

Investigating and Criticizing Software Engineering Practices in Palestine

Mohamed D Almadhoun*

University College of Applied Sciences, Palestine, Gaza

Abstract

Considering good practices of software engineering in ICT sector associations can improve this sector, accelerate development, increase product qualities and enlarge economic investment in country. This research applied a survey to discover weakness and strengths of ICT sector in Palestine, survey consists of different six categories of questions: general information, production type, quality control and standardization, relationships between association and customers, production quality, and production size, every category discusses a dilemma. Results of survey are listed for each category with clarifying and comparing between current situation and the good practices that should be followed. Discussion and recommendations added SWOT analysis for results and changes that should be followed. Data mining techniques were used to try looking at the future and put rules deduced from data, clustering for grouping instances and studying each group properties, and rule induction to deduce the strongest relations between software engineering practices.

Keywords: Software engineering; Investigation; Criticizing; Good practices; Survey; Data mining

Introduction

Software engineering bridges the gap between technology needs of potential customer and delivery of system that satisfies needs. In software engineering formal methods and standard guidelines are used to improve system quality. Practices in Software engineering are those methods used throughout the lifecycle phases of product [1,2].

In Palestine Investment Conference 2010, Dr. Sabri Saidam added that we want to invest in Palestine because we want to change the views about Palestine. Mr. Jamal Yasin added that awareness with regard to IT culture must be spread. Also, the opportunities must be given to creative people and create mechanism to enable business people to control and manage their businesses [3]. This means that increasing the size and quality of ICT products is a target future that should Palestine seeks to it in next economic plan. Good practices in software engineering will enable forcing this trend.

80% of projects are unsuccessful either because they are over budget, late, missing function, or a combination. Moreover, 30% of software projects are so poorly executed that they are canceled before completion. Best practices will help improve the success of a software development project and get better chance of completing project successfully [4]. This confirms the effect of not following good practices in software engineering which will fatigue ICT sector and economy. This paper presents a study of software engineering practices in Palestine, detects weaknesses, and draws the right ways and recommendations of improving software engineering practices. Methodology used was publishing a survey of different classified questions; number of associations that filled the survey was 19. Section 4 will show methodology details, section 5 will show results and comparisons, section 6 will discuss results and gets out recommendation up to international good practices, section 7 will apply data mining techniques and show results for future considerations.

Related Works

Groves et al. [5] reported on the software development techniques used in the New Zealand software industry, paying particular attention to requirements gathering. They surveyed a selection of software companies with a general questionnaire and then conducted in-depth interviews with four companies. Their results show a wide variety in the kinds of companies undertaking software development, employing a wide range of software development techniques. Although their data were not sufficiently detailed to draw statistically significant conclusions, it appears that larger software development groups typically have more well-defined software development processes, spend proportionally more time on requirements gathering, and follow more rigorous testing regimes.

Nikula et al. [6] presented a survey that gives a realistic view of how marginal technology transfer from the research community to the industry has been. It also reveals that the key development needs in industry are (1) development of own RE process adaptations, (2) RE process improvement, and (3) automation of RE practices. Directing efforts to these areas would substantially improve the chances of successful technology transfer and process improvement efforts in industry.

Claudio et al. [7] have designed and carried out a systematic survey based on an extensive WWW-based interactive questionnaire to assure quality, electronic patient record systems (EPRS) are developed using robust Software Engineering (SE) methodologies. Among other things, it asks the respondents (EPRS developers) about SE practices and tools which were used.

Methodology

A survey was published to collect quantified data up to research objectives. Survey contained a set of questions included in six categories. Categories are: general information, production type, quality control and standardization, relationships between association and customers, production quality, production size.

First category (general information) collected information about association field, location, and type (governmental, educational, or private sector), then asked about management roles, experience years, scientific degree, age, sex.

Second category (production type) investigated percentage of using

*****Corresponding author:** Mohamed D Almadhoun, University College of Applied Sciences, Palestine, Gaza, E-mail: mdmadhoun202@ gmail.com

open source products, detected types of programs used during work, which programming languages and development enterprises are most used, software engineering process that person actually work on, trend of services types like customization or development from scratch.

Third category (quality control and standardization) asked about whether if standard forms or special tools or programs are used in requirements specifications step, in design, in planning and management, in testing, in maintenance, do they apply code review in their association, which CASE tools are most used, in which software engineering process uses CASE tools, is there a quality control team and what are practices do they act (like monitoring, assessment of workers' performance), which cost estimation methods are most used, and which version control systems are most used.

Fourth category (relationships between association and customers) questions was interested in appreciating ease of communication between team members who work on the same product, ease of communication between association and customers, if there are support methods after product delivery (as training, and user manual), percentage of those product that are delivered late, and extent of customer satisfaction.

Fifth category (production quality) focused on detecting percentage of projects that exceeds their budget, percentage of products that can't estimate resource for them, percentage of products that can't estimate work progress, percentage of products that need a lot of maintenance, percentage of products that contains lots of errors or bugs that can't be solved easily or cause new bugs when solve them, percentage of high performance working products at delivery, percentage of products that are usable and easy to use, and usability of products.

Sixth category (production size) will show the dominant range of budgets of products, and dominant projects durations.

Results

Results of survey show that software engineering practices are employed in production processes of ICT companies in Palestine, some of these practices are good and some are not, but the majority are good.

Next points will show results of each category questions.

General information

From this set of questions we can note that most workers are of bachelor degree. Workers with age range from 20 to 30 are more than 60%, but most of them are males. The weakness point in appeared in this category that most associations are small with workers less than 6. 70% of associations worked on outsourced projects or parts of projects. There are a big number of workers with good experience years.

Production type

Using open source programs or tools in production stages is considered little; about 50% of them do not use open source products. As for using different types of programs and tools there was 11% only uses activity management programs. As for programming and development languages, most used for web development is PHP, MYSQL is the most used between other databases, windows is most used between other operating systems; Android is most used for mobile applications development. As for tasks done by worker it's notable that most workers do the three tasks analysis, programming, testing. As for types of association tasks the following Table 1 shows results.

Quality control and standardization

Table 2 shows results of surveying the percentage of using standard forms or special tools in software engineering processes.

Maintenance of legacy systems	79%
Development from scratch	95%
Customization	53%
Off-The-shelf	63%

Table 1: Task association percentages.

Requirements Specifications	74%
Design	53%
Planning and Management	53%
Testing	47%
Maintenance	47%

Table 2: Using standard forms percentages.

53% are applying code review. The most used CASE tools are Microsoft Visio, Visual Studio, Rational Rose, Smart Draw, and Altova Respectively. CASE tools are most used for requirements engineering. 70% have a quality management team and the most used tasks in this operation are workers performance assessment and looking for improvement methods. As for cost estimation next table shows usage distribution (Table 3). 50% are using version control systems; most of them use CVS, SourceSafe, and Subversion respectively.

Relationships between association and customers

For communications between team members inside association specially those who are working on the same project changes like 11% hard, 47% moderate, and 37% easy. But for communications with customers especially in requirements collection and review operations, 5% stated that it's hard, 74% moderate, and 16% easy. As for support after project delivery, following Table 4 shows percentages of associations that provide support services.

For late submission of projects, following Table 5 shows projects percentages according to late submissions. For customer satisfaction most associations stated that this is not easy task and some of them described it's very hard to satisfy customers.

Production quality

Answers to question of percentage of projects that exceeds its budget show that 47% of associations suffer from little number of over budget projects and 37% have moderate number of over budget projects. 42% of associations stated that moderate number of projects suffer from hardness in estimating resources. 58% of associations agreed that a moderate number of projects need lot of maintenance and modifications after delivery. 58% of associations stated that little of projects have bugs after delivery, and 32% stated that number of bugs is not little. 47% stated that moderate number of delivered projects is of high performance and good quality, and 47% of associations stated that lots of projects are of a good quality and performance. For ease of use 47% stated that moderate number of projects have high usability, and 37% stated lots of projects have a high usability. Reusability was high in 32% of associations, moderate in 32%, and little in 26%.

Production size

47% of associations are working on projects of budget under $5000, and 53% of associations work on small projects that fall in periods less than 6 months, and 26% of them work on projects between 6 months and one year.

Discussion and Recommendations

To study the last results shown in previous section we have to state SWOT analysis for that and deduce a set of recommendations. Next table lists SWOT points (Table 6).

Using COCOMO	24%
Expert estimation	94%
Using similar projects	71%
Parkinson's Law	41%
Pricing to win	35%

Table 3: Using cost estimation methods percentages.

User training	83%
User manuals	78%
Inline guidelines	56%
Visits	78%

Table 4: Percentages of associated tasks for providing support services.

No late projects	5%
Little of projects were submitted late	42%
Moderate number of projects were submitted late	37%
Lots of projects were submitted late	5%

Table 5: Percentages of late submission of projects.

From weaknesses we have to enforce mechanisms of facilitating communication between team members and between team members and customer. Also strong rule and contracts should prevent submitting late projects to overcome problems between customer and association and increase productivity. Testing should have a bigger chance of software processes to overcome problems of lots of maintenance after delivery. And a very big mistake occur because the same worker do analysis, programming and testing for some project, as this decrease big experience in one field and make testing rapid and weak, and make programming overlap with analysis so lots of conflicts are there in development.

From opportunities we have to exploit the energy of young workers by increasing investment in ICT sector, and support the culture and skills of outsourcing as it seems there is approach for outsourcing as local market is weak. Also good number of associations started in mobile applications development and this is a new trend we have to enforce it.

From threats they have to increase using open source programs as this has extra advantages and to exceed problems, activity management programs should be used for managing ticket issuing and following work progress. And using standard forms is not so wide, while it helps to overcome team changeability problems and have other advantages to make product well documented. Encouraging code review is important to decrease errors and bugs. Using control version systems makes no duplication or removal of work and helps decreasing bugs and contradictions and hence project can win profit. Over budget projects means lose and threat of danger on economy. Small projects don't improve economy, so seeking to win of large projects should be the goal of ICT companies especially those who are working for more than 5 years.

Data Mining and Future Trends

Data mining can find unsuspected relationships and summarize the data in novel ways that are both understandable and useful to the data owner. A set of data mining models were applied on database using rapidminer software to discover rules and associations. A preprocessing step came in first to resolve data from redundant fields, and empty values.

First was clustering which was set to extract three clusters, the main distinguishing factors appeared to differentiate between clusters

Strengths		Weaknesses	
	• Most workers are of bachelor degree. • Most of them are using PHP for web development; MYSQL is the most used between other databases. • 47% of associations stated that lots of projects are of a high quality and performance.		• Most associations are small with workers less than 6. • Communications between team members inside association specially those who are working on the same project changes like 11% hard, 47% moderate, and 37% easy • Communications with customers especially in requirements collection and review operations, 5% stated that it's hard, 74% moderate, and 16% easy • Using inline guidelines percentage is 56%. • 37% stated that moderate number of projects was submitted late. • 58% of associations agreed that a moderate number of projects need lot of maintenance and modifications after delivery. • 37% stated lots of projects have a high usability. • Most workers do the three tasks analysis, programming, testing.
Opportunities		**Threats**	
	• Workers with age range from 20 to 30 are more than 60%. • 70% of associations worked on outsourced projects or parts of projects. • Android is most used for mobile applications development.		• 50% of associations do not use open source products. • 11% only uses activity management programs. • Percentages of using standard forms are mostly less than 60%. • 53% are applying code review. • 50% are using version control systems. • 37% have moderate number of over budget projects • 47% of associations are working on projects of budget under $5000. • 53% of associations work on small projects that fall in periods less than 6 months, and 26% of them work on projects between 6 months and one year.

Table 6: SWOT analysis.

were using standard forms for requirements specification, design, and testing, and the experience. Following graph shows clusters distribution (Figure 1).

Second was rule induction, a set of rules were extract:

• When considering customer satisfaction as a target label, moderate customer satisfaction when number of late projects are moderate, or experience from one to three years of workers, and low satisfaction when percentage of over budget projects is high.

• When considering the percentage of late projects as target label, high percentage of late projects where most found in associations of workers number between one and five, and low percentage when using standard forms for testing.

• When considering over budget as target label, it will be moderate if late projects and needing for maintenance after delivery

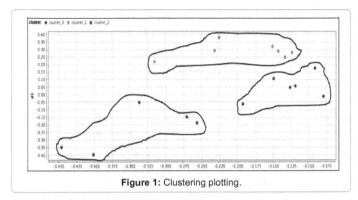

Figure 1: Clustering plotting.

are moderate.

When considering well performed projects as a target label, it will be high if using standard forms in design was high.

Conclusion

This paper draw up the most software engineering practices used in ICT associations in Palestine, SWOT analysis show that a big set of weaknesses and threats are there. Some of good practices are used, most associations suffered from delivery problems. Most associations were small sized and the same thing for projects. Recommendations that can be added here, that government should encourage large projects, government shall outsource its projects to local companies to enforce private sector, very good profile and international relations are needed to bid for big projects outside Palestine because the local market projects are small and this will increase income to country.

References

1. Marianne H (1996) Software engineering practices in Lebanon and suggestions for Lebanese requirements analysis and software testing standards.

2. El-Khalili N, Damen D (2009) Software engineering practices in Jordan. DocPlayer.

3. http://www.pic-palestine.ps/userfiles/file/pdfs/ict_session_en.pdf

4. Perks M (2003) Best practices for software development projects. International Business Machines Corporation.

5. Groves L, Nickson R, Reeve G, Reeves S, Utting M (2000) A survey of software development practices in the New Zealand software industry. Proceedings of Software Engineering Conference, Australia.

6. Nikula U, Sajaniemi J, Kalviainen H (2000) A state-of-the-practice survey on requirements engineering in small and medium-sized enterprises. Telecom Business Research Center.

7. Alves CG, Sabbatini R (2001) A survey of software engineering practices in the development of electronic patient record systems, AMAIA

24

Toward Securing Cyber-Physical Systems Using Exact Cover Set

Sameer Kumar Bisoyi and Hassan Reza*

School of Aerospace Sciences, Department of Computer Science, University of North Dakota, North Dakota, USA

Abstract

Cyber physical systems (CPS) are computer systems that integrate computing, coordination and communication systems in order to monitor physical entities in the physical world. As they interact with the critical systems and infrastructure that may impact real life. There are many issues in design and constructions of these types of systems. One of the key issue that receives so many attention is the security of such systems. Although security solutions for Information Systems handle the security issues associated with Traditional IT security, but the impact of a failure in a cyber-physical system demands a different approach to handle security issues related to the cyber world. In this work, we focus on using a key agreement technique known as Physical Signal Key Agreement (PSKA) technique using the Exact Cover method to generate the random key which will be embedded into an access control model known as the Modified Context-Aware Security The feasibility of our framework (MCASF) to handle both normal and critical situation on demand is demonstrated via a Pervasive Health Monitoring Systems (PHMS).

Keywords: Cyber-physical systems; Trusted computing; Context-aware security; Information security; Exact covering; Modified context-aware security; Framework; Software engineering

Introduction

Cyber-physical systems [1] (CPS) combine the computing and communication capabilities with the entities in the physical world in terms of monitoring as well as control. Typically, Cyber-physical system consists of the cyber systems and the physical world. The physical process can either be natural or artificial. The CPS is a combination of devices that incorporates computing and communication capabilities into physical processes to manage the physical activities of monitoring and control. The communication between the cyber system and the physical process creates new communication channels which make it more vulnerable to security issues. Some examples of such attacks are the recent attack on the air traffic control mission-critical systems [2], an attack on the power system that resulted in power outage [3], CarShark that can turn off a car engine remotely [4], Stuxnet (i.e., a powerful virus which attacked the whole Siemen's networks, almost crippled it, etc. [5]). The most dangerous of all would be a remote hacking on artificial human organs which can control all its activities from outside the body [6].

Cyber-physical Systems are extremely critical in nature due to its close ties with the real-time systems. So the security solutions have to be not only different, but efficient. Though the security solutions for Information Systems provide some level of security, it's still just not enough. For national critical systems like Supervisory Control and Data Acquisition systems (SCADA) that handle national interests like Oil and Natural Gas, Electric Power Grid; any sort of system failure can impact public domain irreparably.

However; it's not only limited to that but also the issue of communicating securely is an important feature of the Cyber Physical Systems in dire need to be addressed. They especially rely on the interoperation of different heterogeneous systems that the traditional systems lack. Although the security of CPS greatly focuses on reliability and prevention, utmost focus of CPS protection is to mitigate malicious cyber-attacks.

To fully analyze the security needs for Cyber Physical Systems, we need to discuss the needs of Secure Control and possible attacks or threats. Although security solutions from Information Security and Network Security measures can help mitigate these issues to some extent, they alone are certainly not sufficient. To achieve this, we need to address the issues that are related to security issues that are prone to malicious cyber-attacks.

At present, there are two security methodologies that work side by side with the CPS Security. Both computer and network security focus on how to prevent faults, however to recover a system already stuck due to unknown faults or uncertainties is addressed by control systems. However, the security of a system against a malicious adversary still needs plenty of work which we are going to outline in this paper.

Background

Even today, the focus on security still relies on improvising the existing mechanisms of traditional IT security for the mission-critical Cyber Physical Systems. Although these solutions work to an extent in providing security, we still need to underline the difference between a traditional Information Systems and a Cyber Physical Systems which will help outlining the security needs that are separately needed in order to ensure that the systems also handle security issues emerging from the attacks or faults in the cyber world. Traditional IT security focuses on central servers while the need for CPS security needs to emphasize on edge clients.

The major issue with CPS is to accommodate the software upgrades or patches. An example of this is the complete system shutdown of a nuclear power plant in Georgia in the year of 2008 [7]. The shutdown was a result of a software patch deployed to a system which was meant for monitoring. The patches reboot the system and reset the data which the system interpreted as a drop in water level of the reservoir meant to cool radioactive nuclear rods and shut down the system [7].

Real-time system properties of CPS pose another challenge [8]. It's not that real-time requirement is the only prerogative of the Cyber Physical Systems, rather it is a requirement of traditional IT systems as well. However; in CPS, the real-time requirement takes the topmost priority as failing to meet a deadline can prove to be completely hazardous, utmost failure of the system. In CPS, the response time to

---

*Corresponding author: Hassan Reza, School of Aerospace Sciences, Department of Computer Science, University of North Dakota, North Dakota, USA
E-mail: reza@aero.und.edu

meet any deadline is absolutely necessary and cannot be compromised at any instant.

Damage to the physical environment, faults in sensors and actuators, response time pose significant challenges that separates a CPS from traditional IT systems.

General Workflow of CPS

There are basically four steps in the workflow for CPS [9].

Monitoring: Monitoring the processes and environment is a primary function of the CPS. It is used to monitor the past activities and predict the future activities of the CPS.

Networking: Networking means collection of data through various means. Multiple sensors can be used to collect data to be aggregated to be analyzed further to provide computing capabilities to the CPS.

Computing: This step deals with the analysis as well as the verification of data which are collected during the Networking phases to see if it satisfies the pre-defined criteria. If the criteria have not been met, then appropriate action has to be taken.

Actuating: This is the final step in the workflow of CPS. This step is meant for actuating real actions formulated during the Computing phase. Actions are determined in terms of whether the criteria have been met.

Security goals and requirements of CPS

Confidentiality: It is an important feature that deals with the prevention of user's private data being revealed to unauthorized users [10]. Confidentiality is not just a requirement of the Information Systems, but also of CPS. To fully understand this, take the example of a banking user. The user has to log in using his own username and password and perform the transactions. These transactions should be revealed only to the user when he logs in. If an unauthorized user is able to view this data by snooping or by any other means, then it is a breach of confidentiality [11]. Though useful, confidentiality alone is not sufficient to handle the issues related to the breach in communication channels between user and controller. For this, the CPS has to impose better security on communication channels.

Integrity: It is the feature that deals with the modification of data with proper authorization [12]. When an unauthorized user or adversary is able to modify data without proper authorization and the user believes it to be true, then integrity is violated [10]. It is achieved by preventing such users to manipulate the existing data to malign the integrity.

Availability: It is the feature that deals with the availability of the system on demand [10]. In CPS, it is vital that the system is available whenever in demand.

Major types of attacks to CPS

We summarize the types of attacks to CPS as follows [9]:

Compromised-key: This attack happens when the secret code to access a CPS is compromised [13]. The adversary can use this key to enter into the system and modify data without authorization and knowledge of the sender or receiver. Along with manipulating data, the adversary can also obtain keys to several other systems by computing the available compromised key and gain access that is not meant for him. Most of compromised key attacks happen with the help of reverse engineering on available physical processes.

Man-in-the-middle: When false messages are sent to the operator, the operator, being unaware of the situation, acts on it. The operator maintains appropriate action based on protocols which are applicable to normal situations whereas that can be disastrous when applied at a time it's not needed or, not applied when it actually is needed. Because the operator fails to recognize a Man-in-the-Middle attack [14], so the actions he takes according to the protocol for normal situations can be hazardous to the CPS.

Eavesdropping: Eavesdropping happens when someone without authorization intercepts data communicated in a system [15]. While eavesdropping, the adversary does not interrupt the communication, rather intercepts the data communicated through the system. As CPS is prone to such attacks, so the eavesdropping usually takes place through the traffic analysis of the monitoring data transferred in the sensor networks that has been collected periodically through monitoring.

Denial-of-service (DoS): The Denial of Service, otherwise known as DoS, is a type of attack that occurs when an adversary is successful in making the system unavailable due to different circumstances [16]. Some of those circumstances are: flooding or blocking the communication channels to deny normal service to the system, sending invalid data to cause abnormal behaviour of the services. In short; DoS interrupts normal work or use of the services and; paralyzes the availability of the system.

Literature Survey of Available Solutions

For our proposed research, we have surveyed variety of solutions that exist today for the security of Cyber Physical Systems, some of which have been described in the following section.

Solution from information security

In this section, we discuss about the existing solutions from the Information Security and their shortcomings [17]. One of the most prominent features that can be used is authentication. It can be used to prevent user personalization so that no one else can impersonate the user. Access Control can also be used to prevent unauthorized access. It is also useful in limiting user's access to how much he/she is allowed to access. Encryption or digital signatures can be used to maintain data integrity. Different tools can also be used to verify the system's correctness and behavior. In case of CPS, principles of redundancy can also be used to prevent a single point of failure, to branch out backups. The system can employ the separation of privilege option to limit access of an unidentified entity that is trying to misuse the system for its own benefit. However; no matter how careful we become, it's impossible to maintain that a system can be a hundred percent full proof of any attack or adversary. Acknowledging that, some tools can be designed specifically with the purpose of intrusion detection and response. Though they are useful, still there can be cases of false alarms and cunning attacks that slip these detections.

However; it's still better to have some security rather than no security. To ensure data confidentiality, some mechanisms of soft cryptography can also be employed.

At the end, an adversary model can be designed in a way to get into an adversary's mindset, get some insight into the real reason of the problem and design a system to overcome such intents.

Though the above mentioned security solutions may mitigate the security issues, there can still be human errors, faulty design or bugs that can make the system vulnerable. To overcome this, we need to be able to design a system that continues even while under attack [18]. The term for this feature is known as Survivability of CPS. Survivability is defined as the graceful degradation of the CPS system when it's facing an attack. Most of the previous techniques that we discussed, focus on availability and integrity of the system under network point of view. They never addressed the issues of deception or DoS attacks on the system. These attacks can affect the estimation and control algorithms, and make the system susceptible to any adversary. Even the tools designed for intrusion detection and response have not considered algorithms for such attacks, especially when the deception attacks are originated from compromised controllers. Furthermore, most of the existing solutions force the design of a human response system. Also; CPS is almost always safety-critical and there is no margin for error. In such situations, waiting for human response to hazardous attacks is a lag in the security. What needs to be done instead, is to design an autonomous, real-time decision making algorithms that gets rid of the response delays by a human response system such that the safety of the safety-critical systems is never compromised.

Lastly, there is still a need of extensive research to fully understand and develop an adversary model so that the real nature of the problem is estimated in time and successive steps can be taken in advance to ensure the safety of the CPS.

Solution from control theory

One of the major problems in Control Theory is to design such a policy in order to keep an unstable system stable under the feedback loop. The major issue of the denial of service (DoS) attack can be raised from the constraints imposed on the CPS such as packet loss, delay in response time, bound capacity etc. Such constraints can lead to a DoS attack which is a major attack on availability which can make the system so vulnerable that it becomes impossible to bring it back to stable. This can also lead to the implementation of incorrect control policies. That is why there is a need to do some extensive research as in how to include network characteristics in case of a control policy design [19,20].

Another problem in Control Theory is the shutting down of the whole system due to a single point of failure. To continue operations while under a failure mode, redundancies need to be incorporated so that a single point of failure does not occur. Whenever a failure occurs, the system should be able to undergo a graceful degradation in performance limiting the negative effects. So, research in fault tolerant control also needs to be addressed [21].

Lastly; there is a need to design distributed algorithms to address distributed estimation for systems that are limited in transmission power and memory [22].

Control Theory is considered to be better than Information Security solutions. However; research on fault tolerant control is still needed. It should be able to provide better security under Deception and DoS attacks. What we mean is that, a robust control and estimation algorithm should be designed to handle such attacks. Under such attacks, worst-case performance should be optimized.

Along with the state of the system, state of communication network should be estimated. Especially; it should address the Quality of Service (QoS) and integrity of the data and control policies. The primary objective should be to optimize performance which is the essential key of the Control Theory.

Redundancies should be addressed properly so that any form of single point of failure does not occur at any moment. Instead these should be combined and let the system degrade its performance gracefully.

While the above redundancies are in place, we should design trust management schemes to handle worst-case performance. So; extensive research is needed to be done not only in designing the control policies, but also in developing a design to include worst-case performance.

Context-aware security framework

In this framework, the context of the application is determined to be incorporated into the system to handle the security features employed by the system. Such security measurements can be encryption, access control, and authentication and so on. This dynamic adapting of the environment by context coupling is known as the Context-Aware Security Framework [9].

Before we move on to further analysis of the framework, we need to define what we actually mean by context. Context is nothing, but a set of environments or physical attributes that determines the system's behavior on the application [23]. Context can be achieved via various sources and can vary from location to system and so on. Context can be divided into four categories which are as follows:

- System Context (CPU, Network etc.)
- User Context (Location, Medical History etc.)
- Physical Environment Context (Weather, Temperature etc.)
- Time Context (Time)

Most focus is on the context that are most applicable to characterize the situation and apply the context to handle the controls to prevent unauthorized access, leak of information, disruption, unwarranted termination of application etc. in order to provide the basic goals of Information Security that are integrity, availability and confidentiality. Under the attack, the system should employ the adversary model as one of its security-relevant contextual attributes. The attributes build the context of the application as in how to choose the most appropriate controls and configuration to mitigate these issues. The values of these attributes determine the choice of controls and configuration under a certain situation.

There are various schemas and security protocols which will be analyzed in the future of Context-Aware Security Framework. Some of which are Context-Aware User Privacy, Context-Aware Mutual Authentication Protocol, Context-Aware Access Control and Context-Aware Intrusion Detection. Context-Aware User Privacy prevents eavesdropping whereas Context-Aware Mutual Authentication Protocol prevents Man-in-the-Middle attacks. Context-Aware Access Control handles problems associated with the access control, and Context-Aware Intrusion Detection manages unwarranted intrusion and DoS attacks.

Trusted Computing in CPS

Trust can be defined as how much a trustor is willing to rely on the CPS even if breach of trust is a possibility. It is the confidence the user has on the performance of the system. When this confidence is justified to satisfy the user needs, it is known as a trusted application or system. The extent to which the user's expectation has been is termed as Trustworthiness [24].

A security model has been proposed to determine the trustworthiness of a system by the following criteria [24]:

The aspects that can affect our systems can never be one hundred percent predicted. Neither can rigorous testing and verification can prove its trustworthiness. So to operate a system successfully, trust to a certain extent on its design and implementation is essential. We can be confident on the functionality of a system based on evidence. Evidence depends on its past usage, performance and level of satisfaction. However; it can never be absolute. Trust is evaluated in context. Based on context or functionality, it can vary within the system.

Even though evidence can generate confidence on trustworthiness, however, the conditions and context of its evaluation is different than that of trustworthiness. So; to justify the trust on the system, only dynamic confirmation is relied upon.

To evaluate trust, evidences that are related to the current context, must be taken into account.

In what follows, we have listed the benefits which justify the use of Trusted Platform Module in securing the CPS [25]:

- CPS uses cloned signatures or session keys to make sure that the sensors and the actuators communicating with them are authentic. So; there is no margin for unauthorized access.

- Sensors collect the data at lower level, and intermediary nodes pass them to the upper level. While transmitting all of the CPS's nodes hold sensitive data. To make sure that the data is safe or protected, we can make use of TPM to encrypt it.

- When a replacement to an existing sensor or actuator is needed, then it has to be peripherally attested first which can be achieved by installing a TPM to the replacement device. Once it asks for a random key, the replacement device has to sign a random number and authenticate.

- CPS has to undergo periodic software and firmware updates. To verify the authenticity of these updates, TPM can be used.

Along with the above mentioned advantages, TPM also supports soft cryptography for encrypting data which is a key feature that makes its stand unique.

We discussed about the advantages of TPM. However; there is still scope for furthermore research. Especially pre-deployment of trusted keys, multilayer security mechanism, incorporating principle of least privileges and redundancy, and managing root and chain of trust in CPS are a few of the issues which does not make Trust computing an ideal choice for the security of CPSs at present. In the following section, we have emphasized the issues with the assumption of pre-deployment of keys to establish trust, which are as such [26]:

- For the key to be pre-deployed at the manufacturing center itself, the whole communication channel has to be trusted from the manufacturing center to the host itself [27].

- For the key has to be deployed by the host itself, important decisions will have to be made about the key which might result in poor quality of the generated keys.

- If the keys are pre-deployed, it would be hard to move or add the keys within the network especially resulting in all keys or nodes being updated within the network. Even removal of a compromised key would be difficult.

Though there are some solutions like message-in-a-bottle approach [27] to manage these problems and many more, they still require some side channels like Faraday's cage or something else to pass the key which makes them unsuitable and unsafe to use them for mission-critical cyber-physical systems.

Modeling and verifying intelligent automotive cyber-physical systems

The authors proposed the use of Machine learning techniques to collect time series data from the sensors of automobile cyber physical systems to record human reaction and behavior. Their proposed approach uses extensive cognitive psychology concepts to design a learning model of conditional probability distributions to maximize expectation and learn the parameters without adding complexity. Along with the theories in psychology, the authors also relied on low abstract learning skills like route selection or steering control to be incorporated [28]. They also developed an algorithm to minimize the overhead by using intelligent automotive cyber physical systems [29,30]. They analyzed the models of the cyber physical systems by proving the correctness of low dimensional abstractions in the linear hybrid automata, which is then used to verify the overall high. They proposed to distribute the verification of low dimensional abstractions as a solution.

Although the model works fine for the automotive intelligent systems, but the time series data have to be available at all times to carry out the proposal. Also, for physiological sensors defining the length for the passkey between the sender and receiver beforehand, though reduces complexity, however increases threats to the security. So, it poses the same threat of exposing the uniform randomness of the passkey to let the hacker be able to reconstruct the appropriate code, just like in the case of chaff points randomized over uniform data in the Fuzzy logic.

Fuzzy extractors

Other approach works with fuzzy Extractors, which rely on reproducing cryptographic keys precisely as well as distributing them in a uniform fashion. Using fuzzy extractors to obtain uniform randomness from the input is nearly optimal till the change in input remains close to the original input. To utilize this feature, the fuzzy vault incorporates error tolerance in practice. When the user provides an input, the extractor pulls some random string from the input, however in a way that it remains noise-tolerant, which means that in the case where another input close, but not the same as the previous input is provided, still the extractor is able to reproduce the string from it. This random string is inverted into a key; however, it is not needed to store this key in the server. It is important to have this feature as it is highly insecure for a key to be stored in a server's long-term storage that is publicly stored.

Secure Sketch can also be used as a tool in fuzzy extractor as well as an independent cryptography construct to reproduce cryptographic keys. Using the secure sketch, it is possible to precisely reconstruct a noisy input. Given an input, a sketch is produced. Then, it is possible to retrieve the input, given another input close to the first one and instead of storing the actual input, only secure sketch is stored to preserve privacy of the input. Advantages also include confidentiality and entropy retention without compromising privacy, however non-uniformity is not addressed.

Therefore, both secure sketches and fuzzy extractors basically provided a fuzzy storage for the cryptographic key such that the actual key is not compromised due to privacy breach [31].

Fuzzy vault

Fuzzy vault was first proposed by Ari Juels and Madhu Sudan in 2002. Fuzzy vault operates in a way to generate a key that is well hidden in the domain of its chaff points. Using a fuzzy vault, a user is able to hide a secret key in an unordered sample. Then a polynomial is chosen to encode the key as well as to evaluate the polynomial on all elements in the sample. The user then has to manually select random chaff points which do not lie on the polynomial. These chaff points, together with the real points construct the secure vault. Usually, the more the number of chaff points, the merrier for the concealing of the genuine key. The degree of the encoding polynomial determines the error-tolerance of the system. To retrieve the key, the user needs to provide a second sample. When the second sample overlaps with the first one, then numerous points in the vault can be identified and when enough points are identified, then an error correction scheme can be utilized to decode the key. If the samples do not overlap with each other in terms of the points, then the fuzzy vault fails to authenticate, however it's not an issue if the samples do not match due to the incorporation of its randomness through its chaff points [32].

Nonetheless; it is still an unsafe choice due to its leaking of vast amount of data regarding the analog of its randomness, almost similar to the secure sketches in case of fuzzy extractors. Though the attacker has to search for valid options of the randomness incurred, it still lacks in a strong definition of the cryptographic object. Also; the storage and computation costs are exponentially high, especially when it comes a large dataset as well as fuzzy vaults without chaff points are discarded. Entropy loss is high and error tolerance only works in case of small Hamming Metric, which calls for better techniques in encoding as well as signal processing [31].

Proposed Approach

In this section, a solution is proposed to make better use of security protocols in two different domains. The first is to establish secure communication within a Body Area Network (BAN) on Pervasive Health Monitoring Systems (PHMS) [33], whereas the second is to develop a proactive access control model to manage a smart infrastructure during emergencies.

Body Area Network constitutes of small-scale sensors that gather the host's vitals, evaluate movements and properties, and send to the base station wirelessly. Body properties usually consist of location, pulse and body temperature. It's usually coupled with PHMS due to its properties in combining remote monitoring with ubiquitous computing. PHMS collects the data gathered by the sensors of BAN and performs real-time health monitoring for mobile patients [34].

These two domains are chosen frequently as they are good representation of CPS because of their environment coupled nature, and they present two variations for CPSs, BAN showing complete physical security, whereas smart-infrastructures demonstrating physical security to a minimum. For the system to be both secure communication and proactive in handling emergency situations, a modified context-aware security framework is proposed which not only takes into account, the context for the subject that requests the access, but the context of the whole system to determine what privileges to be deployed to which set of subjects and for how long depending on the specific kind of environment. To make the communication of privileges for a fixed duration between these nodes secure, we propose using an already established key agreement technique known as Physiological Signal-based Key Agreement (PSKA) [35], but using the exact cover techniques to generate the random key.

PHMS is used to monitor and collect real-time health data of a patient with the help of medical sensors worn by the host or patient. The Body Area Network (BAN) of sensors gather this data and transfer to the system. The sensors can be deployed in the presence of doctors

or by the hosts themselves. As PHMS is becoming popular day by day, even by people with no chronic ailments, for example fitness monitoring, there is need for the use more interoperable sensors. The real overhead for secure communication is key distribution for which there is an urgent need for the development of key agreement technique to preserve the usability. However; this is just one side of the coin. The other side, in this regard to consider, is the response of PHMS in case of the smart-infrastructures or emergencies. Smart-infrastructures are used to provide real-time data to relief workers in order to save lives and property. As the data is sensitive, there is an urn to make the communication more secure from a malicious attack. To achieve this, of course access control techniques are used. However; during emergencies, these access controls are disabled to facilitate emergency management. However; this can be a grave issue as anyone can initiate an emergency to get unlimited access to sensitive info on patient data. So, there is also a need to address this issue by developing an access control model which not only controls access in normal situations, but also adapts its behavior to manage critical situations dynamically.

To overcome security issues related with BANs, an established key agreement solution is presented which is called Physiological Signal-based Key Agreement (PSKA) [35]. It utilizes specific physiological signals as a common key for sensors to enable security. Physiological signals are nothing but stimuli generated by different functions of the human body itself. Examples include the EKG, heart rate etc. Basically; both the communicating sensors specifically agree on one physiological signal, extract features from the signal and convert the features into a set of binary strings, generates a random key, then the sender node concatenates a message authentication code (MAC) to encrypt the data, then hides the key in the previously generated binary string of the physiological signal and sends both the key and data in a single message. The receiver node on the other end, receives the key utilizing a local version of the physiological signal, and checks it by decrypting the data received [36]. If the random key and MAC in both the sender and receiver are matched, then it is accepted, else rejected. Once, the steps are done, there is no need for explicit measurement of physiological signals to establish a secure communication unless the sensors are being reconfigured. It achieves security based on the random key generated by the unique physiological signal at a unique time. A malicious entity who is not in contact with the host will never be able to accurately measure the physiological signal as physiological signals are unique at unique time, so preserving security. This property of physiological signals is known as Time-Variance.

To choose this physiological signal, it has a certain criterion. To be able to get selected for generating the key, the signal has to be long and random, it should be captured in minimal time, it should be distinct and it should possess temporal variance i.e., even if an adversary is able to figure out the physiological signal at present somehow, still future executions of the scheme should not be compromised due to uniqueness of the signal at a time. However; as physiological signals are time-variant and vary unpredictably, so the system needs to ensure that two signals are seeing the same copy of the signal and proper synchronization between sensors needs to be figured out which in case of PSKA is 8mS according to [37]. Though it sounds similar to that of the biometric systems, however, the last feature i.e., Temporal Variance is the property that differentiates a PSKA from the biometric systems as biometric systems depend on not possessing the temporal variance [32].

To generate this key for PSKA, we propose the use of a set cover technique known as the Exact Cover Problem replacing the fuzzy vault in the form of a cryptographic construct [38]. The primary reason behind selecting exact cover techniques to replace fuzzy vault is its flexibility in choosing a length of the set randomly. Also, the combinations in the set to make the cryptographic key is not confined to the scope of the polynomial through the whole time. As soon as a different polynomial is chosen, the combinations can be rearranged accordingly, making the maximum number of such possible combinations to be 2n for length of the set n, below is how the whole process works in terms of an Exact Cover technique.

First; the sender and the receiver sample the physiological signal in current time and make use of the Exact Cover Problem to generate a random set of strings i.e., the polynomial. Given a set of values {1, 2, 3, ..., n} using the concept of natural language processing covering all languages known in the whole world, this scheme first determines the length of the string, which is to be shared by both the sender and the receiver node, and its common factors. Out of all the common factors, two factors are chosen, whose product constitute the length of the set. Out of those two factors, one factor gives the length of the subset and the other factor gives the number of subsets. The polynomial and its order or the number of polynomials are chosen, such that the product of the value of the polynomial and its order, or the order sum of the number of polynomials plus 1, always lie on the factors of the length of the set. However, while choosing the order, we also have to keep in mind that the higher the order, lower will be the chances of exposing the common features. Then the scheme generates a family of subsets in the multiples of nCk, where "k" is the length of the subsets. Among these subsets, the sender finds a subfamily whose union is the set itself such that all the sets in the cover are disjoint which constructs the exact cover with a sum of 2k–1 to be reduced to the subset sum problem to lock the key. Out of all exact covers discovered, the subsets that fulfils the exact cover principle as well as fall on the polynomial, are chosen. Apart from the exact cover, the family also consists of chaff points which are random subsets of the given set, which we are going to use so that the adversary won't be able to figure out the cover the key is constructed upon. Once the subsets are drawn, we will turn these sets into bitmaps of length n where "n" is the length of the set, then interpret these bitmaps to be binary numbers, then find out the disjoint subsets that construct the polynomial, with a sum of 2k – 1, to generate the random key with an exact cover. To unlock this key sent be the sender node, the receiver node constructs the exact cover for the same set and matches it with the set received from the sender node. As the key is pre-agreed between the sender and the receiver node, so the receiver should be able to figure out which are the actual subsets used for locking and which are the chaff point, which in case of the adversary, will be impossible to find out, especially within the given time-frame; as the key will constantly be modified. The chaff points will be used to confuse the adversary to hide the legitimate subsets and the actual set. In a way; it will almost be an almost impossible task for the adversary to reconstruct the polynomial to figure out the key. Once the key is matched, the receiver node can use the Message Authentication Code (MAC) received from the sender to decrypt the data received.

In order to facilitate the solution to manage the problems associated with the smart-infrastructures, we propose an access control model called Modified Context-Aware Security Framework (MCASF) which utilizes the features for emergencies, but with better security mechanisms. The goal of this model is to provide a proactive access control model to address emergency situations, to provide the set of privileges needed by specific subject in a specific situation for a specific amount of time. This awareness will be different from the context-awareness we encountered earlier. Context-awareness decides whether access should be granted to the subject making the access request,

by taking into account the contextual information about the subject itself, whereas modified context-awareness will take into account the contextual information about the whole system. If permitted, then access will be granted without any explicit request for access by the subject. For this, it needs to be both adaptive to facilitate the response actions for the known criticalities and proactive in determining when to execute those actions without any explicit access request by the subject. One might ask how it will be any different than the Critically-Aware Access Control [39].

The Modified Context-Aware Security Framework (MCASF) will not just take the Context of the system and its subject into account, but also the physical interaction of the system with its environment such that not only for the smart-infrastructures, but also for establishing secure communication in case of a Body Area Network (BAN), we will be able to use one set of framework known as the Modified Context-Aware Security Framework. Through its interaction with the physical environment, it will be able to find out the demand of the situation and accordingly deploy the normal or special circumstances features to the system. The privileges will be embedded to the system to follow the two sets of protocols. So, basically it will contain different sets of privileges, one that is provided to subjects under normal situations and many alternate sets of privileges that is provided to subject in case of special circumstances to enable them to handle the urgency. These urgencies will again get subdivided into subcategories based on the type of urgency. The different types of urgencies we are considering in this research will be as follows:

- Urgency Level I: This urgency level will define life-threatening urgencies and notify the relief workers accordingly to prioritize the tasks. The set of privileges will be defined accordingly for the assigned duration to the assigned subjects.

- Urgency Level II: This level will define the level of overload faced by tasks as the next level of urgency and reassign them in the to-do list of relief workers as their next priority. The set of privileges will be defined accordingly for the assigned duration to the assigned subjects.

- Urgency Level III: This urgency level will define the critical tasks that were not able to be executed in proper time due to the faced overload by the system at busy hours. The tasks will be reassigned to appropriate authorities and right set of privileges will be assigned to right set of subjects for a given duration.

So; the initial task for the framework will be to figure out the gravity of the situation using the ductility matrix or flow network and notify the system to release appropriate sets of privileges. If it falls under the category of normal situations, the system will use the key agreement technique generated by the Exact Cover Method to generate the key and communicate the data using the Message Authentication Code (MAC). If the urgent or emergency situation is flagged, then the system will perform system ductility to determine the level of urgency and appropriate set of privileges along with the data will be passed to appropriate subjects with a different set of keys generated through the same technique for a fixed duration. The difference in managing a normal situation and an urgent situation will be that during the whole duration of the emergency situation, the key agreement will be modified such that the keys remains unchanged till the situation is handled or under control. However; in enabling subject for managing urgency, it will not provide them the alternate privileges forever as in case of traditional access control models, rather it will enable the response actions in four phases. Once it identifies gravity of the situation.

- First; it will identify the actions and subjects needed and for how long.

• Then it will enable the appropriate actions by appropriate privileges.

• It will notify the subjects of their responsibilities.

• Finally; once the situation is handled, it will rescind the privileges assigned to the subjects later.

For better clarity in how the system works, we will consider an example as below:

A Case Study: Security of Pacemaker

This section provides a simple case study to show the practicality of our proposed approach. To this end, we have provided an activity diagram as shown in Figure 1 to facilitate the process by which we implement our approach.

The pacemaker would consist of two basic set of components: Sensors and the base station. The patient data will be collected through the sensors and passed over to the base station. There are two types of sensors that will be used in this case. The physiological sensors will collect the physiological data whereas the contextual information such as temperature will be collected by the environmental sensors. The physiological data doesn't have to be collected at a specific rate rather different rates depending on type of sensors and the requirement. However; the environmental data has to be collected frequently to analyze the environmental factors such as temperature, light etc. which can have impact on patient conditions. The base station will maintain a database for storing these data and can be developed using JAVA or C#, depending on convenience. Sensors will follow a two-tier client-server architecture comprising of the collection of data, and the passing over of data to its appropriate destination. A specific topology can be used depending on the number of sensors. The collected data from the sensors will then be passed over to the data storage for storing purposes. Along with storage, the highest tier will also be responsible for detailed analysis and data retrieval. We will choose Oracle or SQL Server for the following scenario.

The base station will be connected to a physical device such as a smartphone to monitor the data on the patient and to allow the patient to move around. The entities responsible for monitoring the activities will be able to do so by querying the central server. The data will pass between the base station and the central served using an IP based

network in XML format to maintain platform independence. No specific technology has to be mandated for the collection and communication of patient information, so long as the required functionalities are met.

Central server will handle multiple ports so that specific ports can be assigned specific entities to query the server at the same time to access current as well as the past data about a patient. Threshold values can also be set for each data received by an entity to trigger an alarm in case of failure.

A pacemaker would work with the proposed system comprised of medical sensors. The sensors will need to monitor and send the data to the base station wirelessly.

They first will exchange some list for the physiological signals measured by the base station to set the measurement for the cryptographic key. The base station will be interfaced to the smartphone to execute the key agreement. To understand the case study better, we will go through a short example.

Suppose the list shared between the sender and the receiver is S = {1,2,3,4,5,6,7,8,9} where n=9 i.e., the length of the set. As shown in Figure 1, the first step will be to generate the exact cover of the list that is all possible combinations that are disjoint and when combined, form the list. For example, in this case, the combinatory subsets can be {(1,3,5), (2,4,8), (6,7,9)}, {(1,2,3), (4,6,8), (5,7,9)}, {(1,4,7), (2,5,8), (3,6,9)} etc. The length is 9 and the factors for length will be 1,3,9.

To select one factor to be considered, the next step in the Figure 1 is to use a random number generator to choose the polynomial instead of determining the length of the key manually as mentioned in using automotive intelligent systems [28]. The sender selects the order of the polynomial(s) or the number of polynomials to be used depending on the factors of length by executing the random number generator algorithm mentioned before.

Populate all the factors into an array.

• Assign the value generated by the new random number generator function Rand () to a new variable.

• Display the new variable.

Out of the three factors, suppose 3 has been chosen to create the first order polynomials such as f(x) = x+3 and f(y) = y+3. Then, product of the value of the polynomial i.e., 3 and its order sum 2 plus 1 constitute to be 9, which is one of the factors of the length of the set as per our approach. So the subsets will be of order (x, y=f(x), z=f(y)), then in the next phase as per the activity diagram, it will generate a family of subsets of nCk, where "k" is the length of the subsets and determine a subfamily of the subsets i.e., the features for the physiological signal using the exact cover techniques with a sum of 2k – 1, which will be as below:

y = f(x) = x + 3, z = f(y) = y+3

So the features will be in the format (x, y, z). Now, the subfamily of subsets according to the polynomial given will be T = {(1,4,7), (2,5,8), (3,6,9)}.

The steps used to generate these sets are given below:

• We turned the sets into bitmaps of length |S|

• Interpreted the bitmaps to be binary numbers as mentioned in Table 1.

As shown in Table 1, each of the features is first turned into a bitmap of 9-bits length. In this case, the set is 9, so in all positions mentioned in

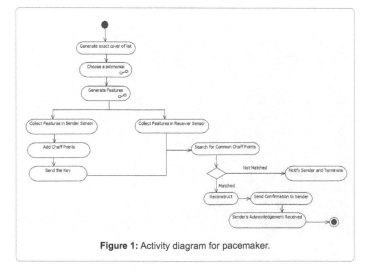

Figure 1: Activity diagram for pacemaker.

Features	9 - bits	Binary Numbers
(1,4,7)	001001001	$2^0+2^3+2^6=73$
(2,5,8)	010010010	$2^1+2^4+2^7=146$
(3,6,9)	100100100	$2^2+2^5+2^8=292$

Table 1: Interpreted the bitmaps to be binary numbers.

a subset, 0 is replaced by 1. Next, bitmaps are converted to binary form to provide the number.

The total of all the binary values is 73+146+292 = 511 which is 29-1 compose of disjoint sets confirming to the exact cover requirements.

When the key is reconstructed based on successful matching of chaff points, then it performs the PSKA and a common key is agreed upon for a specific time period in a range depending upon the type of sensors used which will significantly improve the confidentiality for a given set of sensors in the pacemaker, in a sense to make accomplishment without outside intrusion and privacy violation. After the features are generated based on the polynomial, it is collected by both the sender and receiver node as shown in Figure 1. In the next step, chaff numbers will be added to randomize uniformness on the key as shown below:

Key, K = T + {(1,2,3), (1,4,5), (3,4), (3,4,5,6), (2,6,8)}

= {(1,4,7), (1,2,3), (2,5,8), (1,4,5), (3,4), (3,6,9), (3,4,5,6), (2,6,8)}

Then the sender node sends this key combined with the chaff points and shares the features with the receiver.

A shown in Figure 1, when the key K = {(1,4,7), (3,4), (2,6,8), (3,6,9)} is send, then the receiver will search for the common chaff points added by the sender node, reconstruct the key, and is be able to match the two points (1,4,7) and (3,6,9) with the sender node. Once the key is reconstructed, the confirmation is sent back to the sender and an acknowledgement is received, which establishes the key until the next iteration. However, when the chaff points do not match, then the whole process gets terminated, and the sender sensor receives notification of unauthorized attempt in key establishment.

As soon as the key gets established, the data communication starts in a secure manner. These data will be collected by the base station and will be communicated to the server through secure internet channels, where it will be added to the electronic records pertaining to that patient.

Only the medical professional assigned to that patients will be able to receive input on patient condition or receive the alarm generated, for which the parameters are set by the professionals or attendants beforehand. The example parameter selection is given below:

Generate alarm if any of the following situation arises:

- The blood pressure is more than 140 over 90.

- The blood pressure is less than 120 over 80.

- Heart beat is less than 60 a minute.

- Heart beat is over 100 beats a minute.

To add them as authorized persons, we will use their EMPL IDs and create a sign on using session control as below:

- We will create a hash from the session start combined with the professional's EMPL ID and store it in the data storage on the first request.

- Every time the same user is notified, the hash will be cross verified with the stored hash.

Provided they are authorized to receive it in case of an emergency, they will be able to assist in sending an emergency team or some other emergency solutions.

The emergency team will receive authorization through permission and the session will be generated using the same algorithm as used for medical professionals, and once there is an emergency, the system will integrate its MCASF to enable the emergency team to connect to the server and, query and access the patient's current and past data till the time the patient reaches the facility after which the assigned medical professional takes charge. As soon as the charge is handed over, the session will get destroyed by using session destroy () function.

So, the complexity will be pretty high due to dependency of polynomial on the factors and the dependency of the factors on the length of the set. As the length of the set determines the number of factors to be generated, so the complexity of m is nk for some fixed k, where n is the length of the set and m is the largest value in the set. So the time complexity of the exact cover will be O (n.nm) i.e., O(n2m) [38], however in our case, as m is 2n due to generation of all the features irrespective of length to be fixed, so the complexity will exponential in n(O(n22n) [38], which can be called as pseudo-polynomial time.

Even though the complexity is high i.e., O (n2m) where n is the size of the set and m is the largest value, the integration works smoothly due to the fixed set of physiological signals as a threshold at both the sender and receiver node simultaneously, so in case of an emergency, the agreed key between the sender and receiver takes precedence in order to halt the subset matching.

Conclusion and Future Work

Cyber-physical systems need some additional level of security because of the involvement of the physical domain. The security solutions that have been discussed mostly prompt the user to use Traditional IT Security Solutions in providing security for CPS. Though these can be applied to the security of CPS, there still is need to look at the key difference between an Information System and a CPS before designing a security mechanism specifically for the CPS. Whether Context-Aware Security Framework or Trusted Computing in CPS, both have their advantages, however there are still other security protocols and multilayer security mechanisms that need to be addressed. That's why we proposed a security solution which will use the exact cover problem technique to generate a random key from the physiological signal received from the host and embed this key agreement technique to construct a modified context-aware security framework to manage access control which will make it absolutely hard for a malicious entity to manipulate the system as the key will be constantly modified and erase the traces any past or future instance so that even if the key is compromised at a given instant, the past or future instances are safe from the adversary. However; our proposed techniques still do not take into consideration how to protect the system from the Denial of Service (DoS) attack, which is a direct hit on the properties of availability, nor does it address the issue of interoperability in case of a Cyber-Physical Systems, which are still open areas of research which need to be addressed in the future. Also, the approach needs to be put to experimentation and simulation to prove its feasibility and overhead incurred is big. Also; as most of the authentication techniques require to be time-variant in nature, so scalability poses an issue as it does not take the notion of time into account. As the solutions need to be integrated from a number of domains, the complexity is increased. Also, the system becomes non-deterministic as there is no guarantee as in to provide the key at a specific number of tries because the exact cover might need to repeat itself to come up with another set of numbers to match the key generated.

References

1. Kaiyu W, Man KL, Hughes D (2010) Specification, analyzing challenges and approaches for cyber-physical systems (CPS). Engineering Letters.

2. Elinor Mills (2009) Hackers broke into FAA air traffic control system. The Wall Street Journal.

3. Kelly O'Connell (2008) CIA report: Cyber extortionists attacked foreign power grid, disrupting delivery. Internet Business Law Services.

4. Koscher K, Czeskis A, Roesner F, Patel S, Kohno T, et al. (2010) Experimental security analysis of a modern automobile. Proceedings of the 31st IEEE Symposium on Security and Privacy.

5. Fuhrmans V (2010) Virus attacks siemens plant-control systems. The Wall Street Journal.

6. Leavitt N (2010) Researchers fight to keep implanted medical devices safe from hackers. Computer 43: 11-14.

7. Krebs B (2008) Cyber incident blamed for nuclear power plant shutdown. Washington Post.

8. Alvaro AC, Saurabh A, Shankar S (2008) Research challenges for the security of control systems. HOTSEC.

9. Wang EK, Yunming Ye, Xiaofei Xu, Yiu SM, Hui LCK, et al. (2010) Security issues and challenges for cyber physical system. International Conference on Green Computing and Communications, IEEE/ACM International Conference on Cyber, Physical and Social Computing.

10. Shirey R (2000) Internet security glossary. Network Working Group.

11. Han J, Jain A, Luk M, Perrig A (2007) Don't sweat your privacy: Using humidity to detect human presence. International Workshop on Privacy in UbiComp.

12. Matt Bishop (2003) Computer security, art and science. Addison Wesley.

13. Chalkias K, Baldimtsi F, Hristu-Varsakelis D, Stephanides G (2008) Two types of key-compromise impersonation attacks against one-pass key establishment protocols. Communications in Computer and Information Science 23: 227-238.

14. Saltzman R, Sharabani A (2009) Active man in the middle attacks, a security advisory. IBM Rational Application Security Group.

15. Jung-Chun K, Marculescu R (2006) Eavesdropping minimization via transmission power control in ad-hoc wireless networks. 3rd Annual IEEE Communications Society on Sensor and Ad Hoc Communications and Networks.

16. Pelechrinis K, Iliofotou M, Krishnamurthy SV (2011) Denial of service attacks in wireless networks: The case of jammers. IEEE Communications Surveys & Tutorials 13: 245-257.

17. Cardenas AA, Saurabh A, Shankar S (2008) Secure control: Towards survivable cyber-physical systems. Distributed Computing Systems Workshops, ICDCS International Conference.

18. Marburger JH, Kvamme EF (2007) Leadership under challenge: Information technology R&D in a competitive world, an assessment of the federal networking and information technology R&D program. Technical report, President's Council of Advisors on Science and Technology.

19. Schenato L, Sinopoli B, Franceschetti M, Poolla K, Sastry SS (2007) Foundations of control and estimation over lossy networks. Proceedings of the IEEE 95: 163-187.

20. Hepanha JP, Naghshtabrizi P, Xu Y (2007) A survey of recent results in networked control systems. Proceedings of the IEEE 95: 138-162.

21. Blanke M, Kinnaert M, Lunze J, Staroswiecki M (2003) Diagnosis and fault-tolerant control. Springer-Verlag.

22. Olfat-Saber R (2005) Distributed kalman filter with embedded consensus filter. Proceedings of CDC and ECC, Seville, Spain.

23. Feng Gui (2009) Development of a new client-server architecture for context aware mobile computing. PhD Thesis, Florida International University.

24. Fisher DA (2012) Principles of trust for embedded systems. Technical Note CMU/SEI-2012-TN-007.

25. Moholkar AV (2014) Security for cyber-physical systems. International Journal of Computing and Technology 1: 257-262.

26. Venkatasubramanian KK, Banerjee A, Gupta SKS (2010) PSKA: Usable and secure key agreement scheme for body area networks. IEEE Transactions on Information Technology in Biomedicine 14: 60-68.

27. Kuo C, Luk M, Negi R, Perrig A (2007) Message-in-a-bottle: User-friendly and secure key deployment for sensor nodes. Proceedings of the ACM Conference on Embedded Networked Sensor System (SenSys 2007).

28. Jha SK, Sukthankar G (2011) Modeling and verifying intelligent automotive cyber-physical systems. EECS Department, University of Central Florida, Orlando, USA.

29. Jha SK, Langmead CJ, Ramesh S, Mohalik S (2010) When to stop verification? Statistical trade-off between cost of simulation and possible loss from erroneous designs. IEEE CS.

30. Jha SK (2008) d-IRA: A distributed reachability algorithm for analysis of linear hybrid automata. International Conference on Hybrid Systems Computation and Control, pp: 618-621.

31. Gupta SKS, Mukherjee T, Venkatasubramanian KK (2006) Criticality aware access control model for pervasive applications. Proceedings of the 4th IEEE Conference on Pervasive Computing.

32. Venkatasubramanian KK, Gupta SKS (2006) Security for pervasive health monitoring sensor applications. Proceedings of the 4th International Conference on Intelligent Sensing and Information Processing.

33. Banerjee A, Venkatasubramanian KK, Mukherjee T, Gupta SKS (2012) Ensuring safety, security, and sustainability of mission-critical cyber–physical systems. Proceedings of the IEEE 100: 283-299.

34. Kumbhare YL, Rangaree PH (2015) Patient health monitoring using wireless body area sensor network. International Journal of Engineering and Advanced Technology (IJEAT).

35. Cherukuri S, Venkatasubramanian KK, Gupta SKS (2003) BioSec: A biometric based approach for securing communication in wireless networks of biosensors implanted in the human body. Proceedings of Wireless Security and Privacy Workshop pages, pp: 432-439.

36. Venkatasubramanian KK, Gupta SKS (2010) Physiological value based efficient usable security solutions for body sensor networks. ACM Transactions on Sensor Networks.

37. Elson J, Girod L, Estrin D (2002) Fine-grained network time synchronization using reference broadcasts. Proceedings of the 5th symposium on Operating systems design and implementation 36: 147-163.

38. Papadimitriou CH (2003) Computational complexity. Encyclopedia of Computer Science, pp: 260-265.

39. Dodis Y, Ostrovsky R, Reyzin L, Smith A (2003) Fuzzy extractors: How to generate strong keys from biometrics and other noisy data. Conference Paper in SIAM Journal on Computing 38: 523-540.

25

Assessing and Ranking the Corporate Social Responsibility Behavior of Five Star Hotels in Tehran Using the AHP and FTOPSIS Methods

Jamal Kheiri*
University of Tehran, Tehran, Iran

Abstract

Tourism having 11 percent share of our planet's gross product and as the one of largest industry in the world, has become a major force in our international economies, social lifestyles and understanding of environmental protection. Due to the rising importance of our global interdependence, some concepts like corporate social responsibility (CSR) have a significant role in this dynamic and flourishing industry composed of lodging, transportation and so on. This paper aims at analyzing the concept of CSR as a means of selecting the best practices in the five star hotel brands in Tehran. The three major dimensions of CSR like economic, social and environmental are tried to explain. The paper also presents the results of a study carried out on assessing and ranking the "responsibility level" of these lodging centers. The importance of the criteria used in the CSR-based practices is identified by the analytical hierarchy process (AHP). Moreover, the technique for order performance by similarity to ideal solution (TOPSIS) in the fuzzy environment is used to obtain final ranking of the hotel brands. Results show that among five 5 star hotels in Tehran, Home Hotel takes the best CSR practices. On the contrary, Azadi Hotel is the lowest one in ranking.

Keywords: Corporate social responsibility; five star Hotels; Tehran; AHP; Fuzzy TOPSIS

Introduction

Since the 1950s, due to the increasing awareness of people about their rights, the economical, ecological and social activities and practices of corporates had been addressed by private and institutional stakeholders considerably. The people put pressure on the businesses to move on a responsible way and pay more attention to the impact and consequences of their activities. This phenomenon can be explained because of an increased pressure on certain social and economic factors, the greater need for transparency in organizations, and as a reaction to social and environmental disasters [1,2].

In an effort to prevent the negative views, many businesses began using their resources to address social, economic and ecological issues voluntarily and make their own brand more popular. Consequently, the corporates' practices and programs marked the beginning of Corporate Social Responsibility (CSR) if they desire to sustain in the long run.

Corporate social responsibly is the continuing commitment by corporates to behave according to business ethics and contribute to economic development while improving the quality of the life of the workforce as well as the local community and future generations. They need to think for the society, environment, and all stakeholders of it. More specifically, CSR involves a business identifying its stakeholder groups and meeting their needs and values within the strategic and day-to-day decision-making process.

Despite all definitions of CSR, some authors make clear that the meaning of corporate social responsibility may differ among different stakeholders. On the other hand, the measurement of CSR activities is an additional challenge. Unlike the publication of several methods to measure socially responsible activities, almost all of them have some limitations [3]. Therefore, the methodology must be adjusted to provide a more complete understanding of the current state of CSR.

Since the tourism industry has been labelled "the world's largest industry" [4], yet the lack of CSR in the global tourism industry is "astounding" especially given the negative impacts that tourism can have on stakeholders [5].

In this industry, regarding to the heavy interdependent relationships that exist between tourism and environment and social heritage while contributing to the health and growth of local communities, it is inevitable that all integrated businesses play their responsible role in the long term. As the contemporary tourist becomes aware of the adverse environmental impact, he/she begins to require the tourist product which is used and paid for to be ecologically and socially acceptable.

The development of responsible tourism and the increasing awareness of CSR in the tourism industry causes a strong need to assess and compare the economic, social and ecological performances of tourism companies.

Corporate social responsibility as the micro aspect of sustainable development means integrating environmental, societal and economic concerns into the core business strategy and further into the main business operations. Tourism businesses should behave responsibly in order to contribute to sustainable tourism development [6]. Sustainable development means designing the right mix of economic, social and environmental policies for today and for tomorrow [7].

Therefore, corporates must seek positions that are new, unique, and differentiated from the competitors. In this sense, CSR has become a highly effective attribute for a strategy of differentiation and positioning [8]. Many international initiatives show the growing importance of CSR in the tourism and hotel industry. For instance, Agenda 21 set international guidelines relative to sustainable tourism and was created by the World Travel and Tourism Council (WTTC), the World Tourism Organization (WTO), and the Earth Council [2].

Corporate Social Responsibility (CSR) and its extent has always been a practice usually dictated by the major stakeholders, especially in the industries interconnected closely with the society. As mentioned before, CSR is usually a pledge taken by an establishment or corporation

---

***Corresponding author:** Jamal Kheiri, University of Tehran, Tehran, Iran
E-mail: jamalkheiri@yahoo.com

to set in place socio-ethically responsible policies in areas of work ethics, human welfare, environment and human rights.

Tourism is assumed as an economic phenomenon, but it is actually a human and social activity. The complexity found in tourism is a reflection of complexity and contradictions of today's society, on the one hand, as a consumer good and as spectacle or culture. Economic dimension should have a special importance, but also the other dimensions must be borne in mind in order to gain objective view of the problems that tourism can cause [9].

In the lodging industry, it is expected that most hotels have now incorporated environmental management into their daily operations and implement numerous CSR activities including energy and water conservation, recycling, reusing, and community involvement.

More and more hotels now follow international "green" standards, such as the Green Globe Company Standard and Leadership in Energy and Environmental Design (LEED), when building and operating their properties. For instance, all Novotel hotels, managed by the multinational chain Accor, plan to obtain Green Globe accreditation [10]. Through engaging in CSR programs, hotels can also strengthen their relationships with government. All of this shows that CSR can bring about various benefits to different parties. A CSR strategy is not only needed but highly recommendable [10]. Although CSR is now a global trend in the hotel industry, it is pointed out that a recently as a decade ago, hoteliers were not familiar with the concept . As a matter of fact, the number of relevant studies in this area is quite limited, with most of them carried out in a western context in the US and Europe.

Hotels are as the basic, functional businesses within the tourism industry. All major five star establishments today are owned and run by giant corporations and most of them have adapted a responsible approach of doing business by recognizing that in order to be successful in this current era they will have to focus on the diverse dimensions of CSR. Five star hotels are all spread worldwide and differ based on their comparative and competitive advantage.

Because the way corporates define, design, and implement their CSR policies depends heavily on the contextual features of the context in which they operate, this paper suggests a new scale for measuring CSR in the tourism sector, and 5 star hotels in particular, based on the theoretical framework proposed by some researchers [11]. It should be noted that the researcher conducted the study on the tourism sector, specifically in the hotel segment. With regard to this, it must be stated that the tourism sector has some special particularities because it is possible to identify several subsectors with different characteristics and problems—such as transportation, travel or accommodation [13] that could poentially distort the results of this research if presented together. Since it is expected that 5 star hotels care about the community more and more. This is the main reason why the author decided to focus on a single tourism subsector the lodging sector and more precisely in the Tehtan 5 star hotel sector. The aim of this paper is to assess and rank the responsibility level of five star hotels in Tehran, while using AHP and FTOPSIS model.

This article is divided into four main sections. The first section presents the conceptual framework that forms the structural basis for the study. The second section generally presents the methodology. The third section composes of the proposed model of this paper and its findings, emphasizing the design of the measurement scale. Finally, a brief conclusion arising from this study are included.

Literature Review

Concept of CSR and its three dimensions

Over viewing some last decades' issues, it can be found that the concept of corporate social responsibility was developed in 1953 by Bowen as the obligations of businessmen to pursue those policies, to make those decisions, or to follow those lines of action which are desirable in terms of the objectives and values of the society. In Bowen's opinion, businessmen are "responsible for the consequences of their actions in a sphere somewhat wider than that covered by their profit-and-loss statements" [14].

It was stressed by Davis who gave a definition of CSR as businessmen's decisions and actions taken for reasons at least partially beyond the firm's direct economic or technical interest [12]. In 1962 Friedman argued that few trends could so thoroughly undermine the very foundations of our free society as the acceptance by corporate officials of a social responsibility other than to make as much money for their stockholder as possible [14].

In spite of some skepticism, many authors including Druker and Porter and Kramer [15] have stressed the positive relationships between social responsibility and business opportunities in terms of market opportunities, productivity, human competence and improvement of competitive context [15].

Various studies in economic and organizational theory have reviewed the role of business in society [12]. Despite the fact that CSR is a prominent concept in the literature, it is difficult to formulate a precise and comprehensive definition of the term. As Votaw and more recent authors [16], CSR has a meaning, but its meaning is not the same for everyone. One of the main reasons given is that the meaning of CSR varies depending on the perceptions of the stakeholders involved and on the business sector under study [13,17].

The Freeman's [18] seminal book the focus moved from legitimacy and morals towards a new theory of the firm. Social considerations are thus no longer outside an organization but are part of its purpose of being. CSR thus becomes a question of stakeholder identification, involvement, and communication [19].

Many definitions of CSR are based on two fundamental ideas. The first is that companies have responsibilities beyond their profit-making activities and mere legal liability [13,20]. The second is that these responsibilities apply not only to shareholders but to a broader group of stake holders [1,18]. On the other hand, CSR is defined as a concept by which companies integrate social and environmental concerns in their operations and in their interaction with stakeholders on a voluntary basis (the Commission of the European Communities, 2001). The World Business Council for Sustainable Development [21] interprets CSR as the business commitment for contributing to sustainable economic development, employees, their families, the local community and society to improve their quality of life. The WBCSD also explains that CSR is a continuous commitment by business to behave ethically and contribute to economic development by improving the quality of life of workforce and their families, as well as the local community.

Along all definitions is the definition proposed by some authors, who define his construct as a strategic and proactive way of doing business in a specific context with a synergistic philosophy [22]. This concept of CSR emphasizes the need for firms to design their strategies with particular attention to balancing economic, social, and environmental aspects. However, although CSR is a term commonly used by professionals, methods to formally measure CSR have not been developed among academics [23] .

Corporate responsibility is not restricted to financial initiatives, but transcends borders to integrate with an organization's mission and core values to achieve the Triple Bottom-line Approach of Social, Environmental and Financial performance [24]. Corporations need to constantly adapt and adjust to changing environmental dimensions by closely monitoring changing industry trends and dynamics [25].

A basic assumption of CSR is that companies must adapt their behavior to societal expectations [26]. Complications arise when these expectations vary, depending on the context in which a company operates. Contextual features refer to the specific geographic, social, cultural, and economic policies of the places in which companies carry out their activities [27].

In order to respond in an adequate way to the pressures coming from the society of which companies form integral part, firms should pursue economic, social and environmental goals on the basis of a coordinated approach [28]. Moreover, the EU underlines the need for a holistic approach towards CSR integrated management in order to include social and environmental aspects into corporate planning, measuring and controlling of processes and to define a long-term strategy which minimizes the risks linked to uncertainty.

The dimensions of CSR can be identified from the conceptual framework provided by the theoretical models proposed by some researchers [11]. These authors conceptualize CSR based on sustainable development, establishing that corporate responsibility is a multidimensional construct consisting of economic, social, and environmental dimensions. The United Nations Industial Development Organization emphasizes each of these facets. The economic dimension is based on ensuring viable economic activities in the long term so that all stakeholders receive appropriately distributed socioeconomic benefits. The social dimension refers to a respect for the cultural authenticity of host communities, the preservation of their architectural and living cultural assets and traditional values, and a contribution to intercultural understanding and tolerance. The environmental dimension refers to the optimal use of environmental resources, which is an essential element of tourism development, protecting essential ecological processes and helping to conserve natural resources and biodiversity [29]. Therefore, in this paper, the scope of CSR include economic, social, and environmental factors.

CSR practices in the lodging industry

Despite the fact that tourism represents a very important industry, which contributes to global GDP and creates jobs, it also produces negative and serious impacts at economic, social, and environmental levels, due to uncontrolled development [5,30] which generates a volume of flows higher than the destination carrying capacity [30]. As a consequence, at the beginning of the 1980s, at the same time as the spread of sustainable tourism, the concept of responsible tourism started to emerge.

Since the late 1980s, traditional mass tourism has been gradually replaced by alternative forms of tourism (Timothy and Teye, 2009 cited in [31]. The negative impacts of tourism lead the emergence of new forms of tourism. Many different names has been given to these new forms of tourism such as responsible, soft, green, etc., but in more generic terms, "alternative tourism".

According to the Cape Town Declaration, later reviewed by the Kerala Declaration in 2008, responsible tourism takes a variety of forms, but it always refers to travel and tourism that minimize negative environmental, social, and cultural impacts; that generate greater economic benefits for local people by improving working conditions and access to the industry; that involve local people in decisions that affect their lives and life chances; that make positive contributions to the conservation of natural and cultural heritage and to the maintenance of the world's diversity; that provide more enjoyable experiences for tourists through more meaningful connections with local people and a greater understanding of local cultural and environmental issues; that provide access for physically challenged people; and that are culturally sensitive and engender respect between tourists and hosts [32].

In the hotel industry CSR is still an emerging concept. As part of the tourism industry, the accommodation sector has also put considerable effort into CSR programs over the last twenty years. Understanding the role of hotels in tourism industry can be a crucial factor to the planning of the authorities involved in tourism especially in determining the marketing strategies of lodging sector. Corporate Social Responsibility is a prerequisite for a good and healthy community. The hotel industry's use of CSR in its corporate strategy and daily activities is imperative due to the symbiotic nature of its relationship with the surrounding natural, economic, social and cultural environment [33].

Successful selection and implementation of an integrated CSR program can effectively identify costs and differentiate competitive advantages while contributing benefits to society and other stakeholders [31]. Finally, a hotel's CSR program can be part of its reputation management. To illustrate, innovative green practices have a visible marketing advantage and can be used as a public relations tool. Burke and Logsdon point out that this is one of the strategies derived from the visibility dimension of CSR, which they define as "observable, recognizable credit by internal and/or external stakeholders for the firm" [31].

Some researches explores the kind of information considered by tourists when choosing their holiday destinations and finds that "consumers are already making decisions based on environmental, social and economic quality for day-to-day products and are keen to transfer these habits to the purchase of tourism products" (Miller 2000). Recent research also supports the proposition that both business and leisure travelers have become more aware of environmental attributions when searching for accommodation products.

The reputational scale method usually asks business corporate staffers or managers to evaluate a sample of five star hotels in the form of questionnaire. The focus lies on those institutions that are operating with a combined analytical scheme integrating social, economic and ecologic criteria. On this basis, the primary objective of the survey was to gather descriptive data and information on CSR awareness and the attitude to it shown by 5 Star Hotels in Tehran. By the revised scale consisted of 54 items the respondent indicates his/her opinion on a five-point Likert type questionnaire ranging from "strongly disagree" (1) to "strongly agree"(5).

According to Chen and Fan, the problem with measuring CSR is very similar to a multiple-criteria decision making (MCDM) problem with many quantitative and qualitative attributes [34]. Arrington, Wokutch and Fahey have suggested the use of the AHP for measuring social performance.

However, the measuring and ranking five star hotels in Tehran is a multistep process in decision making and it involves three major dimensions. This resulted the introduction of Multi Criteria Decision Making (MCDM) models such as Analytic Hierarchy Process (AHP) and Technique for Order Preference by Similarity to Ideal Solution (TOPSIS) in fuzzy environment as tools in solving the decision making process. The AHP method was developed by Saaty [35] involves a hierarchical form of the problems that in three levels, which are the goal, the criteria and the alternatives. The Technique for Order Preference by Similarity to Ideal Solution (TOPSIS) is also one of the well-known techniques in MCDM developed by Hwang and Yoon [36] where the method lies on the concept that the selected alternatives should have the shortest distance from the positive ideal solution (PIS) and the farthest distance from the negatives ideal solutions (NIS) in Euclidean distance [36] .

In many problems of decision making that involve human participation, one has to deal with uncertainty and subjectivity since information is normally in the form of perception. Fuzzy approaches have been widely used in decision making when subjectivity and uncertainty are the concerned constraint in the study. The use of fuzzy set theory [37] allows the decision-makers to incorporate unquantifiable information, incomplete information, non-obtainable information and partially ignorant facts into decision model [38].

Research Methodology

Sampling and data collection

The analysis and evaluation of the CSR of hotels was performed through a quantitative study. The 5 star hotel managers and employees with at least five years of experience were considered to be the analysis unit of the study. Each respondent was asked to answer the questionnaire in accordance to the existing actions and behaviors in his/her own business. The sample consisted of 25 respondents from all five star market in Tehran which is five hotels including Laleh International Hotel, Espinas Hotel, Azadi Parsian Hotel, Esteghlal Parsian Hotel, and Homa Hotel Group. In such a sample size, about 48% of respondents were employees and other 52% were managers. Further, regarding gender, 60% of the respondents were men and 40% were women. Over half of the respondents were aged26-35 and approximately 96% had been educated to undergraduate degree level or above. The socio-demographic profile of respondents is summarized in Table 1.

Furthermore, in order to weight the three major factors of CSR, another questionnaire was developed and distributed among six academics and experts in the tourism area. The multidimensionality of the scale was conceptualized based on both a literature review and a qualitative exploratory researches. In this step, three domains were identified as relevant for the CSR of a hotel company: economic,

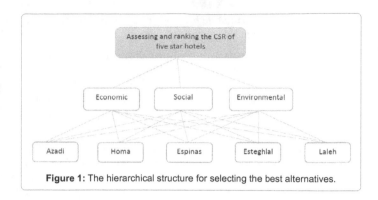

Figure 1: The hierarchical structure for selecting the best alternatives.

social, and environmental factors. According to Martínez and et al [2], these dimensions match up with those defined theoretically by the sustainable development theory [11].

The measurement scale included 54 items. The first twenty two items related to activities aimed at the economic dimension of CSR. The next nineteen items related to the social dimension of CSR. The last thirteen items related to the environmental dimension of CSR. All of the items were measured using a 5-point Likert scale, in which a score of 1 indicate strongly disagree with the statement, and a score of 5 signifies total agreement with the statement. The research has several steps. First, the content of the questionnaire was further enhanced by the literature review and by consulting some experts to enhance the content validity. Second, the questionnaire had been formulated and the sampling method selected. Finally, mathematical computing were conducted to meet the research objectives. In the statistical analysis, descriptive analysis was used to illustrate demographic information about the respondents (Table 1). All the data analysis was carried out using Excel. Figure 1 illustrates the hierarchical structure. Initially, the overall goal of the decision, evaluating the best hotel brand in assuming CSR, is presented in the top level of the hierarchy. The second level consists of three major criteria that are identified to achieve the overall goal. The third level contains the alternative hotels.

AHP model

The AHP is a multi-attribute decision tool that allows financial and non-financial, quantitative and qualitative measures to be considered and trade-offs among them to be addressed. The AHP is aimed at integrating different measures into a single overall score for ranking decision alternatives.

AHP model has the advantage of highlighting the main attributes, strengths and weaknesses of every alternative. This mathematical method stresses the key role of selecting the main criteria and the decision about their importance. In AHP model the priorities are determined by comparing each option with all the others, i.e. making relative comparisons, not absolute assessments.

This section provides an explanation of the AHP model, in particular of the calculation of weights, starting from the paired comparison technique, and of the consistency verification. Determining the weights of each alternative signifies a numerical value that shows the importance compared to each of the criteria. In other words, AHP answer this question whether one criteria is preferable to another and if so, to what extent. The operation has to be entrusted to some experts familiar with the subject, who have been asked to express their personal preferences according to a scale developed by Saaty.

The description is developed in three steps [35].

Gender	%
Male	60
Female	40
Occupation	**%**
Manager	52
Employee	48
Age	**%**
26-35	56
36-45	36
46-55	8
Education	**%**
Diploma	4
BA	80
MA or higher	16

Table 1: Frequency table of demographic profile of respondents (N=25).

Step 1: Compose a pair-wise comparison decision matrix (A)

$$A = [a_{im}] = \begin{bmatrix} 1 & a_{12} & \cdots & a_{1n} \\ \dfrac{1}{a_{12}} & 1 & \cdots & a_{2n} \\ \vdots & \vdots & \vdots & \vdots \\ \dfrac{1}{a_{1n}} & \dfrac{1}{a_{2n}} & \cdots & 1 \end{bmatrix} \quad i, m = 1, 2, ..., n \quad (1)$$

Let C_1, C_2,..., Cn denote the set of elements, while aim represents a quantified judgment on a pair of elements, C_i and C_m. Saaty constitutes a measurement scale for pair-wise comparison. Hence, verbal judgments can be expressed by degree of preference: Equally preferred with 1, Moderately preferred with 3, Strongly preferred with 5, Very strongly preferred with 7 and Extremely preferred with 9; 2, 4, 6 and 8 are used for compromise between the above values.

Step 2: Normalize the decision matrix. Each set of column values is summed. Then, each value is divided by its respective column total value. Finally, the average of rows is calculated and the weights of the decision-maker's objectives are obtained. A set of n numerical weights $w1$, $w2$,..., wi are obtained.

Step 3: Do consistency analysis.

$$A * W_i = \lambda_{max} * w_i, \quad i = 1, 2, ..., n \quad (2)$$

Then consistency index (CI) is calculated as:

$$CI = \frac{\lambda_{max} - n}{n - 1} \quad (3)$$

The consistency index of a randomly generated reciprocal matrix shall be called to the random index (RI), with reciprocals forced. An average RI for the matrices of order 1-15 was generated by using a sample size of 100. The table of random indexes of the matrices of order 1-15 can be seen in.

The last ratio that has to be calculated is CR (consistency ratio). Generally, if CR is less than 0.1, the judgments are consistent, so the derived weights can be used. The formulation of CR is:

$$CR = \frac{CI}{RI} \quad (4)$$

FUZZY TOPSIS model

The Technique for Order of Preference by Similarity to Ideal Solution (TOPSIS) is a multi-criteria decision analysis method, which was originally developed by [36] with further developments by Yoon, Lai and Liu in 1993 [35]. TOPSIS is based on the concept that the chosen alternative should have the shortest geometric distance from the positive ideal solution and the longest geometric distance from the negative ideal solution. It is a method of compensatory aggregation that compares a set of alternatives by identifying weights for each criterion, normalizing scores for each criterion and calculating the geometric distance between each alternative and the ideal alternative, which is the best score in each criterion. An assumption of TOPSIS is that the criteria are monotonically increasing or decreasing. In this paper, the approach of TOPSIS is extended to develop a methodology for solving multi-attribute decision making problems in fuzzy environments.

Considering the fuzziness in the decision data, linguistic variables are used to assess the weight of each criterion and the rating of each alternative with respect to each criterion. The decision matrix is converted into a fuzzy decision matrix and constructed a weighted normalized fuzzy decision matrix once the decision makers' fuzzy

ratings have been pooled. The lower bound value of alternatives has been designed to obtain the distance value of the corresponding alternatives for detecting the fuzzy positive ideal solution (FPIS) and the fuzzy negative ideal solution (FNIS). Then, the fuzzy similarity degree of each alternative is calculated from FPIS and FNIS, respectively. Finally, a closeness coefficient is defined for each alternative to determine the rankings of all alternatives. The higher value of closeness coefficient indicates that an alternative is closer to FPIS and farther from FNIS simultaneously. Some important basic definitions of fuzzy sets and numbers based on recent work by [38] is provided:

Definition 1: A fuzzy set ã in a universe of discourse X is characterized by a membership function $\mu\tilde{a}\ (x)$ which associates with each element x in X, a real number in the interval [0,1]. The function value $\mu\tilde{a}(x)$ is termed the grade of membership of x in ã.

Definition 2: A fuzzy number is a fuzzy subset of the universe of discourse X that is both convex and normal. Figure 2 shows a fuzzy number ãin the universe of discourse X that conforms to this definition.

The triangular fuzzy numbers is used. A triangular fuzzy number ã can be defined by a triplet $(a1, a2, a3)$. Its conceptual schema and mathematical form are shown by Eq (5).

$$\mu_{\tilde{a}}(x) \begin{cases} 0, & x \leq a_1 \\ \dfrac{x - a_1}{a_2 - a_1}, & a_1 < x \leq a_2 \\ \dfrac{a_3\ x}{a_3 - a_2}, & a_2 < x \leq a_3 \\ 0, & x > a_3 \end{cases} \quad (5)$$

Definition 3: Assuming that both ã= $(a1, a2, a3)$ and ã= $(b1, b2, b3)$ are real numbers, then the basic operations on fuzzy triangular numbers are as follows:

$$a \times i a = \times b_1, a_2 \times$$
$$(a_1 \qquad b_2, a_3 \qquad \times b_3) \ for\ multiplication;$$
$$a + a =$$
$$(a_1 \qquad + b_1, a_2 + b_2, a_3 + b_3) \ for\ addition. \qquad (6, 7)$$

Definition 4: A linguistic variable is a variable values of which are linguistic terms [37]. The concept of linguistic variable is very useful in dealing with situations which are too complex or too ill- defined to

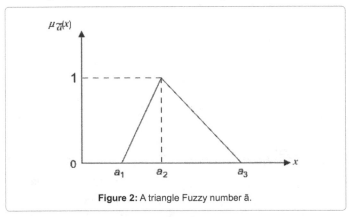

Figure 2: A triangle Fuzzy number ã.

be reasonably described in conventional quantitative expressions [37] . For example, "weight" is a linguistic variable; its values are very low, low, medium, high, very high, etc. These linguistic values can also be represented by fuzzy numbers.

Definition 5: Let $\tilde{a} = (a_1, a_2, a_3)$ and $\tilde{a} = (b_1, b_2, b_3)$ be two triangular fuzzy numbers, then the vertex method is defined to calculate the distance between them.

$$d\left(\tilde{a}, \tilde{b}\right) = \sqrt{\frac{1}{3}\left[\left(a_1 - b_1\right)^2 + \left(a_2 - b_2\right)^2 + \left(a_3 - b_3\right)^2\right]} \quad (8)$$

Definition 6: Considering the different importance values of each criterion, the weighted normalized fuzzy-decision matrix is constructed as.

$$\tilde{V} = \left[\tilde{v}_{ij}\right]_{n \times j}, \quad i = 1, 2, ..., n, j = 1, 2, ..., J \quad (9)$$

Where

$\cdot \tilde{v}_{ij} = \tilde{x}_{ij} \times w_i.$

$\cdot$A set of performance ratings of A_j ($j = 1, 2, ..., J$) with respect to criteria C_i ($I = 1, 2, ..., n$) called

$\tilde{x} = \{\tilde{x}_{ij}, i = 1, 2, ..., n, J = 1, 2, ..., J\}.$

$\cdot$ A set of importance weights of each criterion w_i ($I = 1, 2, ..., n$).(10)

According to briefly summarized fuzzy theory above, fuzzy TOPSIS steps can be outlined as follows:

- Step 1: Choose the linguistic values ($x_{ij} = 1, 2, ..., n, J = 1, 2, ..., J$) for alternatives with respect to criteria. The fuzzy linguistic rating ($\tilde{x}_{ij}$) preserves the property that the ranges of normalized triangular fuzzy numbers belong to [0, 1]; thus, there is no need for normalization.

- Step 2: Calculate the weighted normalized fuzzy decision matrix. The weighted normalized value $\tilde{v}_{ij}$ calculated by Eq. 9.

- Step 3: Identify positive-ideal (A+) and negative ideal (A-) solutions. The fuzzy positive-ideal solution (FPIS, A+) and the fuzzy negative-ideal solution (FNIS, (A-) are shown in the following equations:

$$A^* = \left\{\tilde{v}_1^*, \tilde{v}_2^*, ..., \tilde{v}_i^*\right\} = \left\{\left(\max_j v_{ij} \mid i \in I'\right),\right.$$

$$\left.\times \left(\min_j v_{ij} \mid i \in I''\right)\right\}, i = 1, 2, ..., n \ j = 1, 2, ..., J,$$

$$(11)$$

$$A^* = \left\{\tilde{v}_1^-, \tilde{v}_2^-, ..., \tilde{v}_i^-\right\} = \left\{\left(\min_j v_{ij} \mid i \in I''\right),\right.$$

$$\left.\times \left(\max_j v_{ij} \mid i \in I''\right)\right\}, i = 1, 2, ..., J,$$

where I′ is associated with benefit criteria and I″ is associated with cost criteria.

- Step 4: Calculate the distance of each alternative from A+ and A- using the following equations:

$$D_j^* = \sum_{j=1}^n d\left(\tilde{v}_{ij}, \tilde{v}_i^*\right) j = 1, 2, ..., J \quad (12)$$

$$D_j^- = \sum_{j=1}^n d\left(\tilde{v}_{ij}, \tilde{v}_i^-\right) j = 1, 2, ..., J \quad (13)$$

- Step 5: Calculate similarities to ideal solution.

$$CC_j = \frac{D_j^-}{D_j^* + D_j^-} j = 1, 2, ... J. \quad (14)$$

- Step 6: Rank preference order. Choose an alternative with maximum $CC+j$ or rank alternatives according to $CC+j$ in ascending order.

The proposed model and findings

The methodology applied in this paper is to assess and rank the CSR practices of all five star hotels in Tehran city. The proposed model for assessing and ranking CSR practices in five star hotels in Tehran, composed of AHP and fuzzy TOPSIS methods, consists of three basic stages: (1) identify the criteria to be used in the model, (2) AHP computations, (3) evaluation of alternatives with fuzzy TOPSIS and determination of the final rank.

In the first stage, alternative hotels and the criteria which will be used in their evaluation are determined and the decision hierarchy are formed. AHP model is structured such that the objective is in the first level, criteria are in the second level and alternative hotels are on the third level.

After the first stage, criteria used in CSR are assigned weights using AHP in the second stage. In this phase, pair wise comparison matrices are formed to determine the criteria weights. The experts from decision- making team make individual evaluations using the scale provided in Table 2 to determine the values of the elements of pair wise comparison matrices.

Computing the geometric mean of the values obtained from individual evaluations, a final pair wise comparison matrix on which there is a consensus is found. The weights of the criteria are calculated based on this final comparison matrix. The final matrix can be observed in Tables 3 and 4.

The economic factor is determined the first most important criterion in the computing process by using AHP model. The environmental and social factors are ranked as the second and the third criteria respectively.

Definition	Degree of preference
Equally preferred	1
Moderately preferred	3
Strongly preferred	5
Very strongly preferred	7
Extremely preferred	9
2, 4, 6 and 8 are used for compromise between the above values	

Table 2: Nine-point degree of preference scale and its description.

Inguistic values	Fuzzy numbers
Very low (VL)	(0, 0.05, 0.2)
Low (L)	(0.1, 0.25, 0.4)
Medium (M)	(0.3, 0.5, 0.7)
High (H)	(0.6, 0.75, 0.9)
Very high (VH)	(0.8, 0.95, 1)

Table 3: Membership functions of linguistic values for criteria rating.

Normalizing	Economic	Social	Environmental	average	rank
Economic	0.49	0.54	0.46	0.50	1
Social	0.17	0.19	0.22	0.19	3
Environmental	0.34	0.27	0.32	0.31	2

Table 4: Results obtained with AHP.

On the other hand, hotel ranks are determined by using fuzzy TOPSIS method in the third stage. Linguistic values are used for evaluation of alternative hotels in this step. The membership functions of these linguistic values are shown at Figure 3 [39].

The hotel brand having the maximum *CCj+* value is determined as the optimal brand according to the calculations by Fuzzy TOPSIS. Schematic diagram of the proposed model for hotel brands selection is provided in Figure 4 (Table 3).

The results obtained from the computations based on the pair wise comparison matrix provided before this step are presented in Table 4.

At the stage of evaluating the alternatives and determining the final rank, the decision matrix by comparing alternatives under each of the criteria is established separately. Fuzzy Evaluation Matrix developed by the evaluation of alternative hotels by linguistic variables in Table 4, is presented in Table 5.

NFDM	Economic			Social			Environment		
Azadi	0.251	0.479	0.680	0.249	0.473	0.695	0.102	0.374	0.609
Homa	0.742	0.902	1.000	0.650	0.836	0.981		0.881	1.000
Espinas	0.299	0.518	0.708	0.227	0.457	0.668	0.173	0.393	0.594
Esteghlal	0.670	0.835	0.964	0.661	0.837	1.000	0.557	0.737	0.912
Laleh	0.332	0.585	0.769	0.243	0.513	0.729	0.282	0.538	0.736
w	0.50	0.50	0.50	0.19	0.19	0.19	0.31	0.31	0.31

Table 5: Fuzzy evaluation matrix for the alternative hotels.

NFDM	Economic			Social			Environment		
Azadi	0.125	0.237	0.237	0.048	0.048	0.133	0.032	0.117	0.191
Homa	0.368	0.447	0.496	0.124	0.16	0.188	0.226	0.276	0.313
Espinas	0.148	0.257	0.351	0.043	0.088	0.128	0.054	0.123	0.186
Esteghlal	0.332	0.414	0.478	0.127	0.16	0.192	0.174	0.23	0.285
Laleh	0.165	0.29	0.381	0.047	0.098	0.14	0.088	0.168	0.23
I+	0.368	0.447	0.496	0.127	0.16	0.192	0.226	0.276	0.313
I-	0.125	0.29	0.337	0.043	0.088	0.128	0.032	0.117	0.186

Table 6: Weighted evaluation and similarities for the alternative hotels.

	D+	D-	CC	Rank
Rank				
5	0.469294	0.008737	0.018277	Azadi
1	0.004219	0.471549	0.991131	Homa
4	0.436228	0.040736	0.085406	**Espinas**
2	0.090244	0.391288	0.812589	**Esteghlal**
3	0.359366	0.119697	0.249856	**Laleh**

Table 7: Fuzzy TOPSIS results.

After the fuzzy evaluation matrix was determined, the second step is to obtain a fuzzy weighted decision table. Using the criteria weights calculated by AHP (Table 4) in this step, the Weighted Evaluation Matrix is established. The resulting fuzzy weighted decision matrix is shown in Table 6.

The fourth step solves the similarities to an ideal solution by Eq. (14) [40]. The results can be observes as follows in Table 6. Similar calculations are done for the other alternatives and the results of fuzzy TOPSIS analyses are summarized in Table 7. Based on CCj values, the ranking of the alternatives in ascending order are Homa, Esteghlal, Laleh, Espinas and Azadi Hotel respectively.

Considering the criteria of CSR, the partial ranking demonstrates that Homa Hotel obtain the greatest CC+. This means that Homa Hotel takes the best CSR practices. Homa has the highest fuzzy number grade in economic and environmental factors. On the contrary, Azadi Hotel shows the lowest CC+ in the Table 7. So it indicates that Azadi Hotel may be unable to manage their activities in a economically, socially and environmentally responsible manner.

Conclusion

A strong current trend is the use of sustainable development theory to propose a new dimensioning of CSR composed of not only economic but also social and environmental aspects [11]. Furthermore, as argued in the literature, the application of the principles of CSR is highly conditioned by the contextual features of the sectors to which it is applied [13].

This paper has looked at the concept of CSR in terms of the hotel industry. It adopted a qualitative approach to assessing and ranking the CSR practices in the five star hotels in Tehran, with a view to addressing three major dimensions of CSR i.e. economic, social and

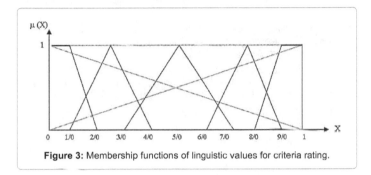

Figure 3: Membership functions of linguistic values for criteria rating.

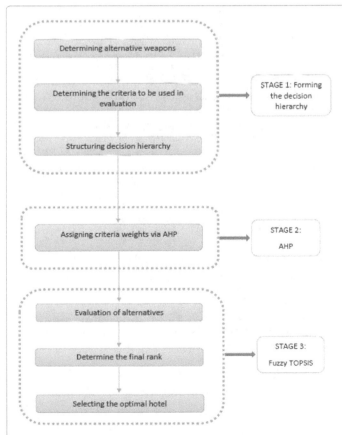

Figure 4: Schematic diagram of the proposed model for hotels' CSR assessing.

environmental factors. For this reason, the study, after underlining the meaning and significance of CSR and its dimensions, has focused on the analysis of the practices of hotels responsibility. Therefore, an effective evaluation approach is essential to improve decision quality. This study, presenting a scientific framework to assess and rank the CSR dimensions using the analytical hierarchy process (AHP) and the triangular fuzzy numbers to express linguistic values that consider the subjective judgments of evaluators. The proposed model is based on the comparisons of hotel brand alternatives according to identified criteria. AHP and fuzzy TOPSIS compound decision-making method has been used in proposed model. AHP is used to assign weights to the criteria to be used in CSR factors, while fuzzy TOPSIS is employed to determine the priorities of the alternatives. The weights obtained from AHP are included in decision-making process by using them in fuzzy TOPSIS computations and the alternative priorities are determined based on these weights. Proposed model has significantly increased the efficiency of decision-making process in hotel rankings. Definitely, this paper may suffer some setbacks. Consequently, some limitations like time and so on should be taken into account. These limitations can be overcome in the direction of the future research.

References

1. Swaen V, Chumpitaz RC (2008) Impact of Corporate Social Responsibility on consumer trust. Rechercheet Applications en Marketing 23: 7-34.

2. Martínez P, Pérez A, Bosque IRD (2012) Analysis of the Corporate Social Responsibility Practice in the Tourism Sector: A Case Study. Cuadernos de Turismo, 309-312.

3. Aupperle KE, Carroll AB, Hatfield JD (1985) An Empirical Examination of the Relationship between Corporate Social Responsibility and Profitability. The Academy of Management Journal 28: 446-463.

4. Miller DGA (2000) Consumerism in Sustainable Tourism: A Survey of UK Consumers. UK Consumer Survey.

5. Kasim A (2006) Socially responsible hospitality and tourism marketing.

6. Jayawardena C (2003) "Sustainable tourism development in Canada: practical challenges."International Journal of Contemporary Hospitality Management 15: 408-412.

7. Strange T, Bayley A (2008) Sustainable Development, Organisation For Economic Co- Operation And Development.

8. Du S, Bhattacharya CB, Sen S (2007) Reaping relational rewards from corporate social responsibility: The role of competitive positioning. Intern J of Research in Marketing 24: 224-241.

9. Nižić MK, Golja T, Vodeb K (2011) The Trend of Economic, Ecological and Social Responsibility Implementation in Tourism. Sustainable Tourism: Socio-Cultural, Environmental and Economic Impact 221-234.

10. Idowu SO, Filho WL (2010) Professionals' Perspectives of Corporate Social Responsibility. Springer Heidelberg, New York.

11. Panapanaan VM, Linnanen L, Karvina MM, Phan VT (2003) Roadmapping Corporate Social Responsibility in Finnish Companies. Journal of Business Ethics 44: 133-148.

12. Martínez P, Pérez A, Bosque IR (2013) Measuring Corporate Social Responsibility in Tourism: Development and Validation of an Efficient Measurement Scale In the Hospitality Industry. Journal of Travel and Tourism Marketing 30: 365-385.

13. Carroll AB (1999) Corporate Social Responsibility: Evolution of a Definitional Construct. Business and Society 38: 268-295.

14. Friedman M (1970) The Social Responsibility of Business is to Increase its Profits. The New York Times Magazine.

15. Porter ME, Kramer MR (2002) The Competitive Advantage of Corporate Philantropy. Harvard Business Review 80: 56-68.

16. Walker M, Heere B, Parent MM, Drane D (2010) Social Responsibility and the Olympic Games: The Mediating Role of Consumer Attributions. Journal of Business Ethics 95: 659-680.

17. Campbell JL (2007) Why would corporations behave in socially responsible ways? An institutional theory of corporate social responsibility. Academy of Management Review 32: 946-967.

18. Freeman RE (1984) Stakeholder theory of Modern Corporation.

19. Mitchell RK, Agle BR, Wood DJ (1997) Toward a Theory of Stakeholder Identification and Salience: Defining the Principle of Who and What Really Counts. The Academy of Management Review 22: 853-886.

20. Salmones MMG, Crespo AH, Bosque IR (2005) Influence of Corporate Social Responsibility on Loyalty and Valuation of Services. Journal of Business Ethics 61: 369-385.

21. WBCSD (1998). Corporate Social Responsibility.

22. Panwar R (2006) Corporate responsibility: Balancing economic, environmental, and social issues in the forest products industry. Forest Products Journal 56: 4-12.

23. Maignan I, Ferrell OC (2000) Measuring Corporate Citizenship in Two Countries: The Case of the United States and France. Journal of Business Ethics 23: 283-297.

24. Sawhny V (2008) Analyzing Corporate Social Responsibility Measurement Parameters.

25. Austin EW, Pinkleton BE (2006) Strategic Public Relations Management. Planning and Managing Effective Communication Program. 2nd edition Lawrence Erlbaum Associates, Publishers, London.

26. Ward H, Borregaard N, Kapelus P (2002) Corporate Citizenship - Revisiting the Relationship between Business, Good Governance and Sustainable Development. International Institute for Environment and Development.

27. Vidal NG, Kozak RA (2008) The recent evolution of corporate responsibility practices in the forestry sector. International Forestry Review 10: 1-13.

28. Tencati A, Perrini F, Pogutz S (2004) New Tools to Foster Corporate Socially Responsible Behavior. Journal of Business Ethics 53: 173-190.

29. UNIDO (2003) The Role of Industrial Development in the Achievement of the Millennium Development Goals.

30. Manente M, Minghetti V, Mingotto E (2012) Ranking assessment systems for responsible tourism products and corporate social responsibility practices. An International Journal of Tourism and Hospitality Research Vol. 23: 75-89.

31. Kucukusta D, Mak A, Chan X (2013) Corporate social responsibility practices in four and five- star hotels: Perspectives from Hong Kong visitors. International Journal of Hospitality Management 34: 19-30.

32. Fabricius M, Goodwin H (2002) Cape Town Declaration on Responsible Tourism.

33. Rodrı´guez FJG, Cruz YdMA (2007) Relation between social-environmentalresponsibility and performance in hotel firms. Hospitality Management 26: 824-839.

34. Chen S, Fan J (2011) Measuring Corporate Social Responsibility Based on a Fuzzy Analytical Hierarchy Process. IJCNIS 3: 13-22.

35. Saaty RW (1987) The Analytic Hierarchy Process-What it is and how it is used. Mathematical Modelling 9: 161-176.

36. Hwang CL, Yoon K (1981) Lecture Notes in Economics and Mathematical Systems. 128-140.

37. Zadeh LA (1965) Fuzzy Sets. Information and Control 8: 338-353.

38. Dagdeviren M, Yavuz S, Kılınç N (2009) Weapon selection using the AHP and TOPSIS methods under fuzzy environment. Expert Systems with Applications 36: 8143-8151.

39. Bojadziev G, Bojadziev M (2007) Fuzzy Logic for Business, Finance, and Management. 2nd edition, World Scientific Publishing Co Pte Ltd, USA.

40. Yang T, Hung CC (2007) Multiple-attribute decision making methods for plant layout design problem. Robotics and Computer-Integrated Manufacturing 23: 126-137.

26

GSM Based E-Notice Board: With Software Interfacing Using ASM Tools

Sachin M Dandage*

Department of Computer Science and Engineering, PLITMS, Buldana, Maharashtra, India

Abstract

Sending SMS through telephone has turned out to be exceptionally broad and on the off chance that we can utilize this SMS to control gadgets and in indicating information. It is conceivable to get or interpret the SMS all around by utilizing GSM, by the any piece of System. We can control and show information on LCD board. In this anticipate we are going to clarifies how a dependable and a true remote correspondence could be effectively settled between a cell telephone and microcontroller utilizing GSM MODEM. This thought will clarifies GSM based e-notice board which can be broadly utilized for numerous of uses including instructive segment, movement control, banks, and open promotions and so on. Moreover we can learn and in addition adjust a portion of the basic uses of GSM MODEM according to the prerequisites and requirements of the clients. Here we will attempt to know the equipment behind the photo.

Keywords: SMS; GSM e-notice; Microcontroller; Telephone

Introduction

This thought is a remote notification board with a GSM modem at the recipients wrap up. So if the client needs to show any message, he can send the data by SMS [1] and in this way overhaul the LCD show thusly. As specialist's primary point is to make life basic with help of learning, this is one stage to rearrange constant taking note.

GSM a computerized portable telephony framework, which is globally gotten to by more than 212 nations and domains. Worldwide framework for portable correspondence is totally enhanced for full duplex voice telephony. At first created for the substitution of original (1G) innovation, now GSM is accessible with heaps of remarkable elements with the consistent up degree of third era (3G) innovation. What's more, now with the organization together of microcontroller, GSM MODEM could be further perfectly customized for some of exceptionally creative applications including GSM based DC engine controller, GSM based home security framework, GSM based robot control, GSM based voting machine control, GSM based stepper engine coordinator and so on. Fundamental Function of GSM Based E-Notice Board [2]:

- Sending message from any of the remote range to the inaccessible found e-notice board utilizing GSM versatile.

- For sending the instant message from remote region we have to interface the cellular telephone with GSM Modem.

- For building up some of GSM based applications we need a few hall peripherals including GSM MODEM, SIM, microcontroller, LCD (Liquid gem show), power supply furthermore some associating wires.

Analysis of GSM Base Electronic Notice Board

Presently a-days declaration is going advanced. The enormous shops and the strip malls use advanced shows now. Additionally, in trains and transports the data like stage number, ticket data is shown in advanced loads up. Individuals are presently adjusted to the possibility of the world readily available. The utilization cellular telephones have expanded definitely over years. Control and declaration has gotten to be vital in all the parts of the world (Figure 1).

This gave us the thought to utilize cellular telephones to get message and afterward show it on an electronic board. The GSM innovation is utilized. GSM remains for Global System for Mobile Communication. Because of this universal meandering ability of GSM, we can send message to beneficiary from any part of the world. It is has the framework for SMS Short Message Service. This thought is a remote

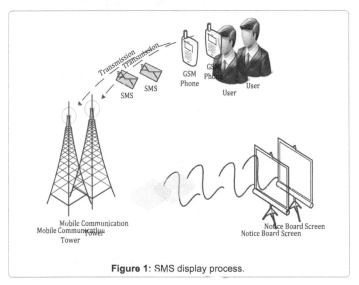

Figure 1: SMS display process.

notification board with a GSM modem at the recipients end. So if the client needs to show any message, he can send the data by SMS and in this manner upgrade the LCD show as needs be [3].

SIM (subscriber identity module)

SIM is a chip-on little card comprising of client's data and in addition telephone directory. Client can modify the administrator on the same handset according to convenience. At present double SIM beneficiaries are additionally accessible in the business sector where we can utilize two administrators on the same handset. The SIM is embedded in a space accessible on the GSM Modem (Figure 2).

Activating a SIM card: Since the greater part of a client's information is attached to the SIM card, just it should be enacted when

---

***Corresponding author:** Sachin M Dandage, Department of Computer Science and Engineering, PLITMS, Buldana, Maharashtra, India
E-mail: dandage.Sachin@gmail.com

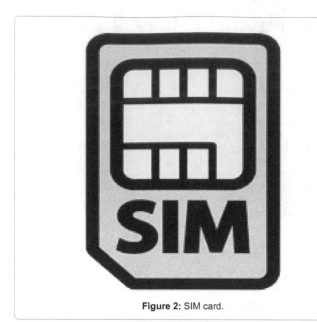

Figure 2: SIM card.

the individual opens a record with a phone administration supplier (additionally called a bearer). Every card has a one of a kind number imprinted on the chip, which the bearer needs to enact it. By and large, the telephone's proprietor can go either to the bearer's site and arrive this number in the reasonable instrument or call the administration supplier specifically from another telephone to get it contorted on. SIM cards are fixing to a specific bearer and must be utilized with an administration arrangement from that transporter.

SIM cards sizes: SIM cards are made in three distinctive sizes to quarter diverse gadgets. Most telephones use smaller than normal SIM or miniaturized scale SIM cards, which are entirely little - the scaled down is 25 mm by 15 mm (0.98 in by 0.59), and the small scale is 15 mm by 12 mm (0.59 in by 0.47 in). Full-sized cards are much bigger, 85.6 mm by 53.98 mm (3.37 in by 2.13 in), and are too huge for generally telephones. All cards are just 0.76 mm (0.03 in) thick, in any case, and the microchip contacts are in the same arrangement. This implies, with the best possible connector, the littler cards can be utilized as a part of gadgets proposed for bigger ones.

GSM modem

A GSM modem is a specific kind of modem which acknowledges a SIM card, and works over a membership to a versatile administrator, much the same as a cellular telephone. From the versatile administrator point of view, a GSM modem looks simply like a cellular telephone. At the point when a GSM modem is associated with a PC, this permits the PC to utilize the GSM modem to convey over the portable system. While these GSM modems are most every now and again used to give versatile web network, huge numbers of them can likewise be utilized for sending and getting SMS and MMS messages. Notwithstanding the standard AT guidelines, GSM modems bolster a developed arrangement of AT orders. These reached out AT orders are characterized in the GSM measures. With the reached out AT summons, you can do things like:

1. Reading, written work and erasing SMS messages

2. Sending SMS messages

3. Monitoring the sign quality

4. Monitoring the charging status and charge level of the battery

5. Reading, written work and seeking telephone directory passages

6. SIM Phonebook administration

7. Fixed Dialing Number (FDN)

8. Real time clock

The quantity of SMS messages that can be prepared by a GSM modem for every moment is low i.e., just around six to ten SMS messages for each moment (Figure 3).

Methodology of e-notice board: A Universal Asynchronous Receiver/Source is a bit of PC equipment that deciphers information amongst parallel and serial structures. UARTs are normally utilized as a part of unification with correspondence principles, for example, EIA, RS-232, RS-422 or RS-485. The all inclusive assignment shows that the information organization and transmission velocities are configurable. The electric flagging levels and techniques, (for e.g., differential flagging and so forth) are taken care of by a driver circuit outside to the UART [4].

A UART is typically an individual incorporated circuit utilized for serial correspondences over a PC or fringe gadget serial port. UARTs are presently normally incorporated into microcontrollers. A double UART, or DUART, joins two UARTs into a solitary chip. Numerous cutting edge ICs now accompany a UART that can likewise convey synchronously; these gadgets are called Universal Synchronous/Asynchronous Receiver/Transmitter (USART).

A UART normally contains the accompanying segments:

- Clock Generator, various of the bit rate to permit examining in center of a bit period

- Input and Output Shift Registers

- Transmit/Receive Control

- Read/Write Control Logic

- Transmit/Receive Buffers (discretionary)

- Parallel Data Bus Buffer (discretionary)

- First-in, first-out (FIFO) Buffer Memory (optional)

Transmitting and receiving serial data: The Universal Asynchronous Receiver/Transmitter (UART) takes bytes of information and transmits the individual bits in a successive manner. At the destination, a second UART re-amasses the bits into complete bytes. Each UART contains a movement register, which is the basic technique for change amongst serial and parallel structures. Serial transmission

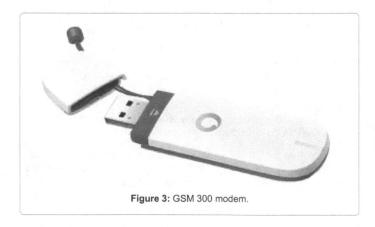

Figure 3: GSM 300 modem.

of computerized data (bits) through a solitary wire or other medium is less unreasonable than parallel transmission through numerous wires.

The UART ordinarily does not specifically produce or get the outside signs utilized between various things of hardware. Separate interface gadgets are utilized to change over the rationale level signs of the UART to and from the outside flagging levels. Outside signs might be of a wide range of structures. Case of norms for voltage flagging are RS-232, RS-422 and RS-485 from the EIA. Verifiably, current (in current circles) was utilized as a part of broadcast circuits. Some flagging plans don't utilize electrical wires. Case of such are optical fiber, IrDA (infrared), and (remote) Bluetooth in its Serial Port Profile (SPP). Some flagging plans use balance of a bearer signal (with or without wires). Cases are adjustment of sound signs with telephone line modems, RF tweak with information radios, and the DC-LIN for electrical cable correspondence. Correspondence might be simplex (in one bearing just, with no procurement for the getting gadget to send data back to the transmitting gadget), full duplex (both gadgets send and get in the meantime) or half duplex (gadgets alternate transmitting and accepting).

Receiving data: All operations of the UART equipment are controlled by a clock sign which keeps running at a various of the information rate, commonly 8 times the bit rate. The recipient tests the condition of the approaching sign on every clock beat, searching for the start of the begin bit. In the event that the obvious begin bit keeps going no less than one-portion of the bit time, it is legitimate and flags the begin of another character. If not, it is viewed as a spurious heartbeat and is overlooked. Subsequent to holding up a further piece time, the condition of the line is again tested and the subsequent level timed into a movement register. After the required number of bit periods for the character length (5 to 8 bits, normally) have slipped by, the substance of the movement register are made accessible (in parallel style) to the accepting framework. The UART will set a banner showing new information is accessible, and may likewise create a processor hinder to demand that the host processor exchanges they got information [5].

Conveying UARTs ordinarily have no mutual planning framework separated from the correspondence signal. Commonly, UARTs resynchronize their inside tickers on every change of the information line that is not viewed as a spurious heartbeat. Acquiring timing data in this way, they dependably get when the transmitter is sending at a somewhat distinctive pace than it ought to. Shortsighted UARTs don't do this, rather they resynchronize on the falling edge of the begin bit just, and afterward read the focal point of each normal information bit, and this framework works if the telecast information rate is sufficiently exact to permit the stop bits to be inspected dependably.

It is a standard component for a UART to store the latest character while accepting the following. This "twofold buffering" gives an accepting PC a whole character transmission time to get a got character. Numerous UARTs have a little first-in, first-out FIFO support memory between the collector shift register and the host framework interface. This permits the host processor much more opportunity to handle a hinder from the UART and forestalls loss of got information at high rates.

Transmitting the data: Transmission operation is less difficult since it is under the control of the transmitting framework. When information is stored in the movement register after culmination of the past character, the UART equipment creates a begin bit, moves the required number of information bits out to the line, produces and attaches the equality bit (if utilized), and annexes the stop bits. Since transmission of a solitary character may take quite a while in respect to CPU speeds, the UART will keep up a banner demonstrating occupied status so that the host framework does not store another character for transmission until the past one has been finished; this may likewise be finished with an interfere. Since full-duplex operation obliges characters to be sent and got in the meantime, UARTs utilize two diverse movement registers for transmitted characters and got characters [6].

Design Approach for E-Notice Board

This is the model for showing sees in schools on electronic notification board by sending messages in type of SMS through versatile; it is a remote transmission framework which has less mistakes and support.

The entire framework is fundamentally isolated into two areas: Transmitting and Receiving. Transmitting segment comprises of only a portable. Any sort of client (SIM Number) can be utilized, as clients are appointed watchword for getting to the framework. Approved clients send the message that they need to show on the notification board to the accepting segment's versatile number and the message will be shown just if the clients have the validation secret word. Accepting segment then again comprises of a GSM modem to get message. Gotten SMS is then extricated by PC with the assistance of a Microsoft Visual Basic .NET Graphical User Interface utilizing AT summons (Figure 4).

Data flow diagram for the e-notice board

This application is design to print the messages on digital [7] board. Here we compare whether the text massage is with prefix. If massages are with prefix then these are considered as emergency notices else normal notices. These messages are transmitted and are processed at MODEM for A/D Conversion. Modem is attached to the computer system analyses the binary signal and display notices on e-notice board. Also it examines the old notices and can delete older one (Figure 5).

Open Issues and Future Scope

This innovation could be further changed and more overhauled according to individual need and intrigue. We have talked about some essential thoughts of this innovation. What's more, contingent upon imaginative applications client can overhaul according to necessity.

1. In data innovation, a booth is a little physical structure including a PC and a showcase screen that presentations data for individuals.

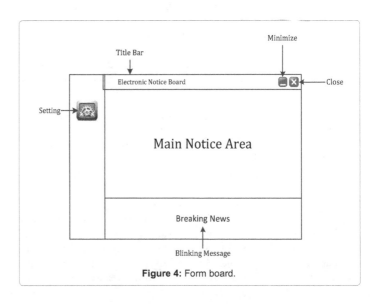

Figure 4: Form board.

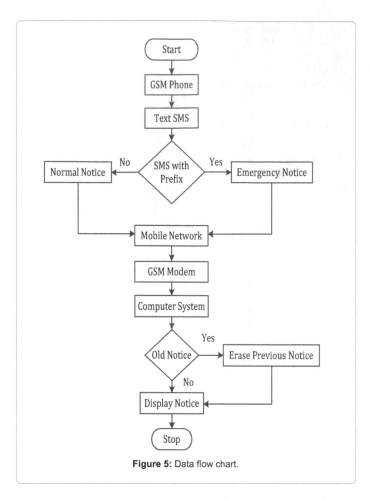

Figure 5: Data flow chart.

2. More modern booths let clients interface and incorporate touch screens, sound and movement video.

3. In future we are attempting to build up a Kiosk for message correspondence so as to show different data on the screen.

4. We will utilize slight customer PC for the same arrangement with Wi-Fi availability alongside GSM network for remote correspondence.

5. A business model ought to have the capacity to show more than one message at once. Right now in our task we are utilizing locally available RAM memory to spare a solitary message. To conquer this deficiency we can interface an EEPROM to spare messages. This not just permits more than one message to be shown at once additionally permits us to recover messages from the EEPROM even after a force disappointment.

6. Alphanumeric LCDs have a constraint on size and additionally no of characters. These can be supplanted with vast LED [8] show sheets which are attractive as well as showcase characters in a moving manner in a steady progression.

Conclusion

By presenting the idea of remote innovation in the field of correspondence we can make our correspondence more productive and speedier, with more noteworthy proficiency we can show the messages and with less blunders and support. This model can be utilized effectively as a part of foundations like chain eateries wherein the request and exceptional rebates can be shown at all branches all the while, in

universities wherein understudies and staffs can be educated at the same time in the blink of an eye. It can be set up at open transport places like railroads, transport station, and airplane terminal furthermore at roadside for movement control and in crisis circumstances, it is cost proficient framework and simple to handle. Inertness required in utilizing of papers as a part of showing of notification is kept away from and the data can be upgraded by the approved persons.

Highlights

1. This thought is an Electronic Notice Board associated with a modem, so that if the client needs to show some messages, The will send the messages in SMS design.

2. The modem in the presentation framework will get the message and upgrade the showcase as indicated by the message.

3. For each message got, the framework will check for the source number and if the source number is right the controller will show the message.

4. Whole screen is partitioned into for the most part two sections, Regular Messages and Breaking News. Additionally gave separate catch to settings.

Application areas

1. Educational institutions and organizations: As of now we depend on setting up papers on notification sheets to illuminate individuals of occasions. This technique can be disposed of by utilizing remote notification loads up to show data continuously.

2. Wrongdoing prevention.

3. Show blocks put on streets will show tips on open security, mischance aversion, data on hoodlums on the run. The board will streak messages, for example, vehicle burglaries as and when they happen.

4. Overseeing traffic: In metropolitan urban areas we as often as possible go over congested roads. One approach to dodge this would be advice individuals heretofore to take backup courses of action. A remote notification board fills well for this need.

5. Notice: In shopping centers we get the opportunity to hear the offers on different items every once in a while. Rather we ceaselessly show the data in regards to the items and related offers on electronic showcase sheets.

6. Railroad station: Rather than reporting the postponement in entry of trains we can show the data.

Significant advantages

1. User friendly: Messages are just to be written on a versatile or PC, which thus are shown remotely on the presentation unit.

2. Eliminates use of printers: Since we don't utilize papers to show data, printers are likewise of no utilization in this framework.

3. Faster means of transferring information: There is no deferral in transmission of data. Messages are shown in a matter of seconds in the wake of writing.

4. Long range: For whatever length of time that we have the required system scope we can send messages from any part of the world.

References

1. Nivetha SR, Pujitha R, Preethi S, Yashvanthini SM (2013) SMS based wireless notice board with monitoring system. International Journal of Advanced

Electrical and Electronics Engineering 2: 58-62.

2. Baby M, Harini P, Eleena SY, Tejaswi Y, Ramajyothi K, et al. (2013) SMS based wireless e-notice board. International Journal of Emerging Technology & Advanced Engineering 3: 106-110.

3. Darshankumar CD, Trivedi N, Kasundra A (2011) Wireless notice board. National Conference on Recent Trends in Engineering & Technology.

4. Kumar P, Bhrdwaj V, Pal K, Rathor NS, Mishra A (2012) GSM based e-Notice Board: Wireless communication. International Journal of Soft Computing and Engineering 2: 601-605.

5. Rich E, Knight K, Nair SB (1991) Artificial intelligence. Mc Graw Hill, New York.

6. Clark AP, Harun R (1986) Assessment of Kalman-filter channel estimators for an HF radio link. IEE Proceedings 133: 513-521.

7. Bernard Sklar (2001) Digital communications: Fundamentals and applications. Prentice Hall, USA.

8. Swiatkowski M, Wozniak K, Olczyk L (2006) Student notice board based on LED matrix system controlled over TCP/IP protocol. Photonics and Microsystems, International Students and Young Scientists Workshop.

27

An Automated Approach for Web Services Architectural Style Selection

Mohsin A*, Fatima S, Khan AU and Nawaz F

Department of Computer Science and Engineering, Air University Multan, Pakistan

Abstract

Selection of an appropriate architectural style is vital to the success a web service. The nature of architecture design and selection for service oriented computing applications is quite complex as compared to traditional software architecture. Web Services have complex and rigorous architectural styles with their own underlying architectural characteristics. Due to this, selection for accurate architectural style for web services development has become more complex decision to be made by architects. Architectural style selection is a multi-criteria decision and demands lots of experience in service oriented computing. There is a huge gap for automated selection of web services architectural styles. Decision support systems are good solution to simplify the selection process of a particular architectural style. Our research suggests an automated approach using DSS for selection of architectural styles while developing a web service to cater FRs & NFRs (Functional & Non Functional Requirements). Our proposed mechanism helps architects to select right web service architectural pattern according to domain, and non-functional requirements without compromising quality. In this paper a rule base DSS has been developed using CLIPS (C Language Integrated Production System) to support decision process in multi-criteria requirements. To select suitable web service, system takes architectural characteristics, domain requirements and software architect preferences for NFRs as input by applying rule base approach. Next Weighted Sum Model has been applied to prioritize quality attributes and domain requirements. Scores are calculated using multiple criterions to choose the final architecture style.

Keywords: Web services; Architectural styles; Rule based; DSS; Multi-criteria requirements; Quality attributes; Automated decisions

Introduction

Software architecture controls how system elements are recognised and assigned, how the elements interrelate to form a system, the amount of communication needed for interaction. Therefore, selection of the suitable architectural style(s) for use in construction of software is of importance. A good Architecture can create a difference between success and failure of web and mobile applications in SOC (Service Oriented Computing) domain.

Service Oriented computing has emerged as top choice for software developers, utilizing the integration of cloud computing and IOTs (Internet of Things). The basic components of SOC are services over distributed networks allowing various devices and software to exchange information. SOC, initially emerged from Service Oriented Architecture(s) an architectural style, it has now become a larger knowledge area consisting of other architectural styles. Because of operational constraints in different environments Quality factors are largely dependent on particular architectural style in use.

A typical Web service is an interface that defines a collection of operations that are network accessible through standardized XML messaging. A Web service is described using a standard, format XML or JSON notion, called its service description [1]. At present we have various architectural styles to choose from to develop a web service each with its own pros and cons.

Software architecture has been a key component in software development in past two decades. Therefore, choosing the correct architecture is a basic task in software engineering phases, concerning quality attributes of a web service. Software Architecture provides abstractions and defines relationships among those abstractions while Architectural Styles impact largely on performance, security, reliability and many others. When we talk about Service oriented computing applications, they are more complex and heterogeneous in nature with respect to different architectural styles. A few traits have been recorded for each style in distinctive writings, however we can't comprehend the degree to what benefits and drawbacks of quality and quality attributes of each architecture are considered [1]; thusly, contrasting capabilities, attributes and benefits of software architecture is a by one means or another difficult task. Apart from Quality requirements other set of requirements make it a tough decision for architects for selection of a particular style to develop a web service.

Figure 1 shows N- tier architectural framework of Web Services. In this figure basic components of a typical web service application are depicted by keeping in mind FRs and NFRs required to support any architectural style, typical web service architecture has been mapped into three layers.

At present when we are conducing this research there are multiple architectural styles available for developing a particular web service like SOAP, RESTFU etc. Each one of these style(s) allows system architects to develop web service to complete a specific functionality with similar and conflicting quality attributes. The general concern of users is performance, security, reliability and related quality attributes. Other most important factor is self-characteristics of architecture to be selected. So, software architect(s) have to consider the self-characteristics as well as domain requirements in addition to NFRs in order to select appropriate architecture according to need of the app being developed. This decision becomes critical to meet different and varying requirements.

At the moment there are various web services styles suitable for different types of web services to design. But there is a lack of work to make distinction which web service style is better for a particular set of requirements. Requirements are of various types i.e. Functional, Non Functional and Domain specific. There is not a single Architectural

---

*Corresponding author: Mohsin A, Department of Computer Science and Engineering, Air University Multan, Pakistan, E-mail: ahmad@aumc.edu.pk

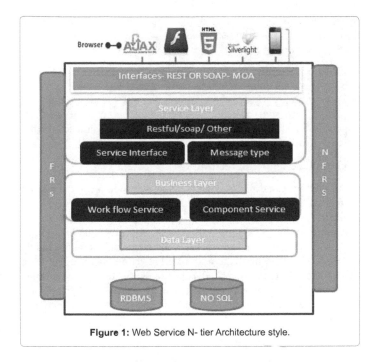

Figure 1: Web Service N- tier Architecture style.

style for a web service which can full fill are the criterion for a given problem set. Some Style are good in terms of Performance but lacks security and vice versa. Architects usually choose a web service style based on its performance in pervious projects, word of mouth or its ease in development. There is no proper framework or any automated system which can recommend for usage of a particular web service style.

Service oriented computing has transformed modern web and cloud computing paradigms. Though there are different architectural styles for developing a web service but here we have considered three different types of web-service architectures which are widely used in industry today. Service Oriented Architecture (SOA), Resource Oriented Architecture (ROA) and Message Oriented Architecture (MOA). These will be explored in later section in detail.

After research we have considered three types of requirements these are Domain Requirements, NFRs and self-characteristics of a particular architectural style(s) in whole decision making process.

For developers and architects there are many architectural choices to choose for a web service. At the moment various architectual patterns exist carrying their own pros and cons for a specific type of a web service development in a particular domain. Architectural style selection is based on various aspects of the system under investigation. There are number of reasons of poor quality but we have considered two that are negligence of NFR (Non-functional requirements) and nature of applications being developed. Architectures have a number of characteristics that must be considered but manual decision and prioir expertise are not enough to make a correct choice.

In this paper, a Rule based Decision Support System (DSS) has been developed which attempts to help the decision making process by keeping in mind different related criteria for web service architecture including quality attributes weightage according to web and mobile app being developed, domain requirements and architectural style characteristics. And base on these criteria suggesting suitable solutions.

Section II presents Literature Review of the related work and Research Challenges. In Section III we shall present proposed DSS

for web service architectural selection; Section IV will show Selecting architecture using proposed DSS. In Section V we will see impact on decision making process, Section VI discusses the advantages and Section VII & VIII will cover future work and conclusions respectively.

Literature Review

In this section we shall review service oriented computing, web service, web service architectural styles, approaches used for selection of architecture in past.

SOC architectural styles

Service-oriented computing is an emerging cross-disciplinary paradigm for distributed computing, which is changing the way software applications are designed, delivered and consumed. At the heart of service-oriented computing are services that provide autonomous, platform-independent, computational elements that can be described, published, discovered, orchestrated and programmed using standard protocols to build networks of collaborating applications distributed within and across organizational boundaries. Web services provide a standard means of interoperating between different software applications, running on a variety of platforms and/or frameworks. The general description of commonly used architectural styles is as follows:

MOA (Message-Oriented Architecture): MOM (Message-Oriented Middleware) or MOA is an alternative to the RPC (Remote Procedure Call) distribution mechanism. This mechanism called Message-Oriented Middleware or MOM provides a clean method of communication between disparate software entities. MOM is one of the foundation stone that distributed enterprise systems are built upon. MOM can be defined as any middleware infrastructure that provides messaging capabilities. A client of a MOM system can send messages to, and receive messages from, other clients of the messaging system. Each client connects to one or more servers that act as an intermediary in the sending and receiving of messages. MOM uses a model with a peer-to-peer relationship between individual clients; in this model, each peer can send and receive messages to and from other client peers. MOM platforms allow flexible cohesive systems to be created; a cohesive system is one that allows changes in one part of a system to occur without the need for changes in other parts of the system [2].

SOA (Service-Oriented Architecture): The service-oriented Architecture (SOA) uses services to support the development of rapid, low-cost, interoperable, evolvable, and massively distributed applications. Services are autonomous, platform-independent entities that can be described, published, discovered, and loosely coupled in novel ways. They perform functions that range from answering simple requests to executing sophisticated business processesrequiring peer-to-peer relationships among multiple layers of service consumers and providers. Any piece of code and any application component deployed on a system can be reused and transformed into a network-available service. Services reflect a "service-oriented" approach to programming that is based on the idea of composing applications by discovering and invoking network-available services to accomplish some task. This approach is independent of specific programming languages or operating systems. It lets organizations expose their core competencies programmatically over the Internet or various networks.

ROA (Resource-oriented Architecture): Resource Oriented Architecture (ROA) or REST Oriented Architecture are used interchangeably and ROA (REST Oriented Architecture) is just a fancy name for a SOA (Service Based Architecture) using REST services. REST was proposed by Roy Fielding. REST is architecture for developing Web services. REST attempts to mimic architectures that use HTTP or similar protocols, by constraining the interface to a set of well-known standard operations (i.e., GET, PUT, POST, and DELETE for HTTP). Here, the focus is on interacting with statefull resources, rather than messages or operations. "REST architecture is designed to show how existing HTTP is enough to build a Web service and to show its scalability". It avoids the complexity and processing overhead of the Web services protocols by using bare http. One important REST concept is a resource, which is a piece of information that has a unique identifier (e.g., a uniform resource identifier (URI)). REST web services architectural style reduces the complexity of transforming data from XML or JSON between sender and receiver.

SOAP vs. RESTfulvs. MOA: Though there is a division among the advocates of two prominent styles in web services but recently a trend has been seen which shows architects and developers favouring RESTful as it is much easy to implement. In a research case study for developing multimedia conference applications both styles were used and results show that RESTful proved itself much better in performance [3]. In another work where performance analysis was done for both styles on different platforms in cloud, RESTful outclassed SOAP style [4]. The new versions of SOAP make it easy to use. One advantage of SOAP is that it uses generic transport protocols while RESTful only uses http/https. REST is best suited in less complex scenario while SOAP is more suitable for complex systems [5]. Message oriented Model has some commonalties with SOAP but differs in architecture and internal complexities.

Architecture selection approaches: The use of Computational intelligence for decision support system in order to solve different problems is much better as opposed manual decisions [6]. A decision support system automates the process for decision making in any domain. There are various approaches for its usage, here we mention few related to our work.

Wang and Yang proposed a selection method for people who lack expertise and experience to select appropriate architecture style for their software systems [7]. The authors collected and categorized a number of common architecture styles, and used Quality Attributes as a criterion to evaluate all those architecture styles. Moreover, they provided a systematic selection process powered by AnalyticHierarchy Process (AHP). It is a widely used theory andprovides a measurement through pair wise comparisons and relies on the judgments of experts to derive priority scales. This method just considers the quality attributes but does not cater the domain and architectural requirements.

Babu et al. [8] presented a method called SSAS (Selection of Software Architecture Styles). It uses analyticnetwork process (ANP) to determine the degree ofinterdependence relationship among the alternatives (architecture styles) and criteria (Requirements). It provides a way of collecting expert group opinion along with stakeholders interests (e.g. reliability, performance) [8]. It should be noted that, the traditional AHP is applied to the problem without considering interdependence property among the criteria.

Moaven et al. [9] explained "A Decision Support System for Software Architecture-Style Selection" presented DSS which makes use of fuzzy logic to represent concepts of quality attributes more precisely and efficiently while considering interaction among them. They constructed a DSS based on knowledge-base which has the ability of updating its knowledge and provides the system architect with suitable choices to select among them. With respect to knowledge base and exploiting expertise of people that work in this domain (e.g. expert architect) some rules have been extracted that can help to surfing the style repository and offering a style or combination of some

styles [10]. This DSS considered NFRs but this DSS not considered the characteristics of architecture to be asked by architect as input for making decision.

Theoretical framework for using a decision maker for cloud based web services architecture selection via rule based engine was presented by Falak et al. [2]. This work only presented framework for choosing an appropriate style among ROA and SOAP. Moreover practical implication of this framework was not provided so impact on the selection process could not be predicted [2].

Architecture selection techniques

Further we can categorize Architecture selection techniques based on manual selection and automated selection. Both techniques help Architects for selecting appropriate architecture. Being a web service a complex entity to be built with diverse requirements, it becomes difficult for system architects to select the one which is most suitable for needs. On the other hand automated selection facilitates software architect to select closely related as per requirements with very short time investment. One can say that manual process for architecture selection is economical but it depends how much domain experience the decision maker has.

The research challenge

Research Challenge: Web Service Architecture Selection in Multicriteria Requirements.

The single most difficult challenge in software development in modern era is the selection of appropriate architectural style and this decision becomes even complex and difficult when it comes to select web services styles. Multiple factors come into play in selection of architecture style for Service Oriented applications. So core Research challenges are:

• Selection of correct architecture style for web services without compromising quality attributes.

• Existence of multiple web services architectural styles.

• Multi-criteria Requirements

• Complex Decision making process

• Diverse Characteristics of different styles

Proposed DSS for Web Service Architectural Selection

Our proposed solution tries to automate the web service architecture selection process by focusing on quality attributes and functional requirements. There are some common features among web service styles but target applications always do require varying quality attributes. So as a solution we have developed a rule based decision support system in CLIPS (C language Integrated Production Shell) to automate the. For this purpose three architecture styles SOA, ROA and MOA are selected and NFRS security, reliability and performance are considered. NFR preferences are taken first along with general characteristics for architectures under question. Weighted sum model is applied with selected characteristics prioritization. This process ends with suitable web service style suggestion based on requirements. The complete process of proposed DSS is depicted in Figure 2.

DSS and its types

Due to the extremely high attention to the computer-based information systems, making use of Decision Support Systems to support and improve decision making has become of importance.

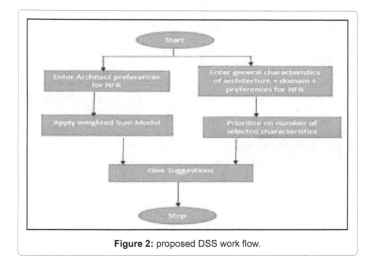

Figure 2: proposed DSS work flow.

Decision making problem is the process of finding the best option from all of the feasible alternatives. DSS is a computer-based system which supports a decision, in any way. DSS will essentially solve or give options for solving a given problem. A DSS provides support for all phases of the (semi-structured and unstructured) decision making process and a variety of decision making processes. It should be easy to use meanwhile providing support for users at all levels to make decision [11]. Decision support systems can be classified in several ways. One well-known classification is to put them into six frameworks [11]:

1) text-oriented which emphasizes on creating, revising and reviewing documents; 2) database-oriented in which the database organization is of importance and the emphasize is most on query capabilities and generating strong reports; 3) spread sheet-oriented which allows the user to develop models to execute DSS analysis; 4) solver oriented DSS which use solver for solving a particular type of problem; 5) rule-oriented DSS in which the knowledge component, which often is an expert system, includes procedural and inferential rules; 6) compound DSS which is a combination of two or more of classifications mentioned above.

Working of proposed DSS

In order to select an architectural style from given choices of architecture styles correctly and precisely, all existing information related to the application should be considered. The proposed DSS will use characteristics of web service architectural styles, domain characteristics of application being developed and NFR (Non-functional requirements) weight age as input for inference and provides appropriate decision complete design of proposed DSS is depicted in Figure 2 in detail [12].

The proposed DSS has five essential components that help in decision making process that are:

- Repositories
- Tool
- Rule-based
- Decision making (CLIPS)
- User interface

Obligations and concerns of every part alongside what they accommodate the DSS is explained as follows.

Repository: We have three types of repositories which are DC (Domain Characteristics), NFRC (Non-Functional Requirements Characteristics) and ASC(Architectural Style Characteristics) [13]. In DC we have characteristics regarding requirements for different domains like e-commerce, banking, health care apps and others. NFRC contains characteristics provided by different quality attributes and also information regarding no. of sub-attributes of quality attribute provided by specific web service architectural style [14]. ASC have information of all the characteristics of web service architectural styles SOA, ROA and MOA respectively. The characteristics considered in repository in proposed DSS are summarized in Tables 1, 2 and 3.

Table 1 shows the characteristics that MOA, SOA and ROA possess in order to fulfill the requirements of app being developed whose nature is SO (Service-Oriented). Now comparison w.r.t NFR characteristics are given in Table 2. Three NFRs are under considerations mainly security, reliability and performance.

Table 2 showing which characteristics of NFR each architectural style possess with assigned weights to be considered as inputs for system.Now comparison w.r.t domain characteristics is summarized in Table 3.

Tools: Domain characteristic and Architectural stylescharacteristics would be prioritized on basis of no. of characteristics selected. After getting all the required information and priorities of quality attributes, the weighted sum model for NFR's would be applied to DSS and no. of characteristics required of specific web service architectural style and domain characteristics would already be counted while gathering information according to the need of app being developed as shown in Figure 3.

Architectural Characteristics	MOA	SOA	ROA
Heterogeneity	Yes	Yes	Yes
Protocol layering	No	Yes	Yes
Loose coupling	Yes	Yes	yes
Integration style	Yes	Yes	Yes
Resource identification	No	No	yes
URI design	No	No	Yes
Resource interaction semantic	No	No	yes
Resource relationship	No	No	Yes
Contract design	No	Yes	Yes
Data representation	Yes	Yes	Yes
Message exchange pattern	Yes	Yes	Yes
Traffic monitoring	Yes	No	No
Traffic determination	Yes	No	No
Traffic transformation	Yes	No	No
Service description	Yes	Yes	Yes
Service identification	Yes	Yes	Yes
Service discovery	Yes	Yes	Yes
Service composition	Yes	Yes	Yes

Table 1: Architectural characteristics comparison.

NFR	Characteristics	MOA	SOA	ROA
Security	Encryption	Yes, 2	Yes ,2	Yes, 1
	Integrity	Yes, 1	Yes, 2	Yes, 1
	Authentication	Yes, 1	Yes, 2	Yes, 1
	Authorization	Yes, 1	Yes, 2	Yes, 1
	Non-repudiation	Yes, 1	Yes, 2	Yes, 1
	Confidentiality	Yes, 1	Yes, 2	Yes, 1
Sum of weight (S)		**7**	**12**	**6**
Reliability	Point-to-Point	Yes, 1	Yes, 1	Yes, 1
	Ordered delivery of msg	No, 0	Yes, 2	Yes, 1
	Delivery status	Yes, 1	Yes, 1	Yes, 1
	Elimination of duplicate message	Yes, 1	Yes, 1	Yes, 1
	Resending message	Yes, 1	Yes, 1	No, 0
	Reliable delivery of msg	Yes, 1	Yes, 2	Yes, 1
Sum of weight (R)		**5**	**8**	**5**
Performance	Caching	Yes, 1	No, 0	Yes, 1
	Clustering	Yes, 1	No, 0	Yes, 1
	Load balancing	Yes, 1	No, 0	Yes, 1
	Throughput	Yes, 1	Yes, 2	Yes, 3
	Response time	Yes, 1	Yes, 2	Yes, 3
	Latency	Yes, 2	Yes, 1	Yes, 3
	Execution time	Yes, 2	Yes, 1	Yes, 3
Sum of weight (P)		**9**	**6**	**15**

Table 2: NFR characteristics comparison.

Domain characteristics	MOA	SOA	ROA
Functionality	Yes	Yes	Yes
App type	Yes	Yes	Yes
Run offline	Yes	No	No

Table 3: Domain characteristics comparison.

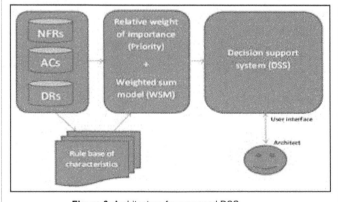

Figure 3: Architecture for proposed DSS.

Where weighted sum model (WSM) is the best known and simplest multi-criteria decision analysis (MCDA) method for evaluating a number of alternatives in terms of a number of decision criteria [2].

In general, suppose that a given MCDA problem is defined on m alternatives and n decision criteria. Furthermore, let us assume that all the criteria are benefit criteria, that is, the higher the values are, the better it is. Next suppose that w_j denotes the relative weight of importance of the criterion C_j and a_{ij} is the performance value of alternative A_i when it is evaluated in terms of criterion C_j. Then, the total (i.e., when all the

criteria are considered simultaneously) importance of alternative A_i, denoted as A_iWSM-score, is defined as follows:

$$A_i^{WSM\text{-}Score} = \sum_{j=1} w_j a_{ij}, \text{ for } i = 1, 2, 3, \ldots, m. \quad (1)$$

In our case architectures SOA, ROA and MOA are alternatives as (A_i) and quality attributes security, reliability and performance are criteria's as (C_j).

General characteristics of architectures are rules in DSS and priority will be given to the highest number of characteristics selected of specific architecture. For example if we have selected 20 characteristics of SOA, 17 of ROA and 10 of MOA then DSS will recommend SOA [15-18].

The rules, which were extracted from architecture styles characteristics, NFRS, domain characteristics, and the priorities, and incorporated by DSS user i.e. system architect, are used as inputs of the tool as in Figure 4.

Rule Base: For extracting decision, there is need of some rules on the basis of our repositories DC, NFRC and ASC. Simply we can say, rules decide which domain characteristics are required, which characteristics of architecture are required, what is the importance level of each quality attribute. These rules would be stored in rule-based engine and then would be obtained with help of repositories. Rule is generally defined as:

$$P \rightarrow Q \text{ or if P then Q} \quad (2)$$

Where P would be characteristics of architecture, domain characteristics or any NFR and Q would be preferred architecture prioritization according to P.

Total 108 rules are implemented in DSS based on characteristics explained earlier

Decision maker (CLIPS): CLIPS has been used for development of rule based Decision Support System as CLIPS is one of the generally utilized AI (Artificial Intelligence) apparatus utilized for Rule-based DSS. CLIPS gives a firm tool to taking care of a wide mixture of information. Rule-based programming permits heuristics, otherwise "thumb rule," that tag a group of activities executed in specified circumstance [7].

CLIPS help in dealing with the obligation of this part, indeed, accepting as well as sending data to and from every segments belong to DSS. Interface is a "data communicator" possesses an obligation to get needs that the DSS user gave to system through client interface as well as give it to tool as an information that is part of DSS for utilization of it. The priorities entered by software architect become inputs for

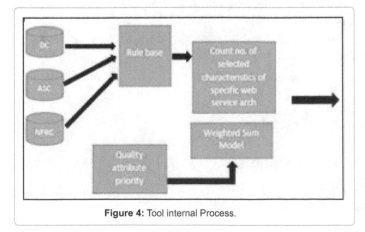

Figure 4: Tool internal Process.

weighted sum model tool that is used for NFRs. Subsequently attaining results after applying WSM, and oblige utilizing different attributes data that are given via software architect, CLIPS inference engine will do surmising on premise of guidelines chain of command. At that point architectural style or may be combination of architectural styles would be suggested for the app under development. The results would be sent to client interface for displaying. Accordingly, DSS dictate recommendations towards the software architect so as to pick most appropriate architecture by utilizing expertise [19,20].

User interface: The user interface is in charge of accepting the data from client in regards to domain qualities needed, which attributes of architectural style are obliged, what is the essentialness level of every quality characteristics as per the way of application being produced; the received data is entered to the decision making tool. In addition, speaking toessential data required by user got via decision making or retrieved via repositories is also the obligation of client interface. The proposed architectural style is spoken to software architect as a recommendation according to need via client interface. The software architect or other vital stake holders could choose the suitable architectural style or styles between proposed one's regarding his insight around the issue.

Actors for interface

The actors for system are as follows:

- Software architect
- Developer
- Technical client

All these actors interact with system by giving desired input i.e. preferred weightage for NFRs security, performance and reliability, then select required characteristics of architecture and domain. Then actors would have recommendations from DSS and can select architecture with highest weightage. The abstract level interface that may appear for actors is depicted in Figure 4. The interface showing the initial inputs.

Automated Architecture Selection

To get a better understanding of our approach we have conducted a hypothetical case study. For this purpose we have identified use case for which architects have to develop web services. In this whole process we consider following Requirements for architectural style selection:

- Business Requirements
- Functional Requirements
- Non Functional Requirements

Along with these requirements we also cater for specific architectural style characteristics and prioritization inputs.

USE CASE: Online Book Order Service

Business requirements: Consider requirements for ordering abook online. Different clients should be able to place online orders for books using this web service in various online stores.

FR01: A client logs onto the book retailer's site and rings a rundown of the obliged articles.

FR02: A request is intended to the "check accessibility" administration which supplies data to the web entrance as to the amount at present in stock.

FR03: The client submits the request for the obliged articles/ books. Order web Service then issues a quotation. The "quotation issue" service demonstrates the cost of the products requested by the individual client making due note of the client status (e.g. rebates, conditions, and so on.).

FR04: In the event that the online payment is done, the payment is acknowledged, and the merchandise are assigned for dispatch. The "send" service exchanges all the essential data to the dispatch system, including the client's conveyance and charging location.

Key Non functional Requirements are:

- NFR01- Security
- NFR02 – Performance
- NFR03 – Reliability

We have considered multicriterian requirements to take input for rule based DSS including general characteristics. A decision problem described over three alternatives A1, A2, A3 namely SOA, ROA and MOA which defined via four criteria C1, C2, and C3 namely Security, Performance plus Reliability. DSS will take weightage of NFR's from architect on basis of the preferences for given case study. The interaction between system and architect is depicted in Figure 5.

The architect would enter weightage for NFR on scale of 1 to 5 where 5 means highly preferred and 1 means less preferred. There are three styles for this use case: Service-Oriented Architecture, Resource-Oriented Architecture also called RESTful, and Message-Oriented Architecture. The satisfaction level of every NFR via different web service architectural styles is summarized in Table 4.

The weightage for each factor is entered as input into system as follows:

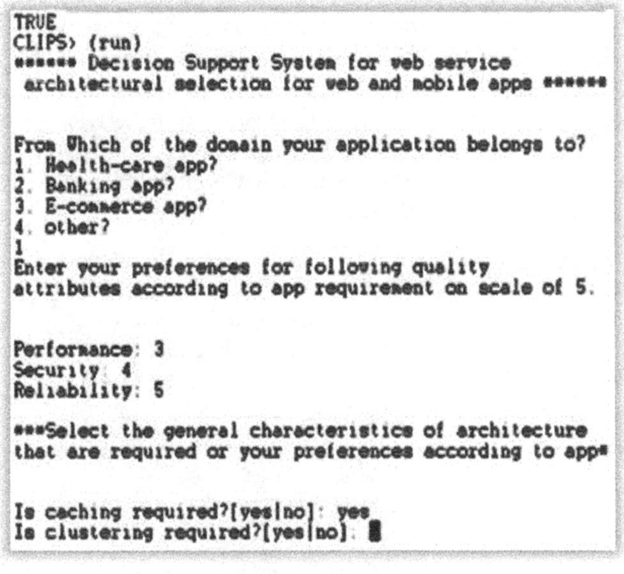

Figure 5: DSS CLIPS interface.

Criteria's	Security	Performance	Reliability
Alternative	--	--	--
SOA	6	6	8
ROA	12	15	5
MOA	7	9	5

Table 4: Satisfaction level.

(C1)Security=5, (C2) Performance= 4, (C3) Reliability= 5

Now subsisting these values in equation (1) derived earlier we get:

(SOA): A1 = w1*a11 + w2*a12 + w3*a13

W(A1) = 5*6 + 4*6 + 5*8 = 94

(ROA): A2 = w1*a21 + w2*a22 + w3*a23

W(A2) = 5*12 + 4*15+ 5*5 = 155

(MOA): A3 = w1*a31 + w2*a32 + w3*a33

W(A3) = 5*7 + 4*9+ 5*5 = 96

Here we have calculated NFR weightage for each architectural style under consideration.

By taking these requirements as input shown in Table 5 the following results are generated by DSS. As represented in Table 6.

At least 21 input for architectural characteristics were taken along with weightage for NFRs. After applying weighted sum model to NFR the final weightage for SOA is at 94, ROA is at 155 and MOA is 96. Similarly from architectural and domain characteristics the weightage is 13 for ROA and SOA and 8 for MOA respectively.

Here we get highest value for ROA in relation to Quality attributes and equal weightage for other characteristics. From these results it is very easy for developers and architects to choose the right architecture as for this use case ROA is more suitable architectural style to choose to develop online Book order web service.

Impact on Decision Making Process

By incorporating different elements involved in manual decision making process into an automated DSS we have streamlined the process for architecture selection for a web service. Decision for selection of a particular architecture for software itself is a complex way and it becomes even more difficult when we are selecting a particular architectural style for web service domain. Here we only considered 03 different types Non-functional requirements for 03 said architectural styles. Here our DSS makes sure to incorporate these NFRs to any selected architectural style by using weighted sum model. Trade-offs analysis may also be done between different NFRs at time of selection of a particular architectural style.

108 different rules were constructed as tree to support various requirements. Now if this process would have been manual or left to system architect without any automation, architecture selection could be subjective depending upon expertise leading to high costs and low quality.

NFR weightage	Architectural + domain characteristics
(SOA): A1	Minimum 21 question asked on the basis of architectural and domain repositories
(ROA): A2	
(MOA): A3	

Table 5: Input by architect.

Architectural Style	Weightage w.r.t NFR	Weightage w.r.t architectural characteristics
SOA	94	13
ROA	155	13
MOA	96	8

Table 6: Results.

Here we discuss some advantages and contribution to the domain with respect to related work.

Advantages

The proposed technique has various advantages which lead towards high quality web services development with reduced, cost and overhead for software development teams. Some of them are:

- Simplified Decision making process
- Un biased decision leading to high quality
- Multi-criterion requirements incorporated
- Automated decision making for architecture selection
- Reduced Risk

Contribution to domain

Though the architecture selection is considered totally a manual process and depends on the knowledge and personal experience of the decision makers. Web services architecture selection is trivial as there are multiple architectural patterns and rate of change in these styles is quite rapid. We believe that there is a criteria as well as a process within architects' mind when they deal with architecture style selection but it is totally based on the judgment of the selector. Our core contribution to this domain is that we present a novel way for architecture selection by incorporating multicriteria requirements. The plus point about our work is that we have considered modern styles which are in use in todays cloud and web development environment. Some researchers have worked in traditional software architecture selection [9] using multicriteria approach but this work lacks the indepth validation of fuzzy path analysis. Booth et al. [11] did work on architectural style selection focusing only on quality attributes by applying AHP technique, though it is a good direction in this domain but they did not consider self characteristics of the styles under question. Our research is quite unique in a sense that we have tried to bring all the aspects in decision making process for web services for example NFRs, domain requirements and above all the self characteristics of these styles. Wieghted Sum Model is a proven approach used in our work for calculating the quality attributes weightage. In a similar work titled "ANP-GP Approach for Selection of Software Architecture Styles" [8] focus on quality attributes and balance among architectural style where goals and objectives are considered in the decision making process. Again this work does not target specific style but applies this method in a general way. In contrast to this work we have targeted modern web services styles and gathered all their characteristics using rule base approach for a better decision making.

Future Work

Web services are everywhere in cloud, big data and IOTs so demand for development and consumption in near future shall increase. In future more architectural styles may be explored and incorporated into this DSS. We have focused key Quality attributes; it can be further enhanced to input other NFRs into system. In future a DSS should be extended to not only suggest architectural style but should be capable to generate suggested architecture style skeleton.

Conclusions

Characteristics of architectural styles are different with each other and, therefore, each one has its own strengths and weaknesses in a problem space. Our research has created new dimensions for architectural selection support. Consequently identifying the Non-functional requirements, architectural characteristics and domain requirements.

In this paper a DSS for web service architectural selection has been developed which considers core requirements. It uses weighted sum model for NFRs and architectural and domain requirements are prioritized on basis of selected characteristics using rule based model as knowledge engine. The results obtained from this DSS would help software architects, teams and developers in making precise and efficient decisions. Subsequently it will help improve the overall quality of web service development process.

References

1. Svahnberg M, Karlskrona K (2003) Supporting Software Architecture Evolution. Blekinge Institute of Technology Dissertation Series.

2. Nawaz F, Mohsin A (2015) Rule-Based Multi-criteria Framework for SaaS Application Architecture Selection. Artificial Intelligence in Theory and Practice IV 465: 129-138.

3. Triantaphyllou E (2013) Multi-criteria decision making methods: a comparative study. Springer Science & Business Media.

4. Riley G (2015) What is CLIPS?.

5. Mumbaikar S, Padiya P (2013) Web Services Based On SOAP and REST Principles. International Journal of Scientific and Research Publications 3: 1-4.

6. Chen Z (1999) Computational intelligence for decision support. CRC Press.

7. Wang Q, Yang Z (2012) A method of selecting appropriate software architecture styles: Quality Attributes and Analytic Hierarchy Process. Bachelor of Science Thesis, University of Gothenburg.

8. Babu KD, Govindarajulu P, Ramamohana Reddy A, Aruna Kumari A (2011) ANP-GP approach for selection of software architecture styles. Int J Softw Eng 1: 91-104.

9. Moaven S, Habibi J, Ahmadi H, Kamandi A (2008) A decision support system for software architecture-style selection. Software Engineering Research, Management and Applications, 2008. SERA'08, Sixth International Conference, Prague.

10. Belqasmi F, Singh J, Melhem SYB, Glitho RH (2012) SOAP-based vs. RESTful web services: A case study for multimedia conferencing. IEEE Internet Computing 54-63.

11. Booth D, Hass H, McCab F (2004) Web Services Architecture, W3C Working Group Note.

12. Fielding RT, Taylor RN (2002) Principled design of the modern Web architecture. ACM Transactions on Internet Technology (TOIT) 2: 115-150.

13. Pautasso C, Zimmermann O, Leymann F (2008) Restful web services vs. big'web services: making the right architectural decision. Proceedings of the 17th international conference on World Wide Web.

14. Wagh K, Thool R (2012) A comparative study of soap vs rest web services provisioning techniques for mobile host. Journal of Information Engineering and Applications 2: 12-16.

15. Muehlen MZ, Nickerson JV, Swenson KD (2005) Developing web services choreography standards—the case of REST vs. SOAP. Decision Support Systems 40: 9-29.

16. Dudhe A, Sherekar SS (2014) Performance Analysis of SOAP and RESTful Mobile Web Services in Cloud Environment. IJCA Special Issue on Recent Trends In Information Security RTINFOSEC: 1-4.

17. Lofthouse H, Yates MJ, Stretch R (2004) Parlay X Web Services. BT Tech J 22: 81-86.

18. Turban E, Liang TP, Aronson JE (2006) Decision Support Systems and Intelligent Systems. Seventh Edition.

19. Curry E (2004) Message Oriented Middleware. Middleware of Communications, John Wiley and sons, Chichester, England.

20. Fielding RT (2000) Architecture Styles and Design of Network based Software Architectures. University of California Irvine.

28

Job Scheduling based on Harmonization between the Requested and Available Processing Power in the Cloud Computing Environment

Elhossiny Ibrahim[1]*, Nirmeen A El-Bahnasawy[1] and Fatma A Omara[2]

[1]Computer Science and Engineering Department, Cairo University, Menouf 32952, Egypt
[2]Faculty of Computers and Information, Cairo University, Egypt

Abstract

The Cloud Computing is a most recent computing paradigm where IT services are provided and delivered over the Internet on demand and pay as you go. On the other hands, the taskscheduling problem is considered one of the main challenges in the Cloud Computing environment, where a good mapping between the available resources and the users's tasks is needed to reduce the execution time of the users' tasks (i.e., reduce make-span), in the same time, increase the degree of capitalization from resources (i.e., increase resource utilization).

In this paper, a new task scheduling algorithm has been proposed and implemented to reduce the make-span, as well as, increase the resources utilization by considering independent tasks. The proposed algorithm is based on calculating the total processing power of the available resources (i.e., VMs) and the total requested processing power by the users' tasks,then allocating a group of users' tasks to each VM according to the ratio of its needed power corresponding to the total processing power of all VMs.

To evaluate the performance of the proposed algorithm, a comparative study has been done among the proposed algorithm, and the existed GA, and PSO algorithms. The experimental results show that the proposed algorithm outperforms other algorithms by reducing make-span and increasing the resources utilization.

Keywords: Cloud computing; Task scheduling; Particle swarm optimization; Genetic algorithm

Introduction

The Cloud Computing allows the users to use the computational resources and services of the data centers (i.e., machines, network, storage, operating systems, application development environments, application programs) through the Internet [1]. The main feature of the Cloud Computing is that it provides self-provisioning of IT resources [2]. The Cloud Computing architecture is categorized as layers; service model, and deployment model (types). The deployment models are public, private, hybrid, community, and federated, while the Cloud Computing services are divided into Software as a Service (SaaS), Platform as a Services (PaaS), and Infrastructure as a Services (IaaS) [3]. By this classification, the users can easily choose the suitable cloud services and types to fit their requirements according to these services [1,3].

The main advantages of the cloud is that servers and IT equipments are collected in a single place or distributed over different data centers and can be access remotely. So, the Users can access the cloud services through the Internet by using mobile, PC, laptop, PDA, etc. (Figure 1) [4].

In the Cloud Computing, there are some issues should be concerned. The main issues are resource management and task scheduling. Therefore, the main function of the Cloud providers is to provide the services to the users by deploying virtual machines (VMs), and defining scheduling policies to allocate VMs to the users' requests [5].

In this paper, a new task scheduling algorithm has been proposed. The main principle of the proposed algorithm is based on calculating the total processing power of the available resources (i.e., VMs) and the total requested processing power by the users' requests,then allocating a group of the users's requests to each VM according to the ratio of its needed power corresponding to the total processing power of all VMs. To evaluate the performance of the proposed algorithm, a comparative study has been done among the proposed algorithm, the existed GA, and PSO algorithms. The experimental results show that our algorithm

outperforms other algorithms by minimizing the total execution time of the users' requests and increasing the utilization of the resources.

The remainder of the paper is organised as follows. In Section

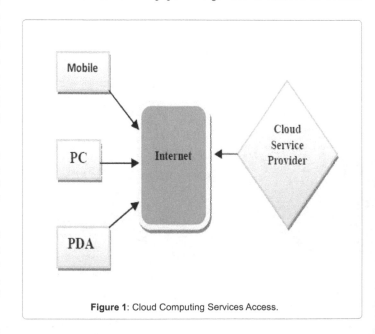

Figure 1: Cloud Computing Services Access.

*Corresponding author: Elhossiny Ibrahim, Faculty of Electronic Engineering, Computer Science and Engineering Department,Cairo University, Menouf 32952, Egypt, E-mail: elhossiny.ibrahim@el-eng.menofia.edu.eg

II, the related work is illustrated followed by the fundamental of our proposed task scheduling algorithm in Section III. In Section IV, the performance evaluation of the proposed algorithm via Cloudsim simulator and the comparative study are discussed. Finally, in Section V, we will conclude our contributions and point out the future work.

Related Work

Yun et al. [6] have proposed an innovative transaction intensive cost-constraint scheduling algorithm to minimize the cost and the execution time. The simulation results proved that this algorithm could minimize the cost while meeting the user designated deadline. Suraj Pandey et al. [7] have proposed a heuristic task scheduling to minimize the cost of task-resource mapping using particle swarm optimization (PSO) algorithm. According to the simulation results, it is found that the proposed algorithm can achieve as much as 3 times cost savings as compared to BRS, and good distribution of workload onto resources. Ke Liu et al. [8] have presented a Compromised-Time-Cost (CTC) scheduling algorithm. The CTC algorithm considers the characteristics of Cloud Computing toaccommodate instance-intensive cost-constrained workflows by compromising the execution time and cost of the users' tasks which areenabled on the fly. The simulation results has demonstrated that the CTC algorithm can achieve lower costwhile meeting the user-designated deadline or reducing the mean execution time within the user- designated execution cost. Parsa and Reza [9] have proposed a taskscheduling algorithm called Resource-Aware-Scheduling (RASA). It is considered an amalgamation of two traditional scheduling algorithms; Max-min and Min-min. Therefore, the deadline of each task, arriving rate of the tasks, cost of the task execution on each of the resource, and cost of the communication are not considered. The experimental results proved that RASA algorithm outperforms the existing scheduling algorithms in large scale distributed systems. Huang [10] has proposed a workflow task scheduling algorithm based on the genetic algorithms (GA) model in the Cloud Computing environment. The experimental results proved that the efficiency of resource allocation has been satisfies, and in the same time, minimized the completion time. Lei Zhang et al. [11] have proposed a PSO algorithm. This proposed algorithm is similar to the genetic algorithms (GA). The aim of this algorithm is to improves the efficiency of resource allocation and minimize the completion time simultaneously. It is noted that the performance of PSO usually spent shorter time to accomplish the various scheduling tasks and specifies better result comparing to the GA algorithm. Also, they have proved that the PSO algorithm can get better effect for a large scale optimization problem. Cui Lin and Shiyong Lu [12] have proposed an Scalable Heterogeneous Earliest-Finish-Time Algorithm (SHEFT) workflow scheduling algorithm to schedule a workflow elastically on a Cloud Computing environment. The experimental results show that SHEFT is not only outperform several representative workflow scheduling algorithms in optimizingworkflow execution time, but also enable resources to scale elastically at runtime. Visalakshi and Sivanandam [13] have presented Hybrid Particle Swarm Optimization (HPSO) method for solving the Task Assignment Problem (TAP) by dynamically schedule heterogeneous tasks on to heterogeneous processors in a distributed setup. The HPSO yields a better result. The experimental result of the HPSO algorithm has proved that the PSO outperforms the GA algorithm. Selvarani and Sudha Sadhasivam [14] have proposed animproved cost-based scheduling algorithm for making efficient mapping of tasks to available resources in the cloud. This scheduling algorithm divides all user tasks depending on the priority of each task into three differentlists. This scheduling algorithm measures both resource cost and computation performance. Also, it

improves the computation/communication ratio. Yang et al. [15] have highlighted theissue of job scheduling in the Cloud Computing with considering hardware/softwarefailure and recovery. They have proposed a Reinforcement Learning (RL(based algorithm that helps the scheduler to define scheduling decision with fault tolerable while maximizing utilities attained in the long term.

The Proposed Algorithm

According to the work in this paper, a new task scheduling algorithm on the Cloud Computing environment has been proposed. The main idea of the proposed algorithm is that allocating the available VMs to the requested tasks according to the following steps:-

1.   Calculate the total available processing power of the available VMs (i.e., VM_MIPS).

2.   Calculate the total requested processing power by the users' tasks (TASKS_MIPs).

3.   Calculate the power factor (PF) of each available resource (VMi)using equation (1).

PF of VMi= (Processing Power of VMi) / (To tal Processing Power of All VMs)   (1)

4.   Calculate the allotment for each existed resource (VMi) as equation (2).

VM_iallotment =PF *(total requested processing power (TASKS_MIPs))   (2)

5.   Search the requested tasks to find a task or a group of tasks which need processing power equal to or less than the allotment of the VMi as calculated in step (4) by considering that the different between the selected tasks processing power and VM allotment to be minimum.

The pseudo code of the proposed algorithm is as follows:

```
Input:
        Number n of cloudlets (i.e., tasks).
        Number m of VMs (i.e., resources).
Output:
Mapping Scheme for the requested tasks (cloudlets) on the available
resources (VMs).
// calculate the total processing power of cloudlets
1 for i=1 to n do
2    Define MIPS of the cloudlet
3 endfor
// calculate the total processing power of VMs.
4 for i=1 to  m do
5    Define MIPS of the  VMs
// calculate the power factor of each VM, and the allotment of each VM
6 for i=1 to m do
7    PF of VMi = processing power of VMi / total processing power
of all VMS
8    VMiallotment =PF *(total requested processing power (TASKS_MIPs).
9    find the sum of set(VMiallotment).
10 endfor
11    Select a set of cloudlets with the sum of their MIPs equal to/
or less VMiallotment.
12    return the set.
```

Performance Evaluation

To evaluate the performance of the proposed algorithm, a comparative study has been done among the proposed algorithm and the GA, PSO, and First-Come-First-Serve (FCFS) algorithms by considering two performance parameters; Make-span, and resource utilization.

Experimental environment

The proposed task scheduling algorithm has been written by java programming language using eclipse program in Intel(R) Core(TM) 2 Duo CPU in 2.10 GHZ of processor and 4.00 GB of RAM, through the CloudSim simulator. On the other hands, CloudSim is an extensible simulation toolkit that enables modeling and simulation of Cloud Computing systems and application provisioning environments. The CloudSim toolkit supports both system and behavior modeling of the Cloud system components such as data centers, virtual machines (VMs) and resource provisioning policies. The Cloudsim Implements generic application provisioning techniques that can be extended with ease and limited efforts [16]. According to the implementation using Cloudsim, the VMs are considered the cloud resources and Cloudlets as tasks/jobs. We have measured the make-span of different algorithms by considering varying the cloudlets while VMs are fixed, as well as, varying VMs.

Cloudlets were generated from a standard formatted workload of a High performance computing center called HPC2N in Sweden as a benchmark. According to this benchmark, Each row in the workload represents a cloudlet where we get the id of the cloudlet from the first column, the length of the cloudlet from the fourth column (the runtime value multiplied by the rating which is defined as 1 MI in CloudSim), and finally the number of the requested processing elements from the eighth column [17].

Experimental results

Two parameters have been used to measure the performance of the task scheduling algorithms; make-span, and utilization ratio. Make-span is the overall completion time needed to assign all the tasks to the available resources (i.e., VMs). Utilization ratio is the average amount of time in which the cloud resources are busy. It ranges from 0 to 1 [4].

Mak-span results

The experimental results of our proposed algorithm, PSO, GA, and FCFS algorithms are presented in Figures 2-4, using different VMs, as well as, different cloudlets (jobs/tasks). According to the experimental results in Figure 2 with considering 5 VMs, it is found that the performance of our proposed algorithm outperforms PSO,

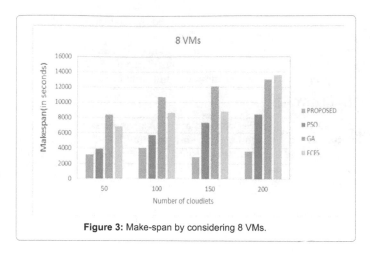

Figure 3: Make-span by considering 8 VMs.

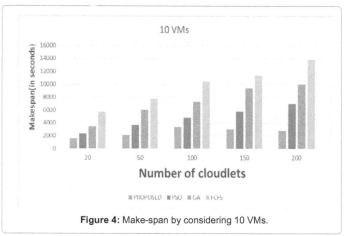

Figure 4: Make-span by considering 10 VMs.

GA, and FCFS algorithms with respect to the total execution time (i.e., makespan) by 59.68%, 71.1%, and 47.2% respectively. The overall performance of the proposed algorithm (i.e., average improvement) is 59.35% relative to the PSO, GA, and FCFS algorithms (Figure 2).

According to the experimental results in Figure 3 with considering 8 VMs, it is found that the performance of our proposed algorithm outperforms PSO, GA, and FCFS algorithms by 53.46%, 30.88%, and 35.97% respectively. The overall performance of the proposed algorithm performance is 40.1% relative to the PSO, GA, and FCFS algorithms (Figure 3).

By considering 10 VMs, the experimental results in Figure 4 proved that the performance of our proposed algorithm outperforms PSO, GA, and FCFS algorithms by 55%, 36%, and 26.46% respectively. The overall performance of the proposed algorithm performance is 39.15% relative to the PSO, GA, and FCFS algorithms.

Generally, by calculating the average performance of our proposed algorithm , SO, GA, and FCFS algorthms, it is found that the proposed algorithm outperforms PSO, GA, and FCFS by 57.7%, 51.2%, and 39.89% respectively. And the overall performance of the proposed algorithm is 49.6% relative to PSO, GA, and FCFS algorithms (Figure 4).

Conclusion and Future Work

Task scheduling is one of the main issues in the Cloud Computing. Efficient task scheduling is essential for saving the time and utilizing the resources. In this paper, a task scheduling algorithm has been

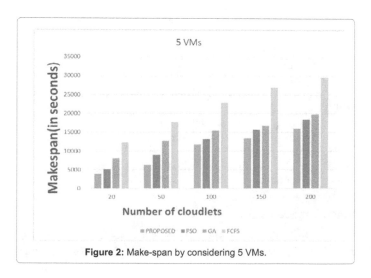

Figure 2: Make-span by considering 5 VMs.

proposed for the Cloud Computing environment. The main idea of the proposed algorithm is that allocating the available VMs to the requested tasks by considering the processing power of VMs and tasks. To evaluate the performance of the proposed algorithm, a comparative study has been done among our proposed algorithm, PSO, GA, and FCFS algorithms. The experimental results prove the efficiency of our proposed algorithm by minimizing make-span by 49.6% , in addition, increasing the utilization ratio. The proposed task scheduling algorithm could be further extended by considering the cost, as well as, the memory size. Also, the proposed algorithm could be modified by considering dependent tasks.

References

1. Soror AA, Minhas UF, Aboulnaga A, Salem K, Kokosielis P, et al. (2009) Deploying Database Appliances in the Cloud. IEEE Data Eng Bull 32: 13-20.

2. Jangra A, Saini T (2013) Scheduling Optimization in Cloud Computing. International Journal of Advanced Research in Computer Science and Software Engineering 3: 62-65.

3. Furht B, Escalante A (2010) Handbook of Cloud Computing. Springer Science+Business Media, LLC.

4. Kaur R, Kinger S (2014) Analysis of Job Scheduling Algorithms in Cloud Computing. International Journal of Computer Trends and Technology 9: 379-386.

5. Pandaa SK, Guptab I, Janac PK (2015) Allocation-Aware Task Scheduling for Heterogeneous Multi-Cloud Systems. Science Direct 50: 176-184.

6. Yang Y, Liu K, Chen J, Liu X, Yaun D, et al. (2008) An Algorithm in SwinDeW-C for Scheduling Transaction- Intensive Cost-Constrained Cloud Workflows. Proc. of 4th IEEE International Conference on e-Science, Indianapolis, USA.

7. Pandey S, Wu L, Guru S, Buyya R (2010) A Particle Swarm Optimization (PSO)-based Heuristic for Scheduling Workflow Applications in Cloud Computing Environments. Proceedings of the 24th IEEE International Conference on Advanced Information Networking and Applications (AINA), Perth, Australia.

8. Ke Liu, Hai Jin, Chen J, Liu X, Yuan D, et al. (2010) A Compromised-Time-Cost Scheduling Algorithm in SwinDeW-C for Instance-Intensive Cost-Constrained Workflows on a Cloud Computing Platform. International Journal of High Performance Computing Applications 24: 445-456.

9. Parsa S, Maleki RE (2009) RASA: A New Task Scheduling Algorithm in Grid Environment. World Applied Sciences Journal (Special Issue of Computer and IT) 152-160.

10. Huang J (2014) The Workflow Task Scheduling Algorithm Based on the GA Model in the Cloud Computing Environment. Journal of Software 9: 873-880.

11. Zhang L, Chen Y, Sun R, Jing S, Yang B (2008) A Task Scheduling Algorithm Based on PSO for Grid Computing. International Journal of Computational Intelligence Research 4: 37-43.

12. Lin C, Lu S (2011) Scheduling ScientificWorkflows Elastically for Cloud Computing. IEEE 4th International Conference on Cloud Computing, Washington.

13. Visalakshi P, Sivanandam SN (2009) Dynamic Task Scheduling with Load Balancing using Hybrid Particle Swarm Optimization. International Journal of Open Problems in Computer Science and Mathematics, ICSRS Publication 2: 476-488.

14. Selvarani S, Sadhasivam GS (2010) Improved Cost-based Algorithm for Task Scheduling in Cloud Computing. IEEE International Conference, Computational Intelligence and Computing Research, India.

15. Yang B, Xu X, Tan F, Parket DH (2011) An Utility- based Job Scheduling Algorithm for Cloud Computing Considering Reliability Factor. Proceedings of the 2011 International Conference on Cloud and Service Computing, IEEE Xplore Press, Hong Kong.

16. Singh S, Kalra M (2014) Task Scheduling Optimization of Independent Tasks in Cloud Computing Using Enhanced Genetic Algorithm. International Journal of Application or Innovation in Engineering & Management 3: 286-291.

17. U. University (2006) The HPC2N Seth log.

29

Software Architecture Methodology in Agile Environments

Mehdi Mekni*, Mounika G, Sandeep C and Gayathri B

Department of Computer Science and Information Technology, St. Cloud State University, St. Cloud, Minnesota, USA

Abstract

Lengthy requirements, design, integration, test, and assurance cycles delay software delivery, resulting in late discovery of mismatched assumptions and system level rework. In response, development methods that enable frequent iterations with small increments of functionality, such as agile practices, have become popular. However, since the business goals and context continuously evolve, the software architecture must also change. Currently, a clear specification in software architecture activities and processes in agile environments does not exist. In this paper, we provide an overview on agile development methodology along with the software architecture related issues in agile environments. Our main contribution is a novel methodology to guide and assist practitioners adopting software architectural design in agile environments.

Keywords: Agile methodology; Software development life-cycle; Software architectural design

Introduction

Software development projects seeking rapid, sustainable delivery are combining agile and architecture practices to manage competing goals of speed in the short term and stability over the long term [1-3]. A software development lifecycle is essentially a series of steps, or phases including requirement specification; software design; software construction; software verification and validation; and software deployment. These phases provide a model for the development and management of software [4].

Software architectural design is the process of applying various techniques and principles for the purpose of defining a module, a process, or a system in sufficient detail to permit its physical coding. The conventional approach to the software design process focuses on partitioning a problem and its solution into detailed pieces up front before proceeding to the construction phase. These up front software architecture efforts are critical and leave no room to accommodate changing requirements later in the development cycle. Some of the issues faced by organizations involved in up front software design efforts are [5,6]:

- Requirements evolve over time due to changes in customer and user needs, technological advancement and schedule constraints.

- Changes to requirements systematically involves modifying the software design, and in turn, the code.

- Accommodating changing software design is an expensive critical activity in the face of rapidly changing requirements.

- Clear specification of activities in the agile software design process is missing and there is a lack of a set of techniques for practitioners to choose from [7].

There is an obvious need for a software architectural design approach in agile environments. To the best of our knowledge, no well-established software design methodology has been proposed in any literature. These are issues of software architecture while fully supporting the fundamentals of agile software development methods.

The rest of the paper is organized as follows: Section 2 provides an overview of existing agile methods. Section 3 details the software architecture design phase as a key part of the software development life-cycle. Section 4 presents the proposed software architectural design methodology in agile environments. Section 5 discusses the outcomes and limits of the proposed methodology. Finally, Section 6 concludes and presents the future perspectives of this work.

Agile Development Methods

The goal of agile methods is to allow an organization to be agile, but what does it mean to be Agile. Agile means being able to "Deliver quickly"; "Change quickly and often" [8]. While agile techniques vary in practices and emphasis, they follow the same principles behind the agile manifesto [9]:

- Working software is delivered frequently (weeks rather than months).

- Working software is the principal measure of progress.

- Customer satisfaction by rapid, continuous delivery of useful software.

- Late changes in software requirements are accepted.

- Close daily cooperation between business people and software developers.

- Face-to-face conversation is the best form of communication.

- Projects are built around motivated individuals who should be trusted.

- Continuous attention to technical excellence and good design.

Agile development methods have been designed to solve the problem of delivering high quality software on time under constantly and rapidly changing requirements and business environments. Agile methods have a proven track record in the software and IT industries. The main benefit of agile development software is allowing for an adaptive process in which the team and development react to and handle changes in requirements and specifications, even late in the development process. Figure 1 illustrates an abstract view of the evolutionary map of main agile development methods.

Through the use of multiple working iterations, the implementation

*Corresponding author: Mehdi Mekni, Department of Computer Science and Information Technology, St. Cloud State University, St. Cloud, Minnesota, USA
E-mail: mmekni@stcloudstate.edu

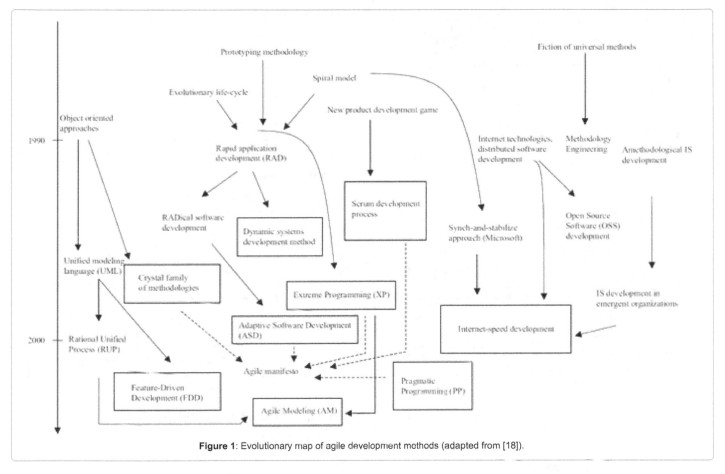

Figure 1: Evolutionary map of agile development methods (adapted from [18]).

of agile methods allows the creation of quality, functional software with small teams and limited resources. The proponents of the traditional development methods criticize the agile methods for the lightweight documentation and inability to cooperate within the traditional workflow. The main limitations of agile development are: agile works well for small to medium sized teams; also agile development methods do not scale, i.e., due to the number of iterations involved it would be difficult to understand the current project status; in addition, an agile approach requires highly motivated and skilled individuals which would not always be available; lastly, not enough written documentation in agile methods leads to information loss when the code is actually implemented. However, with proper implementation agile methods can complement and benefit traditional development methods. Furthermore, it should be noted that traditional development methods in non-iterative fashions are susceptible to late stage design breakage, while agile methodologies effectively solve this problem by frequent incremental builds which encourage changing requirements. We will now describe some common agile methods from a requirements engineering perspective.

Agile modeling (AM)

It is a new approach for performing modeling activities [10]. It gives developers a guideline of how to build models using an agile philosophy as its backbone that resolve design problems and support documentation purposes but not 'over build' these models (Figure 2). The aim is to keep the amount of models and documentation as low as possible.

Feature-driven development (FDD)

It consists of a minimalist, five step processes that focuses on

building and design phases each defined with entry and exit criteria, building a features list, and then planning by feature followed by iterative design by feature and build by feature steps [11]. In the first phase, the overall domain model is developed by domain experts and developers. The overall model consists of class diagrams with classes, relationships, methods, and attributes. The methods express functionality and are the base for building a feature list (Figure 3). A feature in FDD is a client valued function. The feature lists is prioritized by the team. The feature lists are reviewed by domain members [12]. FDD proposes a weekly 30 minute meeting in which the status of the features are discussed and a report about the meeting is written.

Dynamic systems development method (DSDM)

It was developed in the U.K. in the mid-1990s [13]. It is an outgrowth of, and extension to, Rapid Application Development (RAD) practices [14]. The first two phases of DSDM are the feasibility study and the business study. During these two phases the base requirements are elicited (Figure 4). DSDM has nine principles include active user involvement, frequent delivery, team decision making, integrated testing throughout the project life cycle, and reversible changes in development.

Extreme programming (XP)

It is based on values of simplicity, communication, feedback, and courage [15]. XP aims at enabling successful software development despite vague or constantly changing software requirements (Figure 5). XP relies on methods the individual practices are collected and lined up to function with each other. Some of the main practices of XP are short iterations with small releases and rapid feedback, close customer

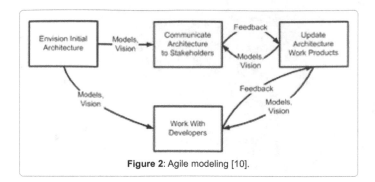

Figure 2: Agile modeling [10].

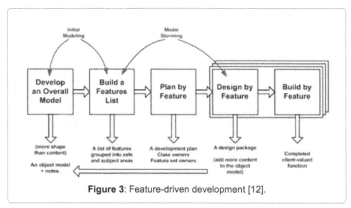

Figure 3: Feature-driven development [12].

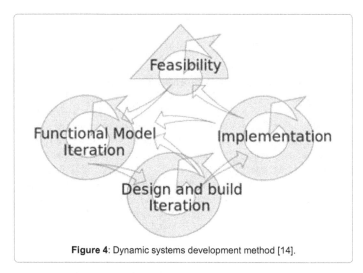

Figure 4: Dynamic systems development method [14].

participation, constant communication and coordination, continuous refactoring, continuous integration and testing, and pair programming [16].

Scrum

Scrum is an empirical approach based on flexibility, adaptability and productivity [17]. Scrum allows developers to choose the specific software development techniques, methods, and practices for the implementation process. Scrum provides a project management framework that focuses development into 30 day Sprint cycles in which a specified set of Backlog features are delivered. The core practice in Scrum is the use of daily 15 minute team meetings for coordination and integration. Scrum has been in use for nearly ten years and has been used to successfully deliver a wide range of products. Figure 6 details the workflow of the Scrum agile software development.

Crystal methodology

It is a family of different approaches from which the appropriate methodologies can be chosen for each project [18]. Different members of the family can be tailored to fit varying circumstances. The members are indexed by different colors to indicate the "heaviness" Clear, Yellow, Orange, Red, Magenta, Blue and Violet [19]. Three Crystal methodologies have been used. These are Clear, Orange, and Orange Web. The difference between Orange and Orange Web is that Orange Web does not deal with a single project [18]. Crystal includes different agile methods fitting the needs of teams with different sizes (Figure 7).

Adaptive software

This development attempts to bring about a new way of seeing software development in an organization, promoting an adaptive paradigm [20]. It offers solutions for the development of large and complex systems. The method encourages incremental and iterative development, with constant prototyping. One ancestor of ASD is "Radical Software Development" [21]. ASD claims to provide a framework with enough guidance to prevent projects from falling into chaos, while not suppressing emergence and creativity.

Internet-speed development (ISD)

It is arguably the least known approach to agile software development. ISD refers to a situation where software needs to be released fast, thereby requiring short development cycles [22]. ISD puts forth a descriptive, management oriented framework for addressing the problem of handling fast releases. This framework consists of time drivers, quality dependencies and process adjustments.

Software Architecture

Definition

Software architecture is a way of thinking about computing systems, for example, their configuration and design. By computing systems, we

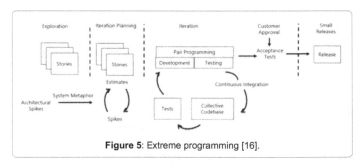

Figure 5: Extreme programming [16].

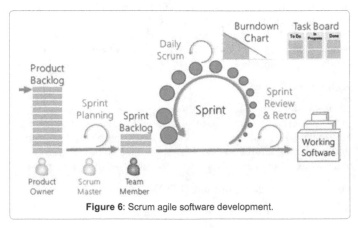

Figure 6: Scrum agile software development.

Methodology	Team (Number of people)
Crystal Clear	2-6
Crystal Yellow	6-20
Crystal Orange	20-40
Crystal Red	40-80

Figure 7: Crystal family.

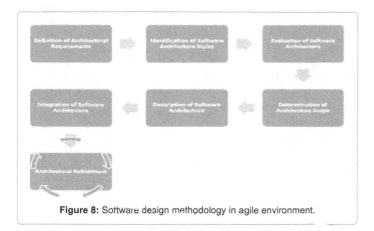

Figure 8: Software design methodology in agile environment.

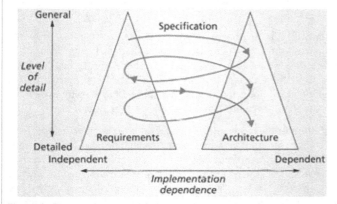

Figure 9: The twin peaks model showing the inter-play of requirements and architecture [50].

mean the hardware, the software and the communication components [6]. A set of components gathered together does not provide us with a problem solution [23]. We must impose a topology for interaction and communication upon them and ensure the components both integrate (physically communicate) as well as interoperate (logically communicate) [24].

Software architecture views

The process of software design and architecture is usually separated into four views: conceptual, module, execution, and code. This separation is based on our study of the software architectures of large systems, and on our experience designing and reviewing software architectures [25]. The different views address different engineering concerns, and separation of such concerns helps the architect make sound decisions about design tradeoffs. The notion of this kind of separation is not unique: most of the work in software architecture to date either recognizes different architecture views or focuses on

one particular view in order to explore its distinct characteristics and distinguish it from the others [23]. The 4+1 approach separates architecture into multiple views [26,27]. The Garlen et al. work focuses on the conceptual view [28]. Over the years there has been a great deal of work on the module view [29].

Moreover, other works focus on the execution view, and in particular explores the dynamic aspects of a system [30]. The code view has been explored in the context of configuration management and system building.

The conceptual view describes the architecture in terms of domain elements. Here the architect designs the functional features of the system. For example, one common goal is to organize the architecture so that functional features can be added, removed, or modified. This is important for evolution, for supporting a product line, and for reuse across generations of a product. The module view describes the decomposition of the software and its organization into layers. An important consideration here is limiting the impact of a change in external software or hardware. Another consideration is the focusing of software engineers' expertise, in order to increase implementation efficiency.

The execution view is the run-time view of the system: it is the mapping of modules to run-time images, defining the communication among them, and assigning them to physical resources. Resource usage and performance are key concerns in the execution view. Decisions such as whether to use a link library or a shared library, or whether to use threads or processes are made here, although these decisions may feed back to the module view and require changes there. The code view captures how modules and interfaces in the module view are mapped to source files, and run-time images in the execution view are mapped to executable files. Some of the views also have a configuration, which constrains the elements by defining what roles they can play in a particular system. In the configuration, the architect may want to describe additional attributes or behavior associated with the elements, or to describe the behavior of the configuration as a whole.

Software architecture activities

Software architecture is comprised of a number of specific architecting activities (covering the entire architectural lifecycle) and a number of general architecting activities (supporting the specific activities) [31]. In the following sections, we provide a short overview on software architecture activities and processes.

The specific software architecture activities are composed of five items:

- Architectural Analysis (AA) defines the problems an architecture must solve. The outcome of this activity is a set of architecturally significant requirements (ASRs) [32].

- Architectural Synthesis (AS) proposes candidate architecture solutions to address the ASRs collected in AA, thus this activity moves from the problem to the solution space [32].

- Architectural Evaluation (AE) ensures that the architectural design decisions made are the right ones, and the candidate architectural solutions proposed in AS are measured against the ASRs collected in AA [32].

- Architectural Implementation (AI) realizes the architecture by creating a detailed design [33].

- Architectural Maintenance and Evolution (AME) is to change an architecture for the purpose of fixing faults and architectural evolution is to respond to new requirements at the architectural level [34-36].

Software architecture processes

An architecture process is composed of the six specific items [32,33]:

- Architectural Recovery (AR) is used to extract the current architecture of a system from the system's implementation [37].

- Architectural Description (ADp) is used to describe the architecture with a set of architectural elements (e.g. architecture views). This activity can help stakeholders (e.g. architects) understand the system, and improve the communication and cooperation among stakeholders [35].

- Architectural Understanding (AU) is used to comprehend the architectural elements (e.g., architectural decisions) and their relationships in an architecture design [38].

- Architectural Impact Analysis (AIA) is used to identify the architectural elements, which are affected by a change scenario [39]. The analysis results include the components in architecture that are affected directly, as well as the indirect effects of changes to the architecture [39].

- Architectural Reuse (ARu) aims at reusing existing architectural design elements, such as architecture frameworks, decisions, and patterns in the architecture of a new system [40].

- Architectural Refactoring (ARf) aims at improving the architectural structure of a system without changing its external behavior [38,41].

Software Design in Agile Environment

The proposed methodology for software architectural design in agile environments is detailed in Figure 8.

Step 1: definition of architectural requirements

Establishing the driving architectural requirements: Driving architectural requirements are obtained by analyzing the business drivers and system context as well as the issues deemed critical to system success by the product stakeholders. The goal is a specification for the architecture directing the architects to create a structure for the system that is sufficient to ensure success in the eyes of the stakeholders. These requirements prevent creation of an architecture that is overly complex or that strives for unnecessary elegance at the expense of critical system properties. The definition of architectural requirements aims to meet the following goals:

- Describe a necessary change to components in an architecture. This might mean adding new components, removing outdated ones, replacing or improving components, or changing the way in which they are organized and how they work together. What is going to change?

- Include the reasoning or motivations behind the change. Why does it need to change? It should explain why the existing components are inadequate, limiting or constraining. What problems, issues or concerns are caused by the current architecture?

- Outline the available options for future architectures that address all concerns. How do alternate target architectures eliminate the problems of the current architecture?

- Explain the benefits, value, risks, costs, opportunities, constraints, and future options associated with each alternative. How do we decide between one alternative and another?

- Outline any alternative routes to close the gaps and get from the current to the target architecture. How do we make the transition or transformation from what we have got now to what we need in the future?

Step 2: identification of software architecture styles

Architectural structures and coordination strategies are developed to satisfy the driving architectural requirements. Alternative architecture solutions may be proposed and analyzed to identify an optimal solution for the product or product line being developed. When product lines are involved, SEI architects also help customer staff adapt the product line architecture to specific product requirements and fully develop the architecture for an individual product. The identification of software architecture styles aims to precise the associated elements, forms, and rationales:

Elements: There are three classes of software elements, namely processing elements, data elements, and connecting elements. The processing elements are those components that take some data and apply transformations on them, and may generate updated or new data. The data elements are those that contain the information to be used, transformed and manipulated. The connecting elements bind the architectural description together by providing communication links between other components. The connecting elements may themselves be processing or data elements, e.g., procedure calls, shared data, or messages.

Forms: The architectural form consists of weighted properties and relationships. The definition implies that each component of the architecture would be characterized by some constraints, generally decided by the architect, and some kind of relationship with one or more other components. Properties define the constraints on the software elements to the degree desired by the architect.

Rational: The rationale explains the different architectural decisions and choices; for example, why a particular architectural style or element or form was chosen. Rationale is tied to requirements, architectural views and stakeholders. Probably all choices are governed by what the requirement is. There are many different external components that have an interest in the system, and expect different things from the same system. We therefore have to consider the different external demands and expectations that affect and influence the architecture and its evolution.

Step 3: evaluation of software architecture

Software architecture evaluation determines when and what methods of architecture evaluation are appropriate. The results of such evaluation are then analyzed and measures are determined and applied to improve the developing architecture.

A formal software architecture evaluation should be a standard part of our software architecture methodology in agile environments. Software architecture evaluation is a cost effective way of mitigating the substantial risks associated with this highly important artifact. The achievement of a software system's quality attributes depends much more on the software architecture than on code related issues such as language choice, fine grained design, algorithms, data structures, testing, and so forth. Most complex software systems are required to be modifiable and have good performance. They may also need to be secure, interoperable, portable, and reliable. Several software architecture evaluation methods exist in literature; Architecture Tradeoff Analysis Method (ATAM) [42], Software Architecture Analysis Method (SAAM) [43], Active Reviews for Intermediate Designs (ARID) [44].

Step 4: determination of architecture scope

Before defining an architecture, the developers determine how many of the system design decisions should be established by the architecture of the system. This scope delimits the activities of application developers, allowing them to concentrate on what they do best. Software architecture scope is a reflection of system requirements and tradeoffs that made to satisfy them. Possible scope determination factors include:

- Performance

- Compatibility with legacy software

- Software reuse

- Distribution profile (current and future)

- Safety, security, fault tolerance, evolvability

- Changes to processing algorithms or data representation

- Modifications to the structure/functionality

Step 5: description of software architecture

An architecture must be described in sufficient detail and in an easily accessible form for developers and other stakeholders. The architecture is one of the major mechanisms that allow stake holders to communicate about the properties of a system. Architecture documentation determines what views of software are useful for the stakeholders, the amount of detail required, and how to present the information efficiently.

Agile methods agree strongly on a central point: "If information is not needed, do not document it". All documentation should have an intended use and audience in mind, and be produced in a way that serves both. One of the fundamental principles of technical documentation is "Write for the reader".

Another central idea to remember is that documentation is not a monolithic activity that holds up all other progress until it is complete. With that in mind, the following is the suggested approach for describing software architecture using agile like principles [45]:

- Create a skeleton document (document outline) for a comprehensive view based software architecture document using the standard organization schemes;

- Decide which architectural views should be to produced, given the software architecture scope (step 4) with respect to available resources;

- Annotate each section of the outline with a list of the stake holders who should find the information it contains of benefit.

- Prioritize the completion of the remaining sections. For example: if a section's constituency includes stakeholders for whom face-to-face conversation is impractical or impossible (e.g., maintainers in an as yet unidentified organization), that section will need to be filled in. If it includes only such stakeholders, its completion can be deferred until the conclusion of the software architecture and design phase.

Step 6: integration of software architecture

The software architecture integration process is a set of procedures used to combine software architectural components into larger components, subsystems or final software architecture [46]. Software architecture integration enables the organization to observe all important attributes that a software will have; functionality, quality and performance. This is especially true for software systems as the integration is the first occurrence where the full result of the software development effort can be observed. Consequently, the integration activities represent a highly critical part of the software development process in agile environments.

Usually, Architecture Analysis and Design Language (AADL) are used in order to build integrated software reliant systems [47]. The AADL is designed for the specification, analysis, automated integration and code generation of real time performance critical (timing, safety, fault tolerant, security, etc.) software. It allows analysis of system designs (and system of systems) prior to development and supports a model based, model driven development approach throughout the software development life cycle.

During software architecture integration, the software architect, checks whether the models provided by the component developers, system deployers, and domain experts as well as his or her own components assembly model are complete. If values are missing, the software architect estimates them or communicates with the responsible role. The result of this step (Integration of Software Architecture) is an overall quality annotated model.

Step 7: continuous architectural refinement

Architectural refinement aims to help provide the degree of architectural stability required to support the next iterations of development. This stability is particularly important to the successful operation of multiple parallel Scrum teams. Making architectural dependencies visible allows them to be managed and for teams to be aligned with them. The architecture refinement supports the team decoupling necessary to allow independent decision making and reduce communication and coordination overhead. During the preparation phase, agile teams identify an architecture style of infrastructure sufficient to support the development of features in the near future. Product development using an architectural refinement most likely occurs in the preservation phase. Architectural refinement is one of the key factors to successfully scale agile.

Describing and maintaining (through refinement) software architectural design enables a system infrastructure sufficient to allow incorporation of near term high priority features from the product backlog. The proposed software architecture methodology in agile environments allows the software architecture and design to support the features without potentially creating unanticipated rework by destabilizing refactoring. Larger software systems (and teams) need longer architectural refinements. Building and rearchitecting software takes longer than a single iteration or release cycle. Delivery of planned functionality is more predictable when the architecture for the new features is already in place. This requires looking ahead in the planning process and investing in architecture by including design work in the present iteration that will support future features and customer needs.

The architectural refinement is not complete. The refinement process intentionally is not complete because of an uncertain future with changing technology orientations and requirements engineering. This requires continuously extending the architectural refinement to support the development teams.

Discussion

Different agile methods cover different phases of the software development lifecycle. However, none of them cover the software architectural design phase. Moreover, the rationalization of phases covered was missing. The question raised is whether an agile method is more profitable to cover more and to be more extensive, or cover less and to be more precise and specific. On one hand, some agile methods that cover too much ground, i.e., all organizations, phases and situations, are too general or shallow to be used. On the other hand, agile methods that cover too little (e.g., one phase) may be too restricted or lack a connection to other methods. Completeness, a notion introduced by Kumar and Welke [48], requires a method to be complete as opposed to partial. In the final analysis it was realized "completeness" is an element associated both with vertical (i.e., level of detail) and horizontal (i.e., lifecycle coverage) dimensions. None of the existing agile methods were either extensive nor precise. Practitioners and experts are still struggling with partial solutions to problems that cover a wider area than agile methods do. In the following subsections, we discuss the limits and perspectives of the architectural refinement process. Finally, we provide an overview on team organization in agile environment in support of software architecture and design activities and processes.

Relationship between software requirements and architectural activities in agile environments

The important feature of agile methods is that they do not assume that there is a sequential process, where each phase of the software development lifecycle is expected to be completed before proceeding to the next one, as for example in a classical water fall process [49]. Thus it is expected that requirements engineering or software architecture phases are not happening just once, but they are rather continuously distributed along the development process. Once there is a first, usually incomplete, set of requirements available, an architect proceeds to the architectural design.

A tighter integration of requirements engineering and software architectural activities is suggested in the twin peak process model [50]. While requirements engineering phases and architectural activities phases alternate in traditional processes, the twin peak model emphasizes that these two activities should be executed in parallel to support immediate continuous feedback from one to another (Figure 9). The goal of this process is that requirement analysts and software architects better understand problems by being aware of requirements and their prioritization non one hand and architecture and in particular architectural constraints on the other hand. Additionally, being able to quickly switch back and forth between the problem to solve (the requirements) and its solution (the architecture) can help to more clearly distinguish the two and to avoid mixing up problem and solution already in the requirements engineering phase.

Team organization

In its simplest instantiation, an agile development environment consists of a single colocated, cross functional team with the skills, authority, and knowledge required to specify requirements and architect, design, code, and testing of the system. As software grows in size and complexity, the single team model may no longer meet development demands.

A number of different strategies can be used to scale up the overall software development organization while maintaining an agile development approach. One approach is replication, essentially creating multiple Scrum teams with the same structure and responsibilities, sufficient to accomplish the required scope of work. Some organizations scale Scrum through a hybrid approach. The hybrid approach involves

Scrum team replication but also supplements the cross functional teams with traditional functionally oriented teams. An example would be using an integration and test team to merge and validate code across multiple Scrum teams.

In general, we recognized two criteria used to organize the teams. First organizing the teams either horizontally or vertically and assigning different teams the responsibility for either components (horizontal) or features (vertical). The second is assigning the teams responsibilities according to development phases.

Conclusion and Future Works

In this paper, we provided an overview on software architectural design related issues in agile environments and proposed a methodology to guide and assist practitioners adopting agile software design in such environments. Our methodology relies on seven processes namely; (1) definition of architectural requirements; (2) identification of software architectural styles; (3) Evaluation of software architecture; (4) Determination of architecture scope; (5) Description of software architecture; (6) integration of software architecture; and (7) architectural refinement. Agile software development methods have evoked a substantial amount of literature and debates. However, academic research on the subject is still scarce, as most existing publications are written by practitioners or consultants. Yet, many organizations are considering future use or have already applied practices that are claiming successes in performing and delivering software in a more agile form. To conclude, we observed that agile methods, without rationalization only cover certain phases of the lifecycle. A majority of them did not provide true support for software architectural design for project management. While universal solutions have strong support in the respective literature, empirical evidence on their adaptation and use in agile environments is currently very limited.

References

1. Erickson J, Lyytinen K, Siau K (2005) Agile modeling, agile software development, and extreme programming: the state of research. J Database Manag 16: 88-100.

2. Bellomo S, Nord RL, Ozkaya I (2013) A study of enabling factors for rapid fielding combined practices to balance speed and stability. International Conference on Soft-ware Engineering (ICSE). pp: 982-991.

3. Martini A, Pareto L, Bosch J (2012) Enablers and inhibitors for speed with reuse. Proceedings of the 16th International Software Product Line Conference 1: 116-125.

4. Dingsøyr T, Lassenius C (2016) Emerging themes in agile soft-ware development: Introduction to the special section on con-tinuous value delivery. Information and Software Technology 77: 56-60.

5. Buchmann F, Nord RL, Ozakaya I (2012) Architectural tactics to support rapid and agile stability. Technical report DTIC Document.

6. Herzog J (2015) Software architecture in practice third edition written by len bass, paul clements, rick kazman. ACM SIGSOFT Software Engineering Notes 40: 51-52.

7. Ambler SW (2001) Agile requirements modeling. The Official Agile Modeling (AM) Site.

8. Edeki C (2015) Agile software development methodology. European Journal of Mathematics and Computer Science 2: 22-27.

9. Lata P (2016) Agile software development methods. International Journal of Computer.

10. Nierstrasz O, Kurš J (2015) Parsing for agile modeling. Science of Computer Programming 97: 150-156.

11. Mahdavi-Hezave R, Ramsin R (2015) Fdmd: Feature-driven methodology development. Evaluation of Novel Approaches to Software Engineering (ENASE). pp: 229-237.

12. Choudhary, Rakesh SK (2016). An approach using agile method for software development. In Innovation and Challenges in Cyber Security (ICICCS-INBUSH) International Conference. pp: 155-158.

13. Awan R, Muhammad S, Fahiem M, Awan S (2016) A hybrid software architecture evaluation method for dynamic system development method. Nucleus 53: 180-187.

14. Lange B, Flynn S, Proffitt R, Chang CY, Rizzo AS (2010) Development of an interactive game-based rehabilitation tool for dynamic balance training. Topics in stroke rehabilitation 17: 345-352.

15. Jaafar NH, Rahman MA, Mokhtar R (2016) Adapting the extreme programming approach in developing ecorrective and preventive actions: An experience. Regional Conference on Science, Technology and Social Sciences (RCSTSS 2014). pp: 801-809.

16. Abrahamsson P, Salo O, Ronkainen J, Warsta J (2002) Agile software development methods: Review and analysis. VTT Publications, Finland. p. 478.

17. Cej A (2010) Agile software development with scrum. EngD Thesis.

18. Abrahamsson P, Warsta J, Siponen MT, Ronkainen J (2003) New directions on agile methods: A comparative analysis. Proceedings 25th International Conference. pp: 244-254.

19. Ramesh B, Cao L, Baskerville R (2010) Agile requirements engineering practices and challenges: An empirical study. Information Systems Journal 20: 449-480.

20. Highsmith J (2013) Adaptive software development: A collaborative approach to managing complex systems. Addison-Wesley, USA.

21. Floyd C (1992) Software development as reality construction. Springer, Germany. pp: 86-100.

22. Baskerville R, Ramesh B, Levine L, Pries-Heje J, Slaughter S (2003) Is internet-speed software development different? IEEE software 20: 70-77.

23. Bass L, Clements P, Kazman R (2012) Software architecture in practice. Addison-Wesley, USA.

24. Kaisler SH (2005) Software paradigms. John Wiley & Sons, USA.

25. Qian K, Fu X, Tao L, Xu C, Diaz-Herrera J (2009) Software architecture and design illuminated. Jones and Bartlett Publishers, USA.

26. Kruchten P (1995) The 4+1 view model of architecture. IEEE Software 12: 42-50.

27. Singh S, Chaurasia M, Gaikwad MH (2016) Importance of 4+ 1 views model in software architecture. Imperial Journal of Interdisciplinary Research.

28. Clements P, Garlan D, Bass L, Stafford J, Nord R, et al. (2002) Documenting software architectures: Views and beyond. Pearson Education, US.

29. Ducasse S, Pollet D (2009) Software architecture reconstruction: A process-oriented taxonomy. IEEE Transactions on Software Engineering 35: 573-591.

30. Magee J, Kramer J (1996) Dynamic structure in software architectures. ACM SIGSOFT Software Engineering Notes 21: 3-14.

31. Yang C, Liang P, Avgeriou P (2016) A systematic mapping study on the combination of software architecture and agile development. J Syst Software

111: 157-184.

32. Hofmeister C, Kruchten P, Nord RL, Obbink H, Ran A, et al. (2007) A general model of software architecture de-sign derived from five industrial approaches. J Syst Software 80: 106-126.

33. Tang A, Avgeriou P, Jansen A, Capilla R, Babar MA (2010) A comparative study of architecture knowledge management tools. J Syst Software 83: 352-370.

34. Systems and software engineering - architecture description. ISO/IEC/IEEE 42010. 2011.

35. Software engineering – software life cycle processes – maintenance. ISO/IEC 14764:2006.

36. Postma A, America P, Wijnstra JG (2004) Component replacement in a long-living architecture: the 3RBDA approach. Proceedings. Fourth Working IEEE/IFIP Conference. pp: 89-98.

37. Malavolta I, Lago P, Muccini H, Pelliccione P, Tang A (2013) What industry needs from architectural languages: A survey. IEEE Trans Softw Eng 39: 869-891.

38. Li Z, Liang P, Avgeriou P (2013) Application of knowledge based approaches in software architecture: A systematic mapping study. Information and Software Technology 55: 777-794.

39. Bengtsson P, Lassing N, Bosch J, Vliet HV (2004) Architecture-level modifiability analysis (ALMA). J Syst Software 69: 129-147.

40. IEEE standard for information technology system and software life cycle processes reuse processes. IEEE Std 1517-2011-51.

41. Babar MA, Brown AW, Mistrík I (2013) Agile software architecture: Aligning agile processes and software architectures. Elsevier.

42. Kazman R, Klein M, Barbacci M, Longstaff T, Lipson H, et al. (1998) The architecture tradeoff analysis method. Engineering of Complex Computer Systems. Proceedings of the fourth IEEE International Conference. pp: 68-78.

43. Tekinerdogan B (2004) Asaam: Aspectual software architecture analysis method. Proceedings of the Fourth Working IEEE/IFIP Conference. pp: 5-14.

44. Babar MA, Zhu L, Jeffery R (2004) A framework for classifying and comparing software architecture evaluation methods. Software Engineering Conference, 2004 Proceedings, Australia. pp: 309-318.

45. Clements P, Ivers J, Little R, Nord R, Stafford J (2003) Documenting software architectures in an agile world. Technical report DTIC Document.

46. S. Larsson (2007) Key elements of software product integration processes. Mälardalen.

47. Feiler P (2013) Architecture analysis and design language.

48. Kumar K, Welke RJ (1992) Methodology engineering: A proposal for situation specific methodology construction. Challenges and strategies for research in systems development. John Wiley & Sons, USA. pp: 257-269.

49. Sommerville I (1996) Software process models. ACM computing surveys (CSUR) 28: 269-271.

50. Nuseibeh B (2001) Weaving together requirements and architectures. Computer 34: 115-119.

30

Server Side Protection against Cross Site Request Forgery using CSRF Gateway

Jaya Gupta* and Suneeta Gola

College of Science & Engineering, Department of Computer Engineering, India

Abstract

The E-Commerce and Social Media has become the new identity for millions of users across the globe. Ease of services for Shopping, Travel, Internet Banking, Social Media, chat and collaboration Apps etc. have become part of one's life where these identities have name, media content, confidential notes, business projects and credit cards. Convenience and connections brings the ease of connectivity and services so does come the concerns related to unauthorized usage and fraudulent transactions that could be lead to loss of money, time, emotions and even life. Web defacement, fake accounts, account hijacking, account lock and unavailability of services has become a common online news and distress for many. There are different Web Attacks and exploits that have sprung up with time and usage for different type of illegal actions performed everyday online. Cross Site Request Forgery Attack is one of the Web top 10 exploited attacks for the past 5 years (Source OSWAP) which can maliciously exploit online services, where unauthorized actions are performed by the fraudulent user on behalf of a trusted and authenticated account for website. It forces the victim user to perform some unauthorized activity on behalf of attacker request. This research work focuses on a new Hybrid strategy that will enhance the server side protection against CSRF attacks. CSRF Gateway, is the proposed solution which provides the Server Side protection against Cross Site Request Forgery (CSRF) Attack.

Keywords: Cross site request forgery; Web application vulnerabilities; CSRF gateway

Introduction

Cross Site Request Forgery (CSRF) is also known as "Session Riding" or "One Click Attack". This attack is a Malicious Exploit type of attack against web application users. This attack has been listed as 7th most exploitable among 10 top Web Attacks [1-3]. CSRF is an attack which allows an attacker to perform unauthorized POST/GET arbitrary HTTP requests on behalf of victim that is currently authenticated to the website. The fraudulent user performs unauthorized activity on behalf of an authorized and authenticated victim user. If the victim is authenticated, a successful CSRF attack effectively by-passes the underlying authentication mechanism. Depending on the web applications, the attacker could send post messages or send emails/message on behalf of the victim or manipulate with the login name or password. Account lock, account hijack, data loss and fake online messages are common fraudulent activities using the CSRF methodologies. Furthermore the results of the attack can be more severe depending the usage scenario. But in contrast other well-known web security attacks such as Cross Site Scripting (XSS) or SQL Injection and Cross Site Request Forgery (CSRF) are appears to be a problem known to the web developers [3].

CSRF attacks are broadly categorized into 2 types. First one is launched from malicious site to a trustful website. In this type, attacker can only send HTTP request to an authentic website but no secret information can be obtained from the true website. The other type of CSRF attack is based on JavaScript and AJAX. It is called the "Multi Stage CSRF attack", which involves a malicious script that generates multiple HTTP requests and secretly sends the generated HTTP requests asynchronously in the background. Detection and prevention of CSRF attacks is challenging from browser's side, the usage of same origin policy (SOP) is not enough to prevent CSRF attack. Same Origin Policy (SOP) is defined as the same scheme, host and the URL of the host. There have been many server and client side protection implementations, few protection plans are still relevant and existing for protection, but unfortunately all these protection plans are not able to protect web application completely for new CSRF exploits that have

come up with time. The Hybrid strategy for server side CSRF Gateway implementation is an attempt to enhance the protection against CSRF exploits with session and token approach.

In this paper, proposed solution called as CSRF Gateway, which provides the Server Side protection to the most Open Source Web Applications. This solution is intended to demonstrate the working of CSRF Attack using different Attack Vectors on the real world examples. This gateway methodology demonstration will provide the clear picture about the subject, so that it will create a better picture to understand the defensive mechanisms [4].

Here are some Real World examples of CSRF Attack

1. ING Direct (ingdirect.com)

2. YouTube (youtube.com)

3. MetaFilter (metafilter.com)

4. The New York Times (nytimes.com)

5. Gmail (gmail.com)

6. Netflix

Related Work

In previous years, there is lot of research work has been done in this field. In the previous researches, researchers had proposed techniques and solutions to prevent and defense against the Cross Site Request Forgery.

*Corresponding author: Jaya Gupta, College of Science & Engineering, Department of Computer Engineering, India, E-mail: mail2me17@gmail.com

Proxy based solution

In this approach, solution to the problem was to decouple the necessary security mechanism from the application and to provide a separate module that can be plugged into existing systems with minimal effort. More precisely, they proposed a proxy that was placed on the server side between the web server and the target application. This proxy was very well sufficient to check and change the requests sent by client and the replies to itself extend applications by using the shared secret technique. In particular, the proxy had to ensure that replies to an authenticated user had to modified in such a way that future requests originating from (through hyperlinks and forms) should contain a valid token, and take countermeasures against requests from authenticated users that did not contain valid token. By decoupling the proxy from the actual application, the XSRF protection could be offered transparently for all applications [5-7].

Referrer privacy guard and defense technique

In this approach, Defense mechanism included 2 techniques for the solution.

Referrer privacy guard: The Referrer Privacy Guard revealed how a constant flow of random HTTP requests could mess up the browsing history at the server side, thus preventing infiltrators from getting access to user browsing trends.

Detection and discouragement: In this section, the focus was on how to detect CSRF signatures in web pages and stop it before commencement. The defense attribute first verified the Client side code before each and every page load and found the CSRF attack involved.

Attack detection using windows form

CSRF attack detection approach that was divided in multiple sections.

Section A: Attack detection framework: In the section they had assumed that a browser could have multiple windows. A trusted website could be viewed by a user in window after performing an authentication process and the session information was saved in the browser. In this section the following processes were followed.

1. Request Checker
2. Window and form checker
3. Request Differentiator
4. Attack Detection policy
5. Attack handler module

Section B: Visibility checking: The proposed notion of visibility relies on examining windows containing web pages and forms presented in a browser. If a request was GET type, they checked whether it contained any query string or not. If no query string was present, no need to examine it further. However, if a query string was present, then tokenize the string to identify the set of parameters and values and related the extracted parameters and values with a webpage containing forms with similar fields and values [7-9]. Note that the form action or target field value should match with the resource file of the suspected request. While examining a webpage, two possible scenarios might arise. These were discussed below:

1. Window and no form
2. Window and form

Section C: Content checking: Content checking relied on the matching of the response of a suspected request with the expected response. A suspected request often resided as part of an HTML tag attribute value or within. A response page might contain various types of elements (static HTML, JavaScript, and Style Sheets). As a result, they relied on the content type of a webpage to differentiate an attack request from a user initiated request based on the identified tag that contained the request. The content type was often specified in the META tag of a page and was accessible from the response header. After that they discussed the comparison of the expected and the actual content type and how to launch a suspected request in next 2 subsections.

1. Comparison between an expected and an actual response content type.
2. Suspected request modification

Section D: Attack detection coverage and attribute checks: The proposed approach was able to detect a variety of CSRF attacks. Some non-exhaustive CSRF examples were highlighted and related with the checks to detect them [10-16].

1. Visible form with field and no value
2. Invisible form with field and value
3. Static/Dynamic HTML tag and URL at tribute
4. Program state retrieval or modification
5. Pre- or post-rendering

CSRF guard

CSRF Guard was verifying the integrity of HTTP requests by inserting a special security token to every active HTTP session established among the authenticated client and the web server. Essentially, the CSRF Guard was doing the filtration of the requests coming in. It was executing following functionalities.

1. Inserted a token to the defined preserved resource.
2. This method did the verification of the token when the preserved resource gets requested. The token origination and certification was used to give the protection against the CSRF attack.

Protection approach

Suggested approach was to protect against CSRF attacks by using some or all of these:

1. Use of random tokens: To use random tokens each time with a form submission could make very difficult for the attacker to guess the next random pattern to fill in the URL.

2. Need to use Post method in form instead of Get: Get and Post are the 2 methods of form submission. Post Method was secure for form submission. In Get method anyone could see the variables and values in URL as a query strings.

3. Limiting the lifetime of authentication cookies: Limit the lifetime to a short period of time. If user was going on other website then the cookies were expired after a short period of time. If the attacker was trying to send any HTTP request to user which he was able to know and he would not fill the password again.

4. Damage limitation: Damage limitation involved those steps which reduced the damage from CSRF. For example if an attacker did manage to perform CSRF on a website then any action done by him was required an authentication every time to limit the damage.

5. Force user to use your form: It was forcing user every time to use the form of website. Use of hidden fields was helpful for this purpose. But this way of protection was easy to bypass.

Labeling mechanism: To prevent the CSRF attack, labeling mechanism called Content Box; was suggested. The Content Box consisted of a labeling function and UCC quarantine policies. The labeling function was used to isolate the UCCs, while the UCC quarantine policy enforces propagation rules for the labeled UCCs. The CSRF attack could be prevented using the Content Box when an untrusted UCC try to access a service that contains sensitive/private information. The main idea was to divide the content into 2 different types. One was called the "trusted contents"; these contents were created by the web server administrator or the content viewer/user. Since these contents were created by the rightful owner, it was that the scripts within the contents were free from the CSRF attack [15]. The other type was called the "untrusted contents" which were created by other users. Since these contents were provided by users other than the rightful owner, the scripts within these contents might cause the CSRF attack. It was important to differentiate the contents of the webpage since the client browser always trusted the contents of a web page provided by the web server even if the authors of the contents were not trusted by the client. In Content Box, they intended to distinguish the untrusted contents and prohibiting the untrusted contents from accessing web services that contain sensitive data.

Initially in web, UCC was the source of the CSRF attack problem. However, most UCCs were harmless providing that if it was created by the current client. This kind of UCC should be classified into trusted contents since the CSRF attack rarely happened when both of the attacker and the victim were identical. Labeling was used to differentiate the contents and ensured that every HTTP request was labeled, provided that the label cannot be disrupted by the client browser. In addition to labeling the contents of a web page, an access control mechanism was required to patrol the accesses of web services.

1. Trusted label had the freedom to access the contents with trusted or untrusted label.

2. Untrusted label could only access the contents with untrusted label.

Once the contents with trusted label were contaminated by untrusted label, its label becomes untrusted.

Overview of CSRF Attacks

A Cross Site Request Forgery is a type of attack that compels an end user to perform unauthorized actions on the web applications on which they are currently authenticated logged in. Specifically, the CSRF is only tangled with state changing requests but not in the theft of data.

Anatomy of cross site request forgery attack

A Cross Site Request Forgery is a type of attack that compels an end user to perform unauthorized actions on the web applications on which they are currently authenticated logged in. Specifically, the CSRF is only tangled with state changing requests but not in the theft of data. This attack typically requires attacker to have prior access to and knowledge of the vulnerable application [13].

To show the Anatomy of Cross Site Request Forgery (CSRF), there is taken an example of the Bank transaction (Figure 1). The User Bob logs into the bank website called "fictitiousbank.com". When the session gets established then cookie sets. Then in between Bob visits a site having malicious IMG tag that followed the site called "somesite. com". Behind the scene this link follows the URL which sends amount to another account using Bob's account authentication. The malicious link can be sent either by GET method or POST method. In the GET action all parameters send in the query string and in the POST parameter goes separately to the server. Then in both the cases HTTP request will be,

If action was a POST

POST/submitpage
Server: server.com

amount=1000&destination=MrHacker

If action was a GET

GET/submitpage?amount=1000&destination=MrHacker
Server: server.com

If attacker can predict all these parameters, then those parameters can be used to get misused. The GET or POST request can be easily forged by using various HTML elements, such as (img), (script) or (iframe), (a) (hyperlink).

If attacker want to misuse GET then the malicious link will be

<img src=".........">
http://server.com/submitpage?amount=1000&destination=MrHacker

If attacker want to misuse POST then the malicious form will be

```
<form name="evil" action=http://server.com/submitpage
action="post">
     <input type="hidden" name="amount" value="1000">
     <input type="hidden" name="destination"
value="MrHacker">
</form>

<Script>document.evil.submit () </script>
```

Because Bob does not know about this malicious link, he submits the request which process the request to get submitted on the server and get the money transfer done. Victim user gets to know only when he see the bank statement or after the action gets committed. In this way Cross Site Request Forgery attack takes place. But unfortunately till that time this action cannot be undone.

Proposed Methodology

The Detection and Prevention of CSRF Attack is Challenging. The previous research work is resulted only limited number of techniques for mitigating CSRF vulnerabilities such as proxy solution, filtering the contents of webpage, using cookies. Such techniques involves moreover much work to perform the task and lengthy process. From the browser perspective Same Origin Policy is not enough to protect against the CSRF attack. Because mostly web applications are using Cross Origin Policy. But even if Cross Origin Policy may not be configured acceptably which can cause the defense or prevent ineffective.

To protect web applications against Cross Site Request Forgery (CSRF) attack, this research work have proposed and implemented

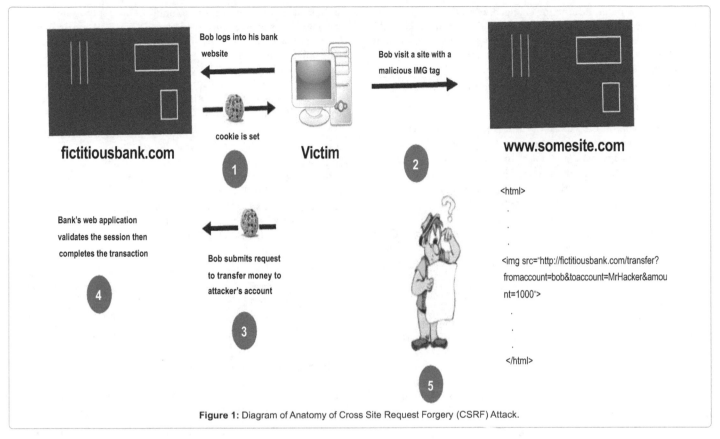

Figure 1: Diagram of Anatomy of Cross Site Request Forgery (CSRF) Attack.

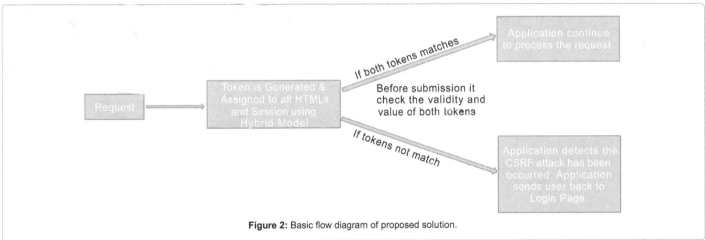

Figure 2: Basic flow diagram of proposed solution.

Hybrid Approach which we named as CSRF Gateway. Below are the key features of CSRF Gateway.

Here is the basic flow diagram of the proposed solution (Figure 2).

Server side protection

CSRF Gateway provides Server Side Protection from Cross Site Request Forgery Attack.

This solution gets installed on the web application. Server side protection is stronger protection approach for control and behavior than client side protection strategies. When the HTTP Request by the user then on the server side, web application creates the session and embeds token to the Session using Custom Tag Library which provides the more secured way to insert the token and in all the forms by newly created Custom Tag <CSRFToken>.

Angular JS anonymity

CSRF Gateway also has Angular JS Anonymity, which sends the CSRF Token anonymously using Angular JS and AJAX in the inner HTML pages like "Add", "Update", "Delete" while Submitting the HTTP Request to the server without refreshing and reloading the web page with updates. This Anonymity creates the secure traversing of the HTTP Request to the server. This makes even more difficult for the attacker to speculate the flow of the request and the parameters. There is no other way in which attacker can predict the supported elements of the attack. Even if the attacker is able to predict the knowledge of request then also request cannot be changed or modified maliciously. In addition, Angular JS Anonymity enhances the Performance of the web solution [1-3]. When the HTTP Requests are traversing so many times to and fro then sometimes server gets overloaded by loading of contents every time, in that case if the Request is very Light Weighted, it gets go over the server very fast to enhance the performance.

Token generation

The key reason for the success of CSRF attack is that attackers can obtain all the parameters of the important operations by analyzing victim request and website and then forge a valid request passing the server-side validation. Thereupon, by adding the hidden token parameter in the operations, (the value which generate random number) so that attackers cannot predict parameters value, and therefore forgery requests cannot pass validation. Using tokens is by far the most effective method to defend against CSRF attacks. CSRF Gateway uses Secure, Random and Unique 32-bit Alphanumeric Token, which makes the token value impossible to predict for forging unauthorized request.

Token insertion

CSRF Gateway uses JSP Custom Tag Library to insert Token in all the HTML pages. Custom Tag Library provides developers more granular control over Token Insertion. This provides more secure way to embed token. More over this strategy is more useful than normal Java Script or any other Token Insertion method. CSRF Gateway has 2 layers of security in additional to traditional token insertion alone (Figure 3).

1. First Token embeds with the each HTML page.

2. Second Token embeds with the Session.

Implementation

We have implemented a proof of concept of our proposed CSRF attack protection approach as a Server Side installation. An application administrator has to embed the solution to the application. We have used Java for the development platform. Java Platform is dynamic, security architecture, standards-based and interoperable. This provides a safe and secure platform for developing and running applications. It includes enforcing runtime constraints through the use of JAVA VIRTUAL MACHINE, a security manager that sandbox untrusted code from the rest of the operating system, and a suite of security APIs that JAVA developers can utilize [7].

We have used Custom Tag Library to insert Random and Unique token to all the HTML pages. Custom tag library is a User defined JSP language element. When a JSP page containing a custom tag is translated into a servlet, the tag is converted to operations on an object called a tag handler. The web container then invokes those operations when the JSP page's servlet is executed. In this way, Custom Tag Library provides the fine grain level of security. The advantage of the Custom Tag over any Java Script is that functionality is never been shown to the end user or attacker.

In the model, the Upper Layer embeds the first CSRF Token to the Session which gets assigned per session. Whenever user requests server for any page first time, session gets created. Server embeds token to the session and sends the request back to the user. This token remains same for the whole session. Then Middle Layer assigns second CSRF Token to all the HTMLs which gets assigned per HTTP request.

In Figure 4, it is shown that how this CSRF Token get inserted into the HTMLs. This CSRF token assigned to the hidden field, and the value of this token gets set in the Custom Tag Handler. Figure 5 shows how the CSRF token value gets displayed in the webpage.

Whenever the user tries to submit any HTTP request to the server then before submitting the request, server verifies the token associated with each request. If both the tokens matches then request get passed to the server, otherwise it assumes that the CSRF Attack has been occurred and then server Logout the user from the application. The Lowest Layer where Angular JS Anonymity plays the most vital role which hides the HTTP Request parameters to get exposed in the request

Figure 3: Diagram of representation of CSRF Token.

Figure 4: Diagram of representation of CSRF Token insertion in HTML page.

```
65
66                                     <tr>
67                                         <td>
68                                             <br/>
69                                         </td>
70                                     </tr>
71                                     <tr>
72                                         <td>
73                                             <input type = "hidden" name = "CSRFToken" value="2bb1d24972f13365291723834f744a81
74 ">
75                                         </td>
76                                     </tr>
77                                     <tr>
78                                         <td>
79                                             <br/>
80                                         </td>
81                                     </tr>
82                                     <tr>
```

Figure 5: Diagram of representation of CSRF Token displayed in HTML page.

```
1
2  var postApp = angular.module("mainModule", []);
3
4  postApp.controller("cRUDController",[ '$scope', '$http', function ($scope, $http)
5    {
6        $http.defaults.headers.post["Content-Type"] = "application/x-www-form-urlencoded; charset=utf-8";
7
8        $scope.sendPost = function()
9        {
10
11           $http({
12               url : 'cRUDController',
13               method : "POST",
14               data :
15               {
16                   'strStudentId' : $scope.strStudentId,
17                   'strStudentName' : $scope.strStudentName,
18                   'strSubjectId' : $scope.strSubjectId,
19                   'strGrade' : $scope.strGrade,
20                   'ctrlAction' : $scope.ctrlAction
21
22               }
23
24           })
```

Figure 6: Diagram of representation of Angular JS Anonymity.

while submitting an important operations to the server by making an anonymous call.

Unfortunately, there is no publicly available test suite for Cross Site Forgery Attack Protection evaluation. Thus, we developed the benchmarked test suite called "Student Grading System" to test the proposed solution. In this test suite, we first put the CSRF TOKEN in the hidden field, so that it will not be visible to the victim or attacker. Then we assign the other CSRF TOKEN to the session. Both the tokens are 32-bit alphanumeric encrypted using SHA1 (32-bit) and MD5 Encryption Technique. This application performs "Insert Faculty", "Add", "Update" and "Delete" student actions. We have put Interceptor Class which intercept each and every request and response. Hence at all the time it check for the tokens associated with session and request to be matched.

We have used OWASP Zed Attack Proxy (ZAP) which is one of the world's most popular free security tools. It can help developers automatically find security vulnerabilities in the web application while developing and testing the application. In our work, we have used this tool to Intercept the Request and test our Proof of Concept. ZAP Proxy tool intercept each incoming and outgoing request. In Figure 6, it is shown how any request can be forged while before submitting it on the server.

Here request can be forged and send back to the server. Figure 7 shows the response of the forged request returned by the server using CSRF Gateway (Figure 8).

Results and Conclusions

We have tested the applications with the proof of concept and we got results over previous research works. We have done the comparison with previous research work.

The new Hybrid technique is deployed for a test application to provide a detailed proof of concept for CSRF Gateway. The results obtained from the previous research works are compared with this gateway technique that is summarized below.

Server side vs client side protection

CSRF Gateway (our research work) provides Server Side Protection against CSRF against which is stronger and powerful than any Client Side Defensive Solution.

Light weighted solution

This is Light Weighted Solution. CSRF Gateway is very easy to install at Server Side. Server Side needs to embed the CSRF token to their application.

Synchronizer token pattern vs other defensive technique

Synchronizer Token Pattern Defensive Technique is most Compatible, Reliable and

Official Technique of Protection against Cross Site Request Forgery. (Source OSWAP Site)

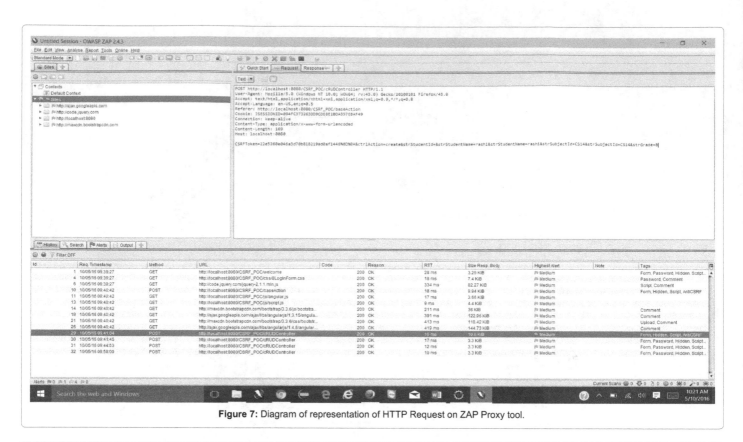

Figure 7: Diagram of representation of HTTP Request on ZAP Proxy tool.

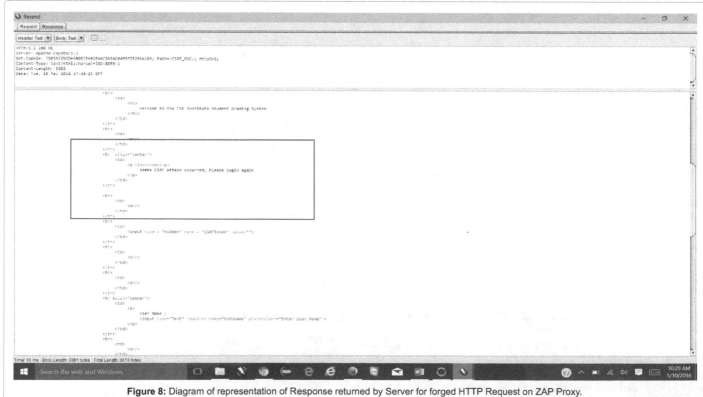

Figure 8: Diagram of representation of Response returned by Server for forged HTTP Request on ZAP Proxy.

Encryption technique

MD5 combined Encryption Techniques used to generate Unique and Random 32-bit Alphanumeric Token. JSP Custom Tag Library is used to embed the Token into the HTML forms, which gives the granular Control over Token Injection. It is more useful strategy over normal Java Script or any other strategy used for Token Injection. AJAX and Angular JS plays an important role to give the great performance

	Application without Protection	Application Protected using CSRF Gateway
GET Request without Malicious Link	Protected	Protected
POST Request without Malicious Link	Protected	Protected
GET Request with Malicious Link	Not Protected	Protected
POST Request without Malicious Link	Not Protected	Protected
Response Content Check	Not Protected	Protected
Reflected CSRF	Not Protected	Protected
Stored CSRF	Not Protected	Protected

Table 1: Requests With & Without Protection in Applications.

because it anonymously all the request parameters to the server. This is very useful for new web services.

This project has implemented keeping an overall efficiency and performance as key factors to cover hidden tags as more secure form of post authorization in a CSRF attack scenario. CSRF Gateway has been designed and implemented to provide robust protection solution against Cross Site Request Forgery using the latest technology for web development that can greatly change the way the traditional proxy based CSRF Gateway was implemented that could itself be a performance throttle for application itself. The solution will become more secure with secure HTTPS transactions to avoid any eavesdropping to ensure the passive data collection are also prevented for user profiling (Table 1).

Future Work

Cross Site Request Forgery (CSRF) attack is a website exploit type of attack. Even though it is very less known to the web developers. As far, we have seen that CSRF Gateway is able to protect against CSRF attack only. In future, we will elaborate this solution to extend to defend the web applications against other threats like Cross Site Scripting (XSS), SQL Injection, and Session Hijacking, Broken Authentication or other less known web attacks.

This Gateway Strategy can be extended to more features and functions for specific web security against server side malicious code detection and protection.

Acknowledgements

Presented thesis work was supported and guided by the faculty members of College of Science & Engineering. We thank you the members of the Silicon valley team in the Bay area who have conducted many security related discussions every month and participating and discussing these methodologies with them gave a new focus and understanding of this project implementation. Also I thank a lot to my project guide and coordinator whose feedback and constant discussion have helped me improve the presentation to provide more detailed feedback.

References

1. Jovanovic N, Kirda E, Kruegel C (2006) Preventing Cross Site Request Forgery Attacks. Securecomm and Workshops 1-10.

2. Alexenko T, Jenne M, Roy SD, Zeng W (2010) Cross-Site Request Forgery: Attack and Defense. Consumer Communications and Networking Conference (CCNC), Las Vegas NV 1-2.

3. Shahriar H, Zulkernine M (2010) Client-Side Detection of Cross-Site Request Forgery Attacks. IEEE 21st International Symposium, San Jose CA 358-367.

4. Open Source Vulnerability Database (OSVDB).

5. Zuchlinski G (2003) The Anatomy of Cross Site Scripting.

6. Siddiqui MS, Verma D (2011) Cross site request forgery: A common web application weakness. IEEE 3rd International Conference 538-543.

7. Sung YC, Cho MCY, Wang CW, Hsu CW, Shieh SW (2013) Light-Weight CSRF Protection by Labeling User-Created Contents. IEEE 7th International Conference, Gaithersburg MD 60-69.

8. Cross-Site Request Forgery (CSRF).

9. http://www.acunetix.com/websitesecurity/csrf-attacks/

10. http://www.veracode.com/security/csrf

11. Gallagher T. Finding and preventing cross-site request forgery. Black Hat Briefings.

12. http://www.toolswatch.org/2016/02/2015-top-security-tools-as-voted-by-toolswatch-org-readers/

13. OWASP Zed Attack Proxy Project.

14. https:/angularjs.org/

15. Defining the Custom Component Tag in a Tag Library Descriptor. The Java EE 6 Tutorial.

16. Boyan C, Pavol Z, Ron R, Dale L (2011) A Study of the Effectiveness of CSRF Guard. IEEF 3rd International Conference, Boston MA 1269-1272.

31

Sw Quality Process Models: An Appraisal

Tanzila Kehkashan, Shahid Yaqub Tabassam* and Nayyar Manzoor

Department of Computer Science, University of Lahore, Sargodha, Pakistan

Abstract

The quality of the software is measured and maintained by the quality models like the Maccalls, Bohem, FURPS, ISO, and CMM. We have given an appraisal of software quality models. The theoretical appraisal is given to select the model on the theoretical base and to augment the theoretical augment the empirical analysis is used. For a given quality criteria the theoretical dealings measure the process quality models. And the experiential appraisal is also developed for evaluating the performance of the models. The theoretical and experiential both procedures evaluate degree which is used in process to measure the quality of the software. Different and many organizations are developing the software these organizations are using different software models. For better quality of the software different models are suggested. We have made a theoretical and the experiential evaluation to measure the quality of the software's.

Keywords: Software; Sw quality process; Quality system

Introduction

The anticipated work is summarized for the proportional estimate of SW quality models. For both the experiential and the theoretical evaluation the process are distinct. The delegate software set is chosen for evaluating the procedures. For specifying the content of quality (relevance to the user need) software results, scope is applied. These procedures evaluate the SW quality models on the experiential base [1].

To measure the notion of the quality the SW quality process are evaluated these processes are selected. For the theoretical evaluation some measures are established for analyzing the content of model theoretically.

The theoretical evaluation defines that either the model is based on the sound theory or not. It also verifies that the measures are not based on exceptions. On the other side the experiential evaluation is applied practically. Validation of the model is done by implementing the model [2]. This defines that the given theory shows a relationship with the observations of real world.

The theoretical evaluation cannot prove the correlation with the real world. The only experiential evaluation also does not identify that the observed process were genuine. So for getting the benefits of both approaches are utilized.

The both approaches for evaluating can be used independent for the success of validation study. So it is advantageous to execute this analysis independently as it's possible.

For integrated approach the results for both approaches can be combined and we can calculate the total validation for the SW quality model.

Theoretical Assessment of SW Quality Models

The theoretical appraisal is an analytical in which the definition of the quality model is used as input and that will result the notion of the quality of the product as the output.

Approaches for theoretical assessment

There are many approaches for measuring the quality but the approach selection is important while considering,

- Contents of model

- Results type of user

Theoretical approach uses the fundamental contents for the model which are theory based so it gives the strongest quality level. The results of this approach cannot be compared. The disadvantage of theoretical approach is that when the model narrates to an indulgent of quality it wants to access the detail of elements of model.

Set of condition is defined for this approach. On the basis of these conditions and requirements the model can be examined. If the SW Quality model is theoretically ideal and it represents all requirements then this model provides some quality measures. So for good quality requirements should be complete and correct [3].

Incomplete requirements set can be used as sample for infinite set. After the analysis the results are compared and the assessment can be made. This approach is indirect measurement of models. This approach does not address the theory directly, only the documents can be utilized by the user. The results by this approach are dependent on the procedure which is selected for the evaluation. While using the analytical method the correctness can be measured in the forms (Table 1).

- Satisfied

- Partially satisfied

- Not satisfied

Approach of user class based appraisal

While developing any software project number of user classes can be identified. Each and every user class performs same roles that an individual performs with content of quality model. This significance can be articulated that requirements are positioned on a SW quality model. Different user classes can share any requirement. Every user class also has a set of requirements. Complete set of requirements for model evaluation is the union of requirements the union of each user class requirements.

For CMM (capability maturity model) software managers, process group's members, practitioners, all are interested to improve the quality

---

*Corresponding author: Shahid Yaqub Tabassam, Department of Computer Science, University of Lahore, Sargodha, Pakistan, E-mail: stabassam54@gmail.com

of software. They all are the audience [4].

User classes are given in the Table 2.

Set of requirements is known as stated in the ideal process quality model and the set of user classes is also known.

Figure 1 illustrates the relationship between user classes and the requirements [5] (Table 3).

There is no upper limit that a unique software process model exists only so we can say that $R \subseteq S$. It is required to maximize the degree to which the association of R concurs with the association of S [6].

R1, R2, R3 represent the user classes Table 1. Table 4 gives the relationship.

T is also other subset of R which has those requirements which are not necessary for R1, R2, R3.

So,

$$R = R1 \cup R2 \cup R3 \cup T$$

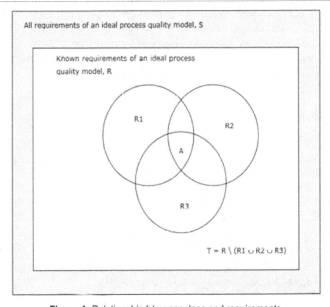

Figure 1: Relationship b/w user class and requirements.

Forms	Remarks
Satisfied	Model completely satisfy all requirements
Partly satisfied	Model satisfies the part of the requirements.
Not satisfied	Model does not satisfy the idea in the requirements.

Table 1: Form of correctness.

User classes	Description
UC1	SW developers
UC2	Manager
UC3	Customers

Table 2: User classes.

S	All requirements in ideal process
R	Requirements known in ideal process.
T	Requirements mapped with no user class
R1, R2, R3	Requirements mapped to specific class
A	Common requirements for all classes

Table 3: Key words for requirements.

R1	UC1(developers)
R2	UC2(process manager)
R3	UC3(customer or client)

Table 4: Relationship b/w user classes and requirements.

$$A = R1 \cup R2 \cup R3 \ T$$

$A = R \setminus (R1 \cup R2 \cup R3)$ $R1 \subseteq R$ $R2 \subseteq R$ $R3 \subseteq R$ $T \subseteq R$ $\forall x. \ x \in T \rightarrow (x \notin R1) \wedge (x \notin R2) \wedge (x \notin R3)$

In the figure the intersecting part of R1, R2, R3 where all are overlapping is the subset of user requirements. This part shows that the issues related to quality are common for all groups in working unit.

So these requirements should be fulfilled by the SW quality model.

The requirements of each class which are not common are for that class users only and issues of quality for these requirements require level of specialization. These are domain specific requirements.

Idyllically, $T = \emptyset$.

Irrelevant requirements are always null because these are cost inefficient.

Experiential Assessment Approach

The main purpose of this approach is to verify the theoretical model on experiments base. The methods in the theoretical approach are implemented. It ensures that the theory correct in the real world. In term of the notion of the quality the experiential approach improves the SW quality processes.

Approaches to experiential assessment

It is not sufficient that the theoretically model is valid it should be suitable for practical use and should produce the valid results. By number of case studies the experiential assessment of a SW quality model is done. The case studies and model definition are inputs of the approach and the quality of the input process is the output of the approach.

The comparative analysis is made on the performance of the output. The quality measure of different models for single process is compared by this approach [7].

The comparative performance is observed in this approach the evaluator is not the content of quality in this approach. Indirect similarity is measured in the contents of quality if two models are producing the similar results they share the common contents. If the results of all SW quality models are same then the any process can be chosen and there is no difficulty to choose any SW quality model for quality. In 2nd case if the results are not similar then we are required to choose that model which is more appropriate in the contents of quality.

Results to obtain by experiential assessment

The results by this approach can be divided in two main categories.

1. Model content dependent

2. Model content independent

Model content dependent results are useful for the analysis of SW quality model. The comparative assessment of model cannot be done in this way. A set of SW quality models and processes is defined in analytical approach. Each and every model is decomposed in individual elements which gives the detail used in that model.

The results are taken when the case study is complete and the form of results could be one for each element. This form could be like:

- Fulfilled

- Partly fulfilled

- Not fulfilled

These results are combined into set. Rating for the process quality is approved by use of the structure of model. The result set and quality measures of the process depend on model contents. For comparison of models the contents of the models are translated. For achieving this, mapping is done b/w each element of the model to the element of a standard model. Subjective measures are difficult to determine correctly.

So we can aspect that the experiential assessment procedure will give way these results [7].

• Process quality measures on the level of model element for process and process quality model.

• Process quality measures on the level of complete model for process and process SW quality model.

• Conformance of measure for case study process to every case study models in a standard format, at the level of the element of standard model.

• Conformance of measure for case study process to every case study models in a standard format, at the level of the complete standard model.

Input resources for experiential assessment procedure

Quality models: Each quality model is known as member of the assessment set of process quality models [8].

Many guidelines are to be monitored while checking for the quality models like:

• Model should be relevant to case study

• Model scope

• Model availability

• Guidelines availability for model application

• Third party resource backing

• How mature the model is

• Stability of the model

• Model Representativeness

• Status of model set

These three quality models were selected on the basis of above guidelines (Table 5). These models are broadly compatible with the evaluation set and with defined evaluation process, so there is no reason that any member from the set of evaluation will be unsuited by this procedure. The given guidelines are applied while measuring the software process model with specific quality model [9].

S.no	Model name
1	ISO 9001:1994/ ISO 9000-3 [8]
2	Spice v1.3 [10]
3	SW-CMM v1.3 [9]

Table 5: The software process model selected.

PReq1	stable process
PReq2	Non trivial process
PReq3	Process is in one production line
PReq4	Multiple workers in the process
PReq5	Software production is main focus
PReq6	Principles of sw engineering are utilized
PReq7	Unified process elements
PReq8	Open for investigation
PReq9	Documentation is available
PReq10	Can be observed
PReq11	Publication info is not restricted
PReq12	Publication not restricted by process
PReq13	It's a real process
PReq14	Software representation
PReq15	Mature process

Table 6: Requirements of a case study process.

Software processes

According to requirements the software process set is selected in 'Appendix N: Case study information'. Every process is in scope of study, and in scope of quality model defined in Table 1. So each process can be used in the experiential assessment procedures. The software process selection is given in Appendix N (appendix summary is given at the end of results below). Two independent processes were selected for the given case study [10]. These requirements were taken in account while working on case study for useable results (Table 6).

Case Study

Case 'A'

The students of the University of Durham implemented the software process while developing a software project in the session 2002-2003 [11]. The software process that these students used was undertaken as case study that is referred to A1, A2, and A3. The level of this organization is that the quality issue does not matter for this organization. Documents of the projects are input in this case study [11,12] and the observation of the process in first time is the experiential implementation.

The process has following characteristics:

- Well defined starts and end points.

- Immutable.

- Fall in the schedule.

Case 'B'

This case is the implementation of the process for the open source GNU GCC project [13]. This is mature project. In this case the latest version that was used in 2017 is discussed. This latest version was launched in 25 May 2017. This case was chosen mainly because the developers were not devolving the new software but they were working on the same software to develop it. In this case the quality is concerned to the organization, and we used this process to our case studies B1, B2, B3. Web site of GCC is Input assets. Because these are open source projects so these are easily available to the researcher.

Case Study Contents

The quality process models are shown in the Table 5 above. In Table 4 pairing for quality process model and software processes is made (Table 7).

Identifier	Name
A	University of Durham [11,12]
B	GNU GCC [13,14]

Table 7: Case studies.

Value	Remarks
n/a	Not applicable
F	Full adequate
P	Partly adequate
L	Large adequate
N	Not adequate

Table 8: Values for spice model.

Value	Remarks
n/a	Not applicable
Satisfied	complete satisfied
Unsatisfied	Wholly not satisfied

Table 9: Values for SW CMM model.

	Software process quality model			
		1	2	3
processes	A	1A	2A	3A
	B	1B	2B	3B

Table 10: Set for case studies.

Measurement Scale for Software Quality Models

Model 1: ISO 9001:1994 / ISO 9000-3

The measurement scale is assigned on three bases in this model:

- Satisfied
- Not satisfied
- Not applicable

Satisfied mean that model elements can be satisfied completely by the process. Not satisfied mean that content elements are not wholly satisfied, not applicable mean that it's a discrete manner.

Model 2: SPICE

Case study assigns a value for each element of model (Table 8).

Model3: SW-CMM

Case study assigns a value for each element of model (Table 9).

Results and Discussion

Standardized set of results for case studies (Table 10).

Case studies (1A, 2A, 3A)

Results set A: ISO 9001: 1994

Each element of ISO 9001:1994 is trivially mapped to itself.

Management responsibility: Satisfied 3 (60.00%), Unsatisfied: 2 (40.00%).

Quality system: Satisfied: 0 (0.00%), Unsatisfied: 3 (100.00%).

Contract review: Satisfied: 2 (50.00%), Unsatisfied: 2 (50.00%).

Design control: Satisfied: 7 (77.78%), Unsatisfied: 2 (22.22%).

Document and data control: Satisfied: 2 (66.67%), Unsatisfied: 1 (33.33%).

Purchasing: Satisfied: 1 (20.00%), Unsatisfied: 2 (40.00%), N/A: 2 (40.00%).

Control product: Satisfied: 0 (0.00%), Unsatisfied: 1 (100.00%).

Product traceability: Satisfied: 1 (100.00%), Unsatisfied: 0 (0.00%).

Process control: Satisfied: 0 (0.00%), Unsatisfied: 1 (100.00%).

Inspection and testing: Satisfied: 1 (14.29%), Unsatisfied: 6 (85.71%).

Inspections and measuring: Satisfied: 0 (0.00%), Unsatisfied: 2 (100.00%).

Test status: Satisfied: 0 (0.00%), Unsatisfied: 1 (100.00%).

Nonconforming control: Satisfied: 0 (0%), Unsatisfied: 2 (100%).

Corrective and preventative action: Satisfied: 0 (0.00%), Unsatisfied: 3 (100.00%).

Handling, and packaging: Satisfied: 6 (100.00%), Unsatisfied: 0 (0.00%).

Quality records: Satisfied: 0 (0.00%), Unsatisfied: 1 (100.00%).

Quality audits: Satisfied: 0 (0.00%), Unsatisfied: 1 (100.00%).

Training: Satisfied: 0 (0.00%), Unsatisfied: 1 (100.00%).

Servicing: Satisfied: 0 (0.00%), Unsatisfied: 0 (0.00%), N/A: 1 (100.00%).

Statistical techniques: Satisfied: 0 (0.00%), Unsatisfied: 1 (100.00%).

Case study 1A: ISO9001/ISO 9000-3 ISO9000-3

Management responsibility: Satisfied: 2 (28.57%), Unsatisfied: 5 (71.43%).

Quality system: Satisfied: 0 (0.00%), Unsatisfied: 5 (100.00%).

Contract review: Satisfied: 2 (50.00%), Unsatisfied: 2 (50.00%).

Design control: Satisfied: 17 (65.38%), Unsatisfied: 9 (34.62%).

Document and data control: Satisfied: 3 (33.33%), Unsatisfied: 6 (66.67%).

Purchasing: Satisficd: 0 (0.00%), Unsatisfied: 3 (100.00%).

Control product: Satisfied: 0 (0.00%), Unsatisfied: 1 (100.00%).

Product traceability: Satisfied: 2 (40.00%), Unsatisfied: 3 (60.00%).

Process control: Satisfied: 4 (66.67%), Unsatisfied: 2 (33.33%).

Inspection and testing: Satisfied: 8 (80.00%), Unsatisfied: 2 (20.00%).

Inspection and measuring: Satisfied: 5 (71.43%), Unsatisfied: 2 (28.57%).

Test status: Satisfied: 2 (40.00%), Unsatisfied: 3 (60.00%).

Nonconforming control: Satisfied: 12 (70.59%), Unsatisfied: 5 (29.41%).

Corrective and preventative action: Satisfied: 0 (0.00%), Unsatisfied: 1 (100.00%).

Handling and packaging: Satisfied: 4 (80.00%), Unsatisfied: 1 (20.00%).

Unsatisfied	55 (44.72%)
Satisfied	61 (49.59%)
n/a	7 (5.69%)
total	123 (100%)

Table 11: Overall results of case study1A: ISO9001/ISO 9000-3 ISO9000-3.

Unsatisfied	163 (46.82%)
Satisfied	167 (47.49%)
n/a	18 (5.17%)
Total	348 (100%)

Table 12: Overall results of case study 2A: SPICE.

Unsatisfied	152 (48.87%)
Satisfied	133 (42.77%)
n/a	26 (8.36%)
Total	311 (100%)

Table 13: Overall results of case study 3A: CMM.

Unsatisfied	53 (43.08%)
Satisfied	70 (56.92%)
n/a	0 (0.0%)
total	123 (100%)

Table 14: Overall results of case study 1B: ISO9001/ISO9000-3.

Unsatisfied	148 (42.52%)
Satisfied	197 (56.60%)
n/a	3 (0.86%)
Total	348 (100%)

Table 15: Overall results of case study 2B: SPICE.

Unsatisfied	133 (42.77%)
Satisfied	171 (54.98%)
n/a	7 (2.25%)
Total	311 (100%)

Table 16: Overall results of case study 3B: CMM.

Quality control record: Satisfied: 0 (0.00%), Unsatisfied: 1 (100.00%).

Quality audits: Satisfied: 0 (0.00%), Unsatisfied: 1 (100.00%).

Training: Satisfied: 0 (0.00%), Unsatisfied: 1 (100.00%).

Servicing: Satisfied: 0 (0.00%), Unsatisfied: 0 (0.00%), N/A: 7 (100.00%).

Statistical techniques: Satisfied: 0 (0.00%), Unsatisfied: 2 (100.00%).

All number of satisfied, N/A, and unsatisfied and process quality model that are mapped are in Table 11.

Case study 2A: SPICE

The data can be provided on demand in order to save the space. All number of satisfied, N/A, and unsatisfied and process quality model that are mapped are in Table 12.

Case study 3A: CMM

The data can be provided on demand in order to save the space. All number and of satisfied n/a and unsatisfied and process quality model that are mapped are in Table 13.

Case studies (1B, 2B,3B)

Case study 1B: ISO9001/ISO9000-3: All number and of satisfied n/a and unsatisfied and process quality model that are mapped are in Table 14.

Case study 2B: SPICE: All number and of satisfied n/a and unsatisfied and process quality model that are mapped are in Table 15.

Case study 3B: CMM: All number and of satisfied n/a and unsatisfied and process quality model that are mapped are in Table 16.

Result graphs of entire mode

We know that for model satisfaction these three values could be seen:

- Satisfied
- Not satisfied
- N/A

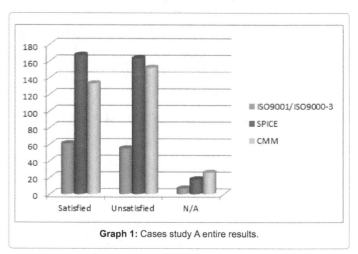

Graph 1: Cases study A entire results.

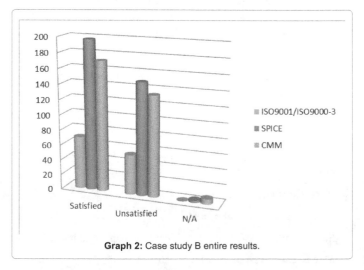

Graph 2: Case study B entire results.

For case study A: Graph 1 indicates the percentage of model necessities. For process A is relatively small, this is very small for results of process assessment [14]. The result range for 'satisfied' models is 42.77% and SW-CMM to 49.59% for ISO 9001:1994 / ISO 9000-3. The SPICE result is found 47.99%.

For case study B: In this graph the range for the 'satisfied' results is in the range 42.77% for SW-CMM to 54.98% and for ISO 9001:1994 / ISO 9000-3. The range size is 56.92% this cannot be disregard in is very efficient value [15]. The SPICE is found as 56.60% in this case study. In this case study all model behave similarly in content of the quality (Graph 2).

Conclusion and Future Work

In this paper a small node is compared to evaluate the quality process models. Many other finding can be calculated as it's a very vide area for getting the information. More case studies can also be included to get the more appropriate finding. In the same work many other aspects can be used for finding. For assessment more process model can be added in the future work. Formalized techniques may be used to find more formal quality process models also. More techniques can be used for pairing of both the process and quality models. These models can also be integrated for the development of the software's.

References

1. Daniel LM, Guttorm S, Terje B, Arne S (2002) Evaluating the Quality of Process Models: Empirical Testing of a Quality Framework. International Conference on Conceptual Modeling, pp: 380-396.

2. Soares MDS, Vrancken J (2008) Model-Driven User Requirements Specification using SysML. J Software 3: 57-68.

3. Aalst W, Desel J, Oberweis A (2000) Business Process Management: Models, Techniques and Empirical Studies. Lecture Notes in Computer Science, Springer.

4. Saavedra R, Ballejos LC, Ale M (2013) Quality Properties Evaluation for Software Requirements Specifications: An Exploratory Analysis. Semantic Scholar.

5. Paulk, M (1993) Comparing ISO 9001 and the Capability Maturity Model for Software. Software Quality Journal 2: 245-256.

6. Kraus T, Zheng Y (2007) Identifying User Needs and Establishing Requirements Interaction Design. Information and Computer Science, pp: 1-24.

7. Becker J, Rosemann M, Uthmann CV (2002) Guidelines of Business Process Modeling. Business Process Management 1806: 30-49.

8. Kitchenham B, Pfleeger SL, Fenton N (1995) Towards a Framework for Software Measurement Validation. IEEE Trans. Software Engineering 21: 929-944.

9. ISO (1994) ISO 9001: Quality systems – Model for Quality Assurance in Design, Development, Production, Installation and Servicing (2nd edn.). International Organization for Standardisation (ISO), Geneva.

10. Paulk M, Weber CV, Curtis B, Chrissis MB (1995) The Capability Maturity Model: Guidelines for improving the software process. Addison-Wesley, Cambridge MA. pp: 441.

11. SPICE Management Board (1995) SPICE Software Process Assessment.

12. http://www.dur.ac.uk/seg.administrator/

13. http://duo.dur.ac.uk/

14. http://www.gnu.org/software/gcc/

15. Raymond ES (1998) The cathedral and the bazaar. Tuxedo, ESR Writings, pp: 1-40.

32

Feature-Based Three-Dimensional Registration for Repetitive Geometry in Machine Vision

Yuanzheng Gong and Eric J Seibel*

Mechanical Engineering Department, University of Washington, Seattle, Washington, USA, 98195

Abstract

As an important step in three-dimensional (3D) machine vision, 3D registration is a process of aligning two or multiple 3D point clouds that are collected from different perspectives together into a complete one. The most popular approach to register point clouds is to minimize the difference between these point clouds iteratively by Iterative Closest Point (ICP) algorithm. However, ICP does not work well for repetitive geometries. To solve this problem, a feature-based 3D registration algorithm is proposed to align the point clouds that are generated by vision-based 3D reconstruction. By utilizing texture information of the object and the robustness of image features, 3D correspondences can be retrieved so that the 3D registration of two point clouds is to solve a rigid transformation. The comparison of our method and different ICP algorithms demonstrates that our proposed algorithm is more accurate, efficient and robust for repetitive geometry registration. Moreover, this method can also be used to solve high depth uncertainty problem caused by little camera baseline in vision-based 3D reconstruction.

Keywords: Iterative closest point (ICP); 3D registration; Machine vision; 3D reconstruction

Introduction

3D machine vision has been widely used in fields of industrial design, reverse engineering, surface defect inspection, manufacturing, virtual reality and even homeland security by its capability of reconstructing 3D surface. There are various optical 3D surface reconstruction methods have been developed, such as time-of-flight [1], structured-light [2], laser scanning [3], structure-from-motion (SfM) [4], multiview stereo vision [5] and etc. These 3D reconstruction methods create different 3D point clouds of various density, efficiency and accuracy. A common attribute is the generation of partial surface of the scanned object or scene in general cases due to the limited field of view of the camera/sensor. To build a complete surface, the 3D surface acquisition system needs to be moved around to capture all the parts of the object/scene from different perspectives. 3D geometrical registration of all of these point clouds that are created from different perspectives, into the same coordinate system is one of the most important and critical steps in 3D reconstruction. The most widely used method for registering 3D point clouds is called ICP [6].

With a proper initial rough alignment and sufficient overlapping 3D points, ICP algorithm obtains an optimal registration solution by minimizing the distance between point-to-point correspondences, known as closest point, in an iterative way [6]. The output of ICP algorithm is a 3D rigid transformation matrix (combination of rotation and translation) from source point cloud to reference cloud such that the root mean square (RMS) between correspondences is minimal. Many improved ICP algorithms have been proposed and studied since introduction of ICP [7]. Different with point-to-point approach, point-to-plane ICP minimizes the sum of the squared distance between a point in the source data and the tangent plane at its correspondence point [8]. Both of the point-to-point and point-to-plane ICP approaches require a good initial coarse alignment, which may be performed manually. Mian et al. developed an automatic pairwise registration of 3D point clouds by a novel tensor representation, which represents semi-local geometric structure patches of the point clouds [9]. Although ICP has become the most popular method for 3D registration, there remains a fundamental problem of ICP-based methods. They do not work well for the 3D registration of plane, cylinder and other objects with repetitive geometric structures. One solution to this problem is by attaching reference marks (RM) on the object [10]. However, the RM methods require preparation work before 3D scanning, and also they are very limited to complex and rough surfaces.

To solve this repetitive geometry issue, a feature-based 3D registration algorithm is proposed in this study to align two point clouds that are generated by vision-based 3D reconstruction, such as SfM, multiview stereo and structured-light scanning. To take advantage of the two-dimensional (2D) texture image of the object, features are detected from the texture images and matched to find the 3D correspondences between the two point clouds, with what 3D registration is much simplified. In this study, a test is performed with multiview stereo vision data. Performance evaluation of our proposed method and ICP-based ones (point-to-point, point-to-plane and Mian's) is performed. The comparison result demonstrates that the proposed method works for the alignment of repetitive geometries and performs more accurate, efficient and robust than ICP-based methods for this example case.

Methodology and Experiment

Figure 1 shows the flow chart of the proposed feature-based 3D registration algorithm, which follows a similar principle as the RM method, but with the ability to automate and generalize using computer vision. Instead of manually attaching physical reference markers on the object surface in RM, our approach detects the unique "markers" (features) from the 2D texture images. By using advanced computer vision algorithms of feature detection and matching, pairs of corresponding feature points are collected. In this study, scale-invariant feature transform (SIFT) [11] detection algorithm was applied to find the unique "markers" from each texture image; Random Sample Consensus (RANSAC) was used to select the robust matching feature pairs by calculating the Euclidean distance in SIFT descriptor space. The

*Corresponding author: Eric J Seibel, Mechanical Engineering Department, University of Washington, Seattle, Washington, USA, 98195
E-mail: eseibel@u.washington.edu

3D coordinates of these correspondences can be easily retrieved from the 3D point clouds. 3D registration problem is then much simplified by only calculating the rigid-body transformation matrix between these 3D correspondences. Unlike the RM method, our approach does not require any preparation work before scanning and is not limited to complex surface or working space.

Internally threaded hole is chosen in this study as the scanning object. Internal threads have repetitive geometry in both axial and angular directions, in Figure 2 and this application has great industrial value. The rapid 3D optical measurement of the internal threads becomes more important nowadays especially in the transportation (automobile) industry since the internally threaded holes in engine are crucial to the safety, longevity and efficiency of modern engines [12]. Our previous work demonstrated that a vision-based 3D reconstruction technique, called axial-stereo vision, could be used for the measurement of small internally threaded holes [13]. However, it only recovered very limited internal profile at the opening of the hole. To generate complete 3D model of threaded hole, 3D registration of such vision-based reconstructed point clouds is mandatory.

In this study, a coarse M8 internal thread was used as the sample. To capture its high topographic relief of internal thread profile, such as the peaks and valleys, a commercial side-view camera (Stryker™ scope #502--503--045) is used in this study, see Figure 2b. This commercial camera provides 45° side-viewing vision of the inner surface of the hole, see Figure 2c, which ensures good and consistent image quality with 1280 x 1024 pixels.

The procedure of generating two point clouds having repetitive profile can be laid out as four steps, see Figure 2d: step 1) placing the camera (center) along the axis of the threaded hole, facing to the side wall; step 2) with the same camera orientation, taking a series of images (the first data set) as the camera moves inwards from the opening to the bottom with constant step distance. We call such sequential images as

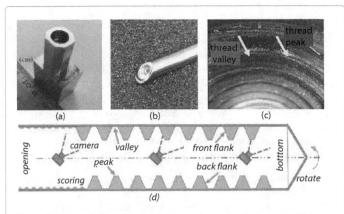

Figure 2: Data collection. (a) shows the aluminum object of coarse M8 internal threads; (b) shows angled tip of the commercial 45° side-viewing Stryker™ scope; (c) shows an image of M8 internal threads captured by the scope. The thread peak and valley shown as bright belt and dark area, respectively; (d) shows the diagram of a full axial scan of an internally threaded blind hole with 45° side-view camera.

a "quadrant"; step 3) repositioning the camera at the hole opening and rotating it along the hole axis at a proper rotation degree to ensure image overlapped with the previously captured quadrant; step 4) repeating the step 2) and collecting the second data set. For 3D reconstruction and registration purposes, the step distance and rotation angle are set as 0.1 mm and 30° respectively in this study to ensure more than 50% image overlap within neighbor images, which are realized by micro-positioning and rotation stages. In this study, the neighbor images that are collected with pure camera linear motion called an "axial neighbor", and the ones that are captured with pure camera rotation are called an "angular neighbor".

Due to the use of micro-positioning and rotation stages, the camera position and orientation data can be collected accurately and slowly. By taking advantage of the known camera pose information, the 3D reconstruction of the threads is accurate and efficient since it only needs to triangulate the 3D point cloud representing the internal surface, called multiview stereo [14]. However, processing all the images at once with state-of-art software VisualSfM [15], OpenMVG [16] or even the customized MATLAB code [17] does not result in a satisfying 3D reconstruction. The reason is that these quadrants are captured with pure camera rotation (the baseline is zero) if the camera center is aligned with the rotation axis, Figure 2d. For this scenario, the complete 3D model can be reconstructed by stacking all the quadrants together with known rotation angles. However, we have to consider the real cases of axes misalignment in the practical applications.

There are three axes in the procedure: hole axis, camera center axis and rotation axis. The misalignment of hole axis with the other two does not affect the reconstruction result. However, the misalignment of camera center line and rotation axis could generate geometrical discontinuity once stacking quadrants together directly. In the practical cases, such misalignment is small and also unknown. Both scenarios of well-alignment and misalignment would generate significant error when triangulating the depth [18], resulting gross reconstruction error. To avoid this, we propose to use axial sequence images to reconstruct the 3D point cloud of each quadrant with a multiview stereo algorithm, and the angular neighboring frames for the 3D registration of neighbor quadrant point clouds. This is one significance of this proposed feature-based 3D registration algorithm that it can solve high depth uncertainty problem caused by little camera baseline in vision-based 3D reconstruction.

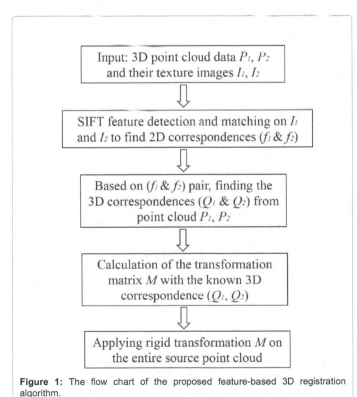

Input: 3D point cloud data P_1, P_2 and their texture images I_1, I_2

⇩

SIFT feature detection and matching on I_1 and I_2 to find 2D correspondences (f_1 & f_2)

⇩

Based on (f_1 & f_2) pair, finding the 3D correspondences (Q_1 & Q_2) from point cloud P_1, P_2

⇩

Calculation of the transformation matrix M with the known 3D correspondence (Q_1, Q_2)

⇩

Applying rigid transformation M on the entire source point cloud

Figure 1: The flow chart of the proposed feature-based 3D registration algorithm.

Given a set of n axial images for the ith quadrant $I_i = \{I_i^1, I_i^2, ..., I_i^n\}$ that are captured with linear motion of camera in one quadrant, feature detection and matching algorithms are applied to find the corresponding points in the image set. Let k_i represent all the features that are detected from I_i and g_i for the features used in the 3D reconstruction. g_i is a subset of k_i, $g_i \in k_i$, since not every feature in an image has correspondences in its axial neighbors. With a priori knowledge of camera extrinsic parameters, two 3D point clouds representing these two quadrants can be generated independently by the multiview stereo vision technique, see the details in [14].

In this experiment, 155 axial images were captured for each quadrant covering the range from the opening through the bottom. Here, we utilized state-of-art software VisualSfM [15] for the processing and visualization for each quadrant, shown in Figure 3, with label of the opening of threaded hole, and the start and end of the threads. The colorful straight line in Figure 3 is the series of camera positions of the line of these axial images as the micro- positioning stage moved inwards.

To register these two generated point clouds, the same feature matching algorithm is applied on the angular neighbor images to find the corresponding features between these two quadrants. Here, f_i is used to represent all the features in k_i that have correspondences in the other data set, so $f_i \in k_i$. For the common features that are used in both 3D reconstruction and 3D registration ($g_i \cap f_i$), their 3D coordinates in their own local coordinate systems are represented by Q_i, which can be retrieved from the reconstructed 3D models. The size of Q is $3 \times m$ where m is the total number of 3D correspondences. To register the first quadrant data (source) to the second one (reference), we have

$$R Q_1^j - t = Q_2^j \qquad (1)$$

for jth pair of 3D correspondence, j=1,2,...,m. In Eq. (1), Q_1 and Q_2 are known; R is a 3×3 rotation matrix from the coordinate system of the first quadrant to the second one. Strictly speaking, det (R)=1. $t = [t_x]^T$ is the translation vector. By subtracting off the respective mean $\overline{Q}$ from data Q_i, the effect of the translation vector t is eliminated. Considering this is an over-determined problem, rotation R can be solved by:

$$\min \|RY_1 - Y_2\| \qquad (2)$$

where $Y_i = Q_i - \overline{Q_i} \cdot R$ can be obtained by taking the singular value decomposition of the covariance matrix $Y_2 Y_1^T$ and t can be calculated by $t = RQ_1 - Q_2$. So far, the registration of these two point clouds is

achieved by applying rotation R and translation t on the entire source point cloud.

Results

To evaluate our proposed feature-based 3D registration algorithm, performances of our method and standard ICP-based (point-to-point, point-to-plane and Mian's) methods are compared. The visualization of the registration results is shown in Figure 4. The initial alignment is shown in Figure 4a by stacking two quadrants together directly. The obvious "discontinuity" of the two point clouds is caused by misalignment between camera center and hole axis in the practical setup. Since these two point clouds were nearly identical and repetitive in geometry, all the ICP-based methods result in a complete overlapping model, see Figure 4c-e. In contrast, the proposed feature-based 3D registration algorithm produced a qualitatively better result, see Figure 4b, with a rough 30° rotation angle and geometrical continuity.

To better understand the significance of the proposed feature-based 3D registration algorithm, two tables were created with more details of the performance comparison of our method and ICP-based approaches. Table 1 shows that our method generated 2.4° error (8%) for the estimation of rotation angle (we consider 30° is the ground truth). All three ICP-based methods generated more than 22° error (>74%) for the rotation angle estimation. These results of ICP-based methods are completely wrong even with root mean square (RMS) error of only about 0.088 mm that is much smaller than the one of our method (0138 mm), see Table 1. Among ICP-based methods, Mian's performs slightly better than the other two. The performance of point-to-point and point-to-plane methods are very close, except computation time. Moreover, our method is much faster than ICPs, allowing over 50,000× improvement by only calculating a rigid transformation with known 3D correspondences.

Table 2 shows the comparison of the robustness of our method and standard ICP-based methods. Five independent tests were performed, following by the same flow chart but with different quadrants data of the internal threads. The comparison result shows that our method keeps a very low estimation error of the rotation angle within a threaded hole. All the algorithms were implemented in MATLAB, running on a Dell Precision 5510 with 2.8 GHz Intel E3-1505M CPUs, 32.0 GB memory in a 64-bit Window operating system.

Discussion and Conclusion

In this study, a feature-based 3D registration algorithm is proposed to solve the repetitive geometry issue for the point clouds that are generated by vision-based 3D reconstruction techniques. The standard ICP-based algorithms do not work well for the geometry with repetitive profiles. By taking advantage of the texture images and the robustness of the SIFT feature, 3D correspondences between these two point clouds can be collected by finding the matching features in the texture images. In this study, two point clouds of the internally threaded hole were generated independently based on multiview stereo. The internally threaded hole in metal is considered as a good test sample since its profile comes with repetitive shape in both axial and angular directions, and has wide-spread industrial applicability. The comparison among our method and ICP-based (point-to-point, point-to- plane, Mian's) methods demonstrated that our approach works much better (less registration error) for this case in a more efficient and robust way.

This proposed feature-based 3D registration method can be used for the registration of point clouds that are not just generated by multiview stereo 3D reconstruction, but also for other vision-based

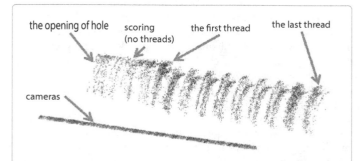

Figure 3: The 3D reconstruction of one quadrant of the recessed internally threaded hole from a sequence of axial images with known camera position and orientation.

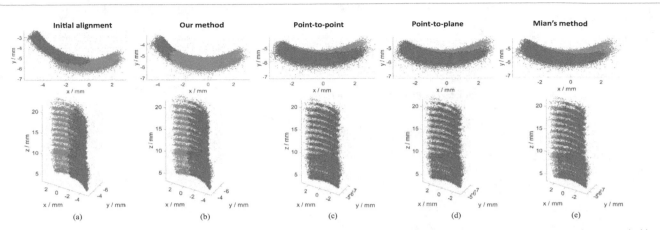

Figure 4: The comparison of 3D registration results by our proposed feature-based method and popular ICP approaches. (a) shows the top and side views of the initial alignment of two differently colored neighbor quadrants with known 30° rotation angle; (b) shows the top and side views of the result of our proposed feature-based 3D registration method, good alignment shows smooth connection between these two data sets; (c) shows the top and side views of the result of the point-to-point ICP method; (d) shows the top and side views of the result of the point-to-plane ICP; (e) shows the top and side views of the result of the Mian's method. ICP-based methods (c)-(e) generated incorrect 3D registration of quadrant views of a threaded hole.

Method	error of rotation angle (°)	computation time (sec)	RMS of registration (mm)
our method	2.4	0.001	0.138
point-to-point ICP	26.7	1574	0.088
point-to-plane ICP	26	1186	0.088
Mian's method	22.2	78	0.087

Table 1: The comparison of our method and ICP approaches.

	our method	point-to-point ICP	point-to-plane ICP	Mian's method
test 1	5.51	28.69	27.98	22.46
test 2	2.44	26.7	26.02	22.16
test 3	4.05	30.27	30.53	18.71
test 4	3.24	27.45	27.45	24.09
test 5	3.1	26.18	26.39	23.29
avg.	3.67	27.86	27.67	22.14
std.	1.18	1.64	1.78	2.06

Table 2: The rotation angle evaluation of our method and ICP-based approaches with multiple tests (°).

3D reconstruction techniques, such as structured-light scanning. The texture images of the object or scene from different perspectives can be generated by three-step phase-shifting algorithm [19]. The same as our proposed approach, feature detection and matching are performed to find the 2D matching features, based on which 3D correspondences are retrieved from individual 3D model at each view. Moreover, this proposed method can be also used to improve the SfM 3D reconstruction. Different with multiview stereo, SfM doesn't require camera information. It estimates all the camera parameters and 3D scene simultaneously by solving a non-linear, non-convex optimization problem [20]. With little camera baseline and therefore high depth uncertainty, the non-convexity of SfM may generate a completely unacceptable 3D model. The strategy proposed here of classifying images as two categories, one for 3D reconstruction and the other for 3D registration, can be used to eliminate the effect of little camera baseline issue.

Acknowledgement

We thank The National Robotics Initiative for providing funding for this project, NIH R01 EB016457, "NRI-Small: Advanced biophotonics for image-guided robotic surgery". The authors appreciate Andrew Naluai-Cecchini (University of Washington, UW), Casey Paus and Sean Mayman (Stryker™ Endoscopy) for their help on providing Stryker scopes at the WWAMI Institute for Simulation in Healthcare (WISH) at UW Medicine, Seattle, USA.

References

1. Amann MC, Bosch T, Lescure M, Myllyla R, Rioux M (2001) Laser ranging: a critical review of usual techniques for distance measurement. Optical engineering 40: 10-19.

2. Gong Y, Zhang S (2010) Ultrafast 3-d shape measurement with an off-the-shelf dlp projector. Optics express 18: 19743-19754.

3. Baltsavias EP (1999) A comparison between photogrammetry and laser scanning. ISPRS Journal of photogrammetry and Remote Sensing 54: 83-94.

4. Mouragnon E, Lhuillier M, Dhome M, Dekeyser F, Sayd P (2009) Generic and real-time structure from motion using local bundle adjustment. Image and Vision Computing 27: 1178-1193.

5. Hartley R, Zisserman A (2003) Multiple view geometry in computer vision. Cambridge university press.

6. Besl PJ, McKay ND (1992) Method for registration of 3-d shapes. International Society for Optics and Photonics in Robotics-DL tentative.

7. Salvi J, Matabosch C, Fofi D, Forest J (2007) A review of recent range image registration methods with accuracy evaluation. Image and Vision computing 25: 578-596.

8. Chen Y, Medioni G (1992) Object modelling by registration of multiple range images. Image and vision computing 10: 145-155.

9. Mian AS, Bennamoun M, Owens RA (2006) A novel representation and feature matching algorithm for automatic pairwise registration of range images. International Journal of Computer Vision 66: 19-40.

10. Franaszek M, Cheok GS, Witzgall C (2009) Fast automatic registration of range images from 3d imaging systems using sphere targets. Automation in Construction 18: 265-274.

11. Lowe DG (1999) Object recognition from local scale-invariant features. The proceedings of the seventh IEEE international conference on computer vision.

12. Hong E, Zhang H, Katz R, Agapiou JS (2012) Non-contact inspection of internal threads of machined parts. The International Journal of Advanced Manufacturing Technology 62: 221-229.

13. Gong Y, Johnston R, Melville CD, Seibel EJ (2015) Axial-stereo 3d optical metrology for inner profile of pipes using a scanning laser endoscope. International journal of optomechatronics 9: 238-247.

14. Szeliski R (2010) Computer vision: algorithms and applications. Springer Science and Business Media.

15. Wu C (2013) Towards linear-time incremental structure from motion. International Conference on 3D Vision.

16. Open Multiple View Geometry Library.

17. Gong Y, Hu D, Hannaford B, Seibel EJ (2014) Accurate three-dimensional virtual reconstruction of surgical field using calibrated trajectories of an image-guided medical robot. Journal of Medical Imaging 1: 035002-035002.

18. Gallup D, Frahm JM, Mordohai P, Pollefeys M (2008) Variable baseline/ resolution stereo. IEEE Conference on Computer Vision and Pattern Recognition.

19. Gong Y, Zhang S (2011) High-resolution, high-speed three-dimensional shape measurement using projector defocusing. Optical Engineering 50: 023603-023603.

20. Gong Y, Meng D, Seibel EJ (2015) Bound constrained bundle adjustment for reliable 3d reconstruction. Optics express 23: 10771-10785.

33

Evaluation of Penetration of Electronic Tools for Pedagogical Purposes in Nigerian Universities Compared to British Universities

Folayan GB* and Folayan KT

Department of Electrical/Electronic Engineering, The Federal Polytechnic, Ado-Ekiti, Nigeria

Abstract

E-learning tools have become important for teaching and learning in universities all over the world. The rate of penetration of these tools into teaching and learning environment in developed and developing countries are quite different. This paper compares the availability of these tools in universities in a developed country and universities in a developing country. This paper will aim to bring to fore the low penetration of e-learning tools in developing countries like Nigeria. Ten universities are picked at random five in the United Kingdom and five in Nigeria. E-learning tools in the countries are then compared to evaluate the rate of appreciation and penetration.

Keywords: E-learning tools; Universities; Penetration; Evaluate; Pedagogical

Introduction

The acquisition or dissemination of Knowledge needs to be effectively done so that the recipient can have a wholesome experience. A wholesome experience can be elusive without communication. The electronic tools used for learning (hereafter referred to as E-learning tools) make communication easier. E-learning includes all forms of electronically supported learning and teaching. The information and communication systems, whether networked learning or not, serve as specific media to implement the learning process [1].

Efficient use of E-learning tools for acquisition, storage, transfer, retrieval, application, and visualization of learning materials often distinguish successful learning environment from the unsuccessful ones. The ability to obtain, assimilate, and apply the right knowledge effectively will become a key skill in the next century. Learning is the key to achieving our full potential. Our survival in the 21st century as individuals, organizations, and nations will depend upon our capacity to learn and the application of what we learn to our daily lives [1].

Research Method

The use of ICT in Nigeria became well known during the late 1990s at the advent of internet facilities in the country for the first time. However, Britain had been using the internet long before the 90s. In order to know the existing e-learning tools in Nigerian universities and then compare with that of British universities, this research work was conducted in Nigeria and Britain. Ten universities were selected at random, five universities in each country. The Nigerian Universities are Ekiti State University (EKSU), Afe Babalola University (ABUAD), Obafemi Awolowo University (OAU), Ladoke Akintola, University of Technology (LAUTECH) and Ahmadu Bello University (ABU) while the British universities include, Teesside University (TU), University of Liverpool (UL), University of Glasgow (UG), University of Aberdeen (UA) and University of East London (UE). The universities are then paired, that is a Nigerian university and a British university so that a comparison can be done.

Questionnaires were distributed in all these schools and the results collated. Schools like Teesside University, University of Liverpool, University of East London, Afe Babalola University and Ekiti State University, were actually visited. Two parameters would be compared: availability and percentage of students that have access. Identified three major types of e-learning tools: curriculum tools, digital library tools and teaching aid tools. All e-learning tools fall under one of these major categories [2]. Some e-learning tools are picked under each category and their deployment and percentage of students' access are then compared.

E-Learning Tools

E-learning is an education via the Internet, network, standalone computer or other electronic devices. E-learning is basically the network- enabled transfer of skills and knowledge. E-learning refers to using electronic applications and processes to learn. E-learning applications and processes include Web-based learning, Computer-based learning, virtual classrooms and digital collaboration. E-learning is when content is delivered via the Internet, intranet/extranet, audio or video tape, satellite TV, and CD- ROM [1].

Before analysing the access of students to the E-learning tools, the most important part to be considered and analysed is the access of students to computers and the internet. Apart from individual computers, universities should make provisions for computers. In the UK universities, computers are made available in the library and in the laboratories. All students in these universities have access to computers always. It should be noted that not all students will use the computer systems at the same time but students' response shows that they have access to computers when needed. In addition to this, these computers hold propriety software's that may be too heavy or expensive for personal computers. In addition to provision of computers, another necessity is the provision of internet access. UK universities have WiFi available all over campus for personal computers and computers in laboratories and library also have internet facilities.

However the case is not the same in Nigerian universities. While access to computers are limited to very few computers, those few computers do not have licensed software's and hardly have software's necessary for simulation and analysis. Internet service exist in some cases but students have to pay extra amount of money to have access. The graph below shows the percentage of access to computers and also percent of access to internet (Figures 1 and 2).

*Corresponding author: Folayan GB, Department of Electrical/Electronic Engineering, The Federal Polytechnic, Ado-Ekiti, Nigeria
E-mail: nattygbengu@gmail.com

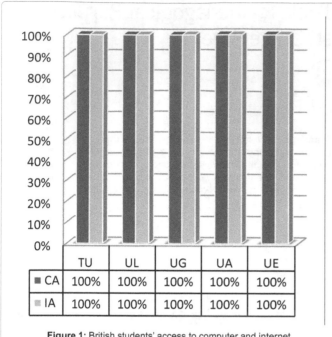

Figure 1: British students' access to computer and internet.

	TU	UL	UG	UA	UE
■ CA	100%	100%	100%	100%	100%
▣ IA	100%	100%	100%	100%	100%

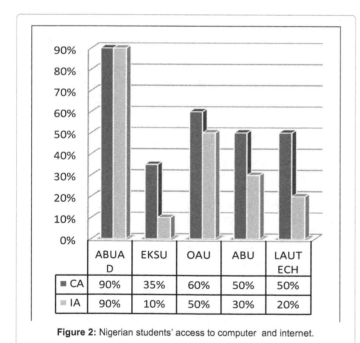

Figure 2: Nigerian students' access to computer and internet.

	ABUAD	EKSU	OAU	ABU	LAUTECH
■ CA	90%	35%	60%	50%	50%
▣ IA	90%	10%	50%	30%	20%

Curriculum Tools

Curriculum tools are widely used in high school and college of education. Materials are selected and organized to facilitate class activities. Additional tools, such as discussion forums and online quizzes, are integrated to support collaboration and evaluation. Other tools include learning progress scheduling and tracking, selftesting and evaluation and even plagiarism check. A very good example for checking plagiarism in the UK universities is software called 'turn it in UK'. The level of plagiarism is checked against the accepted value.

UK universities make use of applications like the Blackboard to make provisions for online collaboration between students and lecturers and among students. Online collaboration provides opportunity for students and lecturers to leave questions and comments that others can later view to further enhance their knowledge. The Blackboard also provides the platform for instructors to leave lecture notes, assignments and other materials available to students. UK students have access to this platform and can easily download notes, supplementary notes as well as view what other students think about an assignment.

Nigerian universities do not have such. The most some universities have like OAU is an e-portal that does not provide for online collaboration or even class materials. Figure 3 shows the percentage of access to online materials between British universities (B S) and Nigerian universities (N S) while Figure shows the percentage of access to online collaboration(Figure 4).

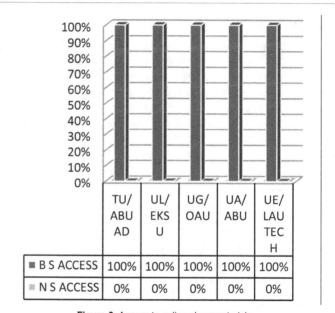

	TU/ ABUAD	UL/ EKSU	UG/ OAU	UA/ ABU	UE/ LAUTECH
■ B S ACCESS	100%	100%	100%	100%	100%
▣ N S ACCESS	0%	0%	0%	0%	0%

Figure 3: Access to online class materials.

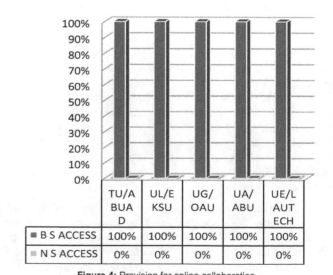

	TU/ABUAD	UL/EKSU	UG/OAU	UA/ABU	UE/LAUTECH
■ B S ACCESS	100%	100%	100%	100%	100%
▣ N S ACCESS	0%	0%	0%	0%	0%

Figure 4: Provision for online collaboration.

Teaching Aids

Teaching aids are electronic materials and tools used to aid teaching in the classroom. These make presentation easier and more organised. Some of them include multimedia projectors and laser pointers, computers with multimedia player for instructors and simulating software's and applications. Research has however shown that electronic teaching aids help students have better grasp of concepts and ideas taught in classrooms. It also boosts student interest and attitude during learning [3].

All classrooms in all universities sampled in the UK use multimedia projectors for teaching the students, the lecture rooms are also provided with computer systems with internet facility for the sole use of lecturers. Of all the universities sampled in Nigeria only ABUAD which is a private university have about 80% of its classrooms fitted with projectors and interactive boards. OAU is next with 40% to aid teaching, simulating software's and applications are also necessary. For instance in Engineering software's like MATLAB are often used for simulation to show how machines behave under certain circumstances and changing variables (Figure 5).

Most students in the UK report that all software's necessary in their courses are available on computers in the laboratory at the very least while some are available in the library. The case is not the same with Nigerian universities. The few universities in Nigeria that have some simulating software's did not obtain the necessary license. Figure 6 shows the comparison between British universities and Nigerian universities.

Library Facilities

Availability and access to E-Books and E- Journals

There is no university or academic institutions without access to reference materials and academic journals and papers. However access has moved from hardcopies to softcopies and hence the need for electronic access to such materials in the library. Universities in the UK have facilities to search for E-books and E-journals. Usernames and passwords are issued to students and they are used to access such. All the universities where research were carried out pointed out the fact that

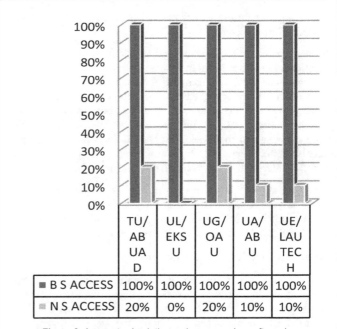

	TU/ABUAD	UL/EKSU	UG/OAU	UA/ABU	UE/LAUTECH
■ B S ACCESS	100%	100%	100%	100%	100%
▪ N S ACCESS	20%	0%	20%	10%	10%

Figure 6: Access to simulating and programming software's.

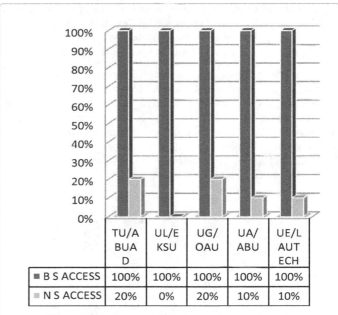

	TU/ABUAD	UL/EKSU	UG/OAU	UA/ABU	UE/LAUTECH
■ B S ACCESS	100%	100%	100%	100%	100%
▪ N S ACCESS	20%	0%	20%	10%	10%

Figure 7: Availability and access to e-books and e- journals

access are even provided to other electronic journals libraries like IEEE, Science Direct and other online libraries. The graph in Figure 7 shows the level of access in both British Universities and Nigerian Universities. As shown Nigerian universities have not made any provisions for e-libraries except at ABUAD and OAU where provisions are made and efforts are being made to populate their e-library.

Online searching of library catalogue and reservation of books

"A Library catalogue is a register of all bibliographic items found in a library or group of libraries, such as a network of libraries at several

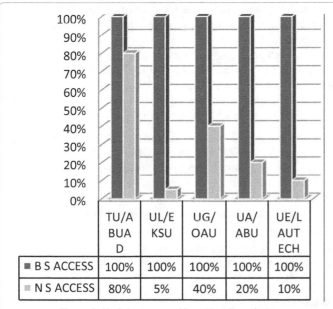

	TU/ABUAD	UL/EKSU	UG/OAU	UA/ABU	UE/LAUTECH
■ B S ACCESS	100%	100%	100%	100%	100%
▪ N S ACCESS	80%	5%	40%	20%	10%

Figure 5: % of classrooms with multimedia projector.

locations. A bibliographic item can be any information entity (e.g., books, computer files, graphics cartographic materials, etc.) that is considered library material" [4].

The card catalogue was a familiar sight to library users for generations, but it has been effectively replaced by the online public access catalogue (OPAC). This makes it possible to search for book and journal online and reserve the book remotely till arrival at the library. In situations where the library have the book but has been borrowed by another subscriber, OPAC makes it possible to view when the book will be available and then make reservation. Physical presence at the library is not necessary to confirm the availability of a particular library material of interest, thereby reducing time wastage.

Figure 8 shows that universities in the UK all have provisions for online searching and reservation of books. Nigerian Universities are not up to scratch about online searching of books and their reservation. ABUAD and OAU lead the pack with just 20% access.

Availability of Self Service Machine

More than ever, libraries throughout both the education and public sectors are looking for ways to make savings while maintaining and improving the service provided to users. Self service systems and other devices that communicate with the library management system.

When installed at libraries, self-service machine enable users to borrow and return items, check their account and make payments quickly and easily. Other machines can sort returned items into library specified categories, speeding up re-shelving. Self service machines operate without staff intervention enabling 24/7 service if required. (Delivering self-service transactions in libraries (no date).

As shown in Figure 9, all the British universities have service machine in their libraries. Students even indicated that they have all at one point or the other used it, indicating a 100% availability and access. Nigerian universities on the other hand have not even started looking into their use. The fact that most university library in Nigeria does not allow students to take books out of the library has partly contributed to their lethargic look into such machines. Figure 9 therefore shows 0% for all the Nigerian Universities in this aspect.

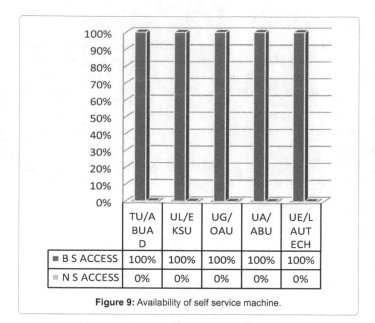

	TU/A BUA D	UL/E KSU	UG/ OAU	UA/ ABU	UE/L AUT ECH
■ B S ACCESS	100%	100%	100%	100%	100%
▪ N S ACCESS	0%	0%	0%	0%	0%

Figure 9: Availability of self service machine.

Discussion

It is obvious from the data available that the penetration and use of electronic tools in Nigerian tertiary education is still very low and in some cases near non-existent. In most tertiary institutions in the country, the fact that ICT facilities and computers are not available is worrisome. It shows that there is a long way to go. When there are no computers, or in some cases where students do not have access to the computers available, you wonder if the institution is planning to make some of these services available. For instance how do students check for the availability of textbooks online?

In the area of teaching, it is in fact very heartbreaking that most students from Nigerian institutions graduate without being taught using a projector or other multimedia tools. It is obvious that it will be difficult for the students to understand some technical graphs and diagrams, and processes that can be explained using a video.

E-learning for smart classrooms (2008) showed that 'The Organisation for Economic Change and Development (OECD 2005) has identified critical factors that determine a nation's economic growth, development and success within a globally competitive market. Outlined was the critical role ICT played in entrepreneurship, innovation and the development of social capital. The capacity of students and teachers to use (digital literacy) and apply ICT (pedagogy) will be key for economic growth and stability in the future.

Similarly, the United Nations Education, Scientific and Cultural Organisation (UNESCO) strongly emphasises the relationship between ICT use, education reform, and economic growth. This is based on assumptions that systemic economic growth is the key to poverty reduction and increased prosperity and that ICT are engines for growth and tools for empowerment with profound implications [5].

While businesses, consumers, students and organisations globally are convinced of the potential and importance of ICT, some educators are still arguing and struggling to accept and adoptlearning through, and with, ICT [6-9].

Conclusion

Most tertiary institutions in Nigeria are being owned by government.

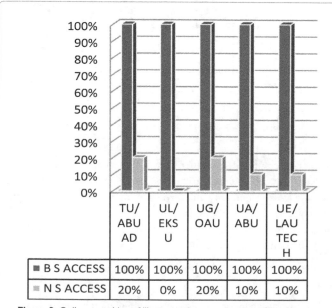

	TU/ ABU AD	UL/ EKS U	UG/ OAU	UA/ ABU	UE/ LAU TEC H
■ B S ACCESS	100%	100%	100%	100%	100%
▪ N S ACCESS	20%	0%	20%	10%	10%

Figure 8: Online searching of library catalogue and reservation of books.

It is therefore urgently necessary for the Nigerian government to stand up to her responsibilities and found institution appropriately. In this age it is really a shame that students in some institutions graduate without even having access to computers. No wonder some graduates cannot even use computers effectively. Management of institutions should also know that most of these electronic platforms are not luxuries but necessities. They help instructors to deliver their classes in a more effective way. Time losses, paper use and loss of information are reduced to the minimum.

References

1. Devajit M, Majidul A (2012) E-learning Objectives, Methodologies, Tools and its Limitation. International Journal of Innovative Technology & Exploring Engineering 2: 46-51.

2. Oye ND, Salleh M, Iahad NA (2012) E.Learning Methodologies and Tools. International Journal of Advanced Computer Science and Applications 3: 48-52.

3. Galy E, Downey C, Johnson J (2011) The effect of using E-Learning Tools in online and Campus based classrooms on Student performance. Journal of Information Technology Education10 : 209-230.

4. Chan LM (2007) Cataloging and classification: an introduction. (3rdedn), Lanham: Scarecrow press.

5. E-learning for smart classrooms (2008).

6. Schacter J (1999) The Impact of Educational Technology on students achievement: What the current research has to say. Milken Exchange on Education Technology Journal.

7. Akhigbe BI (2010) Comparative Study of usage of information and communication Technology in Developed and developing Nations. International Conference on ICT Applications.

8. Aljawarneh S (2010) E-Learning Tools and technologies in Education: A perspective.

9. Bates T (2004) Online Learning tools and Technologies.

Permissions

List of Contributors

Workineh Tesema
Department of Information Science, Jimma University, Jimma, Ethiopia

Duresa Tamirat
Department of Information Science, Medawolabu University, Robe, Ethiopia

Nada O Bajnaid
King Abdulaziz University, Saudi Arabia

Rachid Benlamri
Lakehead University, Ontario, Canada

Algirdas Pakstas
London Metropolitan University, UK

Shahram Salekzamankhani
London Metropolitan University, UK

Shivendra Kumar P, Hari Krishna T and R. K. Kapoor
Department of Computer Application and Research, National Institute of Technical Teachers Training and Research, Bhopal, India

Rajpreet Kaur
CGC, Landran Mohali, Punjab, India

Manish Mahajan
Computer Science and Engineering, CGC, Landran Mohali, Punjab, India

Baroudi Mohammed Yassine, Benammar Abdelkrim and Bendimerad Fethi Tarik
Department of Electrical Engineering and Electronics, University Aboubakr BELKAID Tlemcen, Algeria

Logeshwari R, Ashok D and Karthikayani K
Assistant Professor, Department of Computer Science, SRM University, Chennai, India

Sindhuja A
Assistant Professor, Department of Information Technology, Prathyusha Institute of Technology and Management, Thiruvallur, India

Javed Alam
Research Scholar, Dept. of CS,Mewar University, Gangrar, Chittorgarh, Rajasthan, India

Pandey MK
Director, Computer Science and Applications, AIMCA, Haldwani, Uttrakhand, India

Majid Mehmood
Department of Information Technology, University of Lahore, Gujrat, Pakistan

Kinza Sattar
Department of Computer Science, COMSATS, Abbottabad, Pakistan

Asif Hussain Khan and Mujahid Afzal
Department of Information Technology, University of Lahore, Gujrat, Pakistan

Mohammed El Mokhtar Ould El Mokhtar
Qassim University, College of Science, Departement of Mathematics, BO 6644, Bu- raidah: 51452, Kingdom of Saudi Arabia

Pravin BR and Geetha
P M.E Computer Science Engineering, DhanalaksmiSrinivasan College of Engineering and Technology, Chennai

Odewale OA
Ondo State Information Technology Development Centre (SITDEC), 1, Farm House Aguda Close, Ondo Road Akure, Ondo State, Nigeria

Jiyang Liu, Liang Zhu, Weiqiang Sun and Weisheng Hu
State Key Laboratory of Advanced Optical Communication Systems and Networks, Shanghai Jiao Tong University, Shanghai 200240, China

Ashish Sharma and Mandeep Kaur
Department of Computer Science and Engineering, Guru Nanak Dev University, Regional Campus Jalandhar, India

Novotný R, Kadlec J and Kuchta R
Brno University of Technology, Technická 3058/10, 616 00 Brno, The Czech Republic

Hemant Agrawal, Ajay Thakur, Rajan Slathia and Sumangali K
School of Information Technology and Engineering, VIT University, Vellore, Tamil Nadu, 632014, India

Ajeet Singh
Lecturer in Jagaran Lakecity University, SOET, Bhopal

Alaa Hassan
University of Kirkuk, Kirkuk, Iraq

Ruba Ali Alsuhaymi
Department of Software Engineering, Prince Sultan University, Riyadh, Saudi Arabia

Fayez Fok Al Adeh
The Syrian Cosmological Society, Damascus, Syria

Sagar Soman and Michael Cada
Department of Electrical and Computer Engineering, Dalhousie University, Halifax, NS, Canada

Hassan Khalid, Farhat-ul-ain and Kokab Khushboo
Department of Computer Science, Abdul Wali Khan University, Mardan, Pakistan

Hamed M and Higgett N
School of Art, Design and Humanities, De Montfort University, Leicester, UK

Mohamed D Almadhoun
University College of Applied Sciences, Palestine, Gaza

Sameer Kumar Bisoyi and Hassan Reza
School of Aerospace Sciences, Department of Computer Science, University of North Dakota, North Dakota, USA

Jamal Kheiri
University of Tehran, Tehran, Iran

Sachin M Dandage
Department of Computer Science and Engineering, PLITMS, Buldana, Maharashtra, India

Mohsin A, Fatima S, Khan AU and Nawaz F
Department of Computer Science and Engineering, Air University Multan, Pakistan

Elhossiny Ibrahim and Nirmeen A El-Bahnasawy
Computer Science and Engineering Department, Cairo University, Menouf 32952, Egypt

Fatma A Omara
Faculty of Computers and Information, Cairo University, Egypt

Mehdi Mekni, Mounika G, Sandeep C and Gayathri B
Department of Computer Science and Information Technology, St. Cloud State University, St. Cloud, Minnesota, USA

Jaya Gupta and Suneeta Gola
College of Science & Engineering, Department of Computer Engineering, India

Tanzila Kehkashan, Shahid Yaqub Tabassam and Nayyar Manzoor
Department of Computer Science, University of Lahore, Sargodha, Pakistan

Yuanzheng Gong and Eric J Seibel
Mechanical Engineering Department, University of Washington, Seattle, Washington, USA, 98195

Folayan GB and Folayan KT
Department of Electrical/Electronic Engineering, The Federal Polytechnic, Ado-Ekiti, Nigeria

Index

A

Accounting System, 60
Adaptive Service, 28
Afan Oromo, 1-4
Agile Methodology, 132, 178
Agile Software Development, 5-6, 11, 14-15, 17, 133, 178, 180, 184-185
Ahp, 153-156, 158-160, 168, 172
Architectural Styles, 166-169, 171-172, 184
Architecture, 13, 23, 28-31, 45, 57-58, 69, 71-72, 78, 81-82, 85, 99-100, 102, 127, 150, 152, 166-174, 178, 180-185, 190
Automated Decisions, 166

B

Baseband Receiver, 122
Betweenness, 89-90, 94, 96-97
Bio-capsule Generation, 32-33
Biometrics, 32-33, 35, 152
Bit Error Rate, 81, 85-87

C

Cloud, 23-26, 45-49, 58, 166-168, 172-178, 200-202
Concave Term, 50
Context-awareness, 5, 17, 149
Contextaware Security, 144
Corporate Social Responsibility, 153-155, 160
Critical Exponent, 50
Cross Site Request Forgery, 186, 188-189
Cryptography, 23, 26, 32, 98-99, 145, 147
Csrf Gateway, 186, 189-191
Cyber-physical Systems, 144, 147, 151-152

D

Data Privacy, 23
Deadlock Detection Algorithm, 19, 21-22
Decryption, 98-100, 102
Disable Users, 1
Distribute System, 76
Distributed Software Developments, 127
Distributed Systems, 19, 21-22, 46, 49, 79, 175
Dtdm, 36
Dynamic Adaptation, 28-29, 31

E

E-government, 60, 65, 67-68
E-learning, 5, 17-18, 205, 208-209
Electronic Computations, 117, 119-120

Encryption, 6, 23-27, 65, 98-100, 102, 145-146, 170, 191-192
Entropy, 117-120, 147-148
Error Correction Code, 81, 83, 85-87
Exact Covering, 144

F

Finite Automata, 19-20, 22
Flash Memory, 81-88
Framework, 9-10, 24-25, 28, 31, 49, 77, 92, 96, 116, 127-128, 133, 135-136, 139, 144, 146, 148-149, 151, 154-155, 160-161, 163-164, 166-168, 173, 180, 185, 187, 199
Fusion Algorithm, 32
Fuzzy Topsis, 153, 157-160

G

Genetic Algorithm, 46, 56, 59, 76-80, 174, 177
Global Software Development, 127, 133-134
Gsm E-notice, 161

H

Histogram Equalization, 32-34

I

Information Security, 32, 102, 144-146, 173
Inter-symbol Interference, 122
Internet, 23, 28, 32, 45, 47-49, 58, 60-61, 64-65, 67-68, 75, 89, 98, 111-113, 116, 135-136, 138, 151-152, 166-167, 173-174, 180, 185-186, 205-207
Iterative Closest Point (ICP), 200

L

Linear Prolate Functions, 122, 126
Load Balancing, 45-49, 64, 76, 170, 177

M

Make Span, 47-48, 76
Microcontroller, 161
Minutiae Points, 32-33, 35
Mobile Application, 103
Modified Contextaware Security; Framework, 144
Morphological Operation, 32
Mountain Pass Theorem, 50
Multi Processor, 76
Multi-criteria Requirements, 166, 168
Multi-regression Technique, 127

N

Nearness, 89, 92

Nehari Manifold, 50-51, 55
Network Metadata Structure, 69-71, 74
Network Update, 69-75
News Articles, 111-116
Non-volatile, 81-82, 85, 87

O
Ontology-based Reasoning, 5, 11

P
Particle Swarm Optimization, 58, 174-175, 177
Plagiarism, 111-112, 114, 116, 206
Processing Bandwidth, 122, 124-126
Prolate Filter, 122, 124-126
Provenance, 111-112, 114-116

Q
Qos, 45-49, 56-59, 146
Quality Attributes, 5-6, 17, 134, 166-170, 172-173, 182
Quantum Mechanics, 117, 119-121

R
Reliability, 6-8, 46-49, 76, 79, 81, 83, 86-88, 111, 113, 116, 129, 132, 137, 144, 166, 168-172, 177
Rule Based; Dss, 166

S
Schedule Time, 76, 78-79
Security, 6-7, 12, 23-26, 32, 35, 46, 48-49, 57-58, 62-65, 67, 98-99, 102, 109, 144-152, 161, 164, 166-173, 183, 185-187, 190-191, 200
Service Composition, 31, 56-59

Similarity Relevance, 23
Singular Cylindrical Potential, 50
Sms, 104, 161-165
Social Network, 56-58, 89, 91, 94-96, 134
Social Network Analysis, 56-57, 89, 96
Software Component, 28
Software Defined Networking, 69, 75
Software Design, 103, 121, 133, 178, 181-182
Software Quality Assurance, 5-6, 116
Sse, 23, 26
Surveillance System, 60-61, 63

T
Task Height, 76-77
Text Production, 1, 3
Traffic Congestion, 36, 38, 44
Traffic Urgency, 36, 40-42
Trusted Computing, 144, 146, 151
Tstls, 36, 38-39, 43-44
Tudm, 36, 40-43

V
Vertices, 21, 71, 89-91, 93, 95-96
Visualization, 9, 89-92, 94, 96-97, 202, 205

W
Wait For Graph, 19-21
Web Application Vulnerabilities, 186
Weiner Filtering, 32
Word Completion, 1
Word Prediction, 1-4

CPSIA information can be obtained
at www.ICGtesting.com
Printed in the USA
BVHW050959220519
549014BV00002B/229/P